EATING DISORDERS

A HANDBOOK OF CHRISTIAN TREATMENT

Edward J. Cumella, PhD
Marian C. Eberly,, RN, MSW, LCSW, DAPA
A. David Wall, PhD

SERIES ON EATING DISORDERS

REMUDA Ranch®

Cover Design by Alpha Advertising
Interior Design by Pine Hill Graphics

Published by Remuda Ranch
Packaged by ACW Press
P.O. Box 110390
Nashville, TN 37222
www.acwpress.com
The views expressed or implied in this work do not necessarily reflect those of ACW Press. Ultimate design, content, and editorial accuracy of this work is the responsibility of the author(s).

Publisher's Cataloging-in-Publication Data
(Provided by Cassidy Cataloguing Services, Inc.)

Cumella, Edward J.

Eating disorders : a handbook of Christian treatment / Edward J. Cumella, Marian C. Eberly, A. David Wall. -- 1st ed. -- Nashville, TN : ACW Press, 2008.

p. ; cm.
(Series on eating disorders)
ISBN: 978-1-932124-94-1
Includes bibliographical references and index.

1. Eating disorders--Psychological aspects. 2. Eating disorders--Treatment. 3. Eating disorders--Religious aspects. 4. Faith.
I. Eberly, Marian C. II. Wall, A. David. III. Title.

RC552.E18 C86 2008
616.85/26--dc22 0801

Printed in the United States of America.

We dedicate this book to Ward Keller,
whose vision gave birth to Remuda,
a healing oasis and a sanctuary
from the troubles of the world.
And to the more than 7,500 women
and girls with eating disorders
who entrusted their lives to us,
and who became our teachers.

Contents

Preface

It is with pride and excitement that our authors present this first-ever, multidisciplinary, and comprehensive primer on the Christian treatment of eating disorders. The purpose of this work is to provide a well-rounded, practical handbook for the treatment of eating disorders from a biblically-based and scientifically-valid perspective. The balanced integration of scriptural truth with state-of-the-art, evidence-based therapies for eating disorders, covering the biological, psychological, social/cultural, and spiritual dimensions, has been a multiyear project to which many dedicated Christian healthcare professionals have contributed. We pray that this book will offer as much hope and help to you as we have received in its development.

This book coincides precisely with the mission of Remuda Ranch Programs for Eating Disorders: "*To help individuals suffering from eating disorders with programs that are biblically-based and scientifically-valid.*" As part of the process of fulfilling our mission, we offer this work to more clearly define the essence of Remuda and our successful treatment philosophies.

We realize that our Christian beliefs and approaches to treatment will not be accepted by everyone and may even seem uncomfortable to some. However, after 17 years of successfully treating thousands of eating disorder patients and family members, we believe our superb treatment outcomes lend great credibility to our biblically-based, scientifically-valid approach. As such, this book is intended for both Christian practitioners interested in eating disorders and others who treat Christian patients.

We consider it an opportunity and a privilege that you have opened this book and believe it will be a blessing and a benefit for you in your work with the most fatal of all psychiatric illnesses—eating disorders.

Ward Keller
Founder and CEO
Remuda Ranch Programs for Eating Disorders

Introduction

As trained healthcare practitioners, we join the healthcare community in our conviction that it is essential to rely on evidence-based treatment methods established by scientific research to address the whole person.

Because scientists sometimes approach their work from an atheistic perspective, some Christians dismiss the scientific research. However, Scripture indicates that God reveals truth not only through the Bible, but also through his creation and the study thereof:

> The heavens declare the glory of God; the skies proclaim the work of his hands. Day after day they pour forth speech; night after night they display knowledge...Their voice goes out into all the earth, their words to the ends of the world. (Psalm 19:1-2,4)

> The heavens proclaim his righteousness, and all the peoples see his glory. (Psalm 97:6)

> Ask the animals, and they will teach you, or the birds of the air, and they will tell you; or speak to the earth, and it will teach you, or let the fish of the sea inform you. (Job 12:7-8)

> Since the creation of the world God's invisible qualities—his eternal power and divine nature—have been clearly seen, being understood from what has been made. (Romans 1:20)

By ignoring God's revelation of truth through nature we may forego knowledge God intends for us to have—such as medical knowledge that equips the physician to promote better health. As Christians, we believe that all truths cohere because they derive from the one Truth, Jesus Christ. When individual scientific truths are firmly established according to sound principles and harmonize with Scripture, it is prudent to accept their validity and to benefit from their use, as "every good...gift is from above" (James 1:17), and "every prudent man acts out of knowledge" (Proverbs 13:16).

Christians also believe in revealed truth in the form of sacred Scripture. As Christian healthcare professionals, we endeavor to draw from and harmonize both sources of truth in our work with clients and patients. In keeping with this commitment, Remuda Ranch Programs for Eating Disorders has developed a scientifically-valid, biblically-based model of eating disorder conceptualization and treatment. We call it the bio-psycho-social-spiritual model. Scientific research and the Bible both suggest that human beings are multidimensional creatures—body, soul, and spirit existing in an influential social context.

What science calls illness or disorder, Scripture explains as the result of the fall of man and the broken condition of the world. Where science may ultimately reduce eating disorders only to illness, Scripture makes plain that sin also plays a role. This book explains sin in broad terms, to include not only the broken condition of the world which leads to unhealthy personal choices, but also sins such as abuse and neglect that are perpetrated by various individuals against those with eating disorders.

Science offers a variety of useful tools to address the bio-psycho-social aspects of eating disorders. When screened and applied according to biblical principles, many of these tools are quite effective. Scripture, however, offers a *complete* view of human beings, accurate moral guidance, and information about the unique spiritual aspect of human beings. Thus, through biblical integration with evidence-based patient care, patients' needs—body, soul, social relations, and spirituality—can be addressed with wisdom, truth, and God's transforming love.

In this book, we present a full bio-psycho-social-spiritual conceptualization of eating disorders and treatment approaches appropriate to the full range of dynamically-interactive bio-psycho-social-spiritual needs of eating disorder patients. We have written the material for healthcare providers and other concerned professionals, such as pastors and ministers, and have attempted to explain professional jargon so that members of these helping professions can readily access the material. Lay readers may also find the material accessible and understandable.

We hope you find this work helpful in your efforts to understand eating disorders.

Edward J. Cumella, PhD, CEDS
Marian C. Eberly, RN, MSW, LCSW, DAPA
A. David Wall, PhD

Part I

Scientifically-Valid, Biblically-Based Eating Disorder Model

Chapter 1

Completing the Model: Bio-Psycho-Social-Spiritual

Edward J. Cumella, PhD, CEDS

In 1977, George Engel developed the *bio-psycho-social model* (Engel, 1977). Since he published his groundbreaking work, virtually all health professions have adopted this model as the primary model within which to conceptualize and treat both physical and mental illness.

The bio-psycho-social model recognizes that illness arises from an interactive, dynamic process involving: 1) genetic and biomedical factors, 2) psychological, emotional, behavioral, and cognitive factors, and 3) family, social, and cultural factors. Each area may create a vulnerability to, or protect against, the development of illness. Somewhere among complex bio-psycho-social interactions, illnesses arise, progress, heal, or fail to develop at all.

In spite of this model's broad acceptance in healthcare, when practitioners treat physical and mental illnesses strong tendencies toward reductionism still occur. Among physical illnesses, for instance, it is easy and cost-effective in the short run to treat symptoms biologically with medication and surgery, rather than holistically by exploring psychological, cultural, familial, and environmental factors that may be promoting or sustaining the illness. For example, persons with hypertension and hypercholesterolemia are almost always given medication for these illnesses without referral for psychosocial interventions that could potentially enable these individuals to learn healthier behavioral skills and overcome their physical ailments without the need for long-term medication use. The latter could literally cure the illness, rather than just treat the symptom.

The tendency toward reductionism in treatment recommendations pertains not only to physical illnesses, but to mental illnesses as well. For example, in recent decades healthcare providers have tended to view schizophrenic spectrum disorders as primarily biological in nature. Thus, the treatment received by most people with schizophrenia is medication.

Research suggests that medication should be the first-line treatment in most cases of schizophrenia; however, significant research also suggests that family dynamics reliably predict which persons with a genetic vulnerability to schizophrenia will actually develop the disorder and how often such persons will relapse (e.g., Pourmand, Kavanagh, & Vaughan, 2005).

Although biological vulnerability to schizophrenia is a necessary precursor to the disorder, biological vulnerability alone is often insufficient. Chiefly in certain family systems with particular varieties of emotionally charged communication does the biological vulnerability come alive and lead to actual schizophrenia. In other families, the biological vulnerability may remain latent—never giving rise to the full-blown illness. Furthermore, if families with emotionally charged communication styles receive appropriate family therapy, their newfound communication skills can dramatically reduce the chances that their loved one with schizophrenia will relapse following an initial psychotic break.

In short, even though schizophrenia is a mental illness with a strong genetic/biological foundation and can be treated effectively with long-term use of antipsychotic medications, it is still best understood and treated using the full bio-psycho-social model. Reductionism or overemphasis on just one aspect of this model definitely compromises healthcare. Among those with schizophrenia, long-term antipsychotic use entails multiple and serious side effects, including tardive dyskinesia and affective blunting. A true bio-psycho-social treatment approach might use antipsychotic medication temporarily to treat florid psychotic symptoms, then rely on psychosocial interventions to stabilize the patient's environment and prevent future relapses.

We can generalize from this example. Psychosocial interventions can reliably prevent schizophrenic episodes even in individuals with strong genetic vulnerability to schizophrenia; dramatic interactions between genes and environment are not limited to schizophrenia. Indeed, significant research has demonstrated that psychosocial life experiences alter the expression of our genes and lead to modifications in our neural circuitry (Larkin, 2000). Even our genes, and the biochemistry and structure of our brains, routinely change in response to our life experiences and the environments in which we live (Beitman, Blinder, Thase, Riba, & Safer, 2003). We surely are bio-psycho-social creatures, each dimension interacting with the others. We cannot understand human functioning and illness by focusing on one dimension only.

Accordingly, when we specifically consider eating disorders (EDs), a complex bio-psycho-social picture manifests. From family and genetic studies, we know that genes contribute substantially to the development of both anorexia and bulimia nervosa (Bulik, Sullivan, & Kendler, 2003; Klump & Gobrogge, 2005). Genes explain as much as half the variance in who develops ED. Lest we suddenly jump on the biological bandwagon, let us remember that this leaves approximately half the variance in who develops EDs to be explained by something other than genes. Indeed, we know that EDs have become much more common in the past 30 years. Does this mean that our species has rapidly evolved such that, within the short span of 30 years, ED genes have proliferated in the population? Unlikely. Evolution occurs slowly. Far more likely, human beings have carried ED genes for many generations and now, something in the modern environment is triggering these ancient genes. In particular, we know that people who live in Westernized cultures are much more likely to develop EDs. Hence, in producing EDs a direct etiologic interaction appears to be occurring between genetics and Western culture. One without the other may be insufficient to produce the prevalence of EDs now being observed.

But more than culture interacts with genes to promote ED development. We also know that individual life experiences—experiences unique to each person—can promote EDs. A primary example of this involves childhood sexual abuse. People who have been sexually abused as children are much more likely to develop EDs than those who have not. More specific features, such as the age of the child being abused, and the frequency and violence-level of the abuse also predict ED development, severity, and the precise ED symptoms that will arise (Wonderlich et al., 2000; Wonderlich et al., 2001a; Wonderlich et al., 2001b).

Research has further identified that EDs are more likely to arise in certain family systems (e.g., Minuchin, Rosman, & Baker, 1978). Something about the manner in which people communicate in families appears to interact with individual genetic vulnerabilities to promote ED. In addition, individuals with particular personality traits such as low self-esteem and perfectionism also develop EDs more often. Furthermore, once an ED begins based on this array of interacting bio-psycho-social factors, the ensuing nutrient and calorie deficiencies alter body chemistry, further changing an individual's emotional and social functioning and intensifying their body image distortion, ED rituals and compulsions, and anxiety about food.

In summation, researchers have identified a complex interaction among genetics, individual psychology, family, and culture in the development of EDs and the specific symptoms thereof. EDs are truly bio-psycho-social in nature, as are most medical and mental illnesses. The range of bio-psycho-social factors bring risks, vulnerabilities, predispositions, and influences to the development and maintenance of EDs. Some bio-psycho-social factors offer protective qualities, reducing the likelihood, severity, or longevity of EDs. Bio-psycho-social factors are not simply additive; they are interactive and synergistic. As such, these factors can be likened to a recipe for illness, rather than a static list of ingredients. Bread is not merely yeast plus flour. It is flour transformed by yeast under certain environmental conditions. So with most illnesses, and indeed with EDs.

Let's take a leap from cause to treatment. Just as bio-psycho-social factors dynamically interact to produce a specific kind and severity of ED in each specific individual affected, bio-psycho-social treatment approaches also interact. As such, biological interventions may help address psychological and social issues; psychological interventions may impact biological and social components; and so on. On the one hand, psychotherapy has been shown literally to change brain chemistry and structure (Beitman, Blinder, Thase, & Safer, 2003), and may therefore assist in healing an underlying biological problem that may have arisen in part due to genetics. On the other hand, a biological intervention—serotonin-enhancing medications—may partially correct for serotonin deficits that are due to negative life experiences without ever needing to address those life experiences through traditional talk therapies. In addition, group therapies and approaches—including 12 Step, support groups, and other community-based social experiences such as participation in certain team sports or church youth groups—may counteract the effects of our toxic Western culture and prevent ED development in an otherwise genetically vulnerable child. In a nutshell, the range of interactive possibilities among bio-psycho-social factors is virtually endless.

EDs arise, progress, relapse, and heal within a complex, dynamic, synergistic, and shifting bio-psycho-social landscape. We cannot fully understand any illness—including onset, symptoms, severity, longevity, relapse, and recovery—apart from a bio-psycho-social approach. As Norine Johnson, recent past president of the American Psychological Association, concluded:

> The research is clear—any division between mind and body is arbitrary, capricious, and detrimental to the health of individuals, family, communities, and our nation… [We must] endorse the bio-psycho-social model in health research at all levels… This model integrates mind, body, and culture when discussing health… Behavioral interventions [must] be joined with medical interventions. (Dittmann, 2002)

The Spiritual Dimension

Within the context of the bio-psycho-social model, in the past decade the health professions have embraced the role of spirituality in the development of, recovery from, and protection against mental illness. Renowned psychiatric authorities have published books, and prestigious peer-reviewed journals have offered scientific papers on the importance of spirituality in mental health. Many US medical schools have added courses on spirituality to their standard training (Gundersen, 2000). The "faculty at Harvard Medical School...are teaching medical students how to obtain a spiritual history and how to discuss related concerns with their patients." Americans are also asking for spiritual issues to be addressed in the clinician-patient relationship. Surveys reported by *USA Today* and *Time* indicate that 2/3 of Americans want their health providers to address religion with them. Perhaps as much as 1/2 of Americans want their doctors to pray with them (Gundersen, 2000). More than half of Americans use prayer to control pain, and most say it works (Manning, 2005). Nearly half pray on a regular basis for their health and the health of loved ones (Barnes, Powell-Griner, McFann, & Nahin, 2004).

In short, spirituality has found a place in our bio-psycho-social understanding of mental health and illness. ED professionals likewise have come to recognize that spirituality plays a pivotal role for many ED patients in ED development and recovery. Michelle Lelwica brought together the research and clinical experience surrounding the role of spirituality in EDs in her 1999 book, *Starving for Salvation: The Spiritual Dimensions of Eating Problems Among American Girls and Women* (Lelwica, 1999). A very recent work, *Spiritual Approaches in the Treatment of Women with Eating Disorders* (Richards, Hardman, & Berrett, 2007) continues this work and offers a treatment model for ED women. Although this author finds their recommended treatment model to be limited in applicability and open to ethical criticism (Wall & Cumella, 2007), the decision of the American Psychological Association to publish this work underscores the recognition among ED professionals that spirituality is indeed a significant factor for ED patients.

Because spiritual beliefs influence thoughts and choices and are often shaped in a social context such as family or church, mainstream sources have come to recognize spirituality as an important aspect of individual psychology and social/family functioning. Spirituality is therefore seen as a key part of the "psycho-social" in the bio-psycho-social model. Some have even intimated that the human spiritual impulse is coded into our DNA, suggesting that they have located at least one "religion gene" in the human genome (e.g., Hamer, 2004). Similarly, others suggest that the human brain is wired to experience religious states (e.g., Austin, 1998; Newberg, D'Aquili, & Rause, 2002), and assert that spirituality must therefore be an adaptive trait with a biological basis. As such, some modern scientists see human spirituality as part of the entire bio-psycho-social spectrum.

Christians often view this situation differently. Following biblical teaching, Christians believe that human beings possess a body, a soul, and a spirit. The body clearly corresponds to the "bio" aspect of the bio-psycho-social model. The soul, translated from the New Testament Greek word, *psyche*, corresponds to the "psycho" aspect of the model. In keeping with this, Scripture informs us that human souls consist of emotions, thoughts, and will—each a common aspect of modern scientific psychology. Scripture also reflects man's relational nature. Biblical concepts such as family, congregation, the communal Body of Christ, and national identity express the social dimension and correspond readily to the "social" aspect of the bio-psycho-social model. Hence, Scripture accords well with science in suggesting the importance of a bio-psycho-social model of human functioning and illness.

But many Christians also believe that human beings have a spirit that is distinct from their soul. They assert the existence of an actual spiritual realm and believe that this spiritual reality interacts dynamically with human beings' bio-psycho-social makeup. Christians would therefore propose that spirituality cannot be reduced merely to genes, neurotheology, psychological beliefs, emotional experiences, or church-related social experiences. Spirituality exists above and beyond these documented phenomena. For a Christian, therefore, human beings are bio-psycho-social-*spiritual*, and only a complete bio-psycho-social-spiritual model will fully address all the dimensions of mental health and illness.

Prayer and Healing

Interestingly, focus on the spiritual dimension of humanity as a distinct reality is not only an article of Christian faith, but also a point with potentially emerging scientific validity. For instance, in recent years there has been an effort to study prayer using scientific methods.

Two separate research investigations found scientifically valid evidence that Christian prayer affects the physical world. Together these studies created a frenzy of interest in prayer in the scientific community. At least five additional prayer studies followed. I begin by describing the first two seminal studies.

In 1988, Randolph Byrd published a research paper on prayer in the *Southern Medical Journal* (Byrd, 1988). His paper followed the scientific method to establish a cause-and-effect relationship. In the study, a computer randomly assigned 393 coronary care patients at San Francisco General Hospital either to be prayed for by a prayer group or not. Because the patients were randomly assigned to prayer or non-prayer conditions, the scientific method allows us to assume that there was nothing inherently different about the patients in the two groups. Furthermore, neither the patients themselves nor anyone rendering treatment at the hospital knew to which group the patients had been assigned. The prayer groups were given only the patients' first names. These safeguards created a double-blind study: because no one knew who was receiving prayer, no one could treat the prayer patients differently from the non-prayer patients, nor could the prayer patients benefit psychologically from personal knowledge that someone was praying for them.

In brief, we know that both groups of patients had similar medical histories, received the same medical care, and had similar psychological experiences regarding their medical problem. We must therefore attribute any differences in outcome between the prayer and non-prayer patients to the only known difference between them: the prayer that occurred on behalf of those assigned to the prayer groups. No one possessed enough information to inject any other difference into the groups of patients, so no other cause would present itself in the face of differential outcomes.

After ten months, the results indicated that those receiving Christian prayer were five times less likely to need antibiotics, 2-1/2 times less likely to suffer congestive heart failure, and less likely to suffer cardiac arrest.

Such results suggest that Christian prayer effects some kind of healing power. Because no one knew who was being prayed for (except, presumably, God), the differences between the two groups of patients had to derive from prayer itself and could not have arisen from any human intervention. Only prayer distinguished the groups, and therefore the only cause of the health improvement among those who were prayed for would be prayer itself.

In 1999, William Harris and colleagues at Mid-America Heart Institute in Kansas City conducted a replication of Byrd's 1988 study (Harris, et al., 1999). Harris et al.'s study used very similar methods to Byrd's, but included more patients— 990. In one methodological change, Harris' cardiac patients did not even know that they were in a study at all, whereas Byrd's patients knew that there was a 50-50 chance they were receiving prayer.

Harris et al. used a global measure of clinical outcome, and found that patients who received prayer scored 11% lower on the outcome scale. Lower scores mean better outcomes. The result was statistically significant, again suggesting the healing power of Christian prayer.

Following these two studies on the power of prayer, the popular media offered a flurry of stories on the role of prayer in modern medicine. The scientific community followed suit with additional research, attempting to refine the methodology of the first two studies and to determine whether the healing effects of prayer could be replicated. Replicability of research findings is a hallmark of good science.

Among the five additional studies of which I am aware, three found that intercessory prayer had statistically significant effects on recovery from illness, including AIDS-related illness (Sicher, Targ, Moore, & Smith, 1998), infertility (Cha,Wirth, & Lobo, 2001), and rheumatoid arthritis (Matthews, Marlowe, MacNutt, 2000). Two studies did not find a statistically significant effect (Benson et al., 2006; Krucoff et al., 2005).

Overall, then, of seven studies published, five found statistically significant results for the effect of prayer on recovery from illness. Assessing the evidence, we see that the preponderance of research leans toward supporting the healing efficacy of prayer. Although the evidence is by no means conclusive as yet, it would be difficult to explain away the results of five well-designed studies published in peer-reviewed medical journals. Some have tried (e.g., Chibnall, Jeral, & Cerullo, 2001; Sloan, 2000), but their criticisms are not, in my opinion, of sufficient gravity to invalidate the weight of research evidence that has been amassed for the efficacy of healing prayer.

Church Attendance and Health

A second source of scientific evidence for the reality of the spiritual dimension involves scientific investigations into church attendance. One study was conducted at Duke University (Koenig, et al., 1999) with 3968 elderly North Carolina residents. The study found that those elderly persons who attended church at least once per week were 46% less likely to die during the six-year period of the study than those who attended church irregularly or not at all. We know that those who attend church are healthier than average due to less alcohol and tobacco use, and that they have more social support than others due to fellowship opportunities in their churches. Therefore, the authors used statistical techniques to tease out these differences—medical illnesses, health practices, social support measures, and demographics. Even when the effects of these confounding factors were removed from the picture, the authors still found that church attendance decreased mortality by 28%.

A similar study tracked 5286 California residents (Strawbridge, Cohen, Shema, & Kaplan, 1997) over a much longer time period, 28 years. This study found a concordant result. People who regularly attended Christian services lived longer than those who did not. Once again, the impact of church attendance persisted even after medical conditions, health practices, and social support were accounted for in the statistical models.

Other studies have found that elderly persons who attend church services have healthier immune systems (Koenig, Cohen, George, Hays, Larson, & Blazer, 1997), 56% fewer hospitalizations, 50% shorter hospital stays, and lower overall healthcare costs (Koenig & Larson, 1998). A meta-analysis of more than 80 studies of religious attendance suggested that people who participate in religious services are 60% less likely to experience depression (McCullough & Larson, 1999) than those who do not attend regular church services. Finally, a critical review of the religious attendance research appeared in the *American Psychologist* and concluded that "In healthy participants, there is a strong, consistent, prospective, and often graded reduction in risk of mortality in church/service attendees. This reduction is approximately 25% after adjustment for confounders… church/service attendance protects healthy people against death" (Powell, Shahabi, & Thoresen, 2003).

Because it is difficult to fully measure and tease out the effects of health status and social support from the effects of church attendance per se, these studies on church attendance must be seen as suggestive rather than conclusive. Nevertheless, the church studies meet the standards of evidence expected of most modern social scientific findings. We cannot therefore dismiss them lightly. Together, they may constitute credible support for the reality of a spiritual dimension. In conjunction with the demonstrated efficacy of Christian prayer, fair-minded individuals must acknowledge a possibility that something apparently supernatural may exist and be capable of affecting the visible and measurable bio-psycho-social world.

Reviewing the evidence at hand, Harold Koenig, associate professor at Duke University Medical School, has summarized the situation thus:

> On scientific grounds there is good evidence, in my view, that religious commitment…is associated with better health. And then there's the tantalizing idea that there's something beyond the social support, beyond the lifestyle and the meditation. Scientifically, you would say that's something that we can't explain. A person of faith would say that's the hand of God (quoted in Gundersen, 2000).

To sum up, modern science may be arriving at a view of human beings that harmonizes well with the millennia-old biblical view. Even for a purely secular practitioner who may not accept the reality of a spiritual realm and who may explain the impact of spirituality in purely bio-psycho-social terms, it is nevertheless clear that spirituality matters and plays a role in the understanding, treatment, and prevention of illness. The Christian practitioner might suggest that the Bible through direct revelation, and science through an accurate study of the world God made, are converging on a concordant bio-psycho-social-spiritual understanding of human beings. In either case, we may best understand human experience, functioning, illness, and recovery using a bio-psycho-social-spiritual model.

Spiritual Integration

In light of the scientific evidence, it becomes important to consider how to incorporate spirituality into modern healthcare.

The prevailing view of mainstream authorities who promulgate the role of spirituality is that any spiritual tradition can be incorporated with equal effectiveness into treatment. And, of course, all mental health practitioners would agree that it is essential to respect and to work within patients' existing spiritual beliefs. However, of the many spiritual traditions, by far the greatest quantity of research and theory on the integration of spirituality into mental health has occurred in the Christian tradition.

The field of integration studies endeavors to integrate counseling and Christianity into a unified conceptual and treatment model. Accredited universities and seminaries support this work, as do scientific journals dedicated exclusively or predominantly to this work, such as *The Journal of Psychology and Christianity* and *The Journal of Psychology and Theology*. Thousands of books have been written on the topics of recovery and healing from a Christian perspective. Therefore, the mental health professional wishing to follow the standards of the field and incorporate spirituality into his or her research or clinical work can draw on an extensive literature and emerging evidenced-based content regarding the integration of patient care and Christianity. For other spiritual traditions, this wealth of resources is not available.

This leads us to a key point: Christian-based mental health programs are not only following the standards of current practice by integrating spirituality into treatment, but they are also doing so in perhaps the most scientifically-defensible and valid manner possible given the present state of knowledge. It is from this perspective that this book delineates and disseminates a biblically-based, Christ-centered understanding of the etiology, assessment, and treatment of a specific class of mental illness—EDs.

References

Austin, J. (1998). *Zen and the brain*. Cambridge, MA: MIT Press.

Barnes, P.M., Powell-Griner, E., McFann, K., and Nahin, R.L. (2004). Complementary and Alternative Medicine Use Among Adults: United States, 2002. National Center for Complementary and Alternative Medicine, National Institutes of Health Number 343, May 27, 2004 Advance Data from Vital and Health Statistics.

Beitman, B.D., Blinder, B.J., Thase, M.E., & Safer, D.L. (2003). *Integrating psychotherapy and pharmacotherapy: Dissolving the mind-brain barrier*. New York: W.W. Norton.

Benson, H. et al. (2006). Study of the therapeutic effects of intercessory prayer (STEP) in cardiac bypass patients: A multicenter randomized trial of uncertainty and certainty of receiving intercessory prayer. *American Heart Journal, 151*, 934-42.

Bulik, C.M., Sullivan, P.F., & Kendler, K.S. (2003). Genetic and environmental contributions to obesity and binge eating. *International Journal of Eating Disorders, 33*, 293-98.

Byrd, R.C. (1988). Positive therapeutic effects of intercessory prayer in a coronary care unit population. *Southern Medical Journal, 81*, 826-29.

Cha, K.Y., Wirth, D.P., & Lobo, R.A. (2001). Does prayer influence the success of *in vitro* fertilization-embryo transfer? Report of a masked, randomized trial. *Journal of Reproductive Medicine, 46,* 781-87.

Chibnall, J.T., Jeral, J.M., & Cerullo, M.A. (2001). Experiments on distant intercessory prayer. *Archives of Internal Medicine, 161*, 2529-36.

Dittmann, M. (2002). Fusing mental health and health. *Monitor on Psychology, 33*, 64.

Engel, G.L. (1977). The need for a new medical model: a challenge for biomedicine. *Science, 196*, 129-36.

Gundersen, L. (2000). Faith and healing. *Annals of Internal Medicine, 132*, 169-72.

Hamer, D. (2004). *The god gene: How faith is hardwired into our genes*. New York: Doubleday.

Harris, W. S., Gowda, M., Kolb, J.W., Strychacz, C.P., Vacek, J.L., & Jones, P.G.. (1999). A randomized, controlled trial of the effects of remote, intercessory prayer on outcomes in patients admitted to the coronary care unit. *Archives of Internal Medicine, 159*, 2273-78.

Klump, K.L. & Gobrogge, K.L. (2005). A review and primer of molecular genetic studies of anorexia nervosa. *International Journal of Eating Disorders, 37*, S43-S48.

Koenig, H.G., Cohen, H.J., George, L.K., Hays, J.C., Larson, D.B., & Blazer, D.G. (1997). Attendance at religious services, interleukin-6, and other biological parameters of immune function in older adults. *International Journal of Psychiatry in Medicine, 27*, 233-50.

Koenig, H.G., Hays, J.C., Larson, D.B., George, L.K., Cohen, H.J., & McCullough, M.E.. (1999). Does religious attendance prolong survival? *The Journals of Gerontology. Series A, Biological Sciences and Medical Sciences, 54*, M370-76.

Koenig, H.G. & Larson, D.B. (1998). Use of hospital services, religious attendance, and religious affiliation. *Southern Medical Journal, 91*, 925-32.

Krucoff, M.W., et al. (2005). Music, imagery, touch, and prayer as adjuncts to interventional cardiac care: The Monitoring and Actualisation of Noetic Trainings (MANTRA) II randomised study. *The Lancet,* 366, 211-17.

Larkin, M. (2000). Eric Kandel: Honing in on memory. *The Lancet, 356,* 1250-1.

Lelwica, M.M. (1999). *Starving for Salvation: The Spiritual Dimensions of Eating Problems Among American Girls and Women.* New York: Oxford University Press.

Manning, A. (May 9, 2005). Prayer effective as painkiller? *USA Today.*

Matthews, D.A., Marlowe, S.M., MacNutt, F.S. (2000). Effects of intercessory prayer on patients with rheumatoid arthritis. *Southern Medical Journal, 93,* 1177-86.

McCullough, M.E. & Larson, D.B. (1999). Religion and depression: A review of the literature. *Twin Research, 2,* 126-36.

Minuchin, S., Rosman, B.L., & Baker, L. (1978). *Psychosomatic families: Anorexia nervosa in context.* Cambridge, MA: Harvard University Press.

Newberg, A., D'Aquili, E.G., & Rause, V. (2002). *Why God Won't Go Away: Brain Science and the Biology of Belief.* New York: Ballantine.

Pourmand, D., Kavanagh, D.J., & Vaughan, K. (2005). Expressed emotion as predictor of relapse in patients with comorbid psychoses and substance use disorder. *Australian and New Zealand Journal of Psychiatry, 39,* 473-8.

Powell, L.H., Shahabi, L., & Thoresen, C.E. (2003). Religion and spirituality: Linkages to physical health. *American Psychologist, 58,* 36-52.

Richards, P.S., Hardman, R.K., & Berrett, M.E. (2007). *Spiritual Approaches in the Treatment of Women with Eating Disorders.* Washington, DC: American Psychological Association.

Sicher, F., Targ, E., Moore, D., & Smith, H.S. (1998). A randomized double-blind study of the effect of distant healing in a population with advanced AIDS: Report of a small scale study. *Western Journal of Medicine, 169,* 356-63.

Sloan, R.P. (2000). Should physicians prescribe religious activities? *New England Journal of Medicine, 342,* 1913-16.

Strawbridge, W.J., Cohen, R.D., Shema, S.J., & Kaplan, G.A. (1997). Frequent attendance at religious services and mortality over 28 years. *American Journal of Public Health, 87,* 957-61.

Wall, A.D. & Cumella, E.J. (2007). The spirit is willing but the flesh is weak. A review of *Spiritual Approaches in the Treatment of Women with Eating Disorders* by P. Scott Richards, Randy K. Hardman, & Michael E. Berrett. *PsycCRITIQUES Contemporary Psychology: APA Review of Books, 52.*

Wonderlich, S.A., Crosby, R.D., Mitchell, J.E., Roberts, J.A., Haseltine, B., Demuth, G., & Thompson, K. (2000). Relationship of childhood sexual abuse and eating disturbance in children. *Journal of the American Academy of Child and Adolescent Psychiatry, 39,* 1277-83.

Wonderlich, S., Crosby, R., Mitchell, J., Thompson, K., Redlin, J. Demuth, G., & Smyth, J. (2001a). Pathways mediating sexual abuse and eating disturbance in children. *International Journal of Eating Disorders, 29,* 270-79.

Wonderlich, S., Crosby, R., Mitchell, J., Thompson, K., Redlin, J. Demuth, G., Smyth, J., & Haseltine, B. (2001b). Eating disturbance and sexual trauma in childhood and adulthood. *International Journal of Eating Disorders, 30,* 401-12.

Chapter 2

Four Biblical Factors in Eating Disorder Development

A. David Wall, PhD and Marian C. Eberly, RN, MSW, LCSW, DAPA

A young Christian woman with anorexia nervosa tearfully expressed this statement about her father's views and her anguish that he might be right: Is my eating disorder a result of sin, disease, genes, or something else? Those who work with Christian eating disorder patients will inevitably encounter this tension in their patients. It is important to have a biblical answer to this question. This chapter therefore provides a biblically-based understanding of human nature, illness, and the restorative work of patient care. This biblical model has been carefully developed during Remuda Ranch's seventeen year history by Christians from many backgrounds, and Remuda has applied it effectively in its work with Christian eating disorder patients. We hope that presenting this model may assist others who work with Christian patients to more fully grasp, and effectively and compassionately treat, the complexity of eating disorders.

Biblical View of Human Nature

In the understanding of many Christians, the Bible indicates that human beings are a trinity, like the God in whose image we were made. Genesis lays the foundation for this point-of-view. "The Lord God formed the man from the dust of the ground…" We are physical; *Adam* can mean *from the earth*. The passage continues, "…and breathed into his nostrils the breath of life…" (Genesis 2:8). We therefore also have a spirit. "…and the man became a living being." Finally, we have a soul, which the Bible tells us consists of emotions, thoughts, and will/moral conscience (Romans 2:15). This trinitarian view is confirmed by multiple New Testament scriptures (e.g., Matthew 10:28; Acts 2:31; Romans 8:10; Ephesians 4:4; James 2:26; 1 Peter 2:11), and is expressed frequently in Christian theology.

But human beings are not made up of three segregated parts. In Hebrew thought, humans are unified, indivisible beings, paradoxically or dialectically encompassing all three aspects. All are necessary to form a human being. And each impacts the other within a unified whole (*The New Unger's Bible Dictionary*, 2002).

The Bible also adds one more dimension. Human beings do not exist in isolation from one another. People have an impact on one another, and the people of God were designed to function harmoniously and in unity. "Now you are the body of Christ, and each one of you is a part of it...If one part suffers, every part suffers with it; if one part is honored, every part rejoices with it" (1 Corinthians 12:27,26). In short, our trinitarian human nature is also deeply affected by our social context—family, church, society, and culture.

So why is this biblical understanding of human nature important for dealing with eating disorders?

Human Nature and Eating Disorders

According to Scripture, we live in a broken world due to the fall of man in the Garden of Eden: "Sin entered the world through one man, and death through sin" (Romans 5:12). We are surrounded and impacted by this brokenness in the world: "for the creation was subjected to frustration..." (Romans 8:20). We experience this brokenness within our very organisms: "For in my inner being I delight in God's law; but I see another law at work in the members of my body..." (Romans 7:22-23). This brokenness is often referred to as the fallen or sinful *condition* of the world. As a *condition*, it is not the same as the committing of individual, personal sins. Confusing the two can be the source of hurtful ideas that emphasize judgment and condemnation instead of God's loving redemption.

The fallen or broken *condition* of the world creates vulnerabilities in every aspect of our humanity: body, soul, spirit, and interpersonal relations. We explore these vulnerabilities below.

1. The Body

Vulnerabilities. Scientific research has revealed genetic predispositions to problematic behaviors such as alcoholism, aggression, unhealthy urges, and obsessions. In addition to genes, toxic aspects of our environment—such as stress, nutritional deficiencies, and chemical exposure—can produce biochemical abnormalities within us that dramatically alter our behavior and emotions. Our bodies are also vulnerable to intentional abuse and accidental injuries, including injuries to the brain that result in emotional and behavioral changes. Neuroscience tells us that the developing brain forms an internal map of its environment. Adam and Eve's internal map reflected a creation in total harmony with God—a peaceful and safe environment. Our brains, on the other hand, may grow to reflect a harsh and dangerous environment. In short, many biochemical underpinnings of mental illness—including eating disorders and related pathologies—have been adequately demonstrated and cannot be ignored. Christians often deny this evidence, while secularists may overstate it. A balanced biblical view accepts that these many physiological problems exist because our bodies are part of the fallen world. Physiological problems are not in themselves necessarily the results of personal sin, although they may increase the likelihood that certain personal sins will occur.

Restoration. The biochemistry of an individual with an eating disorder may be out of balance due to the several factors that arise from our fallen world. It is therefore important to treat the body through proper nutrition, exercise, and self-care, as well as the judicious use of medications where indicated. This helps to accomplish the necessary reparative work and to restore the body to an optimal level of functioning.

2. The Soul

Vulnerabilities. Scripture tells us that the soul incorporates three aspects—emotions, thoughts, and will/moral conscience (e.g., Romans 2:14-15). Like the body, the soul is vulnerable to the broken conditions of the fallen world. First, the soul exists in union with a fallen body. Therefore, the physical apparatus through which the soul perceives and interacts with the world may distort reality, promoting negative emotional reactions, thinking patterns, and choices. The soul is also shaped according to what we are taught and the choices and beliefs that have been punished, reinforced, or modeled by others. We are all exposed to and reinforced for unhealthy emotional expressions, negative thinking, and self-centered choices. Shaped by these dysfunctional social influences, the soul may operate according to the distorted principles and beliefs that derive from a fallen world.

Restoration. In working with an eating disorder patient, it is important to address problems in all three aspects of the soul: unhealthy emotional functioning, distorted thoughts, and poor choices. First, providers compassionately validate patients' emotional pain and the reality of the resulting consequences. Constricted patients may need help recognizing and expressing their emotions openly. Emotionally dysregulated or labile patients may need help with emotion regulation skills. Second, providers employ cognitive restructuring to challenge dysfunctional beliefs and thoughts. Patients often need to examine their beliefs, and the social context in which they arose, in order to change unhealthy beliefs to those that are consistent with Scripture. A cultural worldview sees the person merely as "a body" and teaches that one's primary value comes from appearance or ability to perform. Therapists may offer a biblical worldview that values who the person was created uniquely to be by a loving God, helping the Christian patient to establish her true identity in Christ. Finally, treatment is tailored to the patient's motivational level, so that the patient's will is maximally engaged in choosing steps for recovery.

3. The Social Context

Vulnerabilities. We live in a social environment that is hostile to human health because of the pervasive presence of sin in the world. It is not uncommon for patients with eating disorders to have experienced some form of physical, sexual, emotional, and/or spiritual abuse or neglect. Without the sins of others perpetrated against them, it is possible to surmise that the eating disorder may not have developed. In this case, whose sin created the eating disorder? Cultural forces exert tremendous pressures on young women regarding body image and weight control. These pressures sometimes occur even within the church. Wounds perpetrated by others and by cultural forces against the eating disorder patient may therefore play a major role in the development and maintenance of her problems. These wounds are not the result of personal sin, but of a fallen world.

Restoration. Because the social environment can be hostile, the patient is taught how to deal with others more assertively and effectively, to protect herself with healthier boundaries, and to adapt more productively. Healthy, assertive, and emotionally honest relationships can be modeled by providers and supported by other patients in group settings. Because some patients have been deeply wounded by others, it is important to help them grieve losses, begin the forgiveness process, and talk with their families in a context of truth and love (Ephesians 4:15). Education regarding healthy marriage and family life is often needed. Families and marriages also require family therapy to change the systemic relationship patterns that may serve to sustain the patients' eating disorder. Furthermore, patients can be taught how to locate a faith community that will offer the possibility of healthy fellowship and sound biblical doctrine.

4. The Spirit

Vulnerabilities. According to Scripture, at birth our spirits are separated from God's Spirit. This results from the fall in the Garden of Eden, where our spiritual aspect—created to connect us to God—lost its vitality due to the introduction of sin. Apart from God, the human spirit cannot be a source of life or health (Romans 5:12-17). In addition, the human spirit is beset by evil influences that seek to separate us from God and lead us into destructive choices. "For our struggle is not against flesh and blood, but against the rulers, against the authorities, against the powers of this dark world and against the spiritual forces of evil in the heavenly realms" (Ephesians 6:12). As such, individuals often make personal, sinful choices. According to Scripture, we are all born with a sinful nature that is set in rebellion against God. We make choices to maximize pleasure and avoid pain, even when these choices may harm others or ourselves. We all have these tendencies and they make us vulnerable to choosing sin (Romans 7:14-20).

Restoration. To address the needs of the human spirit, it is important to acknowledge that the human spirit can be reborn from above into a living relationship with God (John 3:3-8). Through the indwelling of the Holy Spirit and ongoing sanctification, human beings can flourish in the life-giving fruit of the Spirit (Galatians 5:22-23). To promote sanctification and spiritual health, providers can incorporate Scripture and prayer into treatment, and encourage patients' regular participation in corporate praise and worship. Providers who are committed Christians can model the benefits of an active faith and a personal relationship with Jesus Christ. They can pray for patients throughout the course of treatment. Providers can also invite patients into a deeper relationship with the Father, Son, and Holy Spirit so that patients may continually grow in the grace and knowledge of God.

Because patients have made and will continue to make some sinful choices, counseling should emphasize God's continual offer of loving forgiveness and the life-changing power of repentance. Many eating disorder patients live isolated lives filled with shame and guilt, and believe that they have failed God to the point where He cannot love them anymore. This separation from God is extremely painful. It is therefore essential to help patients understand the concept of grace, to grow beyond a legalistic and judgmental perception of God, and to embrace a Christian life walking in God's beneficent love. From this context of grace, acceptance, and forgiveness, repentance can occur.

Patients can embrace truth, rather than denial about past ineffective choices and actions, and they can take responsibility for recovery, rather than continue in the role of helpless victim. This must occur with wisdom, focusing on responsibility for healing rather than blame for causing the eating disorder. This process is assisted by understanding that eating disorders are almost always unhealthy and irrational ways of meeting what are, at a foundational level, rational, human needs, such as the needs for love and acceptance. It is not productive to blame people for their attempt to meet basic human needs. These underlying needs can be validated, while patients are encouraged at the same time to take responsibility for choosing healthier methods to meet their needs. In short, eating disorder patients recover when they allow themselves to experience the grace of God's unconditional forgiveness and love, and—in this cradle of security and hope—responsibly transform their lives through healthy choices and the continual counsel of the Holy Spirit and caring people.

Views of Human Nature: Implications

In a biblical view, eating disorders result from all four factors, present in varying degrees for different individuals. A thorough assessment, including a spiritual assessment, can reveal which factors predominate for each individual patient and in what proportion and combination. We cannot automatically point to just one element of this complex situation in our efforts to understand an eating disorder. Doing so would overlook critical information about what it means to be human in the present fallen world.

Without realizing it, some Christians subscribe to a nonbiblical view of human nature. They believe that our behaviors and emotions are controlled exclusively by our soul or mind. They therefore endow the soul or mind with a preeminence over the body, spirit, and society. From this perspective, any deviant, pathological, or harmful behaviors are seen purely as personal sins. As such, eating disorders are perceived as sinful, plain and simple. In this case, the patient is believed to be completely responsible for the onset and continuation of her pathological behavior. You cannot medicate sin. You cannot change sin with psychotherapy or treatment. From this perspective, the only thing needed is repentance.

Many Christian patients will either believe this about themselves and/or come from families or churches that do. We need to be prepared to deal with this core belief, because it creates inappropriate shame and guilt and makes the eating disorder more difficult to treat.

On the other hand, some secular authorities remove the soul and spirit completely from the picture and ascribe to a materialistic view of human beings that reduces us to our physical nature alone, like primitive animals. This extreme secular perspective has for the most part removed sin from psychopathology, and focuses exclusively on genes, biochemistry, learning contingencies, and the like. This removal of sin from the equation essentially takes away personal responsibility for one's behavior, because sin involves personal freedom and choice which have no part in such a deterministic model.

Either of these extremes compounds the eating disorder. The first view may engender crippling shame, guilt, and perfectionism. The second may lead to passivity, a victim mentality, and an abrogation of personal responsibility in the healing process. But a biblical view can offer the possibility of comprehensive restoration because it reveals the full complexity of eating disorder pathology.

Conclusions: Practical Integration

So is the eating disorder a sin?

The complex relationship between psychopathology, the fallen world, and personal sin was carefully articulated in a 2002 issue of *Christian Counseling Today*, devoted entirely to this topic. For Christians to perceive eating disorders as chiefly or even exclusively due to personal sin or willful disobedience is to completely misunderstand the complexity of eating disorders in relation to the sinful *condition* of the world with its ubiquitous impact on us. An inordinate emphasis on personal sin is harmful to the human person and is inconsistent with Scripture.

All sickness, physical and emotional, is ultimately due to the fallen condition of the world, which makes us vulnerable in many ways. Eating disorders result from these vulnerabilities in combination. As caring individuals, we must address each aspect of the eating disorder using the best, evidence-based methods available. We must avoid the blame game, compassionately providing treatment to remedy the effects of a fallen world, and offering appropriate spiritual guidance and education to help patients in making healthier personal choices.

It is essential to rely on evidence-based treatment methods established by scientific research in our efforts to address the whole person. Because scientists sometimes approach their work from an atheistic perspective, some Christians dismiss the scientific research. However, Scripture indicates that God reveals truth not only through the Bible, but also through his creation and the study thereof. The Scripture is eloquent in this regard:

> The heavens declare the glory of God; the skies proclaim the work of his hands. Day after day they pour forth speech; night after night they display knowledge… Their voice goes out into all the earth, their words to the ends of the world. (Psalm 19:1-2,4)

> The heavens proclaim his righteousness, and all the peoples see his glory. (Psalm 97:6)

> But ask the animals, and they will teach you, or the birds of the air, and they will tell you; or speak to the earth, and it will teach you, or let the fish of the sea inform you. (Job 12:7-8)

> For since the creation of the world God's invisible qualities—his eternal power and divine nature—have been clearly seen, being understood from what has been made. (Romans 1:20)

By ignoring God's revelation of truth through nature we may forego knowledge that God intends for us to have—such as medical knowledge that equips the physician to promote better health and healing. All truths cohere because they derive from the one Truth, Jesus Christ. When individual scientific truths are firmly established according to sound principles and harmonize with Scripture, it is prudent to accept their validity and to benefit from their use, since "every good...gift is from above" (James 1:17), and "every prudent man acts out of knowledge" (Proverbs 13:16).

Our look at the Bible's understanding of human nature accords with the bio-psycho-social-spiritual model outlined in the companion chapter in this book, Completing the Model: Bio-Psycho-Social-Spiritual. Scientific research and the Bible both suggest that human beings are multi-dimensional creatures, consisting of body, soul, and spirit, and existing in an influential social context. But what science calls illness or disorder, Scripture explains as the result of the fall of man and the broken condition of the world. Where science may ultimately reduce eating disorders only to illness, Scripture makes it plain that there is often an element of personal sin involved as well. Science offers a variety of useful tools for addressing the bio-psycho-social aspects of eating disorders. When screened and applied according to biblical principles, many of these tools can be quite effective. But Scripture offers a complete view of human beings and accurate moral guidance.

In sum, biblical integration supports the judicious use of scientifically-valid treatment methods. It offers a personal relationship with Jesus Christ that can renew the mind through scriptural truth and restore the soul through a covenant of continual forgiveness. Through biblical integration with patient care, the needs of the Christian patient—body, soul, spirit, social relations, and personal sin—can be addressed with wisdom, truth, and God's transforming love.

References

2002. *Christian Counseling Today, 10.* Glen Ellyn, IL: Christian Counseling Resources, Inc.

2002. *The New Unger's Bible Dictionary*. Chicago: Moody Press.

Part II

Biological Dimension of Eating Disorders

Chapter 3

Eating Disorders' Medical Issues

Brenda K. Woods, MD, FAAFP

Among mental illnesses, eating disorders (EDs) have the greatest mortality rate. It is estimated that 6% of patients with anorexia nervosa (AN) succumb to this illness for every decade they are sick (Nielsen, 2001). When we consider that this illness often starts in late childhood or early adolescence, this statistic becomes even more sobering, for it is young people who are dying from AN. Their lives end before they have even begun.

The psalms remind us that we are "...fearfully and wonderfully made..." (139:14). Science confirms what Scripture has long suggested—that the intricacies of human physiology are astounding. Starvation, self-induced vomiting, laxative abuse, and other behaviors associated with EDs can completely disrupt the fine tuning of the human body.

Eating is a normal part of human existence. But those with EDs have a troublesome relationship with food. In EDs, medical and psychiatric issues are interwoven. On the one hand, EDs remain underdiagnosed, because patients often present to primary care physicians with physical symptoms due to the ED but fail to report psychiatric and behavioral symptoms. Many primary care physicians are also reluctant to treat ED patients because they see the diagnosis as psychiatric. It is often the attitude of the medical community that EDs are brought on by patients' own behaviors and choices; they believe that "just eat" is the solution. But this discounts the very real struggles in the patients' lives. On the other hand, psychiatrists are often not comfortable with the medical compromise that is a part of ED. Third party payers want to lump care into mental health benefits, thereby limiting resources available to patients. Clearly, patients, treating professionals, and insurers grapple with questions about EDs, and in many situations this leaves families feeling helpless in negotiating the health care system to obtain the care their loved one needs.

In this context, it is essential that all patients diagnosed with EDs have a primary care physician on their treatment team. The physician's role is to stabilize the patient medically and monitor the ED's ongoing physical sequelae. This enables the remainder of the treatment team to focus on the difficult emotional and psychiatric issues that are so much a part of the ED. Primary care physicians must also be able to recognize and diagnose ED patients in their office when the ED has yet to be acknowledged or disclosed by the sufferer.

This chapter appropriately addresses ED diagnosis in the outpatient primary care setting. I then review medical complications by presenting the pathophysiology of specific ED behaviors. I discuss medical evaluation of ED patients and treatment options. I also offer recommendations for physicians caring for ED patients in general medical hospital wards. Finally, I explore the additional needs of high risk ED populations, such as diabetic, pregnant, and preadolescent patients. Reading this chapter is not intended as a substitute for direct patient contact with a licensed medical provider.

Understanding Eating Disorder Pathophysiology

DSM-IV-TR (American Psychiatric Association [APA], 2000) defines three EDs: anorexia nervosa (AN), bulimia nervosa (BN), and eating disorder not otherwise specified (EDNOS). How does a primary care physician make a diagnosis? How does the physician recognize the ED patient in the office setting?

In order to make the diagnosis, the physician must ask the right questions. EDs are about feelings. This is an area the physician may feel uncomfortable addressing. It is important to assess how the patient feels about weight, size, and food issues. In ED patients, these feelings are very strong. A simple question like, "How do you feel about your weight?" may elicit a strong emotional reaction. ED patients will often verbalize a dislike for their current weight, no matter how low it is. In preventive office visits, it is important to ask the patient if they are currently attempting to change their weight, or if they have been concerned about their weight. These questions may allow the physician to detect a developing ED, and provide some redirection toward healthy lifestyle habits versus dangerous dieting techniques. The SCOFF (Luck et al. 2002) questionnaire, developed in England, is a good screening tool in the primary care setting. The SCOFF has been shown to be of value in quickly assessing patients for potential ED diagnosis:

1. Do you make yourself sick because you feel uncomfortably full?
2. Do you worry you have lost control over how much you eat?
3. Have you recently lost more than 15 pounds in a three-month period?

4. Do you believe yourself to be fat when others say you are too thin?
5. Would you say that food dominates your life?

Any person answering "yes" to two or more of these questions is quite likely to have an ED.

ED patients may also present to their physician with physical symptoms related to an ED, but fail to disclose actual ED behaviors. Table 1 lists common physical findings which may suggest an undiagnosed ED. Presenting physical symptoms include fatigue, weight loss "of unknown etiology," primary or secondary amenorrhea, irregular menses, oligomenorrhea, nausea, vomiting, constipation or diarrhea, nonspecific abdominal pain, edema, sleep disturbance, cold intolerance, chronic diarrhea, depression or anxiety, and syncopal episodes. Because patients are often reluctant to disclose their behaviors, it is important to ask in a safe and nonthreatening manner. If patients disclose behaviors consistent with an ED, unnecessary medical workup may be avoided. Once an ED diagnosis is made, some patients may be relieved to know that their illness has a name and that there are prescribed treatment regimens to help them.

Table 1. Physical Findings Suggestive of an Eating Disorder

System	Symptom
Constitutional	cachexia, overactivity, hypothermia
Dermatological	dry skin, lanugo, thinning hair, periorbital petechiae, callous on dorsum of hand, carotenemia
Head/Ears/Eyes/ Nose/Throat	subconjunctival hemorrhage, angular chelosis, parotid enlargement, dental caries, enamel loss, submandibular adenopathy
Cardiopulmonary	bradycardia, orthostatic tachycardia, orthostatic hypotension, edema, acrocyanosis
Gastrointestinal	abdominal distention
Musculoskeletal	muscle wasting

To best understand ED's medical issues, I review specific ED behaviors and discuss expected or potential medical complications common with each behavior. The medicine is fairly straightforward. If you understand the behavior the patient in engaging in, the expected medical risks are obvious. Each of these behaviors can occur with AN, BN, or EDNOS.

Self-Starvation/Restriction

Self-starvation is the core behavior for certain AN patients who primarily restrict. Patients with AN, by definition, weigh less than 85% of their medically appropriate weight. Malnutrition is expected in this population. The body's primary physiological response to starvation is to reduce energy expenditures. Physiological adaptations occur that enable the body to survive using less energy (Duloo & Jacquet, 1998).

Starvation is associated with reduction in noradrenergic activity in the central and peripheral nervous systems. Cardiovascular changes—bradycardia and hypotension—are typical responses to inadequate nutrition and may be protective in nature. Yet as body weight continues to drop, these symptoms become more dangerous and life threatening (Kriepe & Harris, 1992). Body temperature may drop to 95° F or lower. Lean muscle mass is depleted along with body fat stores. Skeletal muscle myopathies occur with weight loss (McLoughlin et al., 2000). Bone marrow is suppressed, leading to anemia, leukopenia, and thrombocytopenia. Hypoglycemia is common due to depletion of liver glycogen stores. Severe refractory hypoglycemia can lead to coma and death (Rich, Caine, Findling, & Shaker, 1990). Cognitive ability slows and depression develops or is exacerbated. GI motility is sluggish, leading to symptomatic delayed gastric emptying and constipation. Dysregulation of the hypothalamic-pituitary-ovarian axis leads to amenorrhea. Patients on oral contraceptives may continue to have menses in spite of significant underweight. Bone loss is also common in AN: at least 50% of women with AN have evidence of osteoporosis (Levine, 2002).

Table 2. Laboratory/EKG Findings Suggesting an Eating Disorder

Hypercholesterolemia	Hypokalemia	Sinus bradycardia
Leukopenia	Hyperamylasemia	Elevated serum bicarbonate
Hypoglycemia	Prolonged QTc interval	

Many of the effects of chronic caloric restriction resolve as patients refeed and return to healthy weight range. Osteopenia and osteoporosis are two of the complications of starvation that are not necessarily reversible. The effect on bone mineral density typically begins at 12 months after the onset of illness. Castro and colleagues (Castro, Lazaro, Pons, Halperin, & Toro, 2000) noted the following factors related to development of osteopenia: more than 12 months since onset of the disorder, more than 6 months of amenorrhea, body mass index less than 15 kg/m2, calcium intake less than 600 mg/day, less than 3 hours/week of physical activity.

The long-term impact of osteoporosis and osteopenia in this particular population is not well known, but we know from our postmenopausal population that fractures of the hip and compression fractures of the vertebrae are severely debilitating and cause significant issues related to quality of life and life expectancy. It is forecast that these disabling conditions will be impacting ED patients at a much earlier age than typically expected in the postmenopausal population. It is not uncommon for patients with chronic AN to have a history of fragility fractures much earlier than expected.

It had been generally accepted that low estrogen was the cause of low bone density in AN patients. The logical conclusion was that bone loss could be prevented by starting AN patients on oral contraceptives. But even with this practice, AN patients were not being protected from bone loss if they remained underweight and with low body fat. It has since been learned that loss of bone mineral density is multifactorial and related to multiple hormonal aberrations in addition to low serum estrogen, including elevated serum cortisol, decreased insulin-like growth factor 1, and decreased DHEA. Currently, it is not advisable to start AN patients on oral contraceptives unless required for contraception (Golden et al., 2002). The onset of birth control periods can lead to a false sense of security as the patient may not understand that the periods are "artificial" and not evidence of improving physical health. The treatment for decreased bone mineral density is first and foremost weight restoration, normalizing body fat stores, calcium supplementation, and moderate weight bearing exercise. DEXA scans are of value in the ED population. Establishing a baseline Z-score in premenopausal patients allows clinician to monitor patients' bone mineral density during the early years of their recovery.

Starvation with Purging

AN patients who also purge are at much greater risk of developing serious medical complications. This ED diagnosis is referred to as anorexia nervosa, binge-eating/purging type. Some patients binge and purge; others feel compelled to purge after eating only small amounts of food. Purging is most commonly in the form of self-induced vomiting (SIV). SIV causes significant metabolic abnormalities.

With SIV, a metabolic alkalosis develops due to acid losses through the vomitus. Hypokalemia is common and can lead to atrial and ventricular arrhythmias and sudden cardiac death. Ventricular arrhythmias are among the leading cause of death in AN patients with severe potassium deficiency.

Hypovolemia aggravates hypotension with orthostatic blood pressure changes. The occurrence of prolongation of the QTc interval is also worrisome for the potential of cardiac arrhythmia, which can be lethal (Facchini et al., 2006).

Some patients purge with laxatives. This leads to metabolic acidosis due to loss of bicarbonate through the bowel. However, with chronic laxative use, a compensatory metabolic alkalosis may exist. Potassium and magnesium are lost through the diarrhea, along with water. This method of purging is more thoroughly discussed later in the chapter.

Gastroparesis and constipation are often noted due to effects of restriction and purging combined. With all forms of purging, due to dehydration patients often believe they have lost weight. As fluid is replaced, edema occurs, causing patients to feel that they have gained weight. This often leads to further purging behavior.

Laboratory abnormalities mimic those seen with restricting behaviors. Additional abnormalities related to purging include hypokalemia, metabolic alkalosis with vomiting, metabolic acidosis with laxative abuse, hypophosphatemia, hypomagnesaemia, and elevated amylase (Birmingham & Beaumont, 2004). An electrocardiogram may show a prolongation of the QTc interval, which is a warning for possible cardiac arrhythmia leading to sudden cardiac death. It is the author's experience that patients with anorexia nervosa, binge-eating/purging type are the most likely to die from their disorder because they have minimal physiological reserve and chronically teeter on the edge of significant electrolyte disturbances making them vulnerable to a sudden cardiac event.

Bingeing and Purging

Bingeing is defined as eating a larger amount of food than most would consider normal during a limited time period (Malik, Stratton, & Sweeney, 1997). BN is characterized by bingeing along with one or more compensatory mechanisms to eliminate the effects of the bingeing. BN patients may be underweight, normal weight, or overweight. The methods of compensation for binges can be classified as purging or nonpurging. Purging methods are the same as those employed in AN—SIV, laxative use, and diuretics. But BN includes additional risks.

Many patients are able to purge at will, simply by leaning over or applying pressure to the abdominal wall. As tone of the lower esophageal sphincter is lost, patients note increasing gastroesophageal reflux as well as vomiting when not intended. Instrumentation is also used to induce vomiting, such as spoons and toothbrushes. This can cause trauma to the pharynx. There have been cases of these objects being inadvertently swallowed, requiring endoscopic or surgical extraction. Regardless of the method used to induce vomiting, gastric distention and even rupture may occur. Esophagitis and esophageal tears may also occur. Loss of dental enamel and tooth breakage are common. Aspiration of gastric contents may occur during purging, leading to aspiration pneumonitis. Choking deaths have occurred while purging. Patients who repeatedly purge by SIV also face the effects of chronic exposure of the esophagus to gastric acid. This can lead to changes in the esophagus consistent with Barrett's esophagus and subsequent esophageal malignancy (Matsha et al., 2006).

Patients who binge and purge typically report bingeing on high-fat, high calorie food items. Purging does not guarantee elimination of ingested calories from the binge. Chronic overeating can lead to expected effects, such as obesity, lipid abnormalities, cardiovascular disease, and diabetes.

Laxative Abuse

Laxative abuse is a common, albeit ineffective, purging method. The major site of laxative activity is the large bowel. By the time ingested food reaches the large bowel, most caloric value has been utilized, so the primary loss consists of fluids and electrolytes. Fluid loss can be dramatic, reflected by pounds lost on the scale. This effect is short-lived, however, as patients re-hydrate. Fluid loss stimulates the renin-angiotensin system. This leads to an increase in aldosterone and subsequent fluid retention. The fluid shifts cause weight gain, leading patients to purge again. The cycle continues.

Laxative abuse also entails mechanical effects. The Valsalva maneuver, induced by straining over time from laxatives, can lead to prolapse of the rectum and bowel (Malik et al., 1997). Hemorrhoids are common. The normal innervation to the colon can be lost, leading to refractory constipation known as "cathartic colon."

Laboratory abnormalities also occur with laxative abuse. The most common electrolyte disturbance associated with laxatives is a metabolic alkalosis with low serum chloride and potassium. Because of intravascular volume depletion, the BUN and creatinine may also be slightly elevated.

Physical findings with laxative abuse are often those of volume depletion. The patient may have dry mucous membranes and poor skin turgor. Hypotension and tachycardia are associated with dehydration. Orthostatic blood pressure changes may occur. There can be diffuse abdominal tenderness with bloating due to gastroparesis and diminished bowel sounds due to ileus. Bowel sounds may be hyperactive or hypoactive depending on the time frame of last laxative use. Rectal irritation and hemorrhoids are frequent. Stool may contain occult blood.

Treatment of laxative abuse is a difficult patient care issue. In the outpatient setting, laxatives are widely available. It is difficult for patients to abstain from laxatives as they begin to experience the physical discomforts associated with laxative withdrawal. After laxative use, the body is in a state of dehydration. As patients begin to eat and drink again, there can be a rebound accumulation of fluids leading to edema in the GI tract, which leads to feelings of abdominal bloating and fullness. Peripheral edema often occurs. This leads patients to believe that they have indeed gained weight and they will feel the need to use laxatives again. This can lead to a pattern where patients continually relapse in laxative abuse. As such, although not shown to be medically helpful, it may be psychologically helpful to do a laxative taper in outpatient settings. In inpatient settings, this can be approached more aggressively.

Remuda has developed a protocol to assist patients who have developed laxative dependency. This approach has been highly effective in getting patients off laxatives and assisting them in developing normal bowel habits. The protocol is intended to ensure that patients who are abusing laxatives or are laxative dependent are safely withdrawn from laxative use while minimizing physical discomfort which may interfere with ED treatment. In essence, laxatives are discontinued on admission. Bowel functioning is closely monitored. Patients are treated to effectively assist in the return of normal bowel functioning. Below are the details.

A primary care physician completes a History and Physical Exam within 24 hours of patient admission. (See Appendix for detailed template.) Past or present use of laxatives and current bowel functioning are assessed. The exam documents any evidence of current constipation. Orders are written to assist with bowel functioning. Typical starting medications include a stool softener and/or fiber agent. Adequate hydration is important. The patient is educated regarding the process of retraining the bowel and bowel hygiene.

If use of a stool softener and fiber products are not effective, second line medications include osmotic agents such as Miralax or Lactulose. If patient continues to report that bowels are not moving, the physician performs an abdominal exam and considers an abdominal x-ray to quantitate the amount of stool in abdomen. Other alternatives include using glycerin suppository or Fleet's enema to help evacuate stool in the lower rectal vault. In patients with sexual trauma history, suppositories or enemas may be contraindicated. It is preferable to use products which allow the gut to develop normal peristalsis. Evacuating what is in the lower colon allows waste to continue to move through the GI tract. If there is no significant relief with the use of a suppository or enema, an oral cathartic may be indicated. Options include

Fleet's Phosphosoda, MgCitrate, or Go-Lytely. These interventions usually occur after 5 to 7 days with no bowel movement and are not intended for routine use.

Ongoing patient education is required to assist patients in understanding and dealing with this difficult physiological process. The treatment team is kept informed of issues regarding bowel regulation as these may impact patients' compliance with refeeding and may become an issue as patient struggles with body image related to perceived or real abdominal distention.

This cycle of medications, physical exam, x-ray, and eventual use of cathartic medications may need to be repeated as the bowel is being retrained. It is important that the physical evaluation of the patient is continually reassessed to rule out any acute abdominal process during the bowel retraining.

In a laxative abusing or laxative dependent patient, the retraining of the bowels is a very long process. After discharge, the patient may need ongoing follow-up with a primary care physician at home to continue this process. It is important that the patient is advised to not self-medicate for constipation. The patient should allow the physician to manage this process even when only over-the-counter products are needed, due to vulnerability to abuse these products.

Diuretic Abuse

Both prescription and over-the-counter diuretics are used by BN patients. Fluid loss from diuretic abuse leads patients to the perception of weight loss, but the loss is transient. Prescription diuretics can cause significant fluid losses. Furosemide, hydrochlorothiazide, bumetanide, spironolactone, amiloride, and triamterene are all potential drugs of abuse for ED patients. Prescription diuretic abuse is more common in ED patients with a healthcare background. Abuse of these products leads to dehydration, hypokalemia, hypomagnesemia, and hyponatremia. Uric acid and serum calcium may be elevated. Chronic diuretic abuse can lead to hypokalemic nephropathy (Abdel-Rahman & Moorthy, 1997).

Fluid losses through diuretics stimulate the renin-angiotensin system, with the physiological and psychological effects noted above. Over-the-counter diuretics typically contain an herbal diuretic plus pamabrom, caffeine, or potassium salts, and possibly an analgesic such as salicylate or acetaminophen. ED patients often use these products in quantities that exceed dosage recommendations. Therefore, problems with toxicity of acetaminophen, salicylate, or caffeine are possible.

Laboratory abnormalities associated with diuretic abuse are those of volume depletion, including elevated BUN and creatinine. Low specific gravity is seen in the urine. Metabolic alkalosis occurs. The metabolic alkalosis in diuretic abuse is usually milder than with vomiting (Peebles, Wilson, & Lock, 2006). Hyponatremia and hypochloremia may be seen. Hypomagnesaemia and hypercalcemia are also noted. Physical findings are those consistent with dehydration.

Diet Pill Abuse/Stimulant Abuse

Many over-the-counter products are marketed to assist with weight loss. The Dietary and Supplement Health and Education Act of 1994 permits manufacturers to market supplements without providing evidence to the FDA of safety or efficacy (Saper, Eisenberg, & Phillips, 2004). Patients are often attracted to these products because they see them as "natural." Supplements with different mechanisms of action are available. Ephedra alkaloids and caffeine compounds are used to increase energy expenditure. Chromium and ginseng are purported to modulate carbohydrate metabolism. Products with soluble fiber such as psyllium and guar gum are used to increase satiety. Chitosan is purported to block dietary fat absorption. The Internet has opened the door to prescription weight loss drugs, without face-to-face interaction with a physician. Phenteramine, orilistat, and sibutramine can all be ordered easily, although at greater cost than at a traditional pharmacy with a physician's prescription.

Complications from use of these products include myocardial infarction, stroke, hepatic failure, headache, anxiety, and insomnia. Herbal products may interact with other prescriptive medications. It is not uncommon to see these products used in doses that exceed typical dosage regimens, adding to the risk profile.

Drugs of Abuse

ED patients also use many illegal substances to enhance weight loss. Stimulants such as cocaine and methamphetamine are tempting to patients trying to achieve significant weight loss or trying to maintain an unrealistically low body weight. Psychostimulants are abused by ED patients, not to treat ADHD, but to increase energy and decrease appetite. Patients often tell of their drug-seeking behaviors to obtain a psychostimulant prescription to help with their weight loss plan.

When faced with a patient who is abusing a drug such as methamphetamine or cocaine, it is important to determine whether or not the ED is the primary diagnosis. If the patient is suffering primarily from an ED, the treatment needs to focus on the ED as opposed to a primary substance abuse treatment plan. If the ED is not appropriately treated, the patient will soon relapse into substance abuse after the treatment is completed.

Ipecac Abuse

Ipecac is directly cardiotoxic. Its use leads to cardiomyopathy along with peripheral myopathy. It is deposited in muscle and it can require significant time to clear. The cardiotoxic effect is not directly dose dependent. A large study of ED patients indicated that nearly 8% had used ipecac as part of their ED (Greenfield, Mickley, Quinlan, & Roloff, 1993). Another study found that 28% of BN patients reported using ipecac at least once, with 3 to 4% using it regularly (Pope, Hudson, Nixon, & Herridge, 1986). Due to the potential damage to the myocardium, ED patients should always be asked about ipecac use. Urine drug screening can also identify emetine, a principle component of ipecac (Lachman, Romeo, & McComb, 1989). In 2003, the American Academy of Pediatrics issued a statement that ipecac should no longer be used to treat accidental household poisonings. This recommendation was made due to concerns about toxicity and ipecac abuse in the home.

Assessment of Patients with a Presumed Eating Disorder Diagnosis

The medical evaluation is a priority with ED patients. An ED can be immediately life threatening if its complications are not recognized and treated. The first step is therefore a comprehensive history and physical exam.

The physician must understand patients' behaviors in order to assess their physical status. Specific questions are important. The physician must ask to what degree the patient is restricting food intake. Detailed dietary recall from the patient is an important part of the history. Methods of purging and frequency of purging behaviors must be identified. The physician needs to ask specific questions regarding substance abuse as part of the ED. Issues include frequency of use and quantities used. It is not uncommon for patients to report large quantities of various pills to promote weight loss. Substances potentially abused would be laxatives, diuretics, diet pills, appetite suppressants, ipecac, and caffeine. The author finds that patients accept and comfortably respond to questions if they are asked with the assumption that patients are engaging in the behaviors. For example, a physician would ask, "How often do you take laxatives?", rather than, "Do you take laxatives?" This method allows patients to see that you understand their behavior and that you will not be shocked or upset if they respond positively.

After a careful history is obtained, a physical exam needs to be performed. The overall appearance of the patient should be noted. Vital signs should be recorded including orthostatic readings. To prevent weight manipulation, patients should be weighed in a hospital gown with no underclothing. Most authorities believe it is important not to initially reveal the weight to the patient. Accurate height should be measured. The skin is examined for any rashes, lesions, or evidence of skin breakdown, lanugo, poor wound healing, or carotenemia. Evidence of self- injury is not unusual, such as evidence of cutting or picking at the skin. Head/Ears/Eyes/

Nose/Throat exam is looking for parotid gland enlargement, dental status, angular chelosis, or dry mucous membranes. Cardiopulmonary exam is important to assess cardiovascular stability, along with obtaining an EKG. Sinus bradycardia is a common finding and prolongation of the corrected QTc interval is a worrisome finding, suggesting that the patient may be at risk for cardiac arrhythmia. Abdominal exam is important to assess for evidence of obstruction, severe constipation, and abdominal pain. Musculoskeletal exam is performed to look for muscle wasting or any muscle fasciculation from electrolyte abnormalities. The extremities are examined to look for edema and to note peripheral circulation status. As part of a good medical workup, physicians need to ask themselves if any other medical condition could be contributing to the patient's symptoms or physical findings. When a patient reports ED behaviors, this is less complicated. But if a patient is denying ED behaviors and is being evaluated at the request of a concerned parent or spouse, this becomes more important. Many other disease processes can present with symptoms and physical findings similar to presentation of an ED. Experienced clinical judgment is required.

Basic laboratory data should be obtained. It is important to get a CBC with differential, a basic metabolic profile, liver enzymes, albumin and pre-albumin, a lipid profile, phosphorus, magnesium, and calcium, pregnancy test, and urine drug screen as a starting point. In a patient with six months or more of amenorrhea, a DEXA scan should be considered.

At Remuda, a very comprehensive medical history and physical exam is completed at time of patient admission. This level of initial evaluation allows the physician to fully assess patients and rule out any other medical issue which may be mimicking an ED diagnosis.

Medical Intervention with Eating Disorder Patients

The American Psychiatric Association has published a Practice Guideline addressing care of ED patients (Yager et al., 2006). Initial treatment focuses on breaking the cycle of ED behaviors and stabilizing patients' overall medical and nutritional status. Weight restoration is essential to recovery for those below 90% of expected weight.

Refeeding

During the early refeeding phase, care must be taken to avoid refeeding syndrome. This is one of the greatest risks of reintroducing nutrition to the patient who has been severely restricting food intake. This syndrome is characterized by marked fluid and electrolyte shifts with a significant drop in serum phosphorus levels. Because heart mass is reduced with the state of starvation, in refeeding the heart can have difficulty keeping up with the increase in circulatory volume. This can result in congestive heart failure. The heart mass does normalize with weight restoration, but early in the refeeding period the patient needs to be monitored closely.

Changes in serum phosphorus, potassium, and magnesium levels also play a role in the development of refeeding syndrome. Hypophosphatemia may develop when glucose introduced in the diet drives the phosphate into the intracellular space. The resultant low phosphorus levels lead to decreasing contractile properties of the heart, which leads to congestive heart failure. The best treatment for this condition is to prevent it by empiric use of phosphorus supplements early in the refeeding phase rather than waiting until the labs have become abnormal, and carefully monitoring of fluid status. It is essential to work closely with a registered dietician during this phase so that the patient's meal plan is not aggressively increased if the patient is demonstrating signs of refeeding syndrome.

Other labs need to be monitored during this time. It is important to monitor the liver and pancreatic enzymes as refeeding the patient can lead to transient elevation of these enzymes and may indicate a need to reduce the caloric prescription until these enzymes have stabilized. Refeeding pancreatitis can occur with overzealous refeeding. Remuda has established a protocol for refeeding the severely malnourished patient. The purpose of this protocol is to avoid the refeeding syndrome and to safely treat the patient. Details appear below.

Primary care physician completes a history and physical exam within 24 hours of patient admission. Physician assesses risk for refeeding syndrome, including acute weight loss or extreme food restriction during the past 7 to 10 days, significant weight loss over time regardless of pre-morbid weight, or long-standing malnutrition associated with low body weight. Physician reviews initial admission labs and orders supplementation of phosphorus, potassium, and magnesium as indicated by labs. Low serum albumin or electrolyte abnormalities at admission are red flags for refeeding complications. Because serum phosphorus, magnesium, and potassium levels will drop as refeeding is initiated, it is better to proactively treat than to try to catch up once serum levels are evidencing decrease. Consider multivitamin, thiamine, folic acid, and calcium supplementation as indicated by patient's status and other medical conditions.

If nasogastric tube feeding is indicated, write an order to initiate appropriate tube feed protocols. After tube is placed and x-ray is complete, verify appropriate placement of nasogastric tube by looking at x-ray and initiate tube feeding. If nasogastric tube feeding is contraindicated or patient refuses, continue to monitor for refeeding complications. Even without a tube, a refeeding patient may experience medical complications. Order daily weights to monitor fluid shifts. Intake and output may be necessary. Assess patient as often as needed to ensure patient safety and medical stability. Appropriate physical exam in the refeeding patient may include evaluation of vital signs, heart, lung, and abdominal exam, and evaluation for peripheral edema.

Labs may be needed frequently in all refeeding patients. Initially, labs are done daily. After 3 days, if labs are stable, once or twice weekly is typically adequate. Labs which should be monitored in the refeeding patient include CBC with differential, BMP, calcium, magnesium, phosphorus, prealbumin, amylase, lipase, and liver enzymes. Albumin is monitored on a weekly basis as it does not rapidly change. This profile may be expanded or reduced based on patients' current status. If labs are indicating a drop in phosphorus or magnesium, order replacement and advise dietitian so that caloric intake is not increased until labs stabilize. Caloric intake may need to be reduced if labs are indicating instability or there is evidence of rapid weight gain or refeeding edema. Discuss this with the patient's dietitian. Diuretics may be needed with refeeding edema. Spironolactone (Aldactone) is typically the drug of choice as it works with the renin-angiotensin system which is activated in the refeeding patient.

Monitor patients' bowel and gastrointestinal tract functioning. Order bowel medications as indicated to assist with discomfort. Educate patient about gastroparesis which is associated with AN and refeeding. Educate patient regarding normal bowel functioning. Other meds which may help with the gastrointestinal discomfort of refeeding include antacids, proton pump inhibitors, metoclopramide, and antispasmodics.

Continue to monitor weight progress during treatment. Appropriate weight gain goals are two to three pounds per week.

Medication Management

Different classes of medications have been found to be helpful in treating the recovering ED patient. Gastrointestinal symptoms such as gastroesophageal reflux disorder and gastritis respond nicely with the H2 receptor blockers and proton pump inhibitors. Metaclopramide is occasionally helpful in dealing with motility problems, but the patient must be monitored for dystonic reactions. Constipation is managed with stool softeners, fiber agents, osmotic agents, and occasionally laxatives. Supplements, such as potassium, phosphorus, and magnesium may be required early in the process of treatment, or if the patient is continuing to engage in purging behavior. Difficulties with stabilizing the patients' potassium levels can be an indicator that patients are continuing to purge in some fashion, warranting careful observation of such patients and addressing the issue with them directly. In some patients with abdominal bloating and detention with eating, digestive enzymes may be found to be helpful. These enzymes, such as KuZyme or Panrealipase, reduce the workload to the pancreas and may provide some symptomatic relief. These are dosed frequently before meals and snacks. Many patients are started on a once a day multivitamin with minerals due to the depletion that has occurred during the course of their ED. Calcium supplements are frequently prescribed, especially if the patient is at risk for bone loss. It is the goal that as treatment continues and the patients' nutritional status improves, these medications will no longer be needed and can be discontinued.

Eating Disorders and Diabetes

Preteen girls diagnosed with Type I diabetes are at increased risk of engaging in ED behaviors (Goebel-Fabbri, Fikkan, Connell, Vangsness, & Anderson, 2002). Patients with diabetes and EDs also have a greater risk of morbidity and mortality from their illness. In many situations, onset of diabetes occurs at a time in life when patients are also at risk for ED onset. Typically before the diagnosis of diabetes is made, patients will experience significant weight loss associated with the diabetic ketoacidosis state. At time of diagnosis, patients then gain weight as they are rehydrated and insulin therapy is initiated. Patients' families, physicians, dietitians, and diabetic educators may be viewed by patients as controlling their ability to eat as desired. Patients may associate insulin with weight gain. They soon learn that by decreasing insulin intake they can eat whatever they want, and their weight will drop due to their body's inability to adequately utilize the glucose. This leads to a cycle where patients under-dose their insulin as a purging behavior. This behavior is dangerous. Patients engaging in this practice are often found to have uncontrolled hemoglobin A1c levels and repeated episodes of diabetic ketoacidosis. Urgent treatment is required in these patients by a treatment team experienced in the care of the diabetic patients with ED.

Remuda has developed a specific protocol to deal with these high risk patients. Prior to admission, the patient's primary care physician or endocrinologist is consulted regarding the patient's current status and diabetic history and to review any diabetic complications the patient may be experiencing. Upon admission, the patient is immediately assessed by the registered nurse and a finger-stick glucose reading is obtained. A hemoglobin A1c is added to the routine lab work. The urine is checked for microalbumin. The patient is started on a 1200 Kcal diet and insulin is given according to the patient's usual dosage regimen. This often becomes complicated, since many times the patient has not been taking the amount of insulin prescribed, so it is difficult to know how s/he will react to the insulin. Hypoglycemia is a concern. Long acting insulin (Lantis) and a short acting insulin (Humalog) are a typical combination. A sliding scale is utilized if the patient's pre-meal blood sugar is greater than 150 mg/dl. Insulin is given to cover the carbohydrates in the meal. Early in the course of care, the insulin may be held until after the patient eats, to ensure the patient is not overdosed should the patient choose not to eat! Finger-stick glucose readings are obtained multiple times throughout the day and at 2 AM, since it is important to understand how the patient is tolerating insulin and to avoid life-threatening hypoglycemia. Nursing staff is responsible for insulin administration early in the patient's course of care, because the patient has been accustomed to insulin manipulation as part of the ED. As the meal plan is increased to obtain the patient's weight goal, the insulin is adjusted appropriately. As the patient progresses in a recovery program, the patient is allowed to assume more responsibility for the management of the diabetes under nursing and medical supervision and observation. It is the goal that at time of discharge, the patient is properly monitoring blood sugar and making educated decisions regarding insulin dosage adjustments appropriate for his/her meal plan, activity level, and blood sugar readings. It is our experience that at time of discharge, the patient's hemoglobin A1c typically has dropped 2 to 4% from that at admission.

Pregnancy and Eating Disorders

EDs affect women at their peak age of reproductive functioning. It is no surprise that EDs profoundly impact the entire reproductive process. The bottom line is simple: If a woman has AN or BN, she will have a harder time becoming pregnant and carrying a child, and a greater likelihood of either miscarriage or birth defects.

Pregnancy is often difficult to achieve due to the menstrual abnormalities experienced by women with EDs. Women with AN, by definition, have amenorrhea. Fifty percent of women with BN have either scanty or absent menstrual periods. This disruption of the menstrual cycle is a result of caloric restriction, excessive exercise, and/or psychological stress, and it makes pregnancy unlikely. Therefore, in women with EDs pregnancy is far more likely to take place through medication-induced ovulation than through natural means. Even if ovulation and subsequent fertilization occur, the uterine environment is often not conducive to implantation. As a result, one study showed that nearly one in five female patients at an infertility clinic had EDs.

If pregnancy is achieved, the risk is high for obstetrical complications. Pregnant women who continue to practice their ED have a higher incidence of first-trimester miscarriage, still births, low infant birth weights, breech babies, and congenital malformation. Their infants' APGAR scores are lower than the scores of babies born to healthy women.

Pregnancy also poses a variety of physical and emotional difficulties for the woman herself. Physical complications include more vaginal bleeding during pregnancy, a higher likelihood of caesarean deliveries, and greater difficulty healing in the episiotomy area. With AN, the woman will most likely experience little weight gain. With BN, the woman will often gain a great deal of weight, placing her at risk for severe hypertension. The pregnant woman's expanding and changing body often causes profound anguish and emotional conflict. Some women manage to maintain health throughout the pregnancy for the sake of their unborn child, and then make a radical return to their ED immediately after delivery. Others cannot maintain health during pregnancy and must be hospitalized. In such cases, tube feeding may be required to ensure the health of both baby and mother.

Following the birth of the child, women with EDs also have a higher incidence of postpartum depression than other women. They have more problems breast feeding, including insufficient lactation or negative reactions to breast milk in their babies. Inadequate breast milk is often the result of dehydration. For these reasons, women with EDs are more likely to discontinue breast feeding prematurely.

Many women with AN and BN deny that they have an ED. The desire to become pregnant or pregnancy itself does not alter this secrecy. For example, women with BN sometimes claim that their vomiting is due to morning sickness rather than their ED. Therefore, medical professionals must take great care with patients who may have EDs. If AN is suspected, attention must be paid to maternal weight gain and regular ultrasounds must be conducted to determine fetal growth and development. If BN is suspected, particularly if excessive vomiting may be present, maternal electrolyte levels and hydration must be medically monitored to protect the health of mother and child.

In the initial prenatal visit, it is important for the physician to discuss any ED history. A woman with an ED history may struggle more with the expected changes to her body and weight during the course of a normal pregnancy. This can be a point of discussion with the patient to monitor for any relapse of ED behaviors during the pregnancy.

Eating Disorders and Pre-Adolescent Children

ED professionals are observing an increase in EDs among preadolescents. Preadolescent ED patients may present differently than adolescents. Children are more likely to have a shorter duration of illness, but a more substantial weight loss (Peebles et al., 2006). Many times, they do not fully express body image concerns, but are vague about why they are not eating. In some situations, food avoidance is prompted by a choking or vomiting episode, and food is avoided to prevent this from happening again. The child can become ill very rapidly, as they may avoid all food and fluids. Immediate and aggressive treatment is warranted. Along with the usual medical complications of EDs, of concern in the child is the risk of growth failure and permanent loss of height potential due to the ED.

Medical management of the ED child is similar to the ED adolescent and adult, as discussed above. Fluid and electrolyte issues are addressed and weight restoration is promoted with oral and nasogastric tube refeeding. The goal is to get the child back to their ideal weight in a safe fashion and to address the underlying issues which prompted the ED behaviors.

Hospital Management

ED patients occasionally require medical hospitalization. The American Psychiatric Association's Practice Guideline for the Treatment of Patients with Eating Disorders (Yager et al., 2006) indicates that ED patients require inpatient hospitalization according to the indices listed in Table 3.

When ED patients are hospitalized, their care often becomes a frustration to the attending medical and nursing staff. Hospitals are typically not staffed to monitor ED patients. Therefore, special orders need to be written. Below I present a set of suggested routine orders for the patient admitted to hospital for an ED complication.

Admission orders.

- Admit to hospital.
- Diagnosis: Anorexia nervosa or bulimia nervosa.
- Bed rest, with bathroom privileges with staff present. Bathroom to be locked at all other times.
- Orthostatic vital signs three times daily including temperature.
- Weight upon admission and daily with hospital gown only. Patient not to be informed of weight.

Table 3. When to Hospitalize an Eating Disorder Patient

- Medical instability
  - Low heart rate. Adults < 40 bpm. Kids/Teens: heart rate in 40s
  - Low blood pressure. Adults < 90/60 mm Hg. Kids/Teens: < 80/50 mm Hg
  - Kids/Teens: orthostatic blood pressure changes
  - Electrolyte imbalance
    - Hypokalemia (< 3 meq/liter)
    - Hypophosphatemia
    - Hypomagnesemia
    - Hyponatremia or Hypernatremia
  - Low body temperature (< 97 oF)
  - Dehydration
  - Hepatic, renal, or cardiovascular organ compromise
  - Diabetic-insulin dependent
  - Weight < 85% of healthy body weight
- Failure or anticipated failure at lower level of care
  - Outpatient treatment can cost $100,000 if protracted1
  - Inpatient treatment may be more cost-effective at $30,000-$60,000[1]
- Motivation for recovery: Fair or Poor
- Ego-syntonic eating disorder thoughts > 4 hours/day
- Co-occurring psychiatric disorder requiring hospitalization
  - Substance abuse
  - Suicide plan or intent, severe depression
  - Severe anxiety, post-traumatic stress disorder, obsessive-compulsive disorder
- Needs meal supervision or will restrict/binge/purge
- Complete role impairment
- Uncontrolled compulsive exercise
- Severe dysfunctional family system/lack of support system
- Resistant or uncooperative with treatment
- Geographical isolation from treatment services

[1] This indictor of hospitalization need has been established by the National Association of Anorexia Nervosa and Associated Disorders (ANAD) and is not included in The American Psychiatric Association's Practice Guideline for the Treatment of Patients with Eating Disorders.

- Intake and Output.
- CBC with diff, CMP, amylase, lipase, phosphorus, Mg, pre-albumin upon admission.
- CBC with diff, BMP, Ca, Mg, Phos daily to monitor for refeeding syndrome.
- Telemetry for HR less than 50.
- Nutrition consultation: RD and patient to determine meal plan with no substitutions provided by nursing staff. Nursing to keep recording of Kcal eaten. For any food refused, patient to be offered caloric equivalent in form of Ensure.
- Meals to be eaten within 30 minutes of being served with nursing staff monitoring.
- No artificial sweeteners, low-fat, or diet food products.

These preliminary orders give a starting point for caring for ED patients in the inpatient setting, and also offer some guidelines to deal with typical ED behaviors.

Conclusion

It is clear from this chapter that successfully managing the medical aspects of EDs requires physicians to have a good understanding of patient behaviors. Medical concerns are primarily the effects of fluid and electrolyte abnormalities with their inherent risks, along with the abuse of various substances. Left untreated, or sub-optimally treated, mortality and morbidity rates are high. Recovery from EDs is possible for most patients. The first step in recovery is prompt diagnosis and intervention by the physician to stabilize the medical situation and prevent ongoing deterioration of patients' health, including hospitalization if certain conditions arise. Proper treatment includes a team of professionals who specialize in EDs and can treat the nutritional and psychosocial aspects and often complex comorbidities.

The primary care physician is an essential member of the multidisciplinary team caring for ED patients. Their first job is to ensure patients' immediate medical stability. Next the physician monitors patients through the refeeding process to prevent any adverse complications of refeeding. The physician also serves to educate patients about the normal functioning of their bodies, and reassure them when they experience the normal discomforts of refeeding. By working with patients in a nonjudgmental and compassionate manner, the physician helps patients in ways that may not be immediately recognized but are essential to patients' long-term recovery.

Communication with other disciplines is always needed. When team members are reassured that patients are medically stable, they can confidently continue to work on patients' deeper emotional issues. This team concept has proven effective in promoting the long-term recovery of ED patients.

References

Abdel-Rahman, E. M., & Moorthy, A. V. (1997). End-stage renal disease (ESRD) in patients with eating disorders. *Clinical Nephrology, 47*, 106-11.

American Psychiatric Association. (2000). *Diagnostic and Statistical Manual of Mental Disorders, Text Revision* (4th ed.) (*DSM-IV-TR*). Washington, DC: Author.

Birmingham, C. L., & Beaumont, P. (2004). *Medical Management of Eating Disorders.* Cambridge, MA: Cambridge University Press.

Castro, J., Lazaro, L., Pons, F., et al. (2000). Predicators of Bone Mineral Density Reduction in Adolescence with Anorexia Nervosa. *Journal of the American Academy of Child and Adolescent Psychiatry, 39,* 1365-70.

Duloo, A. G., & Jacquet, J. (1998). Adaptive reduction in basal metabolic rate in response to food deprivation in humans: A role for feedback signals from fat stores. *American Journal of Clinical Nutrition, 68*, 599-606.

Facchini, M., Sala, L., Malfatto, G., Bragato, R., Redaelli, G., & Invitti, C. (2006). Low-K+ dependent QT prolongation and risk for ventricular arrhythmia in anorexia nervosa. *International Journal of Cardiology, 106*, 170-76.

Goebel-Fabbri, A. E., Fikkan, J., Connell, A., Vangsness, L., & Anderson, B. J. (2002). Identification and treatment of eating disorders in women with type 1 diabetes mellitus. *Treatments in Endocrinology, 1*, 155-62.

Golden, N. H., Lanzkowsky, L., Schebendach, J., Palestro, C. J., Jacobson, M. S., & Shenker, I. R. (2002). The effect of estrogen-progestin treatment on bone mineral density in anorexia nervosa. *Journal of Pediatric and Adolescent Gynecology, 15*, 135-43.

Greenfeld, D., Mickley, D., Quinlan, D. M., & Roloff, P. (1993). Ipecac abuse in a sample of eating disordered outpatients. *International Journal of Eating Disorders. 13*(4), 411-14.

Kriepe, R. E., & Harris, J. P. (1992). Myocardial impairment resulting from eating disorders. *Pediatric Annals, 11*, 760-768.

Lachman, M. F., Romeo, R., & McComb, R. B. (1989). Emetine identified in urine by HPLC, with fluorescence and ultraviolet/diode array detection, in a patient with cardiomyopathy. *Clinical Chemistry, 35*, 499-502.

Levine, R. L. (2002). Endocrine aspects of eating disorders in adolescents. *Adolescent Medicine, 13*, 129-43, vii.

Luck, A. J., Morgan, J. F., Reid, F., et al. (2002). The SCOFF questionnaire and clinical interview for eating disorders. *British Medical Journal, 325*, 755-56.

Malik, M., Stratton, J., & Sweeney, W. B. (1997). Rectal prolapse associated with bulimia nervosa: Report of seven cases. *Diseases of the Colon and Rectum, 40*, 1382-85.

Matsha, T., Stepien, A., Blanco-Blanco, E., Brink, L. T., Lombard, C. J., Van Rensburg, S., & Erasmus, R. T. (2006). Self-induced vomiting — risk for esophageal cancer? *South African Medical Journal, 96*, 209-12.

McLoughlin, D. M., Wassif, W. S., Morton , J., Spargo, E., Peters, T. J., & Russell, G. F. (2000). Metabolic abnormalities associated with skeletal myopathy in severe anorexia nervosa. *Nutrition, 16*, 192-96.

Nielsen, S. (2001). Epidemiology and mortality of eating disorders. *Psychiatric Clinics of North America, 24*, 201-14.

Peebles, R., Wilson, J. L., & Lock, J. D. (2006). How do children with eating disorders differ from adolescents with eating disorders at initial evaluation? *Journal of Adolescent Health. 39*, 800-805. Epub 2006 Jul 31.

Pope, H. G., Jr., Hudson, J. I., Nixon, R. A., & Herridge, P. L. (1986). The epidemiology of ipecac abuse. *New England Journal of Medicine, 314*, 245-46.

Rich, L. M., Caine, M. R., Findling, J. W., & Shaker, J. L. (1990). Hypoglycemic coma in anorexia nervosa: Case report and review of the literature. *Archives of Internal Medicine, 150*, 894-95.

Saper, R. S., Eisenberg, D. A., & Phillips, R. S. (2004). Common dietary supplements for weight loss. *American Family Physician, 70*, 1731-38.

Yager, J., Devlin, M. J., Halmi, K. A., Herzog, D. B., Mitchell, J. E., Powers, P., et al. (2006). Practice guideline for the treatment of patients with eating disorders (3rd ed.). *American Journal of Psychiatry*. Retrieved November 10, 2006, from http://www.psych.org/psych_pract/treatg/pg/prac_guide.cfm

Appendix

Template of History and Physical Exam for Eating Disorder Patients

Chief Complaint	
Identification/History of Present Illness	
(ED Onset/Development/ ED ER visits and hospitalizations/treatment history/ current treatment and effectiveness)	
ED Behaviors (type, frequency)	**Substance Use:**
Restriction (cals/fat/foods)	Appetite suppressants
Bingeing	Laxatives
Self-induced vomiting	Ipecac
Exercise	Diuretics
Body image issues?	Caffeine
	Water consumption/restriction
	Other substance use to promote weight loss

Weight History		
High Weight	When	
Low Weight	When	
LMP Weight	When	
Desired weight per patient		
Self-weighing frequency		

Habits (Type, frequency of use, patient concerns)
Tobacco
Alcohol
Recreational/Illicit Drugs/Prescription Drug Abuse
Self Harm/ Suicide Attempts

Template of History and Physical Exam for Eating Disorder Patients, cont.

Pertinent History from Outside Source (Doc-to-Doc, preadmission screen, parental report, record review, etc.)		
Past Medical History		
Medical Illnesses (Circle/describe positives)		
CV (CHF, ↑/↓BP, abnormal EKG, ↑ lipids, MI, etc)	**Ortho** (Osteopenia/porosis, Arthritis, Scoliosis, etc)	**Infectious Dis** (TB, serious infection, etc)
Resp (Asthma, Allergies, COPD, abnormal CXR, sinus, etc.)	**Neuro** (HA/Migraine, CVA, Seizure, Syncope, etc.)	**Hem/Onc** (Anemia, Blood transfusion, Cancer, etc)
GI	**Endocrine/Metab** (Diabetes, ↑/↓Thyroid, Electrolyte imbalance, dehydration, etc.)	**Derm** (Acne, etc.)
GU (UTI, kidney disease, stones, etc.)	**Other** (Orthodontic braces, NGTF, TPN, etc.)	Psych diagnosis
Non ED Hospitalizations/ER visits/Accidents/Surgical History/ongoing problems from these issues		
Current Medications (Prescription/ OTC/Naturopathic including dosage and frequency/effectiveness)		
Allergies/Intolerances (Please note type of reaction)		
Meds	Foods	Bee/Wasp sting
Communicable Disease/Exposure History		
Chicken pox	Mono	Strep
TB	Hepatitis	Other
Any other recent exposure to contagious illness:		
Recent travel to third world or remote areas:		
Immunizations ☐ Up to date for age per patient report		

Template of History and Physical Exam for Eating Disorder Patients, cont.

Pain (Current or chronic, rating 1-10, what is usually required for pain management and effectiveness)

Gynecologic History		
Menarche	Frequency	Duration
LMP	LNMP	Amenorrhea/duration
Hormones	Dysmenorrhea	Vaginal Discharge
Sexually transmitted illness	Sexual Activity/current form of contraception	
Last Pap/breast exam/ mammo	Current Breast Feeding	
OB History (include weight gain/loss and postpartum issues)		
Currently Pregnant: Y /N / Unknown		

Developmental History (age 17 and under)				
Birth:	Full-term	Full-term	Post-term	
Complications	Prenatal	Intranatal	Postnatal	
APGAR Scores:	Feeding Problems during infancy/childhood			
Developmental Milestones:		On Time	Other:	
Has required:	PT	OT	ST	
	Educational Assistance			

Family History (Age, Health Hx, Occupation) ❑ Pt is adopted	
Mother	Alcohol/drugs
Father	Other psychiatric illness
Siblings	Hx of AN/BN/obesity
Grandparents	

Template of History and Physical Exam for Eating Disorder Patients, cont.

Social History					
Never married	Married	Divorced	Widowed	Significant other	
Living situation			Work status		
Support system			Church/religious/spiritual affiliation		
Education					
Physical/Sexual Abuse History					

Review of Systems (Circle positives and explain)		
General		
Fatigue	Hot/cold intolerance	Night sweats
Fever/chills/recent illness	Polyuria/-dipsia/-phagia	Insomnia/hypersomnia
History of falls		
Derm		
Body piercing/tattoos	Hair loss	Lanugo
Bruising	Dry skin	Rash
Sores	Moles	Scars
HEENT		
Eyes/vision	Ears/hearing	Sinus
Epistaxis	Glands	Dentition
Oral lesions	Throat	
Resp		
Cough	Hemoptosis	Dyspnea
Wheeze		
CV		
Chest Pain	Palpitations	Lightheadedness
Fainting	Edema	

Template of History and Physical Exam for Eating Disorder Patients, cont.

GI		
Dysphagia	Abd Pain	Nausea
Vomiting	Hematemesis	GERD Reflux
Constipation	Diarrhea	Last BM and BM frequency
Dyschezia	Hematochezia	
Melena	Fecal incontinence	
GU		
Dysuria	Hematuria	Urinary frequency/ hesitancy/urgency
Incontinence	Enuresis	
Muscskel		
Neck pain	Back pain	Joint swelling
Joint pain		
Neuro		
Numbness	Parasthesias	Weakness
H/A	Coord/Balance	
Other		
Physical Examination (Fill-in VS/Measures. Circle *abnormals* and explain)		
General		
NAD	Oriented x 4	Cooperative
Anxious	Cachectic	
VS		
Temp	RR	
P Supine	BP Supine	
P Standing	BP Standing	
Measures		
Ht	Est IBW to be determined by R.D.	
Adm wt	% Est IBW to be determined by R.D.	
1st AM wt	BMI [wt in lbs x 703/ (ht in inches)^2]	

Template of History and Physical Exam for Eating Disorder Patients, cont.

Skin		
Turgor	Discoloration	Rash
Lesions	Piercings	Tattoos
Hair	Lanugo	Scars
HEENT		
NC/AT	PERRLA	EOMI
Fundi	Sclerae/conjunctivae	Auricles
EACs	TMs	Sinuses
Vision Activity	Nose	Mouth
Throat	Hearing	Dentition/gingiva
Parotids		
Neck		
ROM	Tenderness	
Adenopathy	Thyromegaly	
Chest		
LCTA	Wheezes	Rales
Percussion	Chest wall	
Cor		
Rate/rhythm	Murmur/Rub/Gallop	Murmur/Rub/Gallop
Abdomen		
Inspection	BS	Tenderness
Mass(es)	Organomegaly	
Back		
Deformity	Tenderness	ROM
Extremities		
Warm/Cold	Acrocyanosis	Edema
Deformity	Tenderness	ROM
Peripheral pulses	Cap refill	

Template of History and Physical Exam for Eating Disorder Patients, cont.

Joints				
ROM	Swelling		Warmth/Erythema	
Neuro				
CN's	Strength		Sensory	
DTR's	Finger to Nose		Rhomberg	
Gait	Speech/Language			
Breast/GYN				
Other PEx				
EKG				
NSR /Sinus brady/ Sinus tachy/ Irreg Rhythm			Rate	
QTc	ST changes		Other	
Lab				
(Pertinent/abnormal only) ❑ Pending				
Growth Charts: Available N/Y Reviewed: N/Y (Pre-teen only)				
HT/WT/BMI: (Pre-teen only)				
Assessment/Plan:				
ED Diagnosis	AN-R	B/P	BN	EDNOS
Malnutrition (Grade)	Mild	Moderate	Severe	
Other ED-Related Dx				
Obesity	Chest Pain		Hypothermia	
2° Amenorrhea	Dehydration		Irreg Menses	
Bradycardia	Osteopenia/-porosis		Orthostatic Hypotension/ Tachycardia	
Abdominal Pain	Prolonged QTc			
Constipation/Diarrhea	Abnormal EKG		Self mutilation wounds/ Scars	
GERD	Dental Erosions			

Template of History and Physical Exam for Eating Disorder Patients, cont.

Electrolyte Imbalance		
Hyper/Hyponatremia	Hyper/Hypocalcemia	
Hyper/Hypochloremia	Hyper/Hypophosphatemia	
Hyper/Hypokalemia	Hypomagnesemia	Hypercapnia
Hematologic Dx		
Anemia (macro/microcytic)	Leukopenia	
Thrombocytopenia		
Other Lab Abnormalities		
Hyper/Hypoglycemia	Abnormal Thyroid Function Tests	
Elevated LFTs	Hypoalbumin/proteinemia	
Substance Dx		
Polysubstance Abuse for wt loss	Nicotine Abuse/Dependence	
Caffeine Abuse/Dependence	Alcohol Abuse/Dependence	
Appetite Suppressant Abuse	Recreational Drug Abuse (specify)	
Laxatives Abuse/Dependence	Ipecac Abuse	
Diuretics Abuse		
Non-ED Related Dx		
Acne	Dermatitis (specify)	Allergies
Dysmenorrhea	Asthma	Hypothyroidism
Diabetes Mellitus (Type 1/Type 2)		Other
Pain Diagnosis	Headache (specify type)	Other
Fall Risk Assessment:	Low Risk	High Risk

Template of History and Physical Exam for Eating Disorder Patients, cont.

Patient Education The following were discussed with the patient (check what was done):	
❏ Assessments and treatment plans as outlined above	
❏ Medical consequences of ED	❏ Weight restoration/stabilization
❏ Role of PCP in Remuda treatment	❏ Lab draws
❏ PCP visit frequency/need	❏ VS/activity level/activity restrictions
❏ Med changes/new meds	❏ Potential ER/Hospital transfers
❏ PRN meds	❏ NG tube feeding
❏ Other	
❏ Patient voices understanding of discussions noted above	
❏ Patient education appeared effective as evidenced by:	
❏ Patient was offered an opportunity for questions	
❏ Patient understood the plan and agreed.	
Signature:	Date/Time:

Chapter 4

Psychopharmacology in Patients with Eating Disorders

Kevin R. Wandler, MD

This chapter discusses psychopharmacological interventions with eating disorder (ED) patients as well as the role of the psychiatric provider in ED treatment teams. Psychopharmacology with EDs is a complex topic. This chapter is an overview based on the existing research and the experience of psychiatric staff at Remuda Ranch Programs for EDs in treating more than 7000 ED patients over 17 years. It is intentionally written to be readily understood by the nonmedical healthcare provider as well as be a reference for a psychiatrist who is treating patients with EDs. Reading this chapter is not intended as a substitute for direct patient contact with a licensed psychiatric provider experienced in the treatment of EDs.

Psychiatric Medication Philosophy

In this book, we have presented a biblical understanding of EDs. This understanding suggests that we live in a broken world, including genetic abnormalities, toxic environmental conditions, and physical injuries that negatively alter human biochemistry. Many ED patients experience such biochemical alterations. These alterations can lead to emotional and behavioral problems, including depression, anxiety, addictions, obsessive-compulsive behaviors, and EDs. For many patients who are honestly struggling to free themselves from their ED, recovery is more difficult because of these biochemical problems. The words of Jesus reflect such difficulties,"...the spirit is willing, but the body is weak" (Matthew 26:41).

At Remuda, we believe that the best way to restore biochemical health is through proper nutrition, combined with prayer, scientifically-valid and biblically-based psychosocial therapies, and appropriate pharmacological interventions.

The body was designed with certain nutritional requirements. When these requirements are met, the body can often restore itself biochemically. Research has also amply demonstrated that healthy spirituality and psychotherapy both directly affect human biochemistry in positive ways. As described in previous chapters, human beings are bio-psycho-social-spiritual creatures, and these dimensions interact dynamically.

For many persons with EDs, the biochemical issues are substantial enough that additional pharmacological intervention is necessary. Because we are bio-psycho-social-spiritual entities, medication is never a cure-all. But with prudent consideration, a psychiatric provider is often able to find an appropriate medication and the right daily dosage for beneficial effects. Psychiatric medications do not produce artificial euphoria or pleasure, but lessen symptoms such as painful obsessive thoughts, anxiety, insomnia, and depression so that individuals can function normally. Medication can give patients a level playing field to deal with life's struggles.

Some Christian individuals and families have concerns about the use of psychotropic medicines. Although the Bible does not explicitly promulgate the use of such medicines, Jesus confirmed that the sick need a doctor (Matthew 9:12), and Luke, a Gospel writer, was a physician. Billy Graham, a prominent interpreter of Scripture, suggested the following to a mother who was advised that her son needed a prescription for psychotropic medication:

> Much has been discovered in recent years about the human mind, and one finding is that our brains depend on literally hundreds of different chemicals in order to function properly. When one of these is missing or out of balance, it can have a serious effect on our behavior and medications sometimes can help overcome this. While you should be cautious about putting your son (daughter or yourself) on any kind of medication, make your decision in light of your doctor's advice. The Bible does not discourage us from using medicine where necessary.

Remuda's perspective is consistent with Graham's wisdom. We recognize that "every good gift is from above…" (James 1:17). Medications may correct legitimate biochemical problems that cannot be addressed in other ways; therefore, they are among God's good gifts. Remuda does not utilize alternative or homeopathic medicines for the primary treatment of psychiatric conditions as there is insufficient research on these compounds to know whether they are truly effective or not, and how they interact with one another as well as with allopathic medications (O'Mathuna & Larimore, 2001). Because "every prudent man acts out of knowledge" (Proverbs 13:16), with insufficient information about these products it is premature to employ them in treating patients with EDs.

It should also be stressed that habit-forming or addictive medications are rarely needed or used in the psychopharmacological management of ED patients. When prescribed, they are used according to current medical standards to minimize the chances of abuse or habituation. Patients are educated about potential side effects and are monitored closely by medical professionals.

On October 15, 2004, the US Food and Drug Administration (FDA) issued a black box warning regarding the use of antidepressants in children and adolescents, and it later extended this warning to adults (U.S. Food & Drug Administration Center for Drug Evaluation and Research, 2004). (See insert.) The FDA requested that a Medication Guide for each specific antidepressant be provided to all patients or caregivers with every antidepressants prescription.

The black box warning released by the FDA covers all antidepressants. This includes selective serotonin reuptake inhibitors (SSRIs) such as Prozac (fluoxetine), Paxil (paroxetine), Zoloft (sertraline), Celexa (pitalopram), and Lexapro (escitalopram). Additional antidepressants include Wellbutrin (bupropion), Effexor (venlafaxine), Cymbalta (duloxetine), Anafranil (clomipramine), and others.

Remuda follows the FDA guidelines and offers the appropriate information to all parents of adolescents and children. The information is based on *Parents MedGuide, The Use of Medication in Treating Childhood and Adolescent Depression: Information for Patients and Families* (American Psychiatric Association, American Academy of Child and Adolescent Psychiatry, and A National Coalition of Concerned Parents, Providers, and Professional Associations, 2005). The full MedGuide can be found at ParentsMedGuide.org. Additional information may be found at fda.gov. The following are excerpts from the MedGuide.

Suicidality in Children and Adolescents

Antidepressants increase the risk of suicidal thinking and behavior (suicidality) in children and adolescents with major depressive disorder (MDD) and other psychiatric disorders. Anyone considering the use of any antidepressant in a child or adolescent must balance this risk with the clinical need. Patients who are started on therapy should be observed closely for clinical worsening, suicidality, or unusual changes in behavior. Families and caregivers should be advised of the need for close observation and communication with the prescriber. Most antidepressants are not approved for use in pediatric patients except for patients with Prozac for Major Depressive Disorder and Zoloft for Obsessive Compulsive disorder....No suicides occurred in these trials.

WARNINGS - Clinical Worsening and Suicide Risk

All pediatric patients being treated with antidepressants for any indication should be observed closely for clinical worsening, suicidality, and unusual changes in behavior, especially during the initial few months of a course of drug therapy, or at times of dose changes, either increases or decreases. Ideally, such observation would include at least weekly face-to-face contact with patients or their family members or caregivers during the first 4 weeks of treatment, then visits every other week for the next 4 weeks, then at 12 weeks, and as clinically indicated beyond 12 weeks. Additional contact by telephone may be appropriate between face-to-face visits.

Adults with MDD or co-morbid depression in the setting of other psychiatric illness being treated with antidepressants should be observed similarly for clinical worsening and suicidality, especially during the initial few months of a course of drug therapy, or at times of dose changes, either increases or decreases.

At Remuda, we concur with the above warning. All patients are closely monitored when any medications are prescribed. We feel that an inpatient setting gives even more support during the initial 6 to 8 weeks of treatment than recommended by the FDA. We prescribe medications such as antidepressants only when a patient's licensed and trained provider feels such medication is needed. Each individual patient is comprehensively evaluated prior to medication being considered. We exercise caution when we prescribe any medication.

Psychopharmacological Interventions

There are no "magic pills" for the treatment of EDs. The FDA has only approved fluoxetine (Prozac) to treat bulimia nervosa (BN). There are no FDA approved medications for anorexia nervosa (AN). Becker, Hamburg, & Herzog (1998) completed a comprehensive review of the literature on psychopharmacology with ED patients. They found that fluoxetine (Prozac) was helpful to prevent relapse in recovered anorexic patients and that cyproheptadine (Periactin) may help promote weight gain. Kaye &Walsh (2002) have proposed the use of antipsychotic medications, specifically olanzapine (Zyprexa) to treat AN's anxiety symptoms. Another trial included mirtazapine (Remeron), an antidepressant with a common side effect of weight gain. Compliance was an issue due to patient knowledge that the drug caused weight gain and the sedation produced. In April 2006, the Agency for Healthcare Research and Quality issued a comprehensive review of the scientific literature published since 1980, (Berkman et al., 2006) indicating that there are essentially no effective medications for the treatment of anorexia nervosa, but that cognitive-behavioral therapy (CBT) may have benefit.

In this context, it is important to recognize that nearly 100% of ED patients have one or more co-occurring psychiatric conditions, such as depressive and anxiety disorders. Psychotropic medications are frequently used to treat these co-occurring conditions, lessening their interference with ED recovery and their impact on relapse.

Psychopharmacology with Anorexia Nervosa

Antidepressants. In 2006, The American Psychiatric Association revised and updated the Practice Guideline for the Treatment of Patients with Eating Disorders, stating that "psychotropic medications should not be used as the sole or primary treatment for anorexia nervosa. The role of antidepressants is usually best assessed following weight gain" (Yager et al., 2006).

Fluoxetine (Prozac) is recommended for weight recovered AN patients because it has been shown to assist with relapse prevention. Obviously, because of the need to wait until weight restoration, this medication is not helpful in the management of acute AN. Although high doses of fluoxetine have been found to decrease appetite and cause weight loss in normal weight or obese individuals, this does seem to be the case in AN patients. Other SSRIs or selective noradrenergic reuptake inhibitors (SNRIs) may be used as well.

Antihistamines. Cyproheptadine (Periactin) is similar to Benadryl, an antihistamine that causes weight gain. Its side effects include drowsiness and dizziness, especially in weight compromised patients, limiting its utility in AN patients. Hydroxyzine (Vistaril/Atarax), also similar to Benadryl, are antihistamines that have been used to help patients with overwhelming anxiety, not only around food but also due to co-occurring diagnoses.

Atypical antipsychotics. Olanzapine (Zyprexa) and risperidone (Risperdal) have been studied in ED patients in low-dose, short-term use. These medications have been shown to increase weight in AN patients, possibly by affecting metabolism. In addition, antipsychotic medication may facilitate the transition from low weight to an ideal body weight by decreasing the anxiety and body image distortions seen in EDs. AN patients' self-perception of how fat they are is in some ways comparable to a psychotic delusional state. Other atypical medications such as quetiapine (Seroquel) have also been shown to decrease these body image distortions. At Remuda, we generally avoid olanzapine due to weight gain and increased possibility of Type II diabetes. In our experience, risperidone causes lactation in AN patients. While this is not life threatening, it is a concern as it suggests that risperidone affects prolactin levels. Quetiapine (Seroquel), ziprasidone (Geodon), and aripiprazole (Abilify) are used most commonly at Remuda, and they have been very effective in reducing meal and weight gain anxiety and body image distortion, allowing for more compliance with patient meal plans and appropriate weight gain.

Benzodiazepines. Many patients come to Remuda on benzodiazepines such as alprazolam (Xanax), clonazepam (Klonopin), and lorazepam (Ativan) to help control mealtime anxiety. These patients often spend the majority of their treatment detoxifying or weaning off these medications. Our treatment philosophy is to avoid benzodiazepines before mealtimes as every meal and snack is an exposure with response prevention (ERP) activity. If someone is "numbing out" before the meal, ERP cannot occur and meals/food could continue to be experienced as aversive, tolerated only if medicated.

Psychopharmacology with Bulimia Nervosa

Antidepressants. The FDA has approved only fluoxetine (Prozac) for treating BN. An important study (Fluoxetine Bulimia Nervosa Collaborative Study Group, 1992) showed that patients given 20 mg of fluoxetine reduced binge eating by 45% and vomiting by 29%. When the dose was increased to 60 mg, there was a 67% reduction in binge eating and 56% in vomiting. If fluoxetine is not tolerated, a trial with any other SSRI or SNRI should be considered.

Imipramine (Tofranil) and desipramine (Norpramin) are used less often now that safer classes of antidepressants, the SSRIs and SNRIs, have become available. Phenelzine (Nardil) and isocarboxazid (Marplan), antidepressants known as monoamine oxidase inhibitors (MAOIs), are not safe for BN patients. Accidentally bingeing on a food class that interacts with these medications could make patients extremely sick. Also, in treating EDs, it is important to avoid medications that require a restricted diet, so as not to promote additional focus on food.

Bupropion (Wellbutrin) became contraindicated for EDs due to the potentiation of seizure activity in BN patients and AN patients who binge and purge. In the past, we admitted many women who had had seizures on bupropion before admission to Remuda. Bupropion is now available in a sustained release product. We have not seen a history of seizures with the newer formulations. These include a bupropion SR (Wellbutrin SR) given twice daily, and bupropion XL (Wellbutrin XL) given once daily. It has been speculated that due to the time release action, this medication may be less likely to contribute to lowering the seizure threshold than in the regular product.

Anticonvulsants. The Binge Eating Disorder literature supports the use of several anticonvulsants to reduce binge eating and thereby purging. Topiramate (Topamax) and zonisamide (Zonegran) have been shown to reduce bingeing, and thus, in patients with BN and binge/purge AN should decrease purging.

Stimulants. All stimulants suppress appetite. This is well known among ED patients, and becomes a delicate issue when treating a patient with both AN and attention deficit hyperactivity disorder (ADHD). It is counterintuitive to prescribe a medication that decreases appetite in someone who needs to gain weight. Methylphenidate (Ritalin) has been studied in patients with ADHD and BN and was found to be helpful. Modafinil (Provigil), a drug used for narcolepsy, may also be beneficial as it does not significantly decrease weight but has been shown to decrease bingeing. Currently this medication is being studied as an augmenter for depression, for ADHD, and for binge eating disorder.

Opiate antagonists. Naltrexone (ReVia) has been used in the treatment of opiate addiction, alcoholism, cutting, and self-mutilation, and is being studied in the treatment of BN. The challenge in inpatient ED treatment facilities such as Remuda is that most of the patients cannot binge and purge while in treatment because the amount of food to which they have access is limited. If this medication is added during inpatient treatment, it would be virtually impossible to monitor its efficacy. Several patients have come to us on this medication not only for BN but also self-mutilation and alcoholism, and we have continued the medication without incident throughout their treatment.

Psychiatric Comorbidity

Herzog, Keller, Sacks, Yeh, & Lavori, (1992) found that 73% of patients with restricting AN, 82% of those with binge-eating/purging AN, and 60% of those with BN had one or more concurrent comorbid Axis I diagnoses. Others (Zaider, Johnson, & Cockell, 2000) have reported lifetime Axis I comorbidities ranging from 80% and 97% across EDs. Psychiatric comorbidity complicates ED treatment by contributing to ED severity, chronicity, treatment resistance, medical complications, and poor outcome (Blinder, Chaitan, & Goldstein, 1988; Bulik, 2002). Many studies have documented the frequent comorbidity of EDs with mood, anxiety spectrum, and substance use disorders (e.g., Blinder, Blinder, & Sanathara, 1998; Braun, Sunday, & Halmi, 1994; Grilo, Levy, Becker, Edell, & McGlashan, 1996; Herzog, Nussbaum, & Marmor, 1996; Iwasaki, Matsunaga, Kiriike, Tanaka, & Matsui, 2000; Striegel-Moore, Garvin, Dohm, & Rosenheck, 1999; Zaider, et al., 2000). Across investigations, as much as 98% of ED patients have been diagnosed with comorbid mood disorders, 65% with comorbid anxiety disorders, and 55% with comorbid substance use disorders. Recent studies have also begun to emphasize the delusional quality of distorted body perception (e.g., Gordon et al., 2001, Mavrogiorgou, Juckel, & Bauer, 2001; Mehler et al., 2001; Powers, Santana, & Bannon, 2002).

Remuda Ranch data from 6240 patients admitted between January 1990 and December 2006 are consistent with these reported findings. (See Table 1.) As a result of these very high comorbidity rates, it is essential to treat comorbid disorders aggressively during ED treatment to avoid their interference with ED recovery and their negative effects on relapse. There is a substantial role for psychopharmacological interventions in treating the range of co-occurring disorders commonly seen in ED patients. (See Table 1.)

Treating Comorbid Mood Disorders

Tables 2 through 8 provide additional information about a range of pharmacologic agents, their indications for co-occurring disorders, and side effects in ED patients.

Antidepressants are not very effective for patients with extremely low body fat. Most psychotropic medications are lipophilic, which means that they need fat to be absorbed and are stored in the body's fat tissue. If body fat is low, little medication is absorbed. To partially compensate, relatively high antidepressant dosages may be attempted with AN patients and given several times a day. This may increase blood levels and improve efficacy in low weight patients.

Table 1. Co-Occurring Diagnoses of Remuda's Adult & Adolescent Intensive Patients Admitted January 1, 1990 Through December 31, 2005 ($N = 6240$)

Diagnosis	% Patients Diagnosed
Any Depression Diagnosis	89%
MDD	54%
Dysthymia	10%
Depression NOS	38%
Bipolar	4%
Any Anxiety Disorder	56%
OCD	19%
GAD	18%
Social Phobia	5%
Anxiety NOS	29%
PTSD	22%
Substance Abuse/ Dependence	39%
ADHD	7%
Any Personality Disorder	36%

Note. Key to Indication Abbreviations: ADHD—Attention Deficit Hyperactivity Disorder, GAD—Generalized Anxiety Disorder, MDD—Major Depression Disorder, OCD—Obsessive-Compulsive Disorder, PMDD—Premenstrual Dysphoric Disorder, PTSD—Post-Traumatic Stress Disorder, SAD—Social Anxiety Disorder

Depression and anxiety can be described as deficiencies of neurochemicals—hence the common term "chemical imbalance." During times of stress, the body needs more neurochemicals to maintain stability. These neurochemicals come from food. For example, dairy and poultry foods contain the amino acid tryptophan. The body uses tryptophan to manufacture the

Table 2. Selective Serotonin Reuptake Inhibitors (SSRIs)

<table>
<tr><td colspan="4">This group of antidepressants is considered first line in treating "serotonin deficiency" such as depression associated with anxiety, panic, phobias, post-traumatic stress disorder, obsessions, compulsions, or EDs. (Stahl, 2000). With all antidepressants, must use cautiously if the patient has bipolar disorder for risk of making the patient manic.</td></tr>
<tr><th>Brand Name</th><th>Generic Name</th><th>Dose Ranges @ Remuda</th><th>Indication Per PDR</th></tr>
<tr><td rowspan="2">Prozac</td><td>Fluoxetine</td><td>5 – 80 mg</td><td>MDD, OCD, ED (Bulimia Nervosa), Panic/Agoraphobia</td></tr>
<tr><td colspan="3">Prozac is one of two medications that are FDA approved in children for depression. Prozac is the only medication FDA approved for ED—specifically Bulimia Nervosa. May have slight decrease in appetite initially, generally not sedating and well tolerated.</td></tr>
<tr><td rowspan="2">Paxil</td><td>Paroxetine</td><td>10 – 80 mg</td><td>MDD, OCD, SAD Panic/ Agoraphobia, GAD, PTSD</td></tr>
<tr><td colspan="3">Paxil is seldom used at Remuda Ranch. Initially it was banned by the FDA for use in children and adolescents in 2004. It is very sedating.</td></tr>
<tr><td rowspan="2">Zoloft</td><td>Sertraline</td><td>25 – 200 mg</td><td>MDD, OCD, Panic/ Agoraphobia, PTSD, PMDD, SAD</td></tr>
<tr><td colspan="3">Zoloft is one of two medications that are FDA approved in children—specifically for OCD. This medication is weight neutral, not sedating and well tolerated.</td></tr>
<tr><td rowspan="2">Luvox</td><td>Fluvoxamine</td><td>25-300 mg</td><td>OCD</td></tr>
<tr><td colspan="3">Luvox is used seldom used at Remuda Ranch because anecdotally it appeared to cause increase in constipation.</td></tr>
<tr><td rowspan="2">Celexa</td><td>Citalopram</td><td>1-80 mg</td><td>MDD</td></tr>
<tr><td colspan="3">Currently is seldom used at Remuda Ranch due to the compound Lexapro being available which is very similar and appears to be better tolerated and more effective in our patients.</td></tr>
<tr><td rowspan="2">Lexapro</td><td>Escitalopram</td><td>5-20 mg</td><td>MDD, GAD</td></tr>
<tr><td colspan="3">This antidepressant is weight neutral and not sedating and well tolerated.</td></tr>
</table>

Note. Key to Indication Abbreviations: ADHD—Attention Deficit Hyperactivity Disorder, GAD—Generalized Anxiety Disorder, MDD—Major Depression Disorder, OCD—Obsessive-Compulsive Disorder, PMDD—Premenstrual Dysphoric Disorder, PTSD—Post-Traumatic Stress Disorder, SAD—Social Anxiety Disorder

neurochemical serotonin. If a patient has AN and is avoiding food, this could be considered a double stress on brain chemistry. The body needs tryptophan to make serotonin for regular bodily functioning and to deal with the stress of the ED, but because the body is not receiving tryptophan from food, it becomes serotonin depleted. Decreased serotonin leads to "serotonin deficiency syndromes," including depression, anxiety, panic, phobias, post-traumatic stress, obsessions, compulsions, and more ED behaviors (Stahl, 2000).

Many antidepressants work by blocking the normal mechanism that destroys and removes neurochemicals from the brain. The net result is an increase in neurochemicals. For example, fluoxetine (Prozac) works by blocking the reuptake pump in brain neurons that removes serotonin. After a period of weeks, the net effect is an increase in serotonin. Although ED patients may lack sufficient amino acids to complete this cycle due to self-starvation, in an ED treatment facility where caloric intake is carefully monitored and food is ingested regularly, it may be useful to begin antidepressants while patients are in a weight recovery program.

For these reasons and because depression is a life-threatening illness, we typically start depressed patients on an SSRI even during weight restoration. Clinically, most antidepressants take four to six weeks to work. We want to give patients all the tools we can so they are able to be successful when they leave the inpatient setting. With a combination of prayer, nutrition, therapy, and medication, we believe we are giving them the best chance at recovery. I believe it would be negligent to wait for full weight restoration in depressed or anxious AN patients before starting medication. To wait in this manner would mean sending them home on no medications to face what is often a difficult and vulnerable transition period to the stresses of ordinary life.

Many of these medications have been spotlighted in the media, such as fluoxetine (Prozac), sertraline (Zoloft), paroxetine (Paxil), citalopram (Celexa), and escitalopram (Lexapro). All five essentially do the same thing—recycle the naturally occurring neurotransmitter called serotonin. But there are many types of serotonin and serotonin receptors in the brain. As a result, these SSRIs are chemically different from one other and have differing side effects. Clinicians may use some of these other characteristics to choose the specific antidepressant for a particular patient. Fluoxetine is stimulating and would be considered for someone with low energy. Paroxetine is sedating and may be chosen for someone with a sleep disturbance or high anxiety. None of the SSRIs significantly change weight, especially during a relatively short course of treatment. Venlafaxine XR (Effexor XR) and duloxetine (Cymbalta) are also very effective in the treatment of depression, especially

Table 3. Selective Noradrenergic Reuptake Inhibitors (SNRIs)

This group of antidepressants affect patients with "Noradrenergic Deficiency Syndrome," i.e., depression associated with fatigue, apathy, and notable cognitive disturbances, particularly impaired concentration and problems with sustaining and focusing attention (Stahl, 2000). With all antidepressants, must use cautiously if the patient has bipolar disorder for risk of making the patient manic.			
Brand Name	**Generic Name**	**Dose Range @ Remuda**	**Indication per PDR**
Cymbalta	Duloxetine	20-60 mg	MDD, Diabetic Peripheral Neuropathy, MDD
	Cymbalta is relatively new and has not been used significantly at Remuda Ranch. It has both serotonin and norepinephrine reuptake blockade at 40-60 mg		
Effexor XR	Venlafaxine	37.5-300 mg	MDD, GAD, SAD, Panic
	Effexor is frequently used because at low doses (under 225 mg) it acts very much like an SSRI, but at higher doses, it has both serotonin and norepinephrine blockade. Thus it has indications similar to both the SSRI and SNRI medication classes.		
Strattera	Atomoxetine	10-100 mg	ADHD
	This medication has been used in limited amounts at Remuda Ranch primarily due to the fact that we have seen excessive side effects of tachycardia and blood pressure issues especially in anorexic patients who are also ADHD. This medication may have more use when patients are weight restored and you want to avoid a stimulant that could contribute to low appetite.		

Note. Key to Indication Abbreviations: ADHD—Attention Deficit Hyperactivity Disorder, GAD—Generalized Anxiety Disorder, MDD—Major Depression Disorder, OCD—Obsessive-Compulsive Disorder, PMDD—Premenstrual Dysphoric Disorder, PTSD—Post-Traumatic Stress Disorder, SAD—Social Anxiety Disorder

if there is more of a "noradrenergic deficiency syndrome," i.e., depression associated with fatigue, apathy, and notable cognitive disturbances, particularly impaired concentration and problems with sustaining and focusing attention. Antidepressants may provide energy and cognitive improvement as well as improve mood (Stahl, 2000).

Bupropion SR and XL (Wellbutrin SR & XL) work by recycling norepinephrine as well as dopamine, which is helpful for anxiety. Because of the risk of seizures in BN patients, bupropion is used only after SSRIs have been tried and found ineffective. It can be considered for refractory depression if the patient is given a clear explanation of the risk of seizures. Bupropion SR and XL may be the best delivery route for this medication. As a sustained release product, it is absorbed into the bloodstream more slowly, thus posing lower seizure risk. Bupropion-related seizures have not been documented in AN patients. Since the introduction of the SR and XL forms, we have not seen ED patients who have had seizures on the medication. Prior to the sustained release product, we admitted several ED patients a year already taking this medication who indeed had seizures as a result.

Many physicians are prescribing mirtazapine (Remeron) for AN patients. This antidepressant is sedating, and has been shown to cause weight gain. While the weight gain side effect may sound ideal for AN, Remuda's philosophy is not to use psychotropic medications for either weight gain or loss because such use of medication closely resembles the behavior of the ED itself, in which chemical substances are used by patients to manipulate weight and hunger. We do use low doses of mirtazapine on occasion as an augmenting agent to boost the properties of an SSRI, particularly for patients who are not sleeping well at night. However, AN patients are often very fearful of taking anything that might cause weight gain. We inform our patients of this side effect and, as a result, have difficulty convincing them to take mirtazapine (Remeron).

Psychiatrists use anticonvulsants for bipolar disorders as well as severe anxiety and impulsivity. For ED patients, valproate (Depakote) is seldom used due to significant weight gain. In addition, it requires blood tests to watch for anemia and liver changes and assure that the medication remains at a therapeutic level. Lamotrigine (Lamictal) seems to be more weight neutral and is believed to be one of the best medications for mood. There is a risk of Stevens Johnson syndrome, which manifests as a skin rash. This needs to be monitored closely and tends to occur within the first five days of treatment or after eight to twelve weeks. To avoid this, very slow titration is recommended, whereupon the incidence of serious rash is nearly zero (Stahl, 2006). Zonisamide (Zonegran), topiramate (Topamax), oxcarbazepine (Trileptal), and gabapentin (Neurontin) are most commonly used at Remuda, not for bipolar disorders but for mood stabilization. Zonisamide and topiramate have also been shown to reduce bingeing in BN and binge eating disorder.

Lithium was the drug of choice for many years for bipolar disorders. Although it is an effective medication, in many ED patients it is contraindicated. Lithium is a salt and can easily lead to toxicity for patients who restrict or purge food.

Table 4. Miscellaneous Antidepressants

Brand Name	Generic Name	Dose Ranges @ Remuda	Indication (Per PDR)
Anafranil	Clomipramine	25-250 mg	OCD
	This is the first antidepressant approved for OCD. It is in the class of tricyclic antidepressants which increase both serotonin and norepinephrine but is known to have side effects such as weight gain, constipation, blurred vision, and dry mouth. This medication is not well tolerated in high doses. It may be used as an augmentation with an SSRI in low doses and may be used to help with sleep disturbance.		
BuSpar	Buspirone	5 – 60 mg	Anxiety
	This medication is for anxiety and stimulates serotonin receptors. Clinically it is often used as an augmentation medication to assist with severe anxiety and depression. The main disadvantage is that it can take up to four weeks to see effects.		
Desyrel	Trazodone	25 – 300 mg	MDD
	This medication is generally used as an augmentation medication for depression and ultimately given at night for sleep. It is not addicting or habit forming. Most patients respond to low doses for sleep 25-100 mg and it is well tolerated.		
Remeron	Mirtazapine	7.5 mg – 60 mg	MDD
	Remeron is seldom used because of weight gain. If it is used, it would be due to failure of other antidepressants or as an augmentation medication and for sleep.		
Wellbutrin SR & XL	Bupropion	SR – 100-400 mg XL – 150-450 mg	MDD
	This medication has been shown in clinical trials to help with bulimia. The regular formulation, not the SR or XL, was associated with seizures in patients with BN and AN-BP subtype. The FDA has put a warning not to use with patients with an ED.		

Note. Key to Indication Abbreviations: ADHD—Attention Deficit Hyperactivity Disorder, GAD—Generalized Anxiety Disorder, MDD—Major Depression Disorder, OCD—Obsessive-Compulsive Disorder, PMDD—Premenstrual Dysphoric Disorder, PTSD—Post-Traumatic Stress Disorder, SAD—Social Anxiety Disorder

Table 5. Atypical Antipsychotic Medications

There is the potential for weight gain and change in lipid profiles so this must be monitored. It is documented that risperidone and olanzapine causes even more weight gain and thus these two are used less. It is recommended that a screening for movement disorders, such as a DISCUS or AIMS exam, be performed before starting and regularly after initiation. It is also recommended that this medication be discontinued if possible a few months after the patient is discharged and is at home.			
Brand Name	**Generic Name**	**Dose Ranges @ Remuda**	**Indication (Per PDR)**
Risperdal	Resperidone	0.5 – 6 mg	Schizophrenia, Psychosis
	Due to weight gain and lactation from increased prolactin, this medication is seldom used at Remuda Ranch.		
Zyprexa	Olanzapine	1.25 – 10 mg	Schizophrenia, Psychosis, Bipolar
	Due to weight gain and possible Type II diabetes, this medication is seldom used at Remuda Ranch		
Seroquel	Quetiapine	25 – 800 mg	Schizophrenia, Psychosis
	This medication has been used frequently at Remuda Ranch for body image distortion. In addition, when combined with an SSRI it is extremely helpful for treating OCD and anxiety.		
Geodon	Ziprasidone	20 – 160 mg	Schizophrenia, Psychosis
	This medication has been used frequently at Remuda Ranch for body image distortion. In addition, when combined with an SSRI it is extremely helpful for treating OCD and anxiety. Baseline EKG should be obtained due to possibility of causing QTc prolongation.		
Abilify	Aripiprazole	5 – 30 mg	Schizophrenia, Psychosis
	This medication has been used frequently at Remuda Ranch for body image distortion. In addition, when combined with an SSRI it is extremely helpful for treating OCD and anxiety.		

Note. Key to Indication Abbreviations: ADHD—Attention Deficit Hyperactivity Disorder, GAD—Generalized Anxiety Disorder, MDD—Major Depression Disorder, OCD—Obsessive- Compulsive Disorder, PMDD—Premenstrual Dysphoric Disorder, PTSD—Post-Traumatic Stress Disorder, SAD—Social Anxiety Disorder

Treating Comorbid Anxiety Disorders

Tables 2 through 8 provide additional information about a range of pharmacologic agents, their indications for co-occurring disorders, and side effects in ED patients.

Obsessive-compulsive disorder (OCD) is seen in many ED patients. If there is a family history of OCD and the OCD was evident prior to ED onset, this diagnosis will be difficult to treat until the patient is fully weight restored and even then it may take up to twelve or more weeks on therapeutic doses of an SSRI to get a partial reduction in symptoms. Of course, a combination of medication and cognitive-behavioral therapy has been shown to be the most effective treatment for patients with OCD.

In combination with SSRIs, some atypical antipsychotic medications are also effective in reducing the obsessions and anxiety seen with OCD and in allowing weight restoration. They help to control severe agitation and thought distortions—including body image distortions and hallucinations. At Remuda, we have found quetiapine (Seroquel), aripiprazole (Abilify), and ziprasidone (Geodon) to be useful. These medications work on the dopamine and serotonin systems of the brain. They do have side effects that can cause tremors and muscle spasms, generally in high doses, so it is important to monitor patients on these medications regularly for hints of tremor or muscle rigidity. To reduce side effect risk, we generally use low doses of these medications. Unlike the antidepressants, which are generally necessary to take for at least one year, these medications can often be discontinued once a patient is in recovery, often a month or two after returning to an outpatient treatment team.

Hydoryzine (Vistaril or Atarx) has been used for anxiety as well. These are antihistamines and work to treat mild anxiety. They are not addicting. Due to their antihistamine effect, they can cause sedation and impair cognition in high doses.

Patients with a comorbid diagnosis of post-traumatic stress disorder (PTSD) are challenging in that they often evidence depression, anxiety, mood lability, self-mutilation, dissociation, ED symptoms, obsessive-compulsive symptoms, and borderline personality traits. There is no medication or combination of medications that can readily treat all of these symptoms. Some of the SSRI medications have FDA approval for PTSD. Medications such as naltrexone (ReVia) have been shown to help reduce self-mutilation. Antipsychotic medications are helpful for dissociation. An anticonvulsant medication may be necessary to assist with mood lability. zonisamide (Zonegran), topiramate (Topamax), and gabapentin (Neurontin) are most commonly used at Remuda for PTSD mood stabilization. This is where

Table 6. Anticonvulsant Medications

Brand Name	Generic Name	Dose Ranges @ Remuda	Indication Per PDR
Topamax	Topiramate	100-200 mg BID	Partial Seizures/ Migraine Headaches
	This medication has been studied in PTSD, BED, and obesity. It has been known to cause sedation and initially mental confusion. No blood monitoring for levels necessary. It has not been shown to be effective in bipolar disorder.		
Zonegran	Zonisamide	100-600 mg	Partial Seizures
	Studies have shown indications in BED and mood stabilization in PTSD. There is a cross allergy with sulfonamides. This medication has no blood monitoring for levels.		
Lamictal	Lamotrigine	25-200 mg for psychiatric indications	Partial Seizures/ Bipolar
	This medication is weight neutral and felt to be one of the best medications for mood stabilization in bipolar disorder. There is a risk of Stephens Johnson syndrome, which manifests as a skin rash. This needs to be monitored closely and tends to occur within the first 5 days of treatment or after 8-12 weeks. To avoid this, very slow titration is recommended. The incident of serious rash is very low and nearly zero. (Stahl, 2006).		
Neurontin	Gabapentin	300-1800 mg in divided doses	Partial Seizures/pain from Shingles
	Generally considered weight neutral, primary side effect is mild sedation. Used as an adjunct for mood stabilization and anxiety.		
Trileptal	Oxcarbazepine	300-600 mg BID	Partial Seizures
	Generally considered weight neutral, primary side effect is mild sedation. Used as an adjunct for mood stabilization and anxiety.		

Note. Key to Indication Abbreviations: ADHD—Attention Deficit Hyperactivity Disorder, GAD—Generalized Anxiety Disorder, MDD—Major Depression Disorder, OCD—Obsessive-Compulsive Disorder, PMDD—Premenstrual Dysphoric Disorder, PTSD—Post-Traumatic Stress Disorder, SAD—Social Anxiety Disorder

Table 7. Miscellaneous Medications

Brand Name	Generic Name	Dose Ranges @ Remuda	Indication Per PDR
Provigil	Modafinil	100-200 mg	Narcolepsy / sleepiness due to shift work
	Studies have shown that this medication may be useful for BED, ADHD, and augmentation for depression. Weight neutral and nonsedating.		
ReVia	Naltrexone	25-100 mg	Alcoholism and Narcotic Addiction
	Studies have shown that this medication may be helpful for cutting and self-mutilation and bingeing in BED and bulimia nervosa.		
Vistaril/ Atarax	Hydroxyzine	10-200 mg	Allergic reaction
	Antihistamines may be beneficial for sleep and mild anxiety. They are not addicting so may be a good substitute for a benzodiazepine after the benzodiazepine has been stopped.		

Note. Key to Indication Abbreviations: ADHD—Attention Deficit Hyperactivity Disorder, GAD—Generalized Anxiety Disorder, MDD—Major Depression Disorder, OCD—Obsessive-Compulsive Disorder, PMDD—Premenstrual Dysphoric Disorder, PTSD—Post-Traumatic Stress Disorder, SAD—Social Anxiety Disorder

thorough, careful, multidisciplinary assessment and diagnosis become paramount to help clarify symptoms and prioritize treatment strategies and goals.

Benzodiazepines, such as alprazolam (Xanax), lorazepam (Ativan), and clonazepam (Klonopin) may be used when necessary with ED patients, specifically for detoxification or for severe anxiety and panic until an antidepressant medication is stabilized. Due to addiction potential, benzodiazepines are prescribed sparingly and for short durations only.

Psychiatric Providers and Eating Disorder Treatment Teams

Psychiatric providers are most effective when they comanage ED patients along with other members of a treatment team. Primary care providers offer medical management; registered dietitians assist with weight restoration and nutritional counseling; psychologists may help clarify diagnoses and

Table 8. Benzodiazepines

All benzodiazepines listed below have the potential for addiction. Overall they are used for panic disorder and detoxification from alcohol or other benzodiazepines. Generally speaking, long-acting benzodiazepines are suggested for panic.			
Brand Name	**Generic Name**	**Dose Range @ Remuda**	**Indication Per PDR**
Ativan	Lorazepam	0.5 – 6 mg	Anxiety
	Short acting, risk of addiction, well tolerated. It is available as a liquid.		
Klonopin	Clonazepam	0.25 - 4 mg	Epilepsy / Panic Attacks
	Long acting, has been shown better for panic disorder. It is available as a wafer.		
Xanax Xanax XR	Alprazolam Alprazolam Extended Release	0.5- 6 mg 0.5- 6 mg	Anxiety/ Irritable Bowel/ PMDD Anxiety/ Panic
	Has both short and long acting formulation and is tolerated well.		

Note. Key to Indication Abbreviations: ADHD—Attention Deficit Hyperactivity Disorder, GAD—Generalized Anxiety Disorder, MDD—Major Depression Disorder, OCD—Obsessive-Compulsive Disorder, PMDD—Premenstrual Dysphoric Disorder, PTSD—Post-Traumatic Stress Disorder, SAD—Social Anxiety Disorder

treatment needs through interviewing and psychological testing; therapists provide individual and group therapy that work synergistically with the psychotropic medications, as well as feedback on the efficacy of medications in symptom reduction; nurses offer milieu management, close medication monitoring, feedback on symptom reduction, and 24-hour patient support that reinforces the therapeutic work offered by the other members of the treatment team.

When trained in the treatment of ED patients and subtleties of differential diagnosis, psychiatric providers can assist the treatment team in determining which symptoms arise from the ED and which from comorbid psychiatric conditions. Psychiatric providers can give other team members insight into what behaviors and conditions may respond to psychotropic medication, and when pharmacological interventions may be warranted. Psychiatric providers can also apprise the team members about when to expect a response to medications and what responses may occur. In addition, psychiatric providers are key in assessing for improvement and decompensation and making decisions about the appropriate level of care for a given patient. Psychiatric management is one of the foundations for treating the biochemical issues faced by patients with EDs. Most patients with EDs should be evaluated by a psychiatric provider. Because EDs often involve issues across the bio-psycho-social-spiritual spectrum, and because each area affects the others, the treatment of patients' medical needs requires a team approach with open communication among members. In outpatient settings, patients need to sign appropriate releases of information to allow for this effective communication among team members. In inpatient settings, a strongly collaborative team of multidisciplinary specialists is essential for treatment success.

References

American Psychiatric Association, American Academy of Child and Adolescent Psychiatry, & A National Coalition of Concerned Parents, Providers, and Professional Associations. (2005). *Parents medguide: The use of medication in treating childhood and adolescent depression: Information for patients and families.* Retrieved February 23, 2006 from http://www.parentsmedguide.org/.

Becker, A.E., Hamburg, P., & Herzog, D.B. (1998). The role of psychopharmacologic management in the treatment of eating disorders. *Psychiatric Clinics of North America: Annual of Drug Therapy, 5,* 17-51.

Berkman, N.D., Bulik, C.M., Brownley, K.A., Lohr, K.N., Sedway, J.A., Rooks, A. et al. (2006). *Management of Eating Disorders (Evidence report/technology assessment No. 135).* Retrieved February 23, 2006 from http://www.ahrq.gov/clinic/tp/eatdistp.htm.

Blinder, B.J., Blinder, M.C., & Sanathara, V.A. (1998). Eating disorders and addiction. *Psychiatric Times, 15,* 30-33.

Blinder, B.J., Chaitin, B.F., & Goldstein, R. (Eds.) (1988). *The eating disorders: Medical and psychological bases of diagnosis and treatment.* New York: PMA.

Braun, D.L., Sunday, R., & Halmi, K.A. (1994). Psychiatric comorbidity in patients with eating disorders. *Psychological Medicine, 24,* 859-67.

Bulik, C.M. (2002). Anxiety, Depression, and Eating Disorders. In C.G. Fairburn & K.D. Brownell (Eds.), *Eating disorders and obesity: A comprehensive handbook* (pp. 193-98). New York: Guilford.

Fluoxetine Bulimia Nervosa Collaborative Study Group. (1992). Fluoxetine in the treatment of bulimia nervosa. A multicenter, placebo-controlled, double-blind trial. *Archives of General Psychiatry, 49,* 139-47.

Gordon, C.M., Dougherty, D.D., Fischman, A.J., Emans, S.J., Grace, E., Lamm, R., et al. (2001). Neural substrates of anorexia nervosa: A behavioral challenge study with positron emission tomography. *Journal of Pediatrics, 139,* 51-57.

Grilo, C.M., Levy, K.N., Becker, D.F., Edell, W.S., & McGlashan, T.H. (1996). Comorbidity of DSM-III-R axis I and II disorders among female inpatients with eating disorders. *Psychiatric Services, 47,* 426-29.

Herzog, D.B., Keller, M.B., Sacks, N.R. Yeh, C.J. & Lavori, P.W. (1992). Psychiatric comorbidity in treatment-seeking anorexics and bulimics. *Journal of the American Academy of Child and Adolescent Psychiatry, 31*, 810-18.

Herzog, D.B., Nussbaum, K.M., & Marmor, A.K. (1996). Comorbidity and outcome in eating disorders. *The Psychiatric Clinics of North America, 19,* 843-59.

Iwasaki, Y., Matsunaga, H., Kiriike, N., Tanaka, H., & Matsui, T. (2000). Comorbidity of axis I disorders among eating-disordered subjects in Japan. *Comprehensive Psychiatry, 41,* 454-480.

Kaye, W.H., Walsh, B.T. (2002). The Psychopharmacology of Eating Disorders. In K.L. Davis, J.T. Coyle, C.B. Nemeroff, & D. Charney (Eds.), *Neuropsychopharmacology: The Fifth Generation of Progress* (pp. 1675-83). Hagerstown, MD: Lippincott Williams & Wilkins.

Mavrogiorgou, P., Juckel, G., & Bauer, M. (2001). Recurrence of paranoid hallucinatory psychoses after beginning a fasting period in a patient with anorexia nervosa. *Fortschrift Neurological Psychiatry, 69,* 211-14.

Mehler, C., Wewetzer, C., Schulze, U., Warnke, A., Theisen, F., & Dittmann, R.W. (2001) Olanzapine in children and adolescents with chronic anorexia nervosa. A study of five cases. *European Child & Adolescent Psychiatry, 10,* 151-57.

O'Mathuna, D. & Larimore, W. (2001). *Alternative medicine: The Christian Handbook.* Grand Rapids, MI: Zondervan.

Powers, P.S., Santana, C.A., & Bannon, Y.S. (2002). Olanzapine in the treatment of anorexia nervosa: An open label trial. *International Journal of Eating Disorders, 32,* 146-54.

Stahl, S. (2000). *Essential Psychopharmacology, Neuroscientific Basis and Practical Applications,* (2nd ed.). New York: Cambridge University Press.

Stahl, S. (2006) *Essential Psychopharmacology, The Prescriber's Guide.* New York: Cambridge University Press.

Striegel-Moore, R.H., Garvin, V., Dohm, F., & Rosenheck, R.A. (1999). Eating disorders in a national sample of hospitalized female and male veterans: Detection rates and psychiatric comorbidity. *International Journal of Eating Disorders, 25,* 405-14.

U.S. Food and Drug Administration Center for Drug Evaluation and Research. (2004). FDA *Public health advisory: Suicidality in children and adolescents being treated with antidepressant medications.* Retrieved February 23, 2006 from http://www.fda.gov/cder/drug/ antidepressants/SSRIPHA200410.htm

Yager, J., Devlin, M.J., Halmi, K.A., Herzog, D.B., Mitchell, J.E., Powers, P., et al. (2006). Practice guideline for the treatment of patients with eating disorders (3rd ed.). *American Journal of Psychiatry.* Retrieved November 10, 2006, from http://www.psych.org/psych_pract/ treatg/pg/prac_guide.cfm

Zaider, T.I., Johnson, J.G., & Cockell, S.J. (2000). Psychiatric comorbidity associated with eating disorder symptomatology among adolescents in the community. *International Journal of Eating Disorders, 28,* 58-67.

Chapter 5

Nutrition Issues in Eating Disorders: Philosophy, Assessment, and Treatment

Janet K. Carr, MS, RD, Juliet Zuercher, RD, and Marian C. Eberly, RN, MSW, LCSW, DAPA

> *Then Jesus said to his disciples: "Therefore I tell you, do not worry about your life, what you will eat; or about your body, what you will wear. Life is more than food, and the body more than clothes."* (Luke 12:22-24)

Americans worry a great deal about what they will eat and wear (Kilbourne, 1999). Our culture focuses prominently on the body and external appearances. A near-obsession with thinness drives the practice of cyclical dieting and a sizable interest in information related to nutrition and health. Contradictory nutrition messages from sources which vary in accuracy have promoted confusion over healthful eating. The treatment of eating disorders is therefore aided by a biblically-based and scientifically-valid nutrition philosophy that patients can understand and adopt in place of the confusing messages they receive from other avenues. The treatment of eating disorders is also aided by biblically-consistent and evidence-based methods for achieving proper nutrition, healthy weight, and working through eating disorder fears and behaviors.

Nutrition Philosophy

Food Guide Pyramid

The first step in approaching food and meal planning is to establish a foundation for healthful food choices. The Food Guide Pyramid (FGP) is a practical, basic, and easily used eating model designed for the general public and disseminated by the U.S. Department of Agriculture (USDA) and the

U.S. Department of Health and Human Services (1992). From a healthful eating perspective, it promotes the proper distribution of nutrients to efficiently meet the body's needs. It also provides flexible guidelines to allow for food preferences while ensuring proper nourishment. The FGP is a scientifically-valid model; as reasoned elsewhere, relying on scientifically-grounded knowledge is a biblically-consistent practice (Wall & Eberly, 2002). "[E]very prudent man acts out of knowledge" (Proverbs 13:16).

Throughout recent history, models for healthy eating have evolved as new research has emerged in the areas of nutrition and health. Research has likewise led to debate about the current model, the FGP, which is now 15 years old. Proposed changes, derived from research findings, may indeed lead to incremental modifications in the FGP, but not an overhaul as some have suggested. In 2005, the USDA revised the Food Guide Pyramid, developing the MyPyramid to include new nutrient standards, dietary guidelines, food consumption, and composition data.

Recommendations for modification to the FGP include an emphasis on consuming less saturated fat, moderate unsaturated fat, and more whole grains, legumes, fruits, and vegetables to ensure fiber intake. These changes would incorporate guidelines for eating that have already been established. The Dietary Guidelines for Healthy Americans and Healthy People 2010 (Food and Drug Administration and National Institutes of Health, 2003; U.S. Department of Agriculture and the U.S. Department of Health and Human Services, 2000) promote these aspects of healthful eating and have long been indicated as supplements to the FGP. The FGP remains an excellent one-page guide to eating; using the FGP with the accompanying guidelines for health offers a sound foundation for a nutritious eating plan.

All Foods Can Fit

A vital part of a healthful approach to eating and meal planning is the concept that "All foods can fit!" This motto is affirmed by the American Dietetic Association, and is critical in working through the distorted belief systems frequently accompanying eating disorders. In our society, it has become second nature to label foods as "good" and "bad." This may be appropriate to express individual tastes and personal appeal, but confusion often results when these terms are used to define healthful eating. Individuals use different standards for judging the healthiness of food. Labeling foods as "good" and "bad" influences food intake. "Bad" foods are typically avoided, even though these foods may offer beneficial nourishment. Extreme elimination of foods labeled "bad" is a hallmark of anorexia, and clearly leads to serious malnourishment. Those with bulimia often label as "bad" those foods which they most enjoy; avoidance of these foods may lead to an experience of psychological deprivation, followed by food cravings and binge behaviors.

Another danger of labeling foods as "good" and "bad" is inappropriate moral judgment. For example, when a "bad" food is consumed, people may judge themselves "bad" based on their food intake. Statements such as, "I am going to be bad and have a piece of cheesecake" are part of our everyday American parlance. When eating is equated with morality, guilt may mount with each bite of a "bad" food. Likewise, when eating "good" foods, people may perceive themselves as virtuous. In eating disorders, these distorted correlations between food and personal morality/worth are frequent and often extreme. But the truth is simple: Individual foods are neutral and should be viewed as neither "good" nor "bad." The New Testament makes this plain when the distinction between "clean" and "unclean" foods is abolished (Matthew 15:11, Acts 10:15). Furthermore, it is evident from hundreds of scriptures that food is a blessing and eating is intended to be one of humanity's sources of joy (e.g., 1 Chronicles 12:40; Nehemiah 8:12; Esther 8:17 and 9:22). "So I commend the enjoyment of life, because nothing is better for a man under the sun than to eat and drink and be glad. Then joy will accompany him…all the days of the life God has given him…" (Ecclesiastes 8:15).

Promoting the belief that all foods can fit into a healthful meal plan does not mean that all foods are equal. Some foods have greater nutritional benefits than others. For example, fruits are high in fiber and vitamins, and milk is rich in calcium; desserts, candy, and snack foods may offer less nutritional value. But this does not mean that the less nutritionally beneficial foods do not have a purpose and place in a healthful lifestyle and in celebrating and affirming life and God's blessings.

Balance, Variety, and Moderation

How all foods can fit into healthful meal planning is very important to address with eating disorder patients. This occurs under the guidelines of balance, variety, and moderation.

- Balance equates to flexibility: adjusting to hunger, appetite, time, place, people, and food availability.
- Variety simply means eating different foods, consuming the various food groups, and having variety within each group.
- Moderation includes serving size and frequency of consumption. Moderation involves saying both "yes" and "no" to food, knowing

one's nutritional needs, listening to hunger and fullness, and taking personal responsibility and accountability for food choices.

Moderation is the guideline most frequently violated in the American diet. The question should not be whether a food is "good" or "bad," but how much and how often it is consumed. "If you find honey, eat just enough—too much of it, and you will vomit" (Proverbs 25:16).

Following the guidelines of balance, variety, and moderation will promote proper nourishment and proper distribution of calories from nutrients: 50 to 60% carbohydrate, 25 to 30% fat, and 15 to 20% protein. In treating eating disorders, using the FGP with the accompanying guidelines will nourish bodies successfully and facilitate therapeutic progress by effectively challenging food fears and misinformation.

Normal/Intuitive Eating

The ultimate goal for those with or without eating disorders may be referred to as Normal Eating (Satter, 1987) or Intuitive Eating (Tribole & Resch, 1995). A common theme of intuitive eating is "eat when you are hungry and stop when you are full." Listening to the body's cues regarding hunger and satiety is the general rule.

Normal eating includes three meals a day in general. But occasionally it may mean consuming a large, late breakfast or an early, substantial dinner. It may mean eating an extra cookie because they are freshly baked or saving the slice of cake for later because you are too full from dinner. It involves savoring the moment, noticing texture, tasting the food, and simply enjoying it. Normal eating may mean having a bowl of ice cream because it is available and "sounds good," but knowing when to put the spoon down to finish the day's tasks or address underlying emotional issues. Allowing oneself the freedom to occasionally eat beyond the point of fullness because the food is tasty or the meal is part of a holiday celebration, or ending a meal prematurely when still hungry because you are late for an appointment—such things challenge the rigid, black-or-white thinking encountered so often in patients with anorexia and bulimia.

For those with eating disorders or issues, these skills must still be learned or developed. The normal/intuitive eating mind-set leads to flexible, moderate eating behavior and directly confronts eating disorder thoughts. The end result is responsible freedom and autonomy in one's eating practices and the ability to put food in proper perspective, knowing that "[l]ife is more than food..." (Luke 12:23).

The Basics of Nutrition Assessment and Treatment

Nourishing the body properly and achieving a healthy weight are essential for physical and psychological health. "For we are the temple of the living God" (2 Corinthians 6:16). Without appropriate nourishment, the brain does not function properly, and other forms of psychotherapy and counseling are less effective. Proper nourishment and weight are therefore the foundation of treatment with eating disorder patients. The time and course of these foundational interventions are highly individual, but some standard principles apply.

Assessment

The development of individual care plans rests on thorough assessment. This is axiomatic. During the assessment, it is important to establish:

- Recent daily intake (previous 1 to 6 weeks), including both food and fluid consumption
- Frequency of binge and/or purge behaviors
- If purging is present, the methods of purging
- Use of exercise
- Foods that are avoided—"fear foods"
- Weight history
- Lab values
- Medical and psychiatric co-occurring disorders related to the eating disorder.

A weight history—including circumstances and behaviors associated with being at a particular weight, high/low weight, usual weight, length of time at that weight, accompanying feelings and beliefs, and how much the patient currently desires to weigh—assists in determining not only a healthy weight but also what type and amount of support the patient may need during the weight goal progression time period.

Treatment

Nourishing the body.

Current daily intake should be used when establishing the initial meal plan. If the patient has been engaging in severe restriction (<800 cal./day) and/or excessive purging through self-induced vomiting, an initial calorie level between 800 and 1200 is appropriate. Serving foods such as soups, cheese and crackers, and juices helps promote fluid intake and restore electrolyte balance. With less severe restriction and purging, a calorie level between 1500 and 1800 may be initiated.

Calorie progression is tempered by the risk for refeeding complications. For those at risk, daily vital signs—morning weight, pulse, and orthostatic blood pressure readings—and frequent lab studies provide the careful monitoring necessary to identify initial signs of complications and to promote medical stability.

Although common and potentially fatal, refeeding syndrome is highly preventable. Refeeding syndrome refers to severe fluid and electrolyte shifts and associated medical complications that may occur when malnourished patients accept increased nutritional intake. To prevent refeeding syndrome, recommended calorie progression is 300 to 400 every four to five days (Mehler & Andersen, 1999). For the severely underweight patient, monitoring lab values for potassium (K), phosphorous (P), and magnesium (Mg) is critical to prevent refeeding syndrome. Oral supplementation for K, P, and/or Mg under the supervision of a primary care provider may be necessary.

Normal/intuitive eating is the standard for establishing a meal plan. Planning three meals a day with snacks, as appropriate, approximates normal eating. Teaching the patient to ask the following questions will also help the patient to understand and implement normal eating:

- What are my nutritional needs?
- Am I hungry?
- What am I in the mood for?
- What is available?
- What else am I eating today?
- Am I noticing what I am eating (smell, taste, texture)?
- When am I full?

It is also important to understand and discuss with the patient his/her psycho-physiological responses during refeeding. Although listening to hunger and satiety is a goal of intuitive eating, the body will not send appropriate messages during the refeeding process. For those with anorexia, hunger cues are typically absent and a false sense of fullness is continually present. It is important to explain to the underweight patient that hunger and satiety cues will most likely be inaccurate until a healthy weight is achieved, a maintenance meal plan is established for some time, and therapeutic issues are being addressed. For those with bulimia, hunger and satiety cues are unreliable and often dependent upon emotional stress and/or environmental triggers. The first step for those with bulimia is to normalize eating by consuming three meals a day and eliminating binges. Once a consistent meal pattern is established, body signals are more accurate and the patient may begin to practice intuitive eating. But if bingeing with or without a restricting prelude persists, hunger and satiety cues will remain inaccurate.

Several nourishment options should be considered when weight gain is needed. Separating maintenance and weight gain calories can be beneficial. Maintenance calories can be served through meals and snacks while weight gain calories may be served through supplemental options. Supplemental products, such as medical nutrition supplements, provide more nutrients with lower food volume and may be given in the form of shakes, puddings, juices, or cookies. Practically, these are often consumed as snacks.

Another option for the severely malnourished is nasogastric (NG) tube feeding. At Remuda, we have experienced positive results with NG tube feeding in anorexia. Providing weight gain nourishment through an NG tube allows meals and snacks to resemble a maintenance meal plan. NG tube feeding throughout the night distributes satiation levels and decreases gastrointestinal discomfort during the daytime. Other advantages, including more rapid weight gain, accrue to the use of NG tubes.

Remuda staff have published a scientific investigation of NG tube feeding in anorexia (Zuercher, Cumella, Woods, Eberly, & Carr, 2003). The study offers detailed instructions on the use of NG tubes with patients who have anorexia.

The study included 381 female inpatients with a *DSM-IV* (American Psychiatric Association [APA], 1994) diagnosis of anorexia nervosa, both subtypes, with 155 patients receiving tube feeding and oral refeeding and 226 receiving oral refeeding alone. Recovery from the psychological aspects of anorexia was measured by change in Eating Disorder Inventory-2 scores between admission and discharge. Patient satisfaction with treatment was measured using a Patient Satisfaction Questionnaire completed at discharge. Repeated measures and multivariate analyses were performed.

Controlling for severity-of-illness and caloric intake differences between patients with and without tube feeding, patients who received tube feeding gained significantly more weight per treatment week than those who received oral calories alone. Patients who received tube feeding for at least half their length of stay gained 1 kg. (2.2 lbs.) per week versus 0.77 kg. (1.7 lbs.) per week for patients receiving oral refeeding alone. Tube fed patients evidenced no differences in recovery from anorexia's psychological aspects, satisfaction with treatment, or medical complication frequency—suggesting that tube feeding does not have negative psychological or medical consequences for patients.

The study concludes that, in residential psychiatric treatment settings where intensive therapeutic interventions and appropriate medical monitoring can manage potential psychological and medical risks, tube feeding's weight gain benefits may be a viable and safe option in treating anorexia.

Achieving a healthy weight.

Achieving a healthy weight is a critical component of treating an eating disorder, not only in the professionals' mind but also the patients'. Weight history, stage of physical development including adolescent growth charts, and anthropometric data including height and frame size should be obtained. Body Mass Index (BMI) is commonly used to indicate weight appropriateness. Although BMI is useful, some observers believe that it is of limited utility in the treatment of eating disorders because it takes into consideration only height and weight. At Remuda, we obtain body composition measurements, specifically body fat percentage (BF%) and mid-arm muscle circumference (MAMC) through skin-fold caliper methods (Frisancho, 1981; Heyward & Stolarczyk, 1996; Lohman, 1992). This provides a more comprehensive assessment of nutritional status and more thoroughly evaluates the body's response to refeeding. Muscle mass, in particular, is a significant variable when determining a healthy weight. Although refined technical skill is necessary to conduct these measurements, we believe the ensuing weight range is more accurate and individualized. Sharing body composition data with patients can also be very effective in gaining their acceptance of a recommended weight range.

Due to normal weight fluctuation in the human body, establishing a weight range with a midpoint is more useful than focusing on a fixed weight or single number. A 10 lb. weight range is recommended for most women, and an 8 lb. range for children, adolescents, and those at or below 5 feet tall. Having the midpoint as the goal allows for normal, moderate fluctuation (due to temporary dehydration or edema, menstruation, etc.). Weight ranges may need to be reassessed over time for adolescents, in cases of weight restoration after severe emaciation, and to promote continued muscle growth through weight bearing exercise.

The recommended rate of weight gain per week is approximately 1 to 3 lbs. for inpatients and 1 lb. for outpatients. Gaining at a rate much greater than this may indicate edema, constipation, and/or precipitate refeeding complications (Mehler & Andersen, 1999). In our experience, the body replenishes fat and muscle tissue more proportionately at the 2 lbs. per week rate. Average weekly weight gains much below the recommendations may indicate patient resistance and/or an inappropriate level of care. Energy levels to promote weight gain are typically 1000 to 3000 calories greater per day than Basal Energy Expenditure (BEE) with an activity factor of 1.25. Total caloric needs may be as high as 3500 to 4000 per day to promote necessary weight gain (Reiff & Reiff, 1997). This occurs because of the hypermetabolic state needed to rebuild lost tissue and promote homeostasis. Using the calorie progression guidelines offered above in combination with monitoring patient weight progression should promote safe and adequate weight gain.

When weight loss is appropriate, an average of 0.5 to 2.0 lbs. per week is recommended. It is essential to establish and maintain the goals of focusing on the issues of the eating disorder, normalizing eating, eliminating binges, and letting the body heal, and not to concentrate on weight loss. In our experience, normalization of eating and cessation of bingeing promotes weight loss and/or decreases in BF% and increases in MAMC. In bulimia, the metabolism typically functions at a low to normal state. Remaining at or above 1500 to 1600 calories per day will prevent the reduction in metabolic rate associated with restriction and promote rejuvenation of the metabolism.

Achieving weight maintenance is one of the ultimate goals in recovery from an eating disorder. This includes remaining in a healthy weight range and acceptance of weight and appearance. However, as patients begin to eat regularly and gain needed weight, food fears and related issues will likely arise.

Nutrition Counseling with Eating Disorder Patients

> The purposes of a man's heart are deep waters, but a man of understanding draws them out. (Proverbs 20:5)

At one level, eating disorders are self-evidently about food. At another, they are about much more—misinformation, myths, and self-deception; anxiety, fear, and avoidance of problems. Because nutrition counseling seeks to reduce the overt symptoms related to food, nutrition counseling directly challenges patients to face the issues that drive their eating disorder. Therefore, treatment providers must often use creative techniques to discover and address patients' needs. This chapter describes tools that dietitians may use to accomplish this task, assisting patients to work through the myths and fears commonly associated with eating disorders.

Assessment

To begin this process, it is important to assess the patient's level of motivation (Cockell, 2000). A useful way to accomplish this is to evaluate the patient's recovery goals. This establishes the patient's level of readiness to change eating disorder behaviors. If a patient presents with the desire to change but is unsure of how to do so, the dietitian can provide assurance that a primary purpose of nutrition counseling is to assist with this objective. When experiencing ambivalence toward recovery, the patient can prepare a list of the pros and cons of keeping the eating disorder. This list can help to reestablish the value of recovery. Finally, identifying family, social, and environmental influences can help indicate the types of nutrition education and experientials that the patient may need.

Treatment

Nutrition education.

For the patient who is motivated to change, a good starting place is to provide basic nutrition education. Defining nutrition basics such as the function of carbohydrate, protein, and fat in the body can dispel misconceptions and allay common fears, such as the notion that "eating fat makes you fat." Explaining the Food Guide Pyramid teaches not only proper nourishment but also how to include balance, variety, and appropriate portioning in meal planning. Initial education will also involve rejecting the diet mentality and making peace with food; food is not the enemy.

Providing appropriate exercise guidelines supports the importance of exercise and the dangers of overexercising. It may be useful to educate the patient about the exercise guidelines offered by the American College of Sports Medicine (Pollock et al., 1998), which suggest that healthy exercise occurs:

- 3 to 5 times per week
- 30 to 60 minutes per session
- 1 session per day
- Includes aerobic, strength training, and flexibility exercises
- Is motivated by fun and enjoyment

Exploring myths.

Surely you desire truth in the inner parts…(Psalm 51:6)

Frequently, patients with eating disorders take one element of nutrition truth and hold to it as their golden rule, while ignoring other facts and accompanying guidelines. Out of context and with too much emphasis placed on it, this modicum of nutrition truth may transmogrify into a dangerous myth. Therefore, patients will often require nutrition reeducation according to the sound nutrition philosophy. They may also benefit from experientials to help them work through the dieting myths and misinformation which they have absorbed or developed and which have been leading them to make unhealthful eating choices.

One such experiential tool involves an exploration of how eating disorder trends and myths develop. The dietitian can explore with patients various influences on their nutrition beliefs, such as the media, family, sports coaches and trainers, fitness instructors, and the medical community. Discuss if or how any of these influences have affected the patient's thinking. Follow the discussion with a trip to a local bookstore. Visit the health/wellness section and review current books and magazines. Evaluate facts and fiction found in these resources. Offer healthy alternatives to the patient— magazines, books, and Web sites that counter the erroneous claims found in the popular culture. Ultimately, the practitioner should encourage patients to use awareness, discernment, and common sense in evaluating marketing claims. Reinforce healthy eating guidelines and flexibility in eating. This is the best way to maintain balance in the face of an ever-changing health and nutrition field.

Other field trips, such as a trip to a local health food store, can also prove effective in challenging myths about food. Prior to the field trip, discuss the definition of "normal eating." Normal eating is summarized well in Ellyn Satter's (1987) book, *How to Get Your Kid To Eat...But Not Too Much.* Providing information about normal eating in printed form, or referring patients to Satter's book, are both useful avenues of education.

Once at the health food store, examine products and evaluate them for appropriateness. Does this item fit into the definition of normal eating? Why or why not? What health food items are acceptable in a balanced meal plan? Examine nutrition labels and evaluate the claims made by nutritional supplements. Is this accurate information? How do manufacturers sometimes take a kernel of truth and expand it in order to sell products? A critical analysis of several items in a health food store can be a powerful tool for the patient. Learning about health food products may not motivate patients to change behaviors immediately, but may initiate contemplation for change. Ask what the patient's commitment is to changing unhealthy behaviors. Develop a plan together on how to take small steps toward recovery.

Fears and behaviors: exposure therapy.

It is essential for practitioners working with eating disorder patients to understand the role that anxiety often plays in the development of the disorder. Fear promotes self-protective behaviors that may be perceived by others as "controlling" behaviors. When people are fearful, they may take radical steps to manage their fears. Although the spectrum of fears and behaviors is vast, common themes emerge. Anxiety predominantly surrounds the fear of becoming physically fat. This typically results in a focus on dietary fat and/or calories but may generalize to other nutrients as well. Patients are often fearful of: places associated with food, such as grocery stores, restaurants, or kitchens; preparing food; and eating with others. These fears may manifest through a variety of behaviors intended to provide relief from the intense anxiety. Such behaviors include excessive avoidance of food; bingeing; purging; cooking without eating; repeated calorie and/or fat gram counting; frequent weighing; social isolation; excessive exercise; and food rituals. It is essential in treating eating disorders to address the actual fears and behaviors related to eating. In conjunction with a multidisciplinary treatment team, dietitians may address these fears over time through the types of nutrition education described above, through skill enhancement and exposure therapy.

Psalm 23:3-4 reminds us that: "He guides me in paths of righteousness for his name's sake. Even though I walk through the valley of the shadow of death, I will fear no evil, for you are with me." The Lord leads us in paths of righteousness, and sometimes these paths—by his design—journey through terrain of which we are afraid. Yet we may confront what we are afraid of and, with God's guidance, overcome the fear. As the psalm suggests, fear of anything but God is, in truth, a shadow, a myth, and a falsehood from which little good may come. "The LORD is my light and my salvation—whom shall I fear?" (Psalm 27:1). "Do not let your hearts be troubled and do not be afraid" (John 14:27).

For those with eating disorders, overcoming anxiety and fear and learning to make healthful food choices is a process accomplished over time, not overnight. The Lord walks us through the valley. This process involves reeducation, exposure with response prevention, and opportunities to practice newly developed skills to reduce the anxiety associated with food and eating. With the guidance of a professional, eating disorder patients may experience their food and eating-related fears and finish the journey less afraid.

Exposure to fear foods/bulimia group. This exercise may occur individually or in a group. Assemble foods in the center of the room or table. Include a variety of foods, such as pizza, chips, candy, and other "party foods." For patients with bulimia, these may be foods used in binges. Music may be used to create a party atmosphere. Allow each participant to serve herself, encouraging intuitive eating. No specific portions or eating everything on plate required, nor is binge behavior permitted. Eating these foods in a safe setting with peers and therapists provides practice. Not only does this enable patients to see that these foods are permissible, but also that they can eat these foods without binging.

Restaurant experientials. Restaurant settings provide another beneficial venue for patients to face and overcome fears. Restaurants present a challenge for patients for a variety of reasons, including patients' feeling self-conscious while eating in public, not knowing what to order or how much to eat, and not trusting how the food was prepared. Scheduling time to eat with patients in a public setting can provide many clues about the nature of their struggles. Preparation for the restaurant experiential is the key to success. Below we describe some practical tools to aid the practitioner in conducting this experiential.

Create the plan together. Involving the patient in as many aspects of this experiential as possible enhances the chances for success. First, select a restaurant well in advance. This may range from a few days to a few weeks ahead, depending on the patient's anxiety level. Next, establish goals with the patient. For a patient with bulimia, the goals should include: 1) listening to hunger and satiety cues, while 2) eating an appropriate amount, and 3) leaving some food on the plate. For a patient with restricting anorexia, the goals should involve: 1) ordering a fear food as is from the menu, and 2) eating at least half the entrée.

Advise the patient to use the restaurant experience as a challenge to make choices different from those made during the eating disorder. This may mean ordering a food with cream sauce or French fries, or ordering one entrée instead of two or three. Set three to five reasonable goals together prior to the event and discuss the skills that the patient may use to accomplish these goals. Ask what they may need from you to help them succeed. Will you play the role of "food police" at the table, or carry on pleasant conversation as a means of distraction? Establish ground rules before the meal concerning redirection and discussion of ineffective behaviors. The patient may prefer to receive this during the meal or to discuss problem behaviors afterward. Learn how the patient best receives this information. Humor, matter-of-fact confrontation, "code" signals, or a combination of these may be most effective for a particular patient.

Ideally, a counseling session should immediately follow the restaurant outing to provide the patient with support and accountability. Did the patient meet his/her goals? If yes, how was this accomplished? Could the challenge transfer to other areas of recovery or life? If goals were not met, what might have been done differently? When will they have an opportunity to practice again? A restaurant challenge can be an exciting step forward for the patient since this is likely a regular part of life that has been avoided for some time. Affirm the progress made and challenge the behaviors still needing change.

These tools constitute a small sampling of creative interventions used at Remuda Treatment Centers. Additional tools are described in Reiff & Reiff (1997) and Hayes, King, & Kratina (1996).

Eating disorder recovery is gradual; gains are typically made in small steps. Victory occurs with each positive choice that patients make instead of repeating old behaviors. Celebrate these victories and continue to challenge patients toward additional progress.

Conclusion

The range of nutrition interventions detailed in this chapter strongly support the need for inclusion of a registered dietitian as an integral member of an eating disorder treatment team. This position is further established by the American Dietetic Association (Henry & Ozier, 2006) and is an element of best practice in the multidisciplinary treatment of ED patients.

References

American Psychiatric Association. (1994). *Diagnostic and Statistical Manual of Mental Disorders, Text Revision* (4th ed.) *(DSM-IV)*. Washington, DC: Author.

Cockell, S.J. (2000). *A decisional balance measure of readiness for change in anorexia nervosa.* Dissertation Abstracts International. (UMI No. NQ56661).

Food and Drug Administration and National Institutes of Health (2003). *Healthy people 2010: 19. Nutrition and weight.* Retrieved from http://www.healthypeople.gov/document/HTML/Volume2/19Nutrition.html

Frisancho, A.R. (1981). New norms of upper limb fat and muscle areas for assessment of nutritional status. *American Journal of Clinical Nutrition,* 34, 2540.

Hayes, D., King, N., & Kratina, K. (1996). *Moving away from diets.* Lake Dallas: Helm Seminars Publishing.

Henry, B.W. & Ozier, A.D. (2006). Position of the American Dietetic Association: Nutrition intervention in the treatment of anorexia nervosa, bulimia nervosa, and other eating disorders. *Journal of the American Dietetic Association, 106,* 2073-82.

Heyward, V.H. & Stolarczyk, L.M. (1996) *Applied body composition assessment.* Champaign, IL: Human Kinetics Publishers.

Kilbourne, J. (1999). *Deadly persuasion: Why women and girls must fight the addictive power of advertising*. New York: The Free Press.

Lohman, T.G. (1992). *Advances in body composition assessment.* Champaign, IL: Human Kinetics Publishers.

Mehler, P.S. & Andersen, A.E. (1999). *Eating disorders: A guide to medical care and complications.* Baltimore, MD: John Hopkins University Press.

Pollock, M.L., Gaesser, G.A., Butcher, J.D., Després, J-P., Dishman, R.K., Franklin, B.A., & Garber, C.E. (1998). Position Stand of the American College of Sports Medicine: The recommended quantity and quality of exercise for developing and maintaining cardiorespiratory and muscular fitness, and flexibility in healthy adults. *Medicine & Science in Sports & Exercise, 30.*

Reiff, D.W. & Reiff, K.K.L. (1997). *Eating disorders: Nutrition therapy in the recovery process.* Mercer Island, WA: Life Enterprises Publishers.

Satter, E. (1987). *How to get your kid to eat . . . but not too much.* Palo Alto, CA: Bull Publishing Co.

Tribole, E.T. & Resch E. (1995). *Intuitive eating.* New York: St. Martin's Press.

U.S. Department of Agriculture and the U.S. Department of Health and Human Services (2000). *Dietary guidelines for Americans.* Retrieved from http://www.health.gov/dietaryguidelines/dga2000/document/summary/ default.htm

U.S. Department of Agriculture and the U.S. Department of Health and Human Services (1992). *Food guide pyramid.* Retrieved from http://www.nal.usda.gov/fnic/Fpyr/pyramid.html

Wall, A.D. & Eberly, M. (2002). Five biblical factors in eating disorder development. *The Remuda Review,* 1, 6-10.

Zuercher, J. N., Cumella, E. J., Woods, B. K., Eberly, M., & Carr, J. (2003). The efficacy of voluntary nasogastric tube feeding in female inpatients with anorexia nervosa. *Journal of Parenteral and Enteral Nutrition, 27,* 268-76.

Note: The Nutrition Counseling with Eating Disorder Patients section of this chapter is based on an article written for Remuda Ranch Programs for Eating Disorders in part by Shannon Heffern, RD.

Part III

Psychological Dimension of Eating Disorders

Chapter 6

Cognitive-Behavioral Therapy with Eating Disorders: Foundations

A. David Wall, PhD

Cognitive-Behavioral Therapy (CBT) is commonly considered the most scientifically-valid psychotherapeutic approach to eating disorders (Yager et al., 2006). But some Christians have concerns about CBT. They associate it with humanistic psychology in general, and specifically with controversial figures such as Albert Ellis, whose writings–e.g., *The Justification of Sex Without Love* (Ellis, 1966)–raise red flags for Christians.

Remuda believes that CBT can be extraordinarily consistent with, and expressive of, scriptural truth. Indeed, Remuda bases its therapeutic interventions on CBT. We therefore examine: 1) what CBT is, 2) how CBT applies to eating disorders, and 3) why CBT can serve as a primary modality in biblically-based eating disorder treatment. The next chapter in this book focuses in more detail on specific CBT strategies and tools.

What Is CBT?

CBT begins with a behavioral view of human beings. It recognizes that human behavior depends on how our previous behavioral responses to the environment have been reinforced and punished. However, behaviorism asserts that this learning history alone explains human behavior. It denies free choice. But CBT affirms human freedom. According to CBT, when individuals experience stimuli they have only learned *tendencies* to respond in a particular manner. They also have the ability to contemplate and choose a response. In short, CBT asserts that individuals process stimuli cognitively and respond according to their cognitions or thoughts. Hence, CBT is not just behavioral, but *cognitive*-behavioral.

Process and Content

Process. Cognitive processing is simply the mechanism by which human beings handle incoming information to respond to complex stimuli. Cognitive processing itself is neutral—neither healthy nor pathological. It is a fact of brain functioning.

Content. Cognitive processing is guided by well-developed, learned belief systems, known as *schemas.* These belief systems or schemas influence how we perceive reality. For example, a person who comes from a loving family and believes in basic human goodness may perceive an approaching stranger as an innocent tourist needing directions. A person who comes from an abusive family and believes that human beings are dangerous may perceive the approaching stranger as a mugger, a rapist, or a threat of some other kind. By processing the same information from the environment, two different conclusions would be reached because each person is guided by a different schema.

Pathology arises from the content of schemas. Schemas filled with irrational beliefs result in defective and maladaptive behavioral choices. False/irrational assumptions yield false/irrational conclusions. The degree of psychopathology is related to how irrational belief systems are, that is, how inconsistent beliefs and cognitions are with reality and logic. Here is an example.

Rattlesnakes are dangerous. This is a logical and rational conclusion, because in reality people bitten by rattlesnakes suffer deleterious consequences. However, concluding that a caterpillar is dangerous is irrational, because caterpillars do not harm people.

Fear is the emotional response engendered by the belief that something is dangerous. With the rattlesnake, fear is rational emoting, consistent with reality. With the caterpillar, fear is irrational emoting, inconsistent with reality.

Rational emotions are necessary to help us make wise choices, such as avoiding a rattlesnake. Emotions are rational when they flow out of rational, reality-based beliefs and "when they help you achieve [life] goals" (Ellis & Harper, 1975, p. 23). Irrational emotions flow out of irrational beliefs, cause unnecessary psychic pain, and typically lead to behaviors that make things worse; e.g., someone cannot sleep for fear that a caterpillar may crawl into bed. This situation would constitute psychopathology.

CBT's core therapeutic principle is to help individuals distinguish beliefs, perceptions, cognitions, and behaviors that are rational and appropriate from those that are irrational and inappropriate—to change the content of schemas. A variety of methods have been developed to effect these changes.

When schemas become more rational, so do emotions. If I no longer believe that caterpillars are dangerous, I will not experience fear around caterpillars. My psychopathology, my phobia, will be alleviated.

CBT is not defined by specific interventions, such as adherence to a therapy manual or the format of thought journals. Nor is CBT defined by what various authors may opine to be rational versus irrational beliefs. Instead, CBT is defined by the scientific understanding of cognitive processing and by the application of a *variety* of methods that share the common features of examining schemas, determining how beliefs impact current emotional and behavioral functioning, and helping patients to modify schemas to reflect more rational beliefs. CBT's methods may include any intervention that expresses this core therapeutic principle.

Many therapeutic issues arise from situations more complex than fear of a caterpillar. Is it rational or irrational for a female rape victim to conclude that men are dangerous? Such a belief may indeed protect her from a repetition of her trauma. Such a person may need assistance in developing a more complex and sophisticated schema—e.g., the recognition that only some men are dangerous under certain circumstances—and testing this revised schema safely against reality through controlled practice. In some cases, discerning rational from irrational beliefs is less a matter of observable fact and more a matter of moral judgment. For example, is it rational or irrational to have negative cognitions about engaging in premarital sex? Is guilt, in this case, rational or irrational emoting? This depends on the patient's sociocultural and religious experience. Psychotherapists using CBT must be sensitive to the complexities and sociocultural context of each case.

Formation and Function of Schemas

How are schemas formed? Children encounter a multitude of learning experiences. Their brains look for patterns, structures, and cues that make situations predictable. Predictability allows for anticipation. Accurate anticipation permits adaptive responses, enhancing survival and thriving.

The patterns, structures, and cues perceived by the brain are formed into distinct belief systems or schemas. Schemas are mental maps that help individuals interpret situations and choose appropriate responses. Ellis states that schemas help us fulfill life goals (Ellis & Harper, 1975, p. 23). Others suggest that we are born with certain needs and that schemas provide blueprints to meet these needs with minimal risk. Although there is disagreement about what these needs are, they likely include air, water, food, sleep, connections with others, a sense of significance and purpose, a sense of power and autonomy, and love (e.g., Maslow, 1970).

After a schema has been reinforced for a period of time it becomes ingrained and self-perpetuating. A tendency arises to perceive events in such a way that they are consistent with and can be readily assimilated into existing schemas, rather than to change or accommodate schemas to fit events. Information that is consistent with a schema is noticed and even sought after, while inconsistent information is filtered out. Schemas that involve strong emotion, like most eating disorder schemas, are the most difficult to change.

In summary:

1. Schemas are belief systems.
2. Schemas develop through learning as we encounter life situations.
3. Schemas guide how we interpret events.
4. Schemas include beliefs about how to meet our needs.
5. Schemas filter out or interpret as consistent contradictory information—they are self-perpetuating.
6. Schemas most resist change when they are highly emotionally charged.

CBT and Eating Disorders

Recently, I looked at a blueberry muffin and wondered: What has to happen to transform this muffin into a big problem? A muffin can be the stimulus for major power struggles in families. It can make intelligent teenagers cry uncontrollably—irrational emoting. How does this happen?

Self and Eating Disorder Schemas

A central schema, the self-schema, organizes and incorporates what each person has come to believe about him/herself based upon life experiences. Beliefs about intelligence, likeability, beauty, shyness, talents, shame, and other areas are included in this schema.

As children grow and experience more of life, the self-schema changes. Pre- and early teens are constantly searching for information from the environment to define themselves and develop self-schemas that will guide and protect them and meet their needs. The self-schema tends to crystallize as teens get older. New information is assimilated/interpreted to fit the self-schema, rather than the self-schema changing to fit the information. The self-schema—an emotionally charged view of oneself—becomes resistant to change.

Early on, food is simply food. Emotion-generating aspects of food arise from whether or not the food tastes good, features of the caregiver-child relationship, and the context in which the food is given, such as fun at a birthday party. A food schema is developed from these experiences. At some point, especially for girls, a connection is made between food and body image. The food and self-schemas intertwine. Conflicts arise as good-pleasurable food, an approach tendency, collides with the possibility of becoming fat, an avoidance tendency. As girls reach puberty, strong connections are made between body image/physical attractiveness and worth/approval/love. Girls may see what happens to those perceived as thin and attractive versus those perceived as fat. These perceptions are not distortions of reality, but are, unfortunately, rational in light of anti-weight biases in American culture.

Now, when a young woman looks at a blueberry muffin, she no longer sees just a muffin. She sees through a belief system that associates muffins with fat, rejection, and loneliness. So she may avoid the muffin, as well as other foods associated with negative expectations. In some cases, she develops anorexia. In other cases, she eats but learns to purge, developing bulimia.

Illustrative Example

Case history. Lucy is 19 years old. She grew up with a workaholic dad. She cannot recall him ever saying the words "I love you." Dad was also unaffectionate with her mother. However, he provided well and was interested in Lucy's achievements. Lucy watched the joking and affectionate relationships her friends had with their dads, and she longed for this.

Mom had "weight issues" when Lucy was younger. When Lucy was a teenager, her mom became very strict in dieting, a "health-nut." Now Mom is slender and very body focused. Dad has increased his attention to her since she lost weight.

Lucy is very attractive. She began attracting male attention as early as seventh grade. In her sophomore year, she began dating a popular senior, Jared. As a Christian, Lucy had determined not to have sex until marriage. But a year into her relationship with Jared, she was regularly sleeping with him.

Lucy had flirted with an eating disorder for much of her teens. She had experimented with self-induced vomiting, but ultimately found that by exercising two hours a day, and more on weekends, she could keep her weight down without vomiting.

Lucy was certain that Jared was the man she should marry. Whenever he came back to town from the state university regularly; they slept together. Then Lucy heard from a friend that Jared was cheating on her. She refused to believe it until Jared confessed when she confronted him on the phone.

After he hung up on her, she immediately went into the bathroom and threw up due to the emotional shock. She felt slightly better. Before long she was causing herself to vomit. Soon she was bingeing as well.

Case conceptualization. Let's look at Lucy's life from a CBT perspective. What needs did she have? What had she learned from her experiences? What was her self-schema?

Lucy's need for love and attention from males was primary. Unfulfilled over the years, it had grown strong.

Due to her father's lack of affection, she had not learned that she was worthy of love and approval simply because of who she is. In contrast, from her mother's focus on appearance, her father's positive reaction to her mother's weight loss, and her experiences at school she had learned that attention comes primarily from appearance.

Lucy may have concluded: "There is nothing about me that is worth loving, except my body." "I can use my attractiveness to gain love." "If I stop being attractive, I will be rejected."

We interpret events to fit our schemas. Lucy might have seen Jared's rejection of her as his inability to be faithful, but instead she interpreted it according to her schema—as evidence that she is unworthy of love from a man.

When we are insecure, we retreat to areas where we feel most competent. For Lucy, this meant appearance. The more hurt and insecure, the more body focused she became. To her, that was the solution.

Treatment considerations. Eating disorder behaviors often become the primary tool that individuals use to meet needs. Although eating disorders' outward behaviors may look similar across patients, the needs being fulfilled—the function(s) of the eating disorder—usually differ. It is necessary to understand the function(s) in order to effect therapeutic change.

Eating disorders are irrational, unhealthy ways of pursuing what are, at a foundational level, rational, healthy goals. In Lucy's case, she wants to be loved by a man—a rational and healthy goal. She believes that she will receive love primarily for physical attractiveness—a logical conclusion given her experiences. And so she pursues love through compulsive exercise and purging—logical behaviors given her beliefs. These behaviors may work in the short-term. When patients believe that their needs can only be met through an eating disorder, they resist treatment. It is therefore essential to help patients separate the legitimate function(s) of the eating disorder from the eating disorder itself. To accomplish this, rapport and validation are critical. CBT confirms for Lucy that there are rational reasons why she has an eating disorder—a validation of her need for love and the legitimacy of this goal.

In addition to validation, CBT confronts Lucy with the ability—and thus the choice—to change. The ability to change lies in changing her belief systems or schemas. Change-oriented interventions with Lucy might begin by teaching her the basics about how schemas are formed, to connect her past experiences to her current belief system, and to help her see how she interprets events. As she recognizes the logical connection between her experiences and the development of her eating disorder, she will experience a reduction in shame. In the absence of this information, she will explain her eating disorder using her negative self-schema: "I must be a really sick person," "I am hopelessly sinful," "I am a worthless loser."

Parodies of CBT suggest that people can change beliefs simply by looking in the mirror and repeating self-affirmations. Nothing could be further from the truth. Our most significant and often troubling schemas are formed primarily in the context of relationships (Beck & Freeman, 1990), as Lucy's were formed in relation to her father, mother, and boys at school. Thus, schemas can best be transformed in the context of relationships. To focus strictly on changing distorted cognitions apart from a relational context is likely to be ineffective. Furthermore, patients' existing relationships usually reinforce or exacerbate existing schemas. But a directive therapeutic relationship can help transform schemas.

The importance of relationships cannot be overemphasized. It is essential to recognize that the function of eating disorders—the rational goal—is almost always relational. These relational needs are experienced and/or expressed by patients in various ways, such as: I want to connect with others. I don't want to be rejected or attacked. I want to have autonomy and control over my life. I want to be heard. I want attention, to be significant. I want my family to get along. I don't want to be a sexual object. I don't want to be afraid. I want to be loved. For Lucy, the relational goal was the desire to be loved by a man.

CBT helps the patient to see the legitimate relational goal(s) of the eating disorder. It proceeds to assist the person in seeing the cost of using the eating disorder to meet this goal, as well as the eating disorder's ultimate ineffectiveness in achieving the relational goal. CBT then introduces and assists the person to develop new ways of meeting legitimate relational needs, such as skills training and wise mind (Linehan, 1993)—i.e., learning not to have emotions be the primary determinant of reality. Patients cannot give up an eating disorder if they have nothing to replace it with. New skills are essential. Through new skills, CBT helps the person to develop healthier relationships. Healthy relationships better meet the person's relational needs, making the eating disorder obsolete.

In Lucy's case, cognitive restructuring may focus on her self-schema, assisting her to develop an intrinsic sense of worth as a human being and self-esteem based on her many positive qualities apart from her appearance. The therapist can create cognitive dissonance by reflecting how Lucy's values—such as not judging people based on their appearance—conflict with the beliefs she imposes on herself. Cognitive dissonance disrupts homeostasis and motivates the person to resolve the dissonance. Assertion skills training may be needed to help Lucy recognize and appropriately ask for her emotional needs to be met in relationships with men and express her feelings to her family. Lucy may benefit from emotion identification and regulation skills, so that she need not rely on eating disorder behaviors to handle difficult feelings. Other tools will likely be incorporated into treatment.

CBT as a Biblically-Based Treatment Modality

More than many psychological approaches, CBT arose from scientific research. As demonstrated in Part I of this book, because the methods of science study God's creation objectively they are capable of revealing truths that were built into the creation by the Creator. So with CBT.

To begin, scientific research has recognized that the human brain readily packages experiences and information into organized belief systems/schemas and that such schemas allow human beings to manage a wealth of information and respond to the environment in ways that meet basic needs. This inherent schema-building process of the human brain is an intelligent, adaptive function, which Christians would attribute to God's design.

But CBT is consistent with Scripture not merely in describing how the brain was designed by God to function, but also—and more importantly—in recognizing that thoughts and belief systems matter greatly in healthy mental functioning. This truth has long been understood by Christians, and has in a sense been reaffirmed by CBT's scientific research.

The Bible, like CBT, acknowledges the centrality of thought. Scripture indicates that when our thoughts dwell on evil, we are harmed. "Their thoughts are evil thoughts; ruin and destruction mark their ways" (Isaiah 59:7). The Bible accordingly exhorts us to "take captive every thought to make it obedient to Christ" (2 Corinthians 10:5), and instructs that "whatever is true, whatever is noble, whatever is right, whatever is pure, whatever is lovely, whatever is admirable—if anything is excellent or praiseworthy—think about such things" (Philippians 4:8-9). This latter verse resembles a CBT assignment: Change your thoughts to focus on the positive rather than the negative. Strikingly, the Bible teaches that our thoughts define who we are: "For as he thinks in his heart, so is he" (Proverbs 23:7 NKJV).

Perhaps the biblical counsel that most concisely expresses the core therapeutic principle of CBT is this: "Do not conform any longer to the pattern of this world, but be transformed by the renewing of your mind" (Romans 12:2). We see clearly in this verse the biblical perspective: Changing how we perceive reality–renewing the mind–is central to achieving psychological and spiritual health. This is likewise the primary tenet of CBT.

In this Bible verse, two words stand out—*conform* and *transform*.

Conform means to follow the same pattern. We have seen how cognitive processing searches for patterns in the world to form beliefs/schemas about how things work. But the Bible teaches that we live in a broken world. We therefore develop schemas that reflect the limitations of a sin-endowed environment and fallen sociocultural order. We learn that life's primary goals are to gain pleasure and avoid pain, climb and succeed, achieve power and wealth, be physically attractive and sexually active. We are taught that, rather than being created by a loving God, we evolved and are subject to the law of survival of the fittest. All people, including Christians, accept this "world schema" to one extent or another. Girls and women, in particular, absorb distorted beliefs about their bodies and self-worth that can lead them to eating disorders.

According to Scripture, the solution involves a mental transformation, a renewing of the mind. To *transform* means to change form. The New Testament Greek word is *metamorphous*, as in a caterpillar changing form to become a butterfly. The transformation to which the Bible refers involves changing from a schema derived from the fallen world to God's schema or God's way of seeing things. God's schema involves no distortions, misperceptions, denial, or lies. It is truth. It involves natural and easily observable facts as well as deeper spiritual and moral truths revealed in Scripture. " 'For my thoughts are not your thoughts, neither are your ways my ways,' declares the LORD" (Isaiah 55:8).

In Christian CBT with eating disorder patients, mental renewal occurs when patients are offered and build a self-schema from gospel truths. Key truths include:

1) You were created by a loving God with intrinsic value apart from your appearance, gifts, talents, or willingness to do for others. "And even the very hairs of your head are all numbered. So don't be afraid; you are worth more than many sparrows" (Matthew 10:30-31). "…I am fearfully and wonderfully made" (Psalm 139:14). "God is love…" (1 John 4:16).

2) Nothing you have done in the past can change your great worth and value today. "Because of the LORD's great love we are not consumed, for his compassions never fail. They are new every morning; great is your faithfulness" (Lamentations 3:22-23). "There is now no condemnation for those who are in Christ Jesus" (Romans 8:1). "If we confess our sins, he is faithful and just and will forgive us…" (1 John 1:9).

3) Your life has meaning, value, and purpose. " 'For I know the plans I have for you,' declares the LORD, 'plans to prosper you and not to harm you, plans to give you hope and a future' " (Jeremiah 29:11).

4) What you are attempting to achieve through the eating disorder is a legitimate and appropriate need. It is not necessary for you to let go of this need; in fact, God intends to fulfill this need in a life-giving way. "…God will meet all your needs according to his glorious riches in Christ Jesus" (Philippians 4:19). "I have come that they may have life, and have it to the full" (John 10:10).

5) The eating disorder may have worked to some extent in meeting your legitimate needs, but it is costing you much and is killing you. "There is a way that seems right to a man, but in the end it leads to death" (Proverbs 16:25).

6) You are not a powerless victim over the eating disorder or difficult experiences from your past. There is a way out. "In all these things we are more than conquerors through him who loved us" (Romans 8:37). "For God did not give us a spirit of timidity, but a spirit of power…." (2 Timothy 1:7). "…when you are tempted, he will also provide a way out so that you can stand up under it" (1 Corinthians 10:13).

7) The way out includes an examination and transformation of your beliefs and usual ways of perceiving the world, a new schema. "…be transformed by the renewing of your mind" (Romans 12:2). "…take captive every thought to make it obedient to Christ" (2 Corinthians 10:5).

Summary

By assisting patients to renew the mind, Christian CBT promotes a therapeutic transformation: from irrational to rational schemas, emoting, and behaviors that are consistent with God's plan for each person whom he has lovingly made.

References

Beck, A. & Freeman, A. (1990). *Cognitive therapy of personality disorders.* New York: The Guilford Press. [N.B. The notion that schemas are primarily formed in the context of relationships is woven throughout this book.]

Ellis, A. (1966). *Sex without guilt.* Fort Lee, NJ: Lyle Stuart.

Ellis, A. & Harper, R.A. (1975). *A new guide to rational living.* Hollywood, CA: Wilshire Book Co.

Linehan, M.M. (1993) *Cognitive behavioral treatment of borderline personality disorder.* New York: Guilford Press.

Maslow, A.H. (1970). *Motivation and personality* (2nd ed.). New York: Harper & Row.

Yager, J., Devlin, M.J., Halmi, K.A., Herzog, D.B., Mitchell, J.E., Powers, P., et al. (2006). Practice guideline for the treatment of patients with eating disorders (3rd ed.). *American Journal of Psychiatry.* Retrieved November 10, 2006, from http://www.psych.org/psych_pract /treatg/pg/prac_guide.cfm

Chapter 7

Cognitive-Behavioral Therapy with Eating Disorders: Applications and Skills

Marian C. Eberly, RN, MSW, LCSW, DAPA, A. David Wall, PhD, and Dena Cabrera, PsyD

New wine must be poured into new wineskins. (Luke 5:38)

Cognitive-Behavioral Therapy (CBT) is commonly considered the most scientifically-valid psychotherapeutic approach to eating disorders (American Psychiatric Association, 2000; Richards & Baldwin, 2000). It is also particularly consistent with and expressive of scriptural truth (Wall, 2003). One component of CBT found to be especially helpful to eating disorder patients is the learning and practice of specific skill-sets. In learning new skills, maladaptive emotional and behavioral patterns which keep patients entrenched in the eating disorder are replaced with adaptive and effective methods for managing emotions and choosing behaviors.

A recent CBT treatment model includes cognitive and behavioral skills work specifically designed to support patients who struggle with emotional and behavioral regulation problems, such as those with borderline personality or self-injury/parasuicide (Linehan, 1993a). Like these patients, eating disorder patients struggle with an impaired ability to regulate their emotions and frequently demonstrate a lack of ability to tolerate distress. These primary skills deficits require clinical attention if patients are to find relief from the emotional chaos and destructive results of their choices and actions. In our view, after nutritional restoration, attending to these skills deficits is *the single most important ingredient* in the provision of clinical treatment for those with eating disorders. The teaching of biblically-based skill sets supports patients in tangible ways long after termination of treatment.

Between 23% and 80% of eating disorder patients are diagnosed with personality disorders, most often cluster B (dramatic-erratic) disorders, particularly borderline personality disorder or traits (Wonderlich, 1995). At Remuda, we have determined that 99% of patients have one or more indicators of emotion regulation problems, including a personality disorder diagnosis and/or psychological test data suggestive of such problems. As such, eating disorder patients routinely evidence emotion dysregulation issues similar to those suffering from borderline personality. This is clearly not new information for those familiar with eating disorders. The comparison between eating disorder and borderline personality traits is striking. (See Table 1.)

Given this association between borderline personality and eating disorder features, it has become evident that eating disorder patients can benefit from skills training that addresses the common behavioral and emotional

Table 1. Comparison of Borderline Personality and Eating Disorder Traits

BORDERLINE PERSONALITY	*Area of Dysregulation*	EATING DISORDERS
1. Emotional Instability	*Emotional*	1. Emotional Instability, Numbness, Alexithymia
2. Anger Problems		2. Anger, Hostility, Irritability
3. Unstable Relationships	*Interpersonal*	3. Conflictual Relationships
4. Efforts to Avoid Loss		4. Weak Social Support, Isolation
5. Suicide Threats, Parasuicide	*Behavioral*	5. Self-Starvation, Parasuicide, Medical Complications
6. Self-Damaging, Impulsive Behaviors, including ETOH/Drugs, Promiscuity, Shoplifting		6. Impulsive Behaviors, including ETOH/Drugs, Bingeing, Purging, Promiscuity, Shoplifting
7. Cognitive Disturbances, Black-and-White Thinking	*Cognitive*	7. Cognitive Distortions, Black-and-White Thinking, Rigidity
8. Unstable Self and Self-Image	*Self*	8. Low Self-Esteem
9. Chronic Emptiness		9. Lack of Identity

dysregulations. Specifically, the acquisition of biblically-based skills can help to decrease labile emotions, interpersonal chaos, impulsiveness, confusion about self and identity, cognitive dysregulation and distortions, and spiritual confusion; and can serve to increase interpersonal effectiveness, emotion regulation, distress tolerance, and acceptance, as well as awareness of self, environment, and God's action in the patient's life.

The CBT skills training model is predicated on several assumptions regarding these difficult to treat patients (Linehan, 1993b):

- Patients are generally doing the best they can
- Suicidal and borderline individuals' lives are unbearable as they are currently being lived
- Patients may not have caused many of their problems, but have to solve them anyway
- Patients need to do better, try harder, and be more motivated to change
- Patients want to improve
- If patients could do something different, they would
- These patients need to learn new ways of dealing with their thoughts and feelings through the acquisition of skills
- Patients must learn new behaviors in all relevant contexts
- It is essential to believe in patients' ability to get out of the misery and build a life worth living: to instill hope
- Validate whatever you can, truthfully

The model relies on a twofold premise: *acceptance* on the one hand and *change* on the other. These balance and counterbalance one another: We validate patients while challenging them to change the eating disorders' cognitive distortions. This twofold approach is clearly consistent with scriptural wisdom. Jesus often implored us to do *both–and*. In the story of the woman caught in adultery (John 8:1-11), Jesus forgave the woman—validating her worth as a human being; and he also told her to "go and sin no more"—challenging her to change. In essence, this dual message mirrors the essential gospel truth that we are forgiven *and* must also change our ways of thinking and acting to proceed in a new direction.

At Remuda, we have been strategically incorporating an adapted form of CBT skills work into our curriculum since 2000, fully integrating the skills with scriptural truth. Our biblical adaptation has been accomplished without compromising the integrity of the Word of God or the biblical integrative work that is foundational to the Remuda system.

We initially utilized the CBT skills training approach with the most refractory patients to supplement standard treatment interventions. We soon found it to be exceptionally beneficial to the entire patient population. Our front line treatments continue to be nutritional and medical stabilization, family therapy, and traditional CBT. Yet the inclusion of Christian CBT skills training has enhanced our treatment program, influencing and improving our therapeutic outcomes significantly (Cumella, 2003).

CBT Skills Training

The overarching goal of CBT skills training is to modify or replace learned behavioral, emotional, and thought response patterns associated with problems in living, patterns which contribute to the personal and interpersonal misery and distress of the patient and which may impact her health.

For many eating disorder patients, modifying or stopping certain eating disorder behaviors may be incredibly difficult, creating resentment and resistance to therapeutic interventions. Therapeutic suggestions are often met with defensiveness fueled by irrational fears and a perceived threat that the treatment team is attempting to control the patient and intrude on his/her security. At the same time, patients are often aware that the choices they are making are life threatening, and they realize that they are harming themselves. As therapists take the stance of emphasizing validation and acceptance, recognizing how difficult it can be for patients to embrace change, these therapists are able to support patients emotionally as they work through this ambivalence. Skills training then provides an opportunity to objectify patient ambivalence by putting the focus on the need to change maladaptive symptom behaviors and learn techniques/tools to assist with this change. All the while, patients feel validated as persons with legitimate needs—needs they have been attempting to address through their eating disorder.

CBT skills training squarely focuses on these core strategies of validation and problem solving in an attempt to facilitate change. Validating patients' needs provides an empathetic understanding of their difficulties and suffering. Problem solving focuses on developing, enhancing, and building necessary adaptive skills. Thus, the course of therapy includes changing behaviors and incorporating cognitive and behavioral techniques to increase the patients' understanding of the function(s) underlying symptom behaviors. In this process there is an identification of the antecedents that lead to problem behaviors as well as the consequences of those behaviors. Once antecedents are identified, prevention strategies are created to decrease maladaptive behaviors in the future. Because eating disorder patients need to pay attention to modifying their behaviors, not just insight or understanding, skills acquisition results in sustained life changes.

In fact, skills training addresses all three aspects of the human soul—emotions, thoughts, and will (Wall & Eberly, 2002). It helps patients to regulate emotions effectively, to modify thoughts realistically, and—because of its validation of their legitimate underlying needs and dignity as persons—helps them to feel free to choose new behaviors without feeling that their identity is being compromised.

While engaged in skills training, the daily use of a self monitoring tool helps patients keep track of skills they have been using as well as other tools and skills available to them. Other cognitively-focused techniques, such as worksheets and assignments, assist patients in their behavioral progress, accountability, and skill generalization. For instance, in skills training patients are taught how to conduct their own behavior chain analysis, which helps them identify a problem behavior, what may be interfering with solving the problem, and skills that can be used to replace the behavior.

Four CBT skills training modules (Linehan, 1993b) have been reorganized, adapted, and modified for use at Remuda through thoughtful integration with Scripture. The redesigned skills training sessions emphasize two goals: 1) decreasing behaviors likely to interfere with therapy and recovery, and 2) increasing skill knowledge, strength, and generalization. The validation and problem solving strategies are used throughout. Each of the four skill sets is described below.

1. Practicing Presence

The goals of this module are to learn how to observe, describe, and therefore participate more effectively in life.

These goals are achieved by giving your attention to being in control of your own mind, instead of letting the mind be in control of you. "...take captive every thought to make it obedient to Christ" (2 Corinthians 10:5). Patients are encouraged to practice being aware of their environment, thoughts, and feelings: tuned in to potential triggers that may lead to harmful behaviors. They stop and consider the logical outcome of a decision to engage in a particular behavior and learn how to slow down their thoughts to keep them from racing to a preconceived judgment. Then they weigh this consideration against the emotions pushing them toward the behavioral decision, seeking the wisest choice they can make. In this process, Christians are encouraged to seek the mind of Christ and be prayerful and attentive to the Holy Spirit's guidance. In essence, this skill is about learning to be a more careful observer and listener—to oneself, others, and the Holy Spirit.

Jesus modeled staying in the present and not being so future focused that we create distress for ourselves. He said, "...do not worry about tomorrow, for tomorrow will worry about itself" (Matthew 6:34). Practicing the presence of God, being quiet before God, truly attempting to be still, and letting go of distractions are skills that require time and patience but have lasting rewards. These skills can assist in experiencing peace and contentment. "Be still before the LORD and wait patiently for him; do not fret...A little while, and the wicked will be no more...But the meek will inherit the land and enjoy great peace" (Psalm 37:7,10-11).

2. Interpersonal Effectiveness

Both successful/effective and unsuccessful/ineffective people have problems. It is the *attitude toward the problems* that distinguishes one from the other (e.g., Seligman, 1998).

This module's goal is to learn how to meet one's interpersonal objectives, find and maintain positive relationships, and maintain/improve self-respect in the process.

To achieve these goals, patients learn to ask themselves objective questions, e.g.: *What specific results am I trying to attain in this interaction? What do I have to do to get the results I want?* Clear communication techniques are learned and then applied to real-life situations. For example: Learn first to identify what you are feeling or needing and how to express that confidently; then learn to ask for your needs to be met in ways that do not devalue or invalidate the other person or yourself. This exercise, reinforced over time, is similar to teaching assertive communication but with a shift toward operationalizing the concept of interpersonal *effectiveness.* Learning to anticipate a response from others and realizing what is and is not helpful are keys to becoming a socially effective communicator and effective interpersonal problem solver.

In this module there are opportunities to talk about many emotions, especially anger. A scriptural concept frequently cited is: It is appropriate to be angry, but do not sin (Ephesians 4:26; James 1:19). Under certain circumstances, anger can be a healthy emotion, but learning to regulate anger and be kind to those who have hurt you is a challenge. Patients are encouraged to look out for the needs of others as well as for themselves (Philippians 2:4) and are challenged to find this balance by asking the question: *How do I want this person to feel about me after we end this interaction?* Finding this balance is important in helping patients to formulate an other-centered interest.

Overall, Interpersonal Effectiveness Skills help patients learn how to attend to relationships by balancing priorities vs. demands, building mastery in communication, and increasing self-respect.

3. Emotion Regulation

In the Emotion Regulation module, patients develop a greater understanding of emotions, reduce emotional vulnerability, and learn techniques to decrease their emotional suffering.

Emotion regulation involves exercises in cognitive modification and restructuring. Examples of how patients strengthen their ability to regulate emotions include: building on positive experiences, such as choosing to do one thing each day that prompts positive emotions, and accumulating more positive experiences over time; listing small steps toward a goal and taking the first step to achieve that goal; and attending to and repairing relationships. Reaching out to new relationships and working on current relationships serve to increase confidence in one's ability to navigate relationships successfully, which builds positive emotions and enhances social support.

Another emotion regulation skill is to "avoid avoiding." Ambivalence and avoidance often go hand in hand. For those with alexithymia—a condition of emotional unawareness often seen in eating disorders—emotions are a befuddlement. Patients have been successful in emotionally numbing themselves for a long time through the eating disorder, and often are not comfortable with this new skill of "avoiding avoiding." It is not unusual to encounter resistance due to the level of fear that emotions provoke in these patients. However, "avoiding avoiding" is essential to be effective in making and keeping relationships. It is important to teach patients that they are not their emotions, however blunted or out of control they may experience their emotions to be. Patients will often be confronted about faulty thinking, such as: "*Since I feel fat, I am fat; since I feel inadequate, I am inadequate.*" Patients need to return to the basics of observing their emotions first, allowing themselves to experience the emotions, renewing the mind often by recalling that they are not their emotions, and practicing acceptance of their emotions for what they are.

An emotion regulation approach especially helpful for those with anorexia is learning "opposite action" skills. Patients are encouraged to do the opposite of or act contrary to an emotion, but not try to hide or avoid the emotion. Examples include: when feeling afraid, choosing to approach; when depressed, getting active; when angry, behaving with kindness. These opposite action skills teach patients to challenge themselves rather than reinforce familiar ineffective behavioral responses. This is similar to exposure with response prevention, another modality used with severe eating and anxiety disorders. Every time an anorexic patient approaches food and consumes it, s/he learns that despite his/her feelings of fear it is important to approach the food anyway. Over time, because of exposure to the feared object, the anxiety and fear diminish and eating normalizes. Previously, food avoidance was the only way the patient knew how to reduce anxiety. Avoidance was negatively reinforced by the anxiety reduction it afforded. With exposure, however, the avoidance behavior is not reinforced and the anxiety about the feared object diminishes. A similar change occurs when using "opposite action" skills.

To strengthen emotion regulation skills, it can be helpful for patients to study and meditate on the broad range of emotions Jesus exhibited in Scripture—how he appropriately and freely expressed emotions and also used personal restraint and self-control. Jesus became frustrated with his disciples on occasion, yet never attacked them. When hit, the human instinct is to hit back; when forced to go a mile, to express resentment; when robbed, to seek restitution or punish the robber. And yet, Jesus taught us to do the opposite: to turn the other cheek, to walk the second mile voluntarily, and to give to the one who would steal from us. The book of Proverbs also contains wisdom on how to manage emotions.

4. Distress Tolerance

Learning to tolerate distress is not easy for anyone. We are not born with this skill, but must learn it. The task is made more difficult for those who have been raised in invalidating environments. These individuals must learn the art of combating negative self-talk while purposefully remaining in the distress and coping with it.

The focus of Distress Tolerance Skills is learning how to accept life's realities: distressing events will happen. We need tools in our toolboxes to deal with the distressing moments when they occur: crisis survival strategies. Being better equipped to deal with these realities fosters patients' self-efficacy and confidence in their capacity for life management. Patients also learn how to develop a list of pros and cons before making major life decisions that could result in greater distress.

Among Distress Tolerance Skills are acceptance skills—a focus on learning to accept what is happening at the moment. Accepting and tolerating unavoidable suffering is not a new concept for Christians. Jesus said, "In this world you will have trouble. But take heart! I have overcome the world" (John 16:33). In this vein, it is essential to challenge the schema that life is supposed to be easy and to help patients shift to a more mature understanding which recognizes that life includes distress. Patients are more able to make this shift when they develop a relationship with God, who promises to be with them "to the very end of the age" (Matthew 28:20). Such a secure relationship provides an opportunity to confront issues of fear and trust. Also, knowing that one is not alone with one's suffering can alleviate the awfulness of the experience. "I will ask the Father, and He will give you another comforter and He will never leave you" (John 14:16 TLB).

Helping patients to find meaning in suffering or distress can also be useful. Victor Frankl, a holocaust survivor and founder of existential psychotherapy, wrote of how he was able to survive the horrors of the Nazi concentration camps by using this strategy (Frankl, 1997). Helping patients search for the positive in their pain is abundantly supported by Scripture. Christian believers are able to keep troubles in perspective when aware that they have come with a purpose and blessing. Our trials help us to help others and refine our faith and character (1 Peter 1:6-7; 2 Corinthians 1:6). There is often a silver lining in the dark clouds of suffering.

The question of trauma is often brought up in relation to distress tolerance. Can you and should you teach patients to tolerate the distress of an awful trauma? Tolerating distress does not imply an *approval* of the act that created the pain. The trauma needs to be labeled and addressed as trauma. But as awful as the trauma was, the patient now has to deal with the reality of it, including the distress it has led to. There is no way forward without doing so.

By improving Distress Tolerance Skills, patients may ultimately find themselves at a point where they can forgive themselves for things they have done which are creating distress, and also forgive others' failings. In the Christian community, this is an aspect of grace...we receive it unconditionally and we are called to extend it to others. This understanding assists patients to recognize that moral laws exist for our protection; they prevent distress, and so it makes sense to accept them. But, there is also "no condemnation for those who are in Christ Jesus" (Romans 8:1). We are forgiven for our failings, and free to change our ways, making healthier and moral choices that will not likely produce distress but instead produce contentment, peace, and joy.

Of course, when patients are confronted with the need for behavior change, resistance often increases—hence, the infamous "power struggle." The skill of acceptance helps patients to understand that the need for change is not predicated on someone else's will being forced upon them, but rather that certain behaviors result in distressing consequences. Patients are taught that they are accepted just as they are and can accept themselves as they are, but also that they will benefit from change. At Remuda, we recognize the clear parallel between this approach and Christian teaching. Change takes place best in this context of acceptance. "Let us then approach the throne of grace with confidence, so that we may receive mercy and find grace to help us in our time of need" (Hebrews 4:16).

Conclusion

For the thousands of eating disorder patients with whom Remuda has used CBT skills, outcomes have been positive (Cole, 2003). Patients frequently mention on discharge satisfaction questionnaires how much CBT skills training has helped them in recovery. Other eating disorder specialists are recognizing similar efficacy for CBT skills training with eating disorders (e.g., McCabe & Marcus, 2002), with more than 10 papers recently published so demonstrating. These skills therefore appear to be effective additions to more traditional CBT with eating disorder patients. As with all therapeutic models, for Christian practitioners biblical integration is necessary. Parts of CBT skills training have been modified or deleted at Remuda to accomplish such integration and maintain our Christ-centered, biblically-based treatment philosophy.

References

American Psychiatric Association (2000). Practice guideline for the treatment of patients with eating disorders (revision). *American Journal of Psychiatry, Suppl.,* 157, 1-39.

Cole, L. (2003). *The efficacy of skills training with eating disorder inpatients.* Unpublished doctoral dissertation, Argosy University, Phoenix, AZ.

Cumella, E.J. (2003). *Treatment outcome reports: Rio adult intensive center.* Wickenburg, AZ: Remuda Ranch Center for Anorexia and Bulimia, Inc.

Frankl, V. (1997). *Man's search for meaning.* New York: Pocket Books.

Linehan, M. (1993a). *Cognitive behavioral treatment of borderline personality disorder.* New York: Guilford Press.

Linehan, M. (1993b). *Skills training manual for treating borderline personality disorder.* New York: Guilford Press.

McCabe, E.B. & Marcus, M.D. (2002). Is dialectical behavior therapy useful in the management of anorexia nervosa? *Eating Disorders: The Journal of Treatment and Prevention, 10,* 335-37.

Richards, P.S & Baldwin, B.M. (2000). What works for treating eating disorders? Conclusion of 28 outcome reviews. *Eating Disorders: The Journal of Treatment and Prevention, 8,* 189-206.

Seligman, M. (1998). *Learned optimism: How to change your mind and your life.* New York: Free Press.

Wall, A.D. (2003). Cognitive-behavioral therapy with eating disorders: A Christian perspective. *The Remuda Review: The Christian Journal of Eating Disorders, 2,* 1-8.

Wall, A.D. & Eberly, M. (2002). Five biblical factors in eating disorder development. *The Remuda Review: The Christian Journal of Eating Disorders, 1,* 6-10.

Wonderlich, S.A. (1995). Personality and eating disorders. In K.D. Brownell and C.G. Fairburn (Eds.). *Eating disorders and obesity: A comprehensive handbook* (pp. 171-76). New York: The Guilford Press.

Chapter 8

Resistance, Motivation, and Change in Eating Disorders

Marian C. Eberly, RN, MSW, LCSW, DAPA, Dena Cabrera, PsyD, A. David Wall, PhD, and Kari Anderson, MS, LPC

> *I do not understand what I do. For what I want to do I do not do, but what I hate I do...I have the desire to do what is good, but I cannot carry it out.* (Romans 7:15, 18)

"Brittany simply isn't motivated," her therapist sighed. "I've tried everything I know, but she just won't let go of her eating disorder."

"What about talking to her family?" replied the dietitian.

"Done that! She can't seem to surrender her eating disorder. She just hasn't hit bottom yet. I'm very worried about her; I think she needs inpatient treatment."

Brittany was a 19-year-old freshman at a prestigious Midwestern college. She had been a 4.0 honor student in high school and was active in cross country and track. She was always very thin, but her weight dropped dramatically shortly after she went to college. Cindy, Brittany's residence hall counselor, was increasingly concerned. Brittany never showed up for meals, and if she wasn't in the library studying, she was out running or in the gym.

The day after Brittany passed out in class, was taken to the emergency room, given IV fluids, and released, Cindy confronted her.

"Brittany, I want to talk to you about something. I am very concerned about you. I mean..." Cindy struggled for words. "What happened yesterday finally pushed me over the edge. I think you have anorexia!"

"What? Anorexia!" Brittany's disbelieving response was mixed with surprise and anger. "Forget it, I'm fine." She stormed out.

Cindy consulted university administration and Brittany was told that without treatment she could not return to school. Her father upped the ante: "No more money for college until you get help," he told his daughter.

Brittany resisted her inpatient treatment team. Fifty-minute therapy sessions seemed like two hours. She insisted she didn't need help. "How could my parents do this to me?" she complained. "You are not going to make me fat." She remained aloof from the other women in treatment, except for those who shared her anger and denial. The others gave up on confronting her as she consistently responded with sarcasm and anger to any challenge.

Eventually, however, Brittany began to talk about her life, feelings, stress level, and the need to do everything perfectly. Risking vulnerability was new and frightening for her; it required acknowledgment that something might be wrong—that she might be weak. Although she made some progress, she frequently slipped back into defiance.

Brittany rated her motivation for recovery at 5 on a 10 point scale, but at 1 if recovery meant gaining weight. Her anger, stubbornness, and lack of motivation could try the patience of anyone. She seemed willing to go only so far and then dug her heels in.

So is Brittany simply unmotivated? Can this type of resistance be overcome?

Introduction

In addressing eating disorders fully within the bio-psycho-social-spiritual model (Cumella, 2002), it is essential to consider the several aspects of the human psyche, including emotion, cognition, behavior, and will. The last aspect—will—involves the capacity of human beings to make moral distinctions according to their value system and to choose moral, healthful, life-promoting behaviors—or the opposite (Wall & Eberly, 2002). Most professionals recognize that eating disorders are inherently life-compromising, because they constrict emotions and relationships and harm individuals physically. Yet those with eating disorders, like Brittany, often seem unable to choose recovery. For reasons that seem compelling to them, they choose instead the compromises and ravages of the eating disorder. This choice involves the human will.

The motivation to engage in eating disorder behaviors and these behaviors' resistance to change are directly related to the depth and power of the need(s) that eating disorders fill. The greater the need(s), the stronger the motivation to stay sick. Because needs may wax and wane, eating disorder behaviors may also wax and wane. In our introductory example, Brittany's resistance to change tells us that she is very motivated to engage in her eating disorder; the needs it fulfills must therefore be powerful.

In treating eating disorders, it is important to understand why patients may oppose treatment and health and choose illness instead. It is also essential to understand how to work with patients who are not committed to recovery, because such patients deserve competent treatment and access to effective interventions as much as those who are committed to recovery. By understanding the functions an eating disorder may be serving for specific individuals, and hence why they may be choosing eating disorder behaviors, it is possible for treatment providers to offer interventions that make sense to each individual—interventions that patients can actively choose and that will move them closer to recovery. "The wise heart will know the proper time and procedure. For there is a proper time and procedure for every matter" (Ecclesiastes 8:5-6).

Understanding Resistance

"Now there is in Jerusalem near the Sheep Gate a pool...Here a great number of disabled people used to lie—the blind, the lame, the paralyzed. One who was there had been an invalid for thirty-eight years. When Jesus saw him lying there and learned that he had been in this condition for a long time, he asked him, 'Do you want to get well?' " (John 5:2-7). Rather than jumping at the chance to heal, the man responded to Christ's question with excuses and rationalizations for why he had never taken advantage of the healing waters in the pool. Like this man, some will suffer for long periods of time without availing themselves of the healing opportunities that are presented to them.

Resistance to treatment is common in treating eating disorders. It may occur for several reasons.

For patients with eating disorders, the power to control one's life and health can be conceptualized in a distorted manner due to malnourishment. Therefore, biological factors should not be overlooked when creating a treatment plan for resistant patients. For patients experiencing significant cognitive disruption due to malnutrition, more purely behavioral interventions may be needed. Cognitively oriented therapies may be ineffective until a measure of nutrition restoration has been accomplished.

Biological dysfunction in the emotion regulation (limbic) system of the brain may also contribute to long-term resistance. Simply put, researchers hypothesize that brain physiology may accentuate emotional sensitivity in some people—leading them to respond too quickly, intensely, and enduringly to emotional triggers (e.g., Linehan, 2001). Such reactions typically elicit invalidating responses from other people, which reinforce the pattern of emotional dysregulation. Such patients clearly need significant focus on learning new emotion regulation skills or they will be motivated to continue their eating disorder behaviors in an effort to regulate emotions.

Due to the potential biological underpinnings of what treatment teams may label resistance, it should be clear that resistance is not always volitional. Patients may comply with treatment in many ways, yet still be unable to improve despite their best efforts (Hamburg et al., 1989).

On the other hand, some patients do volitionally oppose treatment efforts and refuse to participate for seemingly irrational reasons. Some feel threatened or afraid that in recovery they will not know how to meet basic needs or maintain an identity, so they resist as a self-protective act. Some convince themselves that their symptoms are actually beneficial. Perhaps they feel powerless or helpless over their obsessions and compulsions and are attempting to reduce cognitive dissonance by believing that they have chosen or desire their symptoms. Such beliefs may offer the patient a sense of self-efficacy, mastery, and accomplishment (Yager, 1992). However distorted such beliefs may seem to those who treat resistant patients, it is important to understand these and similar underlying issues which may lead to secondary gain in resistant patients. We must intentionally utilize techniques in treatment that will not add to such resistance or contribute to a pattern of recalcitrance, but will instead lead to an understanding of the root causes of resistance and allow us to work with it effectively.

Whatever the causes, a pattern of enduring resistance, chronicity, and recalcitrance can be complicated by a countertransference response from the treatment team. Jesus' response to the man at the pool had no trace of countertransference; it was not one of frustration or anger or indifference. Instead, Jesus responded with compassion and healed the man in spite of the man's ambivalence about recovery.

Countertransference often manifests as provider frustration, compassion fatigue, and exhaustion, and may lead treatment providers to disengage from the patient and offer less effective or thorough care. Treatment providers can take safeguards against countertransference when working with chronic eating disorder patients.

1. Recognize what is good about the patient's resistance: Reframing the resistance involves recognizing that all defenses serve a purpose. Seek the adaptive function. Sleuthing out the purpose can take time, but it is time well spent. Otherwise, providers may discover their treatment plans have become a revolving door.

2. Choose how you will respond to resistance: Resistance can be a powerful tool in the hands of a skilled clinician. It also has the potential to teach us about ourselves as people and practitioners. If you listen, resistance can

teach you about the judgments you may habitually make and conclusions you unconsciously draw.

Sometimes persistent resistance may not be the patient's problem, but instead a clinician skill issue. The clinician may be reinforcing resistant behavior without realizing it. "The more therapists confronted patients, the more resistance patients exhibited and the less behavior changes" (Patterson & Forgatch, 1985). Since dealing with resistance may be a slippery slope for many practitioners, it is important to know what *not* to do. Several ways to increase resistance in eating disorder patients include (Miller & Rollnick, 2002):

- Arguing for change
- Lecturing
- Assuming the expert role
- Shocking, criticizing, shaming, and blaming
- Labeling what the patient *is* rather than focusing on choices and behaviors
- Being in a hurry

Doing these things will result in a power struggle. But effective therapists help patients figure out how to control their own behaviors rather than attempting to control the patients themselves.

Success in working with resistance has its root in agreeing together with the patient on treatment goals. Stay focused on the goals, and when there is a deviation from them, name it. When behaviors impede the patient's ability to accomplish her goals and create true change in her life, address them as *treatment interfering behaviors.*

Change

It has often been asserted that people don't change because they haven't suffered enough or "hit bottom." But the humiliation, shame, guilt, and angst of hitting bottom are not the primary engines of change. Ironically, these usually immobilize people (Miller & Rollnick, 2002). Instead, people typically change when they connect with something of intrinsic value, something important or cherished.

A framework has been developed to help us better understand behavior change. Prochaska and DiClemente (1992) suggest that people pass through a series of stages as they change their behavior. This process has been appropriately called *stages of change.* The stages of change model includes six specific stages through which patients proceed, generally in this order:

- Pre-Contemplation—“I don’t need to change…I don’t have a problem.”
- Contemplation—“I know I need to change, but…”
- Preparation—“I’ve decided to change.”
- Action—“I am doing what is needed in order to change.”
- Maintenance—“I am committed to my recovery lifestyle and prepared for relapse.”
- Relapse—“I need to review what I need for change to occur.”

Based on scientific research, the stages of change model unfolds in detail a principle of change delineated in Scripture: “I planted the seed, Apollos watered it, but God made it grow” (1 Corinthians 3:6). In relation to truth, particularly the gospel’s life-changing truth, the human soul begins as a barren field needing seed before it can spring to life (pre-contemplation). In offering life-changing knowledge, the health professional scatters good seed on the barren soil, offering the possibility of positive change (contemplation). By providing information and encouragement appropriate to each person’s stage in the process of change, the health professional then waters the seed, which may begin to sprout (preparation). Continued watering through stage-appropriate interventions assists the patient in taking the early and important steps toward change/recovery, allowing the sprouts to grow (action). In a personal relationship with Christ and through the action of the Holy Spirit, the individual develops into spiritual maturity/recovery (maintenance). Finally, all people—regardless of their stage of change or recovery—are vulnerable to relapse and need continual self-examination and restoration: “If we claim to be without sin, we deceive ourselves and the truth is not in us. If we confess our sins, he is faithful and just and will forgive us our sins and purify us from all unrighteousness” (1 John 1:8-9). The professional’s role in the relapse stage is to restore the patient gently (Galatians 6:1).

The ANSOCQ, or Anorexia Nervosa Stages of Change Questionnaire, has been found to be a strong predictor of weight gain in patients with anorexia (Rieger, et al., 2000), suggesting that the stages of change model has direct relevance to treating eating disorders. Other readiness for change research likewise suggests the utility of this approach with eating disorders (e.g., Cockell, 2000; Geller, Cockell, & Drab, 2001; Vitousek, Watson, & Wilson, 1998). At Remuda, we have found that the stages of change model can be an effective therapeutic tool as it can increase the patient’s awareness of her own process as she struggles with recovery. This structured approach reveals much to patients about their ambivalence and provides a framework for therapists to better understand ambivalence, resistance, and motivational issues. Geller (2002) found that clinicians tend to rate readiness to change higher than client's actual readiness. Therefore, when clients state that they want to stop eating disorder behavior, one must be careful not to assume that they are fully ready to change. For example, a client may be quite motivated to stop bingeing and purging, but be unconcerned and unwilling to address her low body weight. It is essential to assess the stage of change *for each symptom* of an eating disorder rather than assume that patients' motivation is uniform for their entire eating disorder (Geller & Drab, 1999). Addressing each at its differential level of motivation is essential for recovery to proceed. The stages of change perspective challenges us to look at each client individually, rather than to assume that every client is ready to change when entering treatment.

Pre-Contemplation Stage

Some patients in this stage are in denial and not thinking about change. Others may be clearly aware and accepting that they have an eating disorder, but their attitude and behavior convey that they are unwilling or uninterested in change. Often patients feel that the consequences of the eating disorder have not become serious enough to warrant change.

In this stage, the eating disorder is ego-syntonic—the patient is comfortable with it and views it as consistent with her values and wishes. Therefore, the goal in this stage is simply for patients to begin thinking about change. Here, interviewing, assessment, and conceptualization are crucial.

Often therapists want to use action-oriented approaches, but these do not account for variances across patients in eating disorder symptoms or motivation. Interventions need to be tailored to patients' specific characteristics and behaviors while keeping in mind the goal of the pre-contemplation stage—for patients to begin thinking about change.

It is valuable at this stage for therapists to take a stance of validation and acceptance. This includes teaching patients that they are accepted regardless of their behavior, identifying feelings, empathizing, and being nonjudgmental. Through this process, patients can begin to self-validate and avoid the recapitulation of guilt and shame. Further, by exploring patients' value systems, therapists may find "a chink in the armor" and utilize it to create useful ambivalence. Creating cognitive dissonance can be powerful in motivating change. Thought provoking questions and assignments help with this process. Questions should consist of internal and external references. For example: If you were to decide to change, what do you imagine might be some advantages? What motivates others to change? Would life be better in any way if you stopped the eating disorder?

An assignment that helps patients to gain insight is to take stock of the emotional, social, and spiritual state they are experiencing at this time. Factual information about their medical condition can present a reality check. However, research demonstrates that shocking or trying to jar a patient into changing does not work. In truth, this is the best way to shut down the change process (Miller & Rollnick, 2002).

Pre-contemplators are most influenced by the eating disorder's cons. These push them into contemplation (Rieger, Touyz, & Beumont, 2002). Focusing on losses— physical, emotional, relational, spiritual, and so on— will make an impact in transition to the contemplation stage.

Contemplation Stage

In a recent study using the stages of change, the majority of inpatients with anorexia were assessed to be in the pre-contemplation or contemplation stage (Treasure & Schmidt, 2001). Overall, most patients with eating disorders are in the contemplation stage in the various domains of their eating disorder.

In the contemplation stage, patients recognize the devastating emotional, physical, social, and spiritual toll the eating disorder has taken. However, they are extremely ambivalent about whether or not to change their behavior. Patients are caught between the desire to stop and the fear of stopping, which creates psychic pain, even agony for some.

At this point, the professional's goal is to assist patients in thinking through the risks of their behaviors and the potential benefits of change and to instill hope that change is possible. As the professional continues to accept, validate, and acknowledge the patients' position, the ultimate goal is to help patients resolve their conflict/ ambivalence.

It is useful to ask thought-provoking questions, such as: What are the benefits and risks of the eating disorder? What concerns you most about stopping? What are the barriers today that keep you from changing? Why do you think you have an eating disorder? Behavioral interventions include visual aids to assist with identifying the pros and cons of the eating disorder. This helps to create imbalance so that the decision not to have the eating disorder becomes more desirable than the decision to have it. In this stage it can also be useful to consider future consequences. Assignments may include having patients write out what their life will be like in five years both with and without the eating disorder. This may provide tremendous insight into what the ambivalence is about for them.

A thorough behavioral analysis of the patient's eating disorder may also be important in understanding the function of the eating disorder. This can help identify skills deficits, emotion regulation problems, and other barriers to change. We have found that often the underlying issue is maturity fears due to reinforcement of dependency by others and/or a lack of life skills. Because of this function of the eating disorder, treatment might focus on enhancing independent living skills.

It is also critical in the contemplation stage to focus on helping patients to build self-efficacy (Rieger, Touyz, & Beumont, 2002). This creates hope and a belief in the patient that "I can really do this." As the pros for recovery increase and individuals develop hope, the likelihood of moving into the preparation stage increases.

ANSOCQ results suggest that the most change occurs between the contemplation and preparation stages (Rieger, Touyz, & Beumont, 2002). The several methods described herein can facilitate this essential change and improve the chances for individuals' recovery.

Preparation Stage

In this stage patients want to quit the eating disorder and begin to prepare emotionally, behaviorally, and physically for doing so. Counseling centers on "change talk"—desire, optimism, hope, advantages of change, and ultimately the intention to change. Patients have made the decision and are determined to recover but have not actually stopped the eating disorder; they are getting ready for behavioral change in the near future.

The goal of treatment in this stage is to help patients formulate a comprehensive plan for decreasing and ceasing their eating disorder behaviors, including identifying support systems, anticipating challenges, and devising ways to address challenges. Areas of intervention include educating the patient about body changes, imbalance, and weight issues, and addressing nutrition and exercise components. It is important to discuss the roles of family and friends in supporting and/or sabotaging success, to increase awareness of eating disorder triggers, and to make plans about which skills will be used to counteract them. Assignments include having patients track changes and modified behaviors, reminding patients of the pros of eating disorder recovery, and encouraging patients to prepare a written commitment to their recovery and to make their commitment public. This helps with accountability and support. While focusing on these interventions, it is imperative to continue building patients' hope and self-efficacy.

Action Stage

This stage requires a considerable commitment in time and energy to modify behavior, environment, and attitude. At this point patients have stopped the eating disorder and are implementing the plan for which they have been preparing. This may be a rewarding stage for the treatment provider, given that patients are motivated and are invested in the outcome of treatment. However, it is important not to equate patient action with recovery per se. With the stages of change model, relapse is a rule rather than an exception. At any time, patients may transition back to a previous stage with one or more symptoms of their eating disorder. Thus, professionals may find that they are working with patients who are simultaneously at different stages of recovery regarding various eating disorder symptoms.

Treatment during the action stage includes carefully listening and affirming that patients are doing the right thing. Praise and affirmation of success are valuable to patients' self-efficacy as well as an inspiration for them to continue in the recovery process. In addition, family and peer encouragement can be very valuable.

It is essential during the action stage to continue teaching about, identifying, and exploring specific relapse triggers that patients have encountered and to discuss what patients did to cope with these triggers. Assignments involve having patients make a list of skills/tools they will need to utilize most, given their individual triggers. Treatment at this stage can involve more experiential exercises, such as art therapy, restaurant eating challenges, and cooking assignments. Treatment also needs to address the grief and loss issues related to giving up the eating disorder. Thought provoking questions include: What do you fear will happen if you are successful? What are you going to miss most by not having an eating disorder? Sometimes these questions are overlooked by providers for fear that patients will relapse if these ideas are brought to the surface. But patients are thinking about and experiencing loss from the adjustments they are making. With careful intervention and support, assignments can safely and directly address patients' grief and loss issues.

Other interventions at this stage will vary depending on patients' diagnostic comorbidity, including Axis I and II disorders. Many times, as eating disorders subside or symptoms diminish, co-occurring symptoms will exacerbate because the stress of living without eating disorder behaviors may be frightening or difficult for patients. For example, as patients demonstrate recovery in their eating disorder, obsessive-compulsive behaviors, impulsive behaviors, or depression may increase. Additional assessment may be needed at this juncture to determine which treatment protocols will assist patients with their co-occurring issues, including psychopharmacological interventions.

Maintenance Stage

In the maintenance stage, patients begin to identify themselves as someone who is "recovering" and in the practice of living without an eating disorder. Patients will occasionally want to engage in eating disorder behaviors, but will instead work on specific countermeasures to cope with their urges and thoughts. The goal is to help patients gain personal insight and continue growing in recovery, focusing on quality of life issues.

Provoking probes to guide patients into this type of exploration include: Let's talk about the person you want to be, or, What are you doing to become more like that person? It is also necessary to discover and explore with patients new issues that may have appeared as they pursue recovery. Assignments and interventions might encourage patients to carry the message of recovery by sharing with others their recovery story. This reinforces their efforts and continues to imbue their pain and struggle with meaning and value through the act of helping others.

Relapse Stage

When in relapse, patients have moved backward in the recovery process, either in behaviors or in previous ways of thinking and feeling. In this stage, patients often experience an incredible amount of embarrassment, guilt, and shame. Patients may isolate and keep their relapse secret, which can hinder chances for reentering recovery.

The goal at this stage is to process the relapse therapeutically and to help patients learn from what has happened. All the while, it is important to validate the patients' pain about relapsing, and convey faith in their ability to move forward. This helps reduce their feelings of shame, imperative at this point in time. Another important objective is to help patients move as quickly as possible through the stages of change from which they regressed during relapse. Thus, reworking activities and assignments from previous stages is recommended. Additional assignments for patients may include having patients take inventory of the barriers to success and doing a thorough review of triggers and vulnerabilities. The frequency of therapeutic sessions should increase as well to maximize skill building.

Bottom Lines

...snatch others from the fire and save them. (Jude 1:23)

The question often arises about whether these motivational approaches can work with the cognitively impaired, severely malnourished, medically compromised patient. We have found that indeed they can and do. Even so, there have to be bottom lines when working with this specialized group of patients (Carney, Wakefield, Tait, & Touyz, 2006).

Bottom lines include state or family guardianship to maintain life and safety, sometimes resulting in involuntary treatment; patient transfer to a higher level of care, such as an inpatient treatment center, locked psychiatric facility, or closely monitored behavioral feeding program; force-feeding through mechanical means; and medical restraint.

Bottom lines communicate safety to the patient: "Here is the limit, this is as far as we go with this particular intervention, and here are the choices available to you now."

When discussing bottom lines it is crucial to maintain a nonpunitive stance of compassion, reassurance, and understanding. Professionals working with clients can create an atmosphere of collaboration and negotiation, reframing the bottom line in the context of promoting the client's health and safety. Obviously, individual autonomy should be promoted as much as possible by presenting the patient with choices and recommending the least restrictive bottom line possible. It is also helpful to maintain a position of advocacy, informing the client throughout the process of her rights and the options being considered to promote her health and safety. Finally, it helps to avoid surprising the patient with abrupt consequences; as bottom lines may potentially become necessary, it is useful to inform the patient of the natural course that treatment may need to take to protect her health and safety.

The goal and hope are that the refeeding accomplished through bottom line interventions will bring improved cognitive and emotional functioning, which will increase the client's motivation for recovery and ability to participate in action-oriented treatments. Bottom lines, when effectively applied, can return the client to treatment more ready to engage and make therapeutic progress.

References

Carney, T., Wakefield, A., Tait, D., & Touyz, S. (2006). Reflections on coercion in the treatment of severe anorexia nervosa. *The Israel Journal of Psychiatry and Related Sciences, 43,* 159-65.

Cockell, S.J. (2000). *A decisional balance measure of readiness for change in anorexia nervosa.* Dissertation Abstracts International. (UMI No. NQ56661).

Cumella, E.J. (2002). Bio-psycho-social-spiritual: Completing the model. *The Remuda Review: The Christian Journal of Eating Disorders, 1,* 1-5.

Geller, J. (2002). Estimating readiness for change in anorexia nervosa: Comparing clients, clinicians, and research assessors. *International Journal of Eating Disorders, 31,* 251-60.

Geller, J., Cockell, S.J., & Drab, D.L. (2001). Assessing readiness for change in the eating disorders: The psychometric properties of the readiness and motivation interview. *Psychological Assessment, 13,* 189-98.

Geller, J., & Drab, D. L. (1999). The readiness and motivation interview: A symptom-specific measure of readiness for change in the eating disorders. *European Eating Disorders Review, 7,* 259-78.

Hamburg, P., Herzog, D.B., Brotman, A.W., et al. (1989). The treatment resistant eating disordered patient. *Psychiatric Annals, 19,* 494-99.

Linehan, M.M. (2001). Dialectical behavior therapy. In N.J. Smelser & P.B. Baltes (eds.), *International encyclopedia of the social and behavioral sciences* (pp. 3631-34). Oxford: Pergamon Press.

Miller, W. R., & Rollnick, S. (2002). *Motivational interviewing: Preparing people for change* (2nd ed.). New York: Guilford Press.

Patterson, G. R., & Forgatch, M. S. (1985). Therapist behavior as a determinant for client noncompliance: A paradox for the behavior modifier. *Journal of Consulting and Clinical Psychology, 53,* 846-51.

Prochaska, J. O., & DiClemente, C. C. (1992). The transtheoretical model of change. In J. C. Norcross & M. R. Goldfried (eds.), *Handbook of psychotherapy integration* (pp. 300-34). New York: Basic Books.

Rieger, E., Touyz, S., Schotte, D., Beumont, P., Russell, J., Clarke, S., et al. (2000). Development of an instrument to assess readiness to recover in anorexia nervosa. *International Journal of Eating Disorders, 28,* 387-96.

Rieger, E., Touyz, S. W., Beumont, P. J. (2002). The anorexia nervosa stages of change questionnaire (ANSOCQ): Information regarding its psychometric properties. *International Journal of Eating Disorders, 32,* 24-38.

Treasure, J. and Schmidt, U. (2001). Ready, willing, and able to change: Motivational aspects of the assessment and treatment of eating disorders. *European Eating Disorders Review, 9,* 4-18.

Vitousek, K.B., Watson, S., Wilson, G.T. (1998). Enhancing motivation for change in treatment resistant eating disorders. *Clinical Psychology Review, 18,* 391-420.

Wall, A.D., & Eberly, M. (2002). Five biblical factors in eating disorder development. *The Remuda Review: The Christian Journal of Eating Disorders, 1,* 6-10.

Yager, J. (1992). *Special problems in managing eating disorders.* New York: American Psychiatric Press.

Chapter 9

Experiential Therapies with Eating Disorders

Edward J. Cumella, PhD, CEDS, David Woods, MBA, and Cheryl Musick, EAPIII

[Jesus] taught them...by parables. (Mark 4:2)

A range of experiential activities have been documented for use with eating disorder patients (Cumella, 2003; Frisch, Franko, & Herzog, 2006; Hornyak & Baker, 1989). We discuss below the application of three common experiential therapeutic approaches: equine therapy, art therapy, and challenge courses.

Equine Therapy with Eating Disorders

Ask the animals, and they will teach you. (Job 12:7)

After God created man, God indicated that "It is not good for the man to be alone" (Genesis 2:18). The first thing God did in response to man's aloneness was to bring the animals he had created to Adam. Long before the fall of man, then, in the perfect order of creation, man was designed to have relationships with animals. Of course, Scripture also makes plain that no animal God created was capable of being a complete and sufficient companion for Adam. Ultimately, to offer man a "suitable helper" (Genesis 2:20), God created woman.

In modern animal-assisted psychotherapy, patients repeat this ancient, God-ordered sequence of events. Although patients may have been too wounded by other people to open to emotionally or spiritually intimate relationships with others, they are often able to trust enough to develop relationships with animals. Because God saw a role for human-animal relationships in the sin-free Garden of Eden, healthy relationships with animals are intended as a meaningful part of a godly human life. Skills learned through human-animal relationships developed during animal-assisted therapy then become stepping stones to authentic relationships with other human beings.

The Bible informs us that animals can be set apart for service in the kingdom of heaven (e.g., Leviticus 27). We see therapy animals in this light. The Bible also informs us that learning about animals can reveal to us God's intentions and attributes, promoting our spiritual maturity. As Job 12:7-8 recommends: "...ask the animals, and they will teach you, or the birds of the air, and they will tell you; or speak to the earth, and it will teach you, or let the fish of the sea inform you." Or as the apostle Paul so eloquently writes: "Since the creation of the world God's invisible qualities—his eternal power and divine nature—have been clearly seen, being understood from what had been made..." (Romans 1:20).

Consistent with this biblical understanding, animal-assisted therapies, particularly equine and canine therapies, have shown evidenced-based efficacy in treating patients with a range of mental illnesses: depression (Francis, Turner, & Johnson, 1985), anxiety (Barker, Barker, Dawson, & Knisley, 1998), attention-deficit/hyperactivity disorder (Katcher & Wilkins, 1994), conduct disorders (Mallon, 1992), dissociative disorders (Arnold, 1995), Alzheimer's disease (Batson, McCabe, & Baun, 1995), dementia (Fritz, Farver, Kass, & Hart, 1995), autism (Campbell & Katcher, 1992), and other chronic mental illnesses (Beck, Seraydarian, & Hunter, 1986; Hundley, 1991). Two psychotherapists (McCormick & McCormick, 1997) demonstrated the efficacy of animal-assisted therapy in treating some of the most profoundly disturbed patients—gang members, psychopaths, and sexual predators. Animal-assisted therapy may therefore be effective not only with a variety of *DSM-IV-TR* (American Psychiatric Association [APA], 2000) Axis I disorders and issues such as those described above, but may also be a powerful adjunct modality in the treatment of patients with the distorted bonding and relational problems predominant in Axis II and eating disorders. In this vein, an article in *Eating Disorders: The Journal of Treatment and Prevention* (Cumella, 2003) suggests that equine therapy may yield a variety of psychotherapeutic benefits for patients with eating disorders. Possible benefits include:

- **Self-Confidence:** The learning and mastery of a new skill—horsemanship—enhances patients' confidence in their ability to tackle new projects, such as recovery.
- **Self-Efficacy:** Learning to communicate and achieve harmony with a large animal promotes the experience of self-efficacy instead of

helplessness and may encourage patients to take on other recovery challenges.

- **Self-Concept:** Riding helps patients to develop a more realistic view of themselves through awareness of their size in relation to the horse. This is especially important in treating the body image misperceptions common in eating disorders.
- **Communication:** Horses' sensitivity to nonverbal communication assists patients in developing greater awareness of their emotions, nonverbal cues, and the role of nonverbal communication in relationships.
- **Trust:** Learning to trust an animal such as a horse also aids in the development, or restoration, of trust.
- **Perspective:** Through grooming and care activities for a specific horse, patients are able to put aside the absorbing focus of their mental illness and direct their attention outwardly toward safe and caring interactions.
- **Anxiety Reduction:** Many studies of human-animal interaction indicate that contact with animals significantly reduces physiological anxiety levels. Some patients initially fear horses, but horses' genuineness and affection allay these fears, which may approximate exposure therapy for anxiety.
- **Decreased Isolation:** For many individuals with mental illness, there is a history of feeling rejected, different, and isolated from other people. Horses' unconditional acceptance may invite patients into relationship and enable them to practice nonverbal relationship skills.
- **Self-Acceptance:** Many patients are concerned that they will embarrass themselves while riding. As patients learn that other participants are engaged in their own equine experiences and observe the comfort of the horses in their own skin, fears of embarrassment are often reduced and self-acceptance increased.
- **Impulse Modulation:** The need to communicate with a horse calmly and nonreactively promotes the skills of emotional awareness, emotion regulation, self-control, and impulse modulation. Research indicates that animal-assisted therapy reduces patient agitation and aggressiveness and increases cooperativeness and behavioral control.
- **Assertiveness:** Communicating effectively with horses requires riders to demonstrate assertiveness, direction, and initiative, potentially enabling patients to express their needs and rights more effectively in other relationships.

- **Boundaries:** Many patients have experienced prior relationships as controlling or abusive. Healing may take place as patients discover that riding occurs within the context of a respectful relationship between rider and horse, and that, although physically powerful, each horse typically operates within the boundaries of this mutually respectful relationship.
- **Creative Freedom:** The playful aspects of riding and team equine activities can help restore spontaneity and the ability for healthy recreation and play in those who are emotionally inhibited or overcontrolled.
- **Spiritual Growth:** Feelings of joy and spiritual connection are often discovered or revived as patients experience the earth's beauty during equine rides and develop an appreciation for the horse as a unique creation.

The article (Cumella, 2003) describes the process of equine therapy with eating disorder patients as follows:

> Patients may participate in one or more Equine Therapy sessions per week, including trail rides, arena sessions focusing on advanced skills, riding to music, team activities, rodeos, and instruction in horse care, grooming, saddlery, and equitation practices. Patients are typically paired with specific horses based on an assessment of patient riding needs and experiences. Safety is addressed in several ways. Patients wear safety equipment and begin Equine Therapy only when approved by a physician. Horses are carefully selected for characteristics that make them suitable to patient contact. Horses receive continuous schooling and training for their participation in Equine Therapy. Experienced Equine Therapists understand the safety issues associated with good horsemanship. Staff may also be trained and certified in Equine Assisted Psychotherapy by the Equine Assisted Growth and Learning Association (EAGALA), a nonprofit organization that promotes, educates, and provides standards of practice, ethics, and safety in Equine Therapy. Staff may obtain continuing education through the Equine-Facilitated Mental Health Association (EFMHA), which sponsors, promotes, and organizes research on the efficacy of Equine Therapy in a mental health context. EFMHA offers publications regarding the effectiveness of Equine Therapy and hosts an annual Equine Therapy training conference.

Below we describe two equine experientials that have occurred at Remuda. Each exemplifies several benefits of equine therapy in treating eating disorder patients.

Temptation Alley: An Equine Experiential Exercise

Instructions. An equine specialist sets up a maze-like alley laced with hay, grain, and escape routes that are tempting to a horse. The goal is for the patient-rider to guide the horse from a starting point through the maze to the end of the alley. Two others stand on either side of the horse and assist the patient by holding the end of lead ropes attached on each side of the halter.

Experience. We set up a temptation alley experiential to mirror the family structure of a patient who was enmeshed with her mother. The patient sat on the horse bareback, without a saddle or reins to assist her. Parents stood on either side of the horse, each holding the end of a lead rope. The family was asked to move the horse through the alley. The family completed the course. Then, however, we disconnected Dad's lead rope. We asked Dad to support his daughter not by being attached but by speaking words of encouragement and responding to her needs when she asked for help. Mom and patient then attempted to complete the course with only Mom connected on one side to direct the horse. With the lead rope now connected only on one side, the patient and Mom ended up going in circles and getting frustrated. After about 15 minutes of struggling to move forward, they realized that being connected in this manner was unbalanced and incapable of promoting progress. Finally, the patient asked: "Mom, would you give me your rope?" The patient then created reins from the lead ropes and was able to direct the horse through the alley, while Mom and Dad came alongside in support. The patient's affect changed dramatically once she realized she was able to problem-solve effectively and complete the goal.

The family discussed the experiential. The patient was overjoyed, stating, "I feel like I have some power and control back in my life." Mom indicated that she felt as though a huge weight had been lifted from her. She realized that she had been taking on more responsibility than she needed to. She compared temptation alley to recovery, realizing that she is there as support but her daughter is the one who has to do it. The patient said that she now feels empowered for recovery and that using this experiential has shown her she is capable of anything.

Overcoming Fear: An Equine Experiential Exercise

She stood on the porch in front of the tack room, tears streaming down her face. Nursing had already notified the equine staff about the terrified patient who might not ever ride a horse. Her peers were concerned and gathered around her to soothe her fears. But she crossed her arms, set her stance, and said: "I am not riding."

I took her aside and gently assured her that I would stay with her. I explained that staff had deliberately selected her horse, Laramie, for his gentle nature. I gave her time to discuss her fears and to hear the calm confidence of my voice, then I challenged her to take just one step at a time rather than looking at the whole picture. Her entire group cheered as she swung her leg over the saddle for the first time.

Her knuckles were white as she tightly gripped the saddlehorn. We encouraged her to stay focused and relaxed.

But her eyes widened with fear as she watched her peers trotting and cantering around the arena. She gripped her saddle, set her jaw, and firmly stated: "I will never do that."

I challenged her again to take just one step at a time.

I fondly remember her family week rodeo. She laughed and took her hand from the saddlehorn waving enthusiastically to the audience. My heart danced with warm pride during her victory lap—a moment to celebrate her successes in recovery. Her face was full of sunshine and joy as she cantered around the arena.

I will always remember the day she said good-bye to her horse. Tears streamed down her face as she wrapped her arms around his neck and choked out the words: "Thank you so much…I'm going to miss you, Laramie."

Art Therapy with Eating Disorders

Art therapy is based on a simple, yet powerful principle: By entering into the creative process, patients experience improved self-awareness, hope and vision for the future, and self-esteem (Dokter, 1994; Ganim, 1999). Through art therapy, patients may awaken or renew a spiritual journey. Because artwork can be a metaphor for difficult feelings and issues, the art therapy process helps patients to discover and find a voice for emotions. This is especially important for eating disorder patients who are often alexithymic, confused about their feelings, and unable to label or articulate feelings verbally (Garner & Bemis, 1985). Eating disorders routinely serve as dysfunctional methods of emotion regulation, relied on because patients are unable to identify or express their emotional turmoil so that it can be approached therapeutically through cognitive-behavioral and other techniques (McCabe & Marcus, 2002).

Art therapy also has deep scriptural roots relating to the core identity of human beings. In Genesis 1:27, we read that "...God created man in his own image..." What is God's image? The Bible begins with these words, "In the beginning God *created*..." (Genesis 1:1, emphasis added), and recounts God's many acts of creation. Thus, the first thing we learn about God is that he is a Creator.

Looking at Scripture's opening verse, we see that God expressed creativity in all that he made. The earth, sea and sky, birds and animals, and men and women are all part of God's creative design. He is the ultimate artist. Not even van Gogh's or Monet's paintings, or Michelangelo's sculpture of David, can match the awesomeness of God's creativity. From a flaming Arizona sunset to the deep blue hues of the Mediterranean Sea; from the ice-covered pines sparkling in the Alaskan sun to the nighttime winter sky and the aurora borealis—God's artistic mastery is matchless.

God is the Creator, and we are made in his image. We, then, are little artists, inherently creative beings. As Ephesians 2:10 says: "We are God's workmanship, in Christ Jesus created to do good works." Art therapists often hear people say that they are not creative. Yet because we are made in God's image, we are indeed creative, each in his or her distinctive way. This truth helps eating disorder patients to discover the "hidden or sleeping artist" within them. And through the expression of their creativity in art, they reclaim their creative identity as artists, discovering emotional truths within their souls and reconnecting their spirits with God's creative nature.

At first, patients will often say that they are "not good at art." To soften their fears and create a safe environment, art therapists gently reinforce the following guidelines:

1) There are no mistakes in art.
2) There is no right or wrong in art.
3) It doesn't have to be perfect.

Patients usually feel relief when hearing these guidelines, and they give themselves permission to not have to be perfect or perform. Patients embark on various projects guided by therapeutic themes. Examples appear below.

Examples of Art Therapy Experientials with Eating Disorder Patients

Anger sculpture, example 1. *Instructions: Use newspaper and masking tape to create an image of your anger.* This patient has anorexia. She labels her sculpture "The Ever-Ready Bunny," expressing the magnitude of her obsessive thoughts to "keep going and going and going." The bunny represents her and holds a can of Ensure. This enables her to talk about anger at herself, at her eating disorder, and at her dietician for "making me drink it." The patient uses a lot of tape in creating her sculpture, and recognizes that this symbolizes her tendency to "stuff my anger and keep it hidden." Through this anger sculpture, the patient identified anger-related issues needing to be addressed in treatment.

Anger sculpture, example 2. *Same instructions as #1 above.* This patient describes her anger as a monster with a sharp red tongue and beady black and red eyes. She states that she struggles with admitting that she has anger and a lack of knowing how to express it. She indicates that the sculpture also represents what it feels like when someone gets angry at her—"it hurts." This anger sculpture assisted the patient in recognizing her extreme discomfort with angry feelings, both her own and those of other people, opening the door for treatment to focus on these issues.

Mask. *Instructions: Create a mask that explores your feelings and/or the face of the eating disorder.* The patient paints the face pink to symbolize how the eating disorder "seduced me into believing that it was good, soft, and pretty, and promised happiness." Horns and black eyes represent its true evil nature. Out of the mouth come its lies and deceit, painted in red and black. The tic-tac-toe on the forehead symbolizes "the mind games which the eating disorder plays with me." When the patient reflects on how much time she spent creating this mask, she is able to identify how much time was wasted by practicing her eating disorder and how angry she is at the eating disorder for stealing her life. The patient also recognizes that she is beginning to see light and goodness in her future, represented in the yellow pupils. This mask served as an excellent summary for the patient of the truth about her eating disorder that she was discovering through treatment.

Canvas collage. *Instructions: Choose three pictures from magazines; create a collage painting to explore connections of the images to your issues.* Through this artwork, the patient describes her desire to be loved and to see herself as beautiful. The rose symbolizes purity and fragility, and the love she experiences from her husband. The Barbie Doll represents beauty and reclaiming her lost childhood. The green garden represents meeting God with peace and serenity; the verse from the Song of Songs describes her renewed relationship with God. The patient states that she is beginning to capture God's love for her and is finding her true identity in him. This collage clearly expressed themes of hope and renewal; it helped the patient to recognize and verbally affirm the healing that was taking place in her and her emerging healthy identity.

Challenge Course with Eating Disorders

A challenge course typically consists of a series of poles or trees connected by rope or cable. Participants accept challenges to cross a span or leap from one place to another. Activities often require teamwork. High ropes activities—20 feet or more in the air—include a zip line, rock climbing wall, trapeze jump, giant ladder, inclined balance beam, and others. During high ropes, participants are connected to a safety line and wear a harness and helmet. Low ropes activities— heights of 5 feet or less—include a horizontal obstacle course, trust fall, balance activities, and others. During low ropes, fellow participants and staff provide a "safety net."

Power of Metaphor

Challenge course activities involve metaphors, as did Jesus' parables. For example, a patient might be asked: "If climbing this wall is recovery, where would you place yourself on it?" During Remuda's challenge course experiences, patients are exposed metaphorically to scriptural truths that will enable them to recover and live life effectively. Other examples:

- An elevated challenge course platform represents the safety of the eating disorder; a trapeze bar, an aspect of recovery. Patients may choose to leave the platform and jump into the air to catch the trapeze bar. In Matthew 8:22, Jesus talks about leaving what is dead behind in order to follow him into life, and in Matthew 11:12 Jesus reminds us to pursue the kingdom of God without hesitation.
- On the challenge course zip line, patients travel rapidly through the air for 270 feet, attached to a cable and a safety line. This gives patients the metaphorical opportunity to leave part of their eating disorder behind without returning to the platform to take it back. This experience reflects Christ's wisdom (Luke 9:62) about embracing the kingdom of God and never looking back.
- As patients begin climbing the challenge course rock wall, they are encouraged to evaluate their approach to achieving their goal. It is wise to get a boost from a teammate rather than to expend great energy merely to get started on the rock wall. In Luke 14:28, Jesus offers a parable about the importance of assessing one's resources before beginning a task.

Multichannel Learning

In addition to their ability to teach through the power of metaphor, challenge courses are beneficial because they offer multichannel learning—auditory, visual-nonverbal, and kinesthetic/tactile. Each individual learns differently. Not everyone learns best through traditional verbal therapy. Challenge course experiences offer a range of learning modalities that reinforce and supplement verbal therapeutic interventions.

As people approach a challenge course, they hear instruction and direction. They hear others' comments about their experiences, concerns, and excitement. The challenge course is visually stimulating because it is often unfamiliar, even foreboding. The experience is full of visual cues and requires visual assessments. People touch, climb, hang on, let go, jump, and ride—a cornucopia of kinesthetic/tactile experiences. As such, challenge courses embody this wisdom: "Tell me and I will forget; show me and I may remember; involve me and I will understand."

Circumventing Familiar Defenses

Some patients have become adept at saying the right things in clinical settings, but have difficulty "walking the walk" or making real behavioral progress. Challenge courses are often unfamiliar; they invoke the common human fear of heights and therefore increase patients' disequilibrium. In this situation, patients are off balance and cannot react with the typical defenses they erect in traditional therapy settings (Fletcher & Hinkle, 2002). They discover new possibilities.

Participants often find that they can do more than they thought. By experiencing and triumphing over the course's challenges, they begin to look at life's problems with a new perspective, knowing they can use problem-solving skills and feedback from peers to move forward. They practice effective communication skills to express needs and set boundaries. They have opportunities to increase trust as they participate in activities where their very physical safety involves other people. These applications allow individuals to discover more effective attitudes and behaviors specific to eating disorder recovery and adaptive living in general.

Remuda patients have been benefiting from challenge course lessons for years. Patient comments and objective ratings indicate a significant benefit to their recovery.

References

American Psychiatric Association. (2000). *Diagnostic and Statistical Manual of Mental Disorders, Text Revision* (4th ed.) *(DSM-IV-TR)*. Washington, DC: Author.

Arnold, J.C. (1995). Therapy Dogs and the dissociative patient: Preliminary observations. *Dissociation, 8,* 247-252.

Barker, S.B., Barker, R.T., Dawson, K.S., & Knisley, J.S. (1998). The effects of aminal-assisted therapy on anxiety ratings of hospitalized psychiatric patients. *Psychiatric Services, 49,* 797-801.

Batson, K., McCabe, B. W., & Baun, M. M. (1995). The effect of a therapy dog on socialization and physiologic indicators of stress in persons diagnosed with Alzheimer's disease. Animals, Health and Quality of Life: Abstract Book. Paris, France: AFIRAC.

Beck, A., Seraydarian, L., & Hunter, G. F. (1986). The use of animals in the rehabilitation of psychiatric inpatients. *Psychological Reports, 58,* 63-66.

Campbell, C., & Katcher, A. (1992, July). *Animal assisted therapy dogs for autistic children: Quantitative and qualitative results.* Presented at the Sixth International Conference on Human-Animal Interactions. Montreal, Canada.

Cumella, E.J. (2003). Is equine therapy useful in the treatment of eating disorders? *Eating Disorders: The Journal of Treatment and Prevention, 11,* 143-47. Permission was obtained to reproduce the material quoted above.

Dokter, D. (1994). *Art therapies and clients with eating disorders.* London: Jessica Kingsley Publishers Ltd.

Fletcher, T.B. & Hinkle, J.S. (2002). Adventure based counseling: An innovation in counseling. *Journal of Counseling and Development, 80,* 277-85.

Francis, G., Turner, J.T., & Johnson, S.B. (1985). Domestic animal visitation as therapy with adult home residents. *International Journal of Nursing Studies, 22,* 201-206.

Frisch, M.J., Franko, D.L., & Herzog, D.B. (2006). Arts-based therapies in the treatment of eating disorders. *Eating Disorders: The Journal of Treatment and Prevention, 14,* 131-42.

Fritz, C.L., Farver, T.B., Kass, P.H., & Hart, L.A. (1995). Association with companion animals and the expression of noncognitive symptoms in Alzheimer's patients. *Journal of Nervous and Mental Disease, 183,* 459-463.

Ganim, B. (1999). *Art and healing: Using expressive art to heal your body, mind, and spirit.* New York: Three Rivers Press.

Garner, D.M. & Bemis, K.M. (1985). Cognitive therapy for anorexia nervosa. In D.M. Garner & P.E. Garfinkel (Eds.), *Handbook of psychotherapy for anorexia nervosa and bulimia* (pp. 107-46). New York: Guilford Press.

Hornyak, L.M. & Baker, E.K. (Eds.). (1989). *Experiential therapies for eating disorders.* New York: Guilford Press.

Hundley, J. (1991). Pet Project: The use of pet facilitated therapy among the chronically mentally ill. *Journal of Psychosocial Nursing and Mental Health Services, 29,* 23-26.

Katcher, A.H., & Wilkins, G.G. (1994). The use of animal assisted therapy and education with attention-deficit hyperactive and conduct disorders. *Interactions, 12,* 1-5.

Mallon, G.P. (1992). Utilization of animals as therapeutic adjuncts with children and youth: a review of the literature. *Child and Youth Care Forum,* 21, 53-67.

McCabe, E.B. & Marcus, M.D. (2002). Is dialectical behavior therapy useful in the management of anorexia nervosa? *Eating Disorders, 10,* 335-37.

McCormick, A., & McCormick, M. (1997). *Horse Sense and the Human Heart: What Horses Can Teach Us About Trust, Bonding, Creativity and Spirituality.* Deerfield Beach, FL: Health Communications, Inc.

Note: The art therapy section of this chapter is based on an article written for Remuda Ranch Programs for Eating Disorders by Brenda J. Fox, MS, ATR. The section, Temptation Alley: An Equine Experiential Exercise, is based on an article written for Remuda Ranch Programs for Eating Disorders by Bradley Hoffman, EAPI. Written authorizations were secured from patients whose artwork is reproduced here.

Part IV

Social Dimension of Eating Disorders

Chapter 10

Family Dynamics in Eating Disorders

Carolyn Newsome, MA, LPC

> *The* Lord *God said, "It is not good for the man to be alone..." For this reason a man will leave his father and mother and be united to his wife, and they will become one flesh...God blessed them and said to them, "Be fruitful and increase in number..."*
> (Genesis 2:18,24; 1:28)

And now a word to you parents. Don't keep on scolding and nagging your children, making them angry and resentful. Rather, bring them up with the loving discipline the Lord himself approves, with suggestions and godly advice. (See Ephesians 6:4 TLB).

From many biblical passages, Christians have long understood the critical role of the family in shaping children and forging a healthy society. Mental health professionals began to discuss the importance of family during the 1950s and 1960s, with pioneering work by scholars such as Virginia Satir and Salvador Minuchin. Although every person lives in many social contexts—such as society, culture, religion, and friendship circles—the family is often the most influential. Satir (1972) echoed this ancient scriptural wisdom when she recognized through her work that the family is the "factory" where people are made and that parents are "people-makers."

In 1978, Minuchin, Rosman, and Baker treated 53 cases of anorexia nervosa with family therapy. They obtained a 90% improvement rate with positive results maintained for years. These findings dramatically demonstrated that family dynamics contribute significantly to eating disorders. Through the present time, the importance of family dynamics in the etiology and maintenance of eating disorders is widely understood. Family therapy continues to be associated with better outcomes than individual treatment alone (Howatt & Coombs, 2003). Although much individual work is clearly necessary in treating eating disorders, family therapy must be a consideration for successful and thorough treatment. When carefully integrated with Scripture, family therapy theories, conceptualizations, assessments, and skills can prove invaluable with eating disorder patients.

This chapter therefore examines some of the major constructs of family therapy and demonstrates the necessity and potential efficacy of family therapy with eating disorders as opposed to a strictly individual approach.

Perspectives on the Family

The body is a unit, though it is made up of many parts; and though all its parts are many, they form one body...God has arranged the parts in the body, every one of them, just as he wanted them to be...God has combined the members of the body...so that there should be no division in the body, but that its parts should have equal concern for each other. If one part suffers, every part suffers with it; if one part is honored, every part rejoices with it. (1 Corinthians 12:12,18,24-26)

Just as God designs the Body of Christ to function with an integration of different talents, gifts, structures, and roles, he designs families to operate similarly. When the family is not operating as designed, problems ensue. "If one part suffers, every part suffers with it" (1 Corinthians 12:26). Problems play out within the family as a whole and in the lives of its individuals. The family is therefore a crucial element in understanding many difficulties faced by individuals, including eating disorders. Several family therapy theories and constructs express well the biblical concept of "one body, many parts" and offer detailed frameworks for understanding how the parts interact and influence one another within the whole.

General Systems Theory (GST)

A main theoretical underpinning of family therapy models is GST. By definition, a system is a set of elements which interact with one another and their environment (Bertalanffy, 1956). These interactions tend to occur in a patterned manner through time despite changes in the environment (Benjamin, 1982). If the patterned manner is not healthy or functional, it can contribute to ongoing problems within the individual elements or the system.

Following GST, family systems theories focus on each member of the family, the relationships represented in the family, and the dynamic processes occurring within the family. Looking at individuals' issues without considering their relationships within the family system misses important etiologic and maintaining factors of dysfunctional behaviors. Thus, although eating disorders are rarely only about family issues, families can greatly contribute to eating disorder dynamics and addressing the family effectively can enhance the possibility of recovery.

Just as systems tend to resist change, families have homeostatic mechanisms that attempt to maintain a balance or certain way of doing things even when unhealthy (Becvar & Becvar, 1982). If therapeutic work is occurring only with an individual, the system may interfere. For example, if a wife is working on her fears of intimacy by trying to draw closer to her husband, he may sabotage the increased intimacy out of his own fear of intimacy. Therapy with the wife alone would probably not work. Working on the family system is important in this situation to address both partners' fears of intimacy and assist them in developing ways to seek a deeper relationship with one another.

Family Structure

Family structure is another element to understand when working with families. Structure includes several concepts, including power, hierarchies, coalitions, alliances, boundaries, and subsystems. Structural family therapy views changing a family's unhealthy structures as critical in resolving problems (Minuchin, 1974). Changing the structure means changing specific ways of relating within the family.

A healthy structure entails a family with appropriate internal and external boundaries; a balance of power within the marital dyad; and parents who are in charge and who foster age-appropriate responsibility, privileges, and freedoms in their children. This ideal is frequently skewed. Common in families where there is an eating disorder is a power imbalance. The parental subsystem is either overly passive with too little power, or overly controlling with too much power.

The overly passive style forces children into maturing too quickly, does not equip them with tools to handle adult responsibilities, and leaves them confused about who is in charge. In this situation, an eating disorder may be the child's method of getting the parents to take charge and act like adults.

The overly controlling style prevents children from developing confidence in their ability to be independent and from learning to benefit from failure. It may lead to anger, resentment, and rebellion against parental control. In this situation, an eating disorder may be used to gain more power or to rebel.

Family therapy helps render power relations appropriate for the child's age. Teaching parenting skills, assertiveness, boundaries, and how to equip children to become responsible adults is often part of the therapeutic process.

Also common in eating disorder families are unhealthy alliances or coalitions. If the marital subsystem is weak, frequently a child becomes a surrogate spouse and provides emotional support to one or both parents. This can evolve into an unhealthy coalition where one parent/child is pitted against the other parent. Although the child may enjoy the specialness of the surrogate role, eventually resentment builds, along with feelings of pressure to maintain the role and a realization that the role has detached the child from the other parent. Guilt over abandoning the needy parent for whom the child is a surrogate may nevertheless keep the child in this role. An eating disorder may arise in this situation for several reasons. By suppressing secondary sexual characteristics, it is a symbolic way for the patient to remain childlike and avoid the confusion of being a surrogate spouse who is sexually maturing. The eating disorder delays maturation so the child can remain in the surrogate relationship indefinitely and need not deal with the desire to separate from the needy parent. The eating disorder can also be a way for the child to bring the parents together and to focus their energies back on the child rather than on themselves.

Family therapy illuminates these dynamics and provides direction to create healthier structure. In this scenario, marital therapy would strengthen the marital subsystem and parental dyad, and empower the needy parent to find more appropriate emotional support. Therapy would work with the family to create a healthier role for the child and would also help in bridging the emotional gap between the child and the distanced parent.

Multigenerational Patterns

Family therapy looks not only at the current context in which individuals live, but also at past generational contexts. It is common for patterns of relating to be passed down through the generations and to influence behavior without awareness. For eating disorder patients, the disorder may serve to influence a spouse to conform to inherited relational expectations. For example, a wife who experiences her husband as insufficiently nurturing or protective compared with multigenerational expectations may obtain additional nurturance/protection from him through the sick role associated with the eating disorder. In family therapy, it is possible to explore together what the multigenerational patterns have been for each spouse. The couple can be helped to create a shared, realistic, and healthier vision of their relationship. The underlying function of the eating disorder can then be fulfilled instead through mutually satisfying relational choices.

Relational Skills

Common in eating disorder families are communication problems, including lack of emotional communication, an unsafe environment for emotional openness, an invalidating environment, indirect or unclear communication, communication triangles, and lack of communication in general. An eating disorder may be a way of suppressing emotions so as not to express them verbally in this unsafe atmosphere, or a way of communicating something indirectly. If a girl with anorexia becomes angry with her father but cannot express this openly, she can punish him by not eating and thus lead him to feel worried and helpless.

There are many resources on effective communication and conflict resolution skills. It is important to teach the family these skills as a whole because they work best if everyone is using the same skills and coming from the same frame of reference/understanding. Family therapy can assist the family in creating a validating and safe environment for honest communication and can be the context in which new communication skills are practiced until the family trusts itself as a haven for honest expression. As healthier communication develops, the eating disorder is no longer needed as a voice or passive-aggressive expression.

Family Life Cycle

Developmental issues are often part of eating disorder etiology or maintenance. Hence, understanding both individual and family life cycle development is important. Each developmental stage brings its own challenges, obstacles, and joys. Proceeding successfully to the next stage depends largely on accomplishing the previous stage's tasks and feelings/beliefs about the next stage (Carter & McGoldrick, 1989).

Individuals with eating disorders often fail to develop age-appropriate psychological independence from their family of origin (e.g., Root, Fallon & Friedrich, 1986). The reasons for this difficulty are many, including individual, social, and familial factors. The process of growing up is complicated in modern societies, necessitating an integration and resolution of numerous social, intellectual, financial, and technological pressures on adolescents. Consequently, today's parents have a difficult job in steering their children through the tasks necessary to become psychologically independent. Teenagers, likewise, have more difficulty finding a functional balance between autonomy and parental support/closeness. This developmental impasse within the family system is usually characterized by suppressed feelings—particularly anger, grief, and dependency needs. These emotions may be suppressed because they conflict with the family's understanding of ideal behavior.

Not surprisingly, then, eating disorders develop most often around the time of transition to high school or college. Puberty can be frightening because of past sexual abuse which makes becoming a woman terrifying or because of growing distance in a girl's relationship with her father due to his inability to relate to a daughter with a mature body. Frequently 18 year olds fear becoming adults. Some may have been overprotected and not adequately prepared for adulthood. Others may fear failure due to perfectionistic standards. Still others may fear what will happen to their family if they leave home. Will a depressed mom be okay if the patient leaves? If the family was a child-focused family, what will happen to the parents when the last child leaves? Does that child feel responsible for keeping the parents together? An eating disorder may be a way of keeping the child at home or dependent on the family for any of these reasons.

Life cycle dynamics of this kind can often be assessed and addressed most effectively through family therapy because they involve subtle communications between parents and children and messages that therapists may have difficulty uncovering without the opportunity to observe the family interacting.

Family Types Common in Eating Disorder Development

There is not a single type of family in which eating disorders arise. However, in our experience treating thousands of families we have found that families with an eating disorder member are often repressed emotionally and stuck in rigid roles and expectations. They may be unaware of these roles and expectations and the impact they are having on the eating disorder. We briefly describe five types of families commonly discussed in the literature and their relationship to eating disorder development.

The Perfect Family

The perfect family is similar to the idealized all-American family and embodies many positive qualities. Obviously, there is really no such thing as a perfect family, but there can be a sense that people *view* the family as perfect. In this circumstance, the child may feel imperfect and unable to live up to the high behavioral expectations of the family.

Perfect families are usually intact. The children feel loved and generally report closeness to the family. Achievement is valued highly. The dysfunction of the family occurs most in its prohibition of negative feelings, minimization of interpersonal problems, and promotion of fairy-tale endings to problems. Upon close inspection, many perfect families' closeness is a sign of enmeshment or the stifling of individuality out of fear that it may threaten the family's identity. An imbalance between autonomy and closeness prevents teenagers from moving into adulthood.

In these families, the eating disorder may become the patient's voice. It may be the patient's attempt to become physically perfect to fit into this perfect family. Or it may be a conscience-pleasing rebellion: "I love my family and would never embarrass them by becoming a drunk or drug addict. An eating disorder is a nice way to rebel."

The perfect family often does not see its dysfunction and is unwilling or unable to talk about what is happening within the family. This family is at times so rigidly structured that it takes what Nichols & Schwartz (1995) refer to as "therapeutic dynamite" to change them. Effective family therapy with such families requires powerful interventions, including activities that promote emotional experiencing.

The Overprotective Family

The overprotective family provides a safe and secure physical and psychological environment for children. The major dysfunction lies in the parents' inability to change the rules to encourage independent behavior in a timely, age-appropriate manner and to support children's need for increased autonomy during adolescence. These families provide so much for their children that children feel indebted and guilty for being angry and wanting to grow up. With too few opportunities to learn by trial and error, it is premature for children from overprotective families to leave at any age since they feel incompetent and ill-equipped to deal with the world.

In an overprotective family, eating disorders may be a means to gain independence from overcontrol. "You have controlled everything else in my life...you CAN'T make me eat!" The eating disorder may also be experienced by patients as a protective cocoon—a sense of security with rigid rules and requirements to hold onto as they are transitioning from the protective family into the scary world.

The Chaotic Family

The chaotic family moves from crisis to crisis. "When is someone going to get sick again, drunk again, scream and yell again...when are we going to move again?" Or the family schedule is so busy, rushing from soccer practice to piano lessons to church activities, that there is little routine or stability. This family experiences constant change. At times, someone consciously or unconsciously creates crisis because the family functions only in chaos. Inconsistent rules, explosiveness, and multiple problems among members also characterize this family. This family lacks role models for limit setting, resulting in an inconsistent, changeable balance between autonomy and closeness that severely interferes with the development of trust in self and others.

In this context of unpredictability and insecurity, an eating disorder can become the one predictable factor. Children have been unable to develop trust in themselves or anyone. The eating disorder becomes something they learn to trust. It is always there for the child; no one can take it away. It sets rules on how to use one's time, what are good and bad behaviors, etc.

The Enmeshed Family

Enmeshed families are overly close and dependent on one another. There are poor emotional boundaries and little privacy. There is a strong message, spoken or unspoken, that "our family is all you need." In the enmeshed family, the child cannot develop a separate, autonomous life. In this context, an eating disorder can become the patient's voice, as s/he perceives no right to have opinions other than the family's. An eating disorder can establish an identity apart from the smothering enmeshment the patient is feeling. Being "the bulimic one" is at least an identity that distinguishes the patient from the rest of the family. The eating disorder can also fulfill the need for separation and individuation, since its behaviors clearly violate the family's rules and norms and allow patients to make their own choices.

The Disengaged Family

In contrast to the enmeshed family, relationships in the disengaged family are overly distant and independent. Self-sufficiency is an important virtue in this family. Home is primarily a place to eat and sleep, and relationships are superficial. Using the common analogy, in the disengaged family there is insufficient strength in the children's roots so they cannot develop strong wings. They may be launched into flight without sufficient security.

In this context, an eating disorder brings people together because a loved one is ill, and it gives the person with the disorder much needed attention and support. At times, we have heard patients say that they do not want to give up their eating disorder because "My dad won't talk to me again. He was too busy for me until I got anorexia." Sometimes patients fear their parents will divorce if they recover, because they have experienced the eating disorder bringing the parents together and working hard to communicate whereas parents were not communicating prior to the eating disorder.

Common Themes Across Family Types

Although these five family types are different in significant ways, they also have similarities that can promote eating disorders.

- In each family type, individuation is impeded, whether by the uniformity of the perfect family, the dependency of the overprotective family, or the lack of consistency in the chaotic family.
- Each family type becomes rigidly closed to outsiders when their rules of functioning are threatened. The perfect family shuts strangers out by exceedingly high and rigid expectations and intolerance for differences. The overprotective family has an implicit assumption that no one is good enough for their child. The chaotic family's internal organization is marked by an inconsistent rules structure that allows the family to create convenient rules to exclude anyone who threatens them.
- In each family type, there is incongruence between nonverbal and verbal communication regarding feelings, especially anger, grief, and dependency. This incongruence between nonverbal and verbal communication impedes children's trust in their perceptions and feelings; repeated experiences of incongruence lead to a fragile sense of identity and self-esteem.
- Each family type has difficulty resolving conflict, often pulling children into marital conflicts and failing to teach children how to effectively deal with real-world conflicts.
- In each family type, parents may be inappropriately dependent on their children. In perfect families, there may be too much dependence on children to affirm parents' identities. In overprotective and enmeshed families, there is often a dependence on the child for companionship. In chaotic families, there is physical and emotional dependence on children for responsibilities, including caretaking of parents with multiple social and occupational problems. With all forms of dependency, the child does not have permission to be psychologically autonomous—a necessary internal condition for successfully leaving home.

The distinct and common dysfunctions combined in these family types are significant enough to derail the families' ability to launch their children into psychological independence. The therapist is therefore challenged to help these families allow their children to grow up.

Concluding Thoughts

It is not easy to work with most eating disorder families. Family members often distrust the therapist, fearing they will be blamed for their loved one's disorder. They feel shame, which they mask with myriad well-developed and sophisticated defenses; they are fearful of being judged. These feelings are intensified because they are scared their loved one might die. Furthermore, the conflict between verbal and nonverbal communication within these families, the closed nature of the family system when it is threatened, and some of the families' ability to appear to function better than they actually do—each of these confound traditional, verbal therapeutic communications.

These families need to experience grace if they are to open up, be free to expose their shame, talk about their feelings, and receive healing. Jesus was able to confront the woman at the well with her dysfunctional relationship patterns because he did it with grace (John 4:6-30). He showed her acceptance and respect, which she was surprised to receive. She was then able to deal with her shame and to tell others both about her history of dysfunction and her healing experience. Jesus spoke the truth in love, which is what hurting families need (Ephesians 4:15,25).

Consistent with this scriptural understanding, Satir (1972) held that demonstrating caring and acceptance is the key to helping people overcome their fear, reveal their experiences, and open up to each other. In our experience, families with eating disorders desperately need this caring and acceptance. A willingness to understand and accept—rather than an anxious eagerness to change the family—enables therapists to help people discover and acknowledge deeply held, but poorly understood, fears, desires, and family dynamics. When therapists break the family system's rule by talking openly about shame and the issues that cause it, they break the invisible bondage that entraps the family members, helping the family to take steps toward self-respect and integrity.

As Gerald May (1991) expressed: "Grace is the most powerful force in the universe. It can transcend repression, addiction, and every other internal or external power that seeks to oppress the freedom of the human heart. Grace is where our hope lies." Family therapists are privileged to bring God's grace into family sessions, transcending repression and opening the hearts of family members to experience freedom.

In short, without looking at family issues in eating disorder patients, important etiologic and sustaining elements can be missed. Although much individual work needs to occur with eating disorders, family therapy better addresses some of the key elements. There are obviously no perfect families, but families that function more in keeping with God's design for the family can liberate blessings that God intends for families to give and profoundly support the recovery of individuals with eating disorders. "If one part suffers, every part suffers with it; if one part is honored, every part rejoices with it" (1 Corinthians 12:26).

References

Becvar, R. J., & Becvar, D. S. (1982). *Systems theory and family therapy: A primer.* Lanham, MD: University Press of America.

Benjamin, M. (1982). General systems theory, family systems theories, and family therapy: Towards an integrated model of family process. In A. Bross (Ed.), *Family therapy: Principles of strategic practice* (pp. 34-88). New York: Guilford Press.

Bertalanffy, L. (1956). General systems theory. *Behavioral Systems, 4,* 1-10.

Carter, B., & McGoldrick, M. (1989). Overview of the changing family life cycle: A framework for family therapy. In B. Carter & M. McGoldrick (Eds.), *The changing family life cycle* (pp. 3-28). Boston: Allyn and Bacon.

Howatt, W. A, & Coombs, R. H. (2003). Psychosocial recovery tools for addictive disorders. *Counselor: The Magazine for Addiction Professionals, 4,* 58-61.

May, G.G. (1991). *Addiction & grace.* New York: Harper Collins.

Minuchin, S. (1974). *Families and family therapy.* Cambridge, MA: Harvard University Press.

Minuchin, S., Rosman, B. L., & Baker, L. (1978). *Psychosomatic families: Anorexia nervosa in context.* Cambridge, MA: Harvard University Press.

Nichols, M.P., & Schwartz, R.C. (1995). *Family therapy: Concepts and methods* (3rd ed., p. 300). Boston: Allyn and Bacon.

Root, M.P.P., Fallon, P., & Friedrich, W.N. (1986). *Bulimia: A systems approach to treatment.* New York: Norton Books.

Satir, V. (1972). *Peoplemaking.* Palo Alto, CA: Science and Behavior Books.

Note: We thank Jim Schettler, MMFT, LMFT for his contributions to an earlier version of this chapter.

Chapter 11

Christian Family Therapy with Eating Disorders

Guy Braem, MD, MA, CMFT

> *But we are meant to hold firmly to the truth in love, and to grow up in every way into Christ, the head.* (Ephesians 4:15; Phillips Modern English)

This verse is the basis for Remuda's family therapy interventions. Teaching, modeling, and practicing the application of this verse within families enables family members to nourish each other "to grow up in every way into Christ."

Remuda's week-long, intensive family therapy program consists of four major components:

- *Education and preparation*— Communicating information to families about eating disorders, basic family structures/roles, and family contributions to the development, maintenance, and recovery from eating disorders.
- *Family therapy sessions*—Called Truth-in-Love sessions, these follow Remuda's intensive family therapy format. Format incorporates elements of family systems, structural, conjoint, transgenerational, cognitive-behavioral, 12-Step, and psychodynamic approaches integrated with biblical Christianity.
- *Formal/informal sharing among families and patients*—Sharing among several families to learn from and encourage one other, discover that they are not alone with their experiences, and offer accountability throughout the day and evening so that the five-day Family Week is truly intensive and fully therapeutic.
- *Family outings*—Opportunities for each individual family and patient to be together, unsupervised within the community, to practice recently-learned relationship and communication skills and to enjoy a new freedom in being with one another.

This chapter focuses on one of these four components: family therapy sessions following Remuda's Truth-in-Love format. Through this format, Remuda addresses the family issues outlined in the previous chapter in this book.

Family Therapy Sessions: The Remuda Format

Following Ephesians 4, Remuda's family therapy sessions are called Truth-in-Love sessions. They focus on teaching, modeling, and practicing open and honest communication in a loving way. Such communication promotes an atmosphere of safety and healing, as well as personal and family change.

In his book, *Family Love*, Alfred Ells (1995) writes:

Studies of family life indicate that being truthful in a loving and appropriate way is a common characteristic of healthy families. But hurtful communication and denial of truth are major traits of unhealthy families. Truth without love is destructive. So is love without truth.

In his book, *The Peacemaker: A Biblical Guide to Resolving Personal Conflict*, Ken Sande (1997) includes a chapter titled, "Speak the Truth in Love." His development of this idea was independent of Remuda's, but similar. He states: "With God's help, you can learn to speak the truth in love by saying only what will build up others, listening responsibly to what others say, and using principles of wisdom. 'The tongue of the wise brings healing' (Proverbs 12:18)."

Eating disorders generally foster secretiveness, withdrawal, and isolation. Patients hide what they are doing and who they are. Speaking the truth in love breaks through the secrets and isolation in a gentle yet powerful way.

Following Ephesians 4, a Truth-in-Love session involves two parts.

Truth-in-Love: Part One

A Truth-in-Love session begins with speaking the truth, or *confrontation*: communicating and presenting one's history and story in a factual and informative manner. Many families have little idea what has been going on in the patient's life with the eating disorder and some families do not learn that their loved one even has an eating disorder until just weeks or days before their loved one enters treatment. Likewise, parents have sometimes chosen not to share important personal information or marital issues with their children. Through the Truth-in-Love process, problematic family dynamics and structures—such as those outlined in the previous chapter of this book—are discussed and addressed openly in language accessible to everyday people. With open disclosure, there is an honest look at the reality of what the eating disorder and the underlying issues have done to the patient and family. This is only possible when the patient and family experience a sense of love and safety from the professionals involved and each other.

Confrontation is followed by *confession*. "Therefore confess your sins to each other and pray for each other so that you may be healed" (James 5:16). The families and patients learn a step-by-step process that helps them to talk about wounds and hurts, apologize, and ask for forgiveness. This process is healing and emotionally freeing. It brings relief from years of pain, blame, and shame. Sometimes our family therapists see a physical change in patients from before the Truth-in-Love to afterwards. Patients may stand straighter, look up more, make better eye contact, smile and interact more freely, and evidence greater energy. Guilt and shame may be hard masters, but freedom from them offers a powerful release.

Many times a patient's divorced parents have not spoken to each other for perhaps a decade and cannot stand to be in the same room with each other. They come to Family Week and act civilly to one other because of the love they have for the patient. At times, through the process of Family Week, these parents ask forgiveness from one another, heal old wounds, and release years of bitterness.

We end Truth-in-Love sessions with *validation*: families validate and build each other up, showing that relationships consist not merely of faults but also of strengths and mutual appreciation.

This Truth-in-Love process, consisting of confrontation, confession, and validation, helps reduce the power of the secrets, shame, and fear that have paralyzed the patient and family, sometimes for years.

Truth-in-Love: Part Two

The second aspect of a Truth-in-Love session reflects the latter part of Ephesians 4:15, "to grow up in every way…" As noted in the previous chapter in this book, patients with eating disorders experience difficulties in the developmental process. Those with eating disorders tend to function emotionally behind their chronological age. They are often afraid to progress because it would mean facing something fearful: more responsibility, the possibility of failure, feelings of guilt and worthlessness, a mature female body, sexuality, trauma, grief, and loss.

Eating disorder patients are overwhelmed by these feelings and do not have the means to cope with them. Ironically, they are also frightened of asking for help because they are afraid they will be hurt if they open up. Their fear is founded: People do hurt us, and the patients have been hurt in past relationships. But the means to healing relationally is also through people, the very avenue through which we have been hurt. This can seem like a double-bind or no-win situation, which can be paralyzing. Eating disorders provide a way to cope with this double-bind by numbing its anxiety and confusion and narrowing patients' focus to something over which they feel they have control—food and weight. But using the eating disorder to cope leads to further paralysis because the original dilemma is never resolved. It is repressed and avoided and continues to control the patient.

In *One-Way Relationships*, Ells (1990) says that, "Family is the single most powerful influence in shaping our relationships." To heal the deep relational problems of eating disorder patients, Remuda therefore focuses on the family. The Truth-in-Love format offers patients the safety needed to uncover the relational truths they have been avoiding and, by unfreezing their emotional paralysis and that of their family, to grapple with and grow through their feared, repressed experiences. The developmental process is restarted and the patient can continue toward separation-individuation and adulthood.

To grow up, one needs a direction to grow toward. Remuda's therapies respect individuals and their choices. Many therapy models operate on the principle that the therapist's job is to provide a stimulus to provoke change, but then to trust the client to discern through prayer, meditation, counsel, and life experiences to know which change(s) to make and in which direction. This approach engages personal will and responsibility and relies on the guidance of the Holy Spirit speaking within the person's conscience. Such an approach is consistent with a scriptural understanding of human beings.

How do growth and maturity occur within families?

First, truthful and loving speech leads to a maturing of relationships. It brings honesty, respect, and self-respect into relationships and inherently believes in the capacity of the persons involved and their relationships to handle the truth and its implications.

Second, family connection and belonging form the foundation for growth, providing the freedom, safety, and stimulus to grow (Cloud & Townsend, 1992). Ephesians 4 lays out the keys to developing this sense of family belonging and connection in a child. It says: "the body...builds itself up in love." Love is the most basic need that human beings have (1 Corinthians 13:4-7,13). In a loving environment, people grow. Scripture makes plain that a loving environment includes: people who believe in us, are kind and compassionate, encourage, provide safety, are honest with us, and don't give up on us. These characteristics are the very definition of love itself (1 Corinthians 13).

Families usually come to Remuda's Family Week out of love. The pain, fear, crises, and helplessness that families and patients have been through have stripped away denial and superficial concerns and have refocused the family on crucial issues. Coming face to face with a loved one's possible death from an eating disorder creates a turning point in people's lives. The things that really matter come into sharp focus and people become more willing than they have been at previous times to make difficult decisions and take needed actions. Families' love for the eating disorder patient is awakened by this crucial moment in time; this love is encouraged, brought forward, laid bare, and intensified by the Family Week environment and experiential exercises. "Above all, love each other deeply, because love covers over a multitude of sins" (1 Peter 4:8). This deep love breaks through years of dysfunctional habits of behavior and motivates families to change. Decisions, commitments, and actions are taken that break old patterns of enmeshment, criticism, overprotection, etc., and open family systems to offer experiences of connection and belonging so that they support the patient's development.

Third, Ephesians 4:29 continues: "Do not let any unwholesome talk come out of your mouth, but only what is helpful for building others up according to their needs…" The intent of this verse is modeled and practiced during Family Week. In loving each other, we take actions and speak words that promote the best interests of other people, to help them grow and become who God created them to be. During Family Week, families and patients work hard at the separation-individuation process. The acceptance and understanding they experience from the therapists and other families build them up and help them to see the value in this scary work. For many families, their fear can be summarized in these words: "If I can't control what happens to my child, something bad will happen or my child may die." When families learn how hard patients have been working toward recovery and they experience open, mature, healing communication with the patient, it helps them to believe in the patient's ability to grow. They become hopeful and find the power to let go.

Fourth, Ephesians 4:16 states: "Each part does its work…" This expresses the idea of appropriate roles and boundaries within a family system. Family members have a specific job to do—to support, listen to, and understand the patient, and to provide models of healthy living and relationships. It is not the work of the family to play the role of caretaker, therapist, food police, problem-solver, or fix-it person for the patient's life and problems. This understanding reemphasizes the process of separation-individuation. Often families have to learn in truth to say "no" as well as "yes."

Finally, another way of looking at the developmental process is as integration or reintegration. As discussed in the previous chapter in this book, each person is formed to be a contributing and meaningful part of a healthy, loving whole or system. No baby is born with the belief that s/he is worthless or has no purpose; no one is born with shame and guilt. As we grow, we learn these things and they isolate us from family and relationships. We forget who we are and what we feel because we no longer like ourselves or our emotions.

The Truth-in-Love process helps people to reintegrate from this isolation, both internally and externally. Families and participants validate one another, teaching each other loving and truthful self-understandings. In addition, since God created us, through his Word we learn critical truths about ourselves and our lives. Such truths are woven into the Truth-in-Love process. Through these identity-building affirmations, the Truth-in-Love process gives patients tools to deal with fear and heal shame. It helps patients to challenge beliefs that may not be true (e.g., "I am worthless") and to learn what is true about themselves in a way that builds them up and sets them free to journey into recovery, maturity, and adulthood.

Family Perceptions of Family Week

Over 7000 patients and 20,000 family members have gone through Remuda's Family Week program. With few exceptions, they validate the benefit of the Truth-in-Love process. Their ratings on satisfaction surveys indicate that they are, on average, extremely satisfied with their Family Week experiences. Their comments, in their own words, bring life to the numbers:

> *"Our family learned how to communicate."*

> *"We never talked before. In the Truth-in-Love we discussed taking responsibility and asking forgiveness. It changed all our relationships and I feel I have a real relationship instead of a superficial one."*

> *"We started to incorporate the Truth-in-Love methods into our lifestyle."*

> *"My family did not believe in therapy. It made a believer out of them and they went home and got in therapy themselves. It changed my family. It's OK to cry, to feel. It brought my whole family closer."*

"Coming to Family Week was the first time they took time for me."

"I felt safe."

"I benefited from each and every experience."

"I was skeptical of how this would work, but was highly impressed."

"Family Week was an amazing opportunity to provide clarity, understanding, hope, unity, and love."

"Family Week was amazing in assisting us to communicate with each other."

References

Cloud, H. & Townsend, J. (1992). *Boundaries.* Grand Rapids, MI: Zondervan.

Ells, A.H. (1995). *Family love.* Nashville: Thomas Nelson.

Ells, A.H. (1990). *One-way relationships.* Nashville: Thomas Nelson.

Sande, K. (1997). *The peacemaker.* Grand Rapids, MI: Baker Books.

Chapter 12

Peers, Schools, and Eating Disorder Development

Edward J. Cumella, PhD, CEDS

Become wise by walking with the wise; hang out with fools and watch your life fall to pieces. (Proverbs 13:20 MSG)

In a shopping mall I noticed a group of 12-year-old girls. Each wore an identical tube top reading, "Dare to be Different!" This ironic image captures the epitome of adolescence: the need to belong, coupled with the need to be unique.

Erik Erikson (1980) characterized the essential developmental issue of adolescence as a conflict between identity and role confusion. As children move beyond the primary social influence of the family, they develop individual identities separate from their identities as members of their family. To do so, children look to peers for messages about who they are. Successful maneuvering of this stage leads to fidelity to one's own values and an integrated sense of self. But successful adolescent development can be hampered by social and academic forces that may lead to a variety of problems, including eating disorders.

Peers

It is common knowledge that peer group influences are profoundly important for teenagers because belonging is of such high priority for them. Fitting in allows teenagers to feel acceptable. Being different, however, can come with a high price—becoming an outcast. Yet because each teenager is an individual, they experience within themselves and observe in others differences that they often devalue rather than prize. Puberty especially has the ability to render one utterly self-conscious. Physical changes become painfully apparent, particularly for girls, who experience breast development, emerging curves, and necessary weight gain. Girls who experience pubertal onset earlier than average are at greater risk for adjustment problems and often feel negatively toward their bodies, perhaps because they tend to weigh more than average (Brooks-Gunn & Reiter, 1993). Dating and sexual experimentation are further domains of teen life that spotlight teens' physical attributes and often promote the angst of self-consciousness.

Trusted friends may offer teens the acceptance they desperately crave and need. Less kind peer groups/cliques may be downright cruel and ostracizing. "Kind words heal and help; cutting words wound and maim" (Proverbs 15:4 MSG). Recent television reports suggest that 2/3 of violent school crimes committed by students are carried out by those who have been bullied, mocked, or tormented by their peers. School violence is obviously an externalized expression of complex emotions including rage toward peers and self-hatred born of ridicule. For some, an eating disorder may be an internalized expression of similar emotions.

I have worked with many eating disorder adolescents who have the cruel remarks of peers ringing in their ears—the result of peer maltreatment due to childhood obesity. For some, an extreme fear of humiliation by peers results in avoidant personality disorder or features thereof. The response of these wounded children can sometimes be an "I'll show you"—communicated nonverbally but resoundingly through an emaciated body. Often, too, there is a second response: the depths of depression and a lacking will to live.

On the other hand, some adolescents with eating disorders have never struggled with weight. Some have done well in school and didn't cause trouble. Their vulnerability consists of a lack of social skills needed to be effective in relating to peers. By default, these children are often discounted by their peers as "weird" and relegated to the fringe. In more extreme cases, some develop social phobia; others have schizotypal or even schizoid personality disorders/features. Lonely and often confused about what they ever did to alienate their peers, such students may develop eating disorder behaviors unconsciously to achieve a variety of potential goals.

- Some are looking for a consistent companion and release from the loneliness of having no friends. Patients often refer to their eating disorder as their best friend. The eating disorder sets rules about good and bad behavior, offers rewards and punishments, occupies the mind with food and caloric obsessions, and distracts from emotional pain.
- For some, eating disorder behaviors may supply an outlet for unidentified and ill-managed feelings—a form of emotion regulation. The

core symptoms of eating disorders—bingeing, purging, restricting, compulsive exercise—can release endorphins, create temporary euphoria, and/or lead to emotional numbness. The negative feelings with which these teens need to cope include loneliness, despair, self-hatred, and anger related to their frustrated experiences with peers, as well as fears of sexuality.

- Other teens have felt demoralized and hopeless that their social circumstances will change. For them, eating disorders may indeed be experienced as "something I can control." Counting and recounting calories, fat grams, and carbohydrates; finding novel ways to reduce food intake or eliminate consumed calories; keeping track of weights and body measurements—all these endeavors have structure, rules, logic, and direction that can offer an arena of control when the rest of life feels beyond their control.
- For some, eating disorders are an attempt to become like admired or envied peers based on the perception that thinness equals beauty and popularity. Some are literally copying an admired peer or public figure who has an eating disorder; others are seeking to attain a similar look or body by way of eating disorder behaviors. The underlying rationale is often: "If I look like her/him, I will also be accepted by other people just like she/he is."

Other avenues also exist connecting problematic peer relations with the onset of eating disorders.

In contrast, some adolescent girls with eating disorders seem to have everything in place socially: an appearance that mirrors America's cultural ideals of beauty, boyfriends, teachers' favor, popularity, and many friends. But adolescence, even for successful teens, poses many challenges, such as dating, athletics, academic success, and possible competition to maintain popularity and status. Some teenagers with a high measure of status also feel pressured to be everything to everyone. Some have narcissistic personality disorder or features. These pressures may intensify adolescents' focus on external appearance and drive for perfection, gradually leading to more and more eating disorder behavior.

If she is in a peer group that is highly weight conscious, compares body sizes, or even exhibits eating disorder behaviors, a teenage girl may seek ever-increasing thinness and engage in extreme dieting, compulsive exercise, and a variety of eating disorder behaviors. Without realizing it, she may find herself caught in the quagmire of an eating disorder.

Schools

In addition to social and peer experiences, attendance at school challenges children with academic pursuits. For those with perfectionistic tendencies, the demands of the high school workload may appear to mount, sometimes joined by performance pressures from well-meaning teachers, coaches, and parents. The performance expectations and perhaps coaching/training styles associated with certain sports that require a lean physique, such as gymnastics or figure skating, also place students at higher risk for dieting behavior and possible eating disorder development (Zerbe, 1995). Although perfectionism is not a requirement for an eating disorder, studies—beginning with Hilda Bruch's classic work on anorexia (Bruch, 1973)—have consistently demonstrated that perfectionism is a hallmark personality trait of those with eating disorders. In fact, one recent study concluded that in high school girls, stress intensifies the association between perfectionism and desires/plans to lose weight (Ruggiero, Levi, Ciuna, & Sassaroli, 2003).

For teens, the future may appear to be on the line with college admissions or the pursuit of meaningful post-high school employment. A perfectionist may conceptualize this experience in an equation such as: "failure to get an A in ninth grade geometry = a lost future." Part and parcel of perfectionism is a frequent if not persistent experience of personal ineffectiveness and helplessness in spite of success in other people's eyes. This can lead to eating disorder behavior for two interconnected reasons: 1) eating disorders narrow one's focus to food and body issues over which some sense of control/efficacy can be achieved; and 2) eating disorders offer a subjective experience of success as measured by eating disorder standards—e.g., weight lost, caloric restriction achieved.

The private school setting adds another dimension to the typical school pressures. A study by Lesar, Arnow, Stice, and Agras (2001) indicates that both girls and boys in private schools demonstrate a higher level of eating pathology and are at higher risk for developing bulimia than their public school counterparts. While the authors posit that one explanation for this difference may be family driven or modeled, they do not discount the atmosphere within private school life itself as a likely contributing factor. Private schools may offer a different subculture than public schools, with more pronounced peer pressure and demands for students to achieve cultural ideals, including body weight and shape.

Many private schools have a Christian foundation. Sometimes—as is also seen in church environments—Christianity can be expressed legalistically or with expectations of perfect behavior. Groups of Christian students and teachers together may hold one another to impossibly high standards—standards, like body ideals, that may derive from a broken, misguided culture. This additional pressure may readily promote eating disorder behaviors.

In Christian school settings, it is important for teachers and administrators to reflect on and promote a culture that mirrors an essential Christian teaching. "For we fix our eyes not on what is seen, but on what is unseen. For what is seen is temporary, but what is unseen is eternal" (2 Corinthians 4:18). "You were taught, with regard to your former way of life, to put off your old self…to be made new in the attitude of your minds; and to put on the new self, created to be like God in true righteousness and holiness; …so from now on, we regard no one from a worldly point of view" (Ephesians 4:22-24; 2 Corinthians 5:16). There should be no distinction between "Greek or Jew" (Galatians 3:28), fat or thin, for all are "one in Christ Jesus" and all have value as unique creations of God.

Implications for Eating Disorder Prevention and Treatment

Recognizing the complexities of the modern teenagers' social and academic world assists our understanding of how eating disorders may emerge. This has implications for eating disorder prevention and treatment efforts.

Research is indicating that peer-based primary prevention strategies in the school setting can be effective in reducing the incidence of eating disorders. McVey et al. (2003) found that middle school girls experienced increases in weight-related esteem and decreases in dieting behaviors after completing a 10-session intervention group program. This study suggests that, with guidance and education, peer influence on teens' body image and eating behaviors can be favorable rather than pathogenic. In fact, an additional study shows that merely asking questions of teens about risky weight control behavior and attitudes can discourage such behavior (Celio, Bryson, Killen, & Taylor, 2003).

For those teenagers with eating disorders, it is important to recognize the power of positive peer culture in the recovery process. Group therapy and education, peer recovery support groups, and other healthy peer affiliation groups such as church groups or certain team sports, can greatly assist eating disorder teenagers to develop positive self-esteem and body image and to adopt healthful eating behaviors and attitudes.

References

Brooks-Gunn, J. & Reiter, E. O. (1993). The role of pubertal processes. In S. S. Feldman & G. R. Elliott (Eds.), *At the threshold: The developing adolescent* (pp. 16-53). Cambridge, MA: Harvard University Press.

Bruch, H. (1973). *Eating disorders: Obesity, anorexia nervosa, and the person within.* New York: Basic Books, Inc.

Celio, A. A., Bryson, S., Killen, J. D., & Taylor, C. B. (2003). Are adolescents harmed when asked risky weight control behavior and attitude questions? Implications for consent procedures. *International Journal of Eating Disorders, 34,* 251-54.

Erikson, E. H. (1980). *Identity and the life cycle.* New York: W.W. Norton & Company.

Lesar, M. D., Arnow, B., Stice, E., Agras, W. S. (2001). Private high school students are at risk for bulimic pathology. *Eating Disorders: The Journal of Treatment & Prevention, 9,* 125-39.

McVey, G. L., Lieberman, M., Voorberg, N., Wardrope, D., & Blackmore, E. (2003). School-based peer support groups: A new approach to the prevention of disordered eating. *Eating Disorders: The Journal of Treatment & Prevention, 11,* 169-85.

Ruggiero, G. M., Levi, D., Ciuna, A., & Sassaroli, S. (2003). Stress situation reveals an association between perfectionism and drive for thinness. *International Journal of Eating disorders, 34,* 220-26.

Zerbe, K. J. (1995). *The body betrayed: A deeper understanding of women, eating disorders, and treatment.* Carlsbad, CA: Gurze Books.

Note: This chapter is based on an article written for Remuda Ranch Programs for Eating Disorders by Noëlle Kerr-Price, PsyD.

Chapter 13

The Demise and Restoration of Intimacy

David J. Rogers, MA, LPC

Intimacy: Theological and Spiritual Considerations

The Merriam-Webster dictionary (2003) defines intimacy as: "close, familiar, and affectionate personal relationship; close association with, or deep understanding of; sexually familiar." Intimate is defined as: "showing a close union or combination...inmost, personal; of, pertaining to, or characteristic of the inmost or essential nature; intrinsic." In short—intimacy means "to know and be known."

From a Christian theological perspective, the Trinity is the basis of intimacy: three distinct personalities in perfect union (1 John 5:7 KJV). When human beings, as distinct individuals, live in union with one another, we reflect God himself and his nature: unity in diversity (cf. 1 John 5:7; 1 Corinthians 12:4-27). Moreover, we then live according to God's design for humanity. As Jesus said: "I pray...that all of them may be one, Father, just as you are in me and I am in you" (John 17:20-21; emphasis added).

Even more foundational to intimacy among ourselves, Christians believe that human beings were created to live in intimate relationship with God as the core of their existence: "From one ancestor he made all nations...he allotted the times of their existence and the boundaries of the places where they should live, so that they would search for God and perhaps grope for him and find him, though he is not far from each one of us. For in him we live and move and have our being" (Acts 17:26-28 NRSV. See also Genesis 1:27; 2:7; Psalm 139:1-18; 145:13b-19; 1 Corinthians 13:12). Theologians have long spoken of the "I-Thou" relationship. For adolescents and adults, this personal interface between God and self is the experiential foundation of all intimacy.

Awareness of the contrast between, yet union of, myself and God—divine and mortal, infinite and finite, Creator and created, Savior and redeemed, holy and broken, Father and child, lover and beloved—is the birthplace of intimacy. The understanding that God has full comprehension of all my thoughts, feelings, motives, intentions, desires, and past, present, and future failings, yet loves me with inseparable love is the basis on which I can be fully disclosing, fully honest with myself and another (Romans 8:29-39).

In short, intimacy is about self revelation combined with the experience of being accepted. God has initiated this entire process by revealing himself to us in the person of Jesus Christ (John 1:14; 14:9), by searching and knowing us deeply, and by accepting us just as we are:

> O LORD, you have searched me and you know me. You know when I sit and when I rise; you perceive my thoughts from afar. You discern my going out and my lying down; you are familiar with all my ways. Before a word is on my tongue you know it completely, O LORD (Psalm 139:1-4). "Accept one another, then, just as Christ accepted you..." (Romans 15:7).

Trust and Identity: Psychological Foundations of Intimacy

The interplays between trust and fear, identity and shame, are critical to both the demise and restoration of intimacy in eating disorders.

Trust

Erikson (1980) identified trust as the first and primary task in psychosocial development. He posited that trust is so foundational that if it is not attained, further development derails. In worst-case scenarios involving abuse, abandonment, and neglect, individuals' capacity to trust is so damaged that permanent impairment can occur, preventing significant attachment or bonding to others throughout the lifespan. Simply put: no trust, no intimacy.

For women, research suggests that eating disorders often begin during the onset of adolescence, ages 12 to 14, or at its end, ages 17 to 19. Children face multiple developmental challenges during these ages—puberty, relinquishing childhood, embracing adolescence, increasing responsibility, separation/individuation, acceptance/rejection by peers, identity formation, competence, sexuality, and early adulthood. Teens need intimate relationship support during this time. In fact, the capacity for intimacy is one of the most critical resources needed for young people to successfully navigate adolescence. Individuals' ability to develop intimacy during adolescence is directly related to the trust achieved earlier in life.

Without trust and intimate support during these transitional milestones, young people are vulnerable to arrested development and reliance on unhealthy coping strategies. Eating disorders are part and parcel of these two difficulties. Anorexia virtually maintains or restores physiological childhood by eliminating menses and secondary sexual characteristics, by stopping physical growth, and by rendering the person physically diminutive. The primary features of eating disorders—bingeing, purging, restricting, and compulsive exercise—increase endorphin levels and promote temporary euphoria or emotional numbing, functioning as a form of emotion regulation or unhealthy coping. Both anorexia and bulimia can represent attempts to meet other legitimate developmental needs through maladaptive methods. For example, self-starvation leads to thinness and the subjective perception of acceptance in lieu of actual peer relationships; purging prevents weight gain and can be experienced as the solution to anticipated peer rejection; eating disorders can become companions to the lonely; eating disorder behaviors can be forms of rebellion against family expectations and, as such, a method of separation/individuation. Other variants exist.

Identity

Erikson (1980) considered identity formation as the stage of psychosocial development occurring at the time of puberty. Identity formation specifically means learning to be oneself and to share oneself.

At this stage, adolescents start to more formally separate from family. They seek peer group belonging to find out who they are as unique and distinct from their family of origin. Identity is therefore shaped in the context of relationships.

Identity formation can be likened to growing up in a house of mirrors. Early in development children look to their families for input and affirmation about who they are and their value as people. If the early mirrors are healthy and accurate, the likelihood of internalizing/believing reality-based and affirming input about oneself is higher. If the early mirrors are shaming or distorted—akin to a circus mirror—the likelihood of incorporating inaccurate inputs into the self-concept rises proportionally. Of course, we know from psychological research that some people are prone to hear the most negative messages about themselves and to screen out the positive. Nevertheless, the nature of the mirroring we receive—the quality and tone of the messages about ourselves that others communicate to us—has a definitive impact on the development of our identity.

Once negative or shaming messages have been internalized as core to someone's identity—a condition sometimes called "the shame base"—intimacy becomes frightening. The person's inner dialogue will resemble this: "I know how bad and unacceptable I am; therefore, I cannot risk letting someone truly know me. If I do, they will find me out, reject me, and I will not be able to bear it." Herein lies the linkage between shame-based identity and fear of rejection. This fear can become virtually paralyzing for young women with significant internalized shame about who they are and their lack of value as people.

From a Christian perspective, even the healthiest mirroring by other people cannot provide us with a complete and accurate identity. For Christians, God and the Bible are the ultimate, accurate, and most penetrating mirrors. It has been said that we will never truly know who we are until we know who God is. "Anyone who listens to the word but does not do what it says is like a man who looks at his face in a mirror and, after looking at himself, goes away and immediately forgets what he looks like. But the man who looks intently into the perfect law that gives freedom, and continues to do this, not forgetting what he has heard, but doing it—he will be blessed in what he does" (James 1:23-25). In short, true identity is lost when we are provided only man-made mirrors—when we "go away" from the ultimate mirror, God.

Sociologists inform us that culture is also a powerful mirror. The mirrors in US culture are heavily shaped by materialism and economic concerns. Alexis De Tocqueville (2000), who intensely studied emerging American culture in the 1800s, concluded that "materialism breeds violence." Consider, for example, the mirrors our culture holds up for young women to look into during the vulnerable time of adolescence. On any night, American television offers messages, images, and mirrors about what women are, should and need to be, look like, and weigh in our culture in order to fit in. Often absent are spiritual virtues such as faith, hope, love, grace, mercy, justice, truth, wisdom, self-restraint, character, and integrity (Kilbourne, 1999; Knapp, 2003). Materialism cheapens humanity and personhood by lowering people to objects of utility—to be assessed as useful or not, visually pleasing or not, acceptable or not.

Such messages militate against the intrinsic worth given us by God himself, since we are created in his image. Such messages ignore that we are the intended recipients of Christ's redemptive suffering and resurrection: "For God so loved the world..." (John 3:16; emphasis added). If a young woman's identity and worth are built upon visual, material foundations, her true femininity and personhood will be lost because, at their core, true femininity and personhood are immaterial, spiritual, and unseen.

> Your beauty should not come from outward adornment, such as braided hair and the wearing of gold jewelry and fine clothes. Instead, it should be that of your inner self, the unfading beauty of a gentle and quiet spirit, which is of great worth in God's sight. For this is the way the holy women of the past who put their hope in God used to make themselves beautiful. (1 Peter 3:3-5)

The unseen virtues (above) are the very things which keep the seen (material aspects) in their proper place—safe and adequately anchored. Moreover, young women who are starving for self-respect and seeking this through visual acceptability wind up doing violence to themselves and their relationships through diets, extreme measures to change the body and looks, and even eating disorders. These efforts are perceived by the women so affected as more proof that they really are flawed and not worth knowing. The internal dialogue runs thus: "I must try harder and be perfect, or just give up and isolate to stay safe from being known."

In Alcoholics Anonymous (AA) there is an interesting play on words regarding intimacy; AA calls it "in-to-me-I-see." This expresses the notion that before we can be intimate, we must first understand and accept ourselves. How can a young woman share with another what she is unclear about herself? The barrier here is that a young woman, affected as described above, is petrified to look inside of herself for fear of what she will find: shame and unacceptability. In our materialistic culture, it may seem easier to focus on changing something she knows how to change—such as her body—than on something she does not know how to change—i.e., the intangible aspects of her soul, character, identity, and virtues. Eating disorders readily arise from such desperate efforts to change the outer appearance, or to become symbolically invisible, as in anorexia, so that the fear of intimacy can be avoided.

Sexual and Marital Intimacy

The capacity for sexual and marital intimacy arises similarly to intimacy in general, but with additional features. For sexual and marital intimacy, critical foundations are established especially in the father-daughter relationship. This is commonly the first and most formative experience a girl has with the opposite sex. In essence, the father or father figure is the girl's prototype for the entire male gender. He is the girl's first exposure to, and model of, committed love from the opposite sex, and forms the template of her future interactions with men.

In this father-daughter relationship develop the girl's identity and sense of personal value in opposite-sex relationships. This can occur through the interface and contrast of the father's masculine characteristics with the girl's feminine characteristics, as well as the extent to which the girl is affirmed as cherished and worthy of protection, provision, and sacrificial love by her father. Because the deepest levels of intimacy are spiritual—soul to soul and heart to heart—it is the father's responsibility to not only teach the girl in words, but also to provide her with actual experiences of what such connection and tenderness look like in the absence of romantic contact. When this is handled well, the girl has a clear, healthy reference against which to measure future interactions with the opposite sex.

From a Christian perspective, relationships that are solely physically/sexually-based inevitably cheapen and devalue people. We are told that "the Spirit gives life; the flesh counts for nothing" (John 6:63). And we are exhorted to "love one another deeply, from the heart" (1 Peter 1:22; emphasis added). Sexually-based relationships eventually destroy true intimacy because they derive from and focus on the material and sensual aspects of humanity only, and exclude the emotional and spiritual aspects of who we are. There is no wholeness in such relationships, and thus the whole person cannot be affirmed by such forms of intimacy. In fact, the excluded dimensions of the human person may be indirectly or even directly dismissed, devalued, and damaged by relationships that focus solely on sex. In addition, sexually-based relationships may neglect the interpersonal respect and trust which are critical for true intimacy and its soul-nurturing benefits. A father or father-figure can give a girl a priceless gift by showing her such respect and trust in his relationship with her throughout her developmental years, and by valuing her far beyond her body or appearance, so that she will seek and expect these essential components in her future relationships with men.

Yet the physical aspects of the human person do matter as well. They are not separate from the person, but integral to the whole bio-psycho-social-spiritual person. Author John Eldredge (2001) writes that a question which women carry within themselves is: "Am I lovely?" Although this question may sound a bit stilted to modern ears, it captures something important about body image—a woman's need to feel accepted and comfortable with her physical presence in the world. God has answered this question with a resounding "yes!" "How beautiful you are, my darling! Oh, how beautiful!" (Song of Solomon 1:15).

If a father has faithfully modeled Christ's love to his daughter, the question about body image will have been largely settled for her, leaving her far less vulnerable to seeking the answer from potentially inadequate or disruptive sources, such as other males or cultural influences. However, if this question has not been settled by puberty, a young woman may be dangerously vulnerable regarding her body image and who, or what, she will look to for affirmation of her identity. A woman may look solely to her partner/husband to answer this question, but this will place excessive pressure on him, even though his acceptance may partially heal such a void. Her search will conclude successfully only when the answer resides within her and derives from her Creator, who made her beautiful in his all-meaningful eyes.

For some women, eating disorders are clearly an effort to answer Eldredge's question, "Am I lovely?", in the absence of a healthy, self-validating answer from within. But an emaciated body, or one contorted into artificial thinness by purging and compulsive exercise, can never satisfy a question so deep and intrinsic to the human soul. Such women may also evidence relational instability and promiscuity—companion efforts to answer this fundamental question about their sexual identity.

Restoring Intimacy in the Recovery Process

To begin, trust must be firmly established between the patient and therapist in order for the patient to feel safe enough to examine the pain, shame, and fear inside without feeling judged. Then, the specific relationship between the patient's core underlying issues—e.g., identity, shame, fear of rejection—and eating disorder behaviors must be clearly identified and understood by both patient and clinician. You cannot address what you do not understand. Patients are typically relieved to discover that their behaviors are actually methods/attempts to meet legitimate underlying needs, such as the desire to be intimately accepted by self and others and the need to know truly who they are.

Shame causes people to hide in darkness—to not be known, to be rejected. Therefore, once a strong therapeutic alliance/bond has been established, the patient must take a risk to bring the hidden into the light. Healing occurs when shame-laden content is disclosed by the patient and accepted (though not necessarily endorsed) by the therapist. Most importantly, regardless of the content disclosed, the patient herself must experience that she is fully accepted verbally and relationally by the therapist. In this moment the patient actually experiences the opposite of the rejection/abandonment that the shame convinced her she would receive if she ever opened up. This experience reinforces her initial risk/impetus toward intimacy and also provides the mechanism for restoring intimacy to her relationships: trust–disclosure–acceptance–to know and be known.

Many of us have responses and reactions to intimate encounters, some of which we are unaware of, that block intimacy or repel others from pursuing further intimacy with us. The patient may therefore need the therapist's assistance in how to receive acceptance and experience emotional intimacy. Maintaining and cultivating intimacy will also inevitably entail points of conflict. The ability to tell another the truth in love is often difficult and requires training and practice, involving such skills as conflict resolution/management, forgiveness, reconciliation, and the distinctions between the latter two. Joint sessions with those closest to patients may be helpful in assisting patients further to develop their newfound relationship skills and generalize them from the therapy context to real life situations. But patients' trust–disclosure–acceptance experiences occurring in therapy serve as a starting point from which patients can build intimacy with others and the skills needed to invite and maintain intimacy in their everyday lives.

References

De Tocqueville, A. (2000). *Democracy in America.* Chicago: University of Chicago Press.

Eldredge, J. (2001). *Wild at heart: Discovering the secret of a man's soul.* Nashville: Thomas Nelson.

Erikson, E. (1980). *Identity and the life cycle.* New York: W. W. Norton & Company, Inc.

Kilbourne, J. (1999). *Deadly persuasion: Why women and girls must fight the addictive power of advertising.* New York: The Free Press.

Knapp, C. (2003). *Appetites: Why women want.* New York: Counterpoint.

Merriam-Webster, et al. (2003). *Merriam-Webster's collegiate dictionary* (11th ed.). Springfield, MA: Merriam-Webster, Inc.

Chapter 14

American Culture and the Production of Eating Disorders

Edward J. Cumella, PhD, CEDS

> *Entrepreneurs made millions exploiting her...the merchants of the earth grew rich from...articles of every kind...and bodies and souls of men.* (Revelation 18:3, 12-13 MSG; NIV)

Because of their biblical commitment, Christians have historically supported freedoms for individuals and groups, including groups formed for economic pursuits. Simultaneously, Christians promulgate the biblical values of truth, justice, morality, resource and planetary stewardship, and Christ's perfect, all-encompassing commandment to "love your neighbor as yourself" (Matthew 22:39). Economic interests that fail to incorporate these essential biblical values depart from the will of God and have the capacity to distort cultures and do violence to people and God's earth. Well-respected Christian and secular leaders have lamented the immoral and destructive influences that certain untempered economic interests are having on American culture (e.g., Burkett, 1996; Kilbourne, 1999; Lucado, 2001; Pipher, 1994; Swenson, 1992). In this chapter, we will briefly explore these problematic influences on American culture and the manner in which they may promote the debilitating symptoms of eating disorders.

Culture and Advertising

When patients in Remuda's body image groups watch the film, "The Ad and the Ego," they often walk out angry—angry that they have apparently been deceived by subtle messages in advertising. As one teenager wrote of this situation:

> Messages about our bodies not being good enough...[are] heard and seen on radios, TVs, billboards, news, articles, movies, fashion

> runways, and magazines everywhere. The result so far of the bombardment of "If you don't look like this you don't belong" is nothing but low self-confidence and self-worth...and in some death. (Fuller, 1999)

Jean Kilbourne has devoted her life to studying the insidious effects of advertising on people's identities and emotions. Her critique of American culture resounds when she calls our nation "the United States of Advertising" (Kilbourne, 1999). What she captures so succinctly in this phrase is the following sequence of events, chronicled by multiple scholars (e.g., Ewen, 1988; Jacobson & Mazur, 1995; Jhally, 1991).

- By the 1950s, more than enough products were being inexpensively mass produced in the US to meet most essential human material needs
- Therefore, producers could no longer assume that there would be markets for new products
- To address this economic shift, advertising began to focus on creating consumers for new, less essential products and services
- The creation of markets for less essential products has typically involved three factors:
    1) Making people feel discontent, doubt, and anxiety about everyday human experiences, bodily needs, and their appearance
    2) Encouraging people to compare themselves to other people, to feel as though they are in competition with others for acceptance and self-esteem
    3) Suggesting that particular products can offer deliverance from this discontent and anxiety, bringing acceptance and self-esteem

A women's advertisement that perfectly exemplifies this phenomenon runs as follows: "Your breasts may be too big, too saggy, too pert, too flat, too full, too far apart, but at least you can have your hair the way you want it." This ad clearly suggests to women that they can never be comfortable with their bodies; it creates discontent and anxiety where none should be present. The ad further suggests that if women buy a particular product to groom their hair, their physical deficiencies will be less noticeable and they will fare well in comparison to other women. The product in question offers deliverance from artificially fomented discontent and anxiety about one's body. There is no native, necessary market for this product; the market has been fabricated by assaulting women's self-esteem regarding something as intimate and personal as their breasts. Messages of this kind are a far cry from the biblical exhortation: "Do not let any unwholesome talk come out of your mouths, but only what is helpful for building others up according to their needs, that it may benefit those who listen" (Ephesians 4:29). Rather, messages of this kind suggest that, at least for some, "their hearts are greedy for unjust gain" (Ezekiel 33:31).

Additional developments occurring in the past 20 years have intensified Americans' experience of discontent in their own skin. First and foremost, advertising has become so ubiquitous that it occupies almost every space in which Americans commonly find themselves. Advertisers have aggressively pursued the idea that saturation and repetition lead to product recognition and sales. Advertisements are appearing in more and more places that were long considered out of reach for marketing—including public schools and children's textbooks. Advertising has so invaded the crevices of everyday life that it has become our primary environment—something, like air, that we often do not even see or experience consciously, but which nevertheless dominates our senses.

Kilbourne and others suggest that the pervasive, repeated messages of advertising have become a system of public education. The average American comes in contact with more than 3000 advertisements per day and spends two years of their life watching television ads. The average American child spends more time watching television than in school. One can argue that advertising has therefore become the dominant channel through which messages about normal life are offered and digested.

Evidently, advertising is effective in creating markets and consumers for a multiplicity of products. The fact that corporations spend $250 billion a year on advertising suggests its efficacy. America's economic success also testifies to this. But what does this have to do with eating disorders? According to Ewen (1988), the human images seen in advertisements have become increasingly extreme. Images of an idealized, supertall, superthin female body with elegant hair, large eyes, high cheekbones, large mouth, white straight teeth, plump lips, and perfectly proportioned arms, legs, and abs are constantly paired with images of wealth, pleasure, friendship, flourishing sexuality, self-confidence, and success. The message communicated through this constant association is that, to fulfill these intrinsic human desires, one must have an absolutely flawless body. Increasingly in recent years, images of idealized male bodies are being presented and associated with the same expressions of human fulfillment. Not surprisingly, some experts believe that there is a concomitant increase in eating disorders among men in the US (Cumella, 2003).

It is worth noting that the kind of supertall, superthin idealized female body consistently portrayed in advertising exists in less than 2% of the US population (Smolak, 1996). The remaining 98% of women, because of their genetics, cannot obtain this unusual look. Hence, the female models portrayed in advertising are very poor role models indeed. They may even be considered "anti-models," since they represent an image that is virtually impossible for most women to achieve. Furthermore, most of the images are pure fiction. They are computer-enhanced composites of multiple women's body parts. The beautiful woman on the magazine cover does not even exist. Celebrity role models routinely have multiple body doubles, whose inclusion in film and print media reinforces the illusion that the super-thin, super-tall body is not only attainable but an ordinary ingredient of success—a patent falsehood.

When girls and women are repeatedly exposed to these unattainable and frankly alien images of female beauty, the result is a powerful experience of self-criticism and discontent for the 98% who cannot achieve the vaunted look. Producing discontent in 98% of the population may create huge markets for products purporting deliverance from this discontent. But it also leads to wide scale body-hatred. America is sadly a nation in which the large majority of women suffer body image dissatisfaction. Some pursue extreme measures, such as eating disorders, to contort their bodies into an unnatural, idealized shape, in the desperate quest for self-esteem and acceptance. The body hatred starts early, with advertising targeting ever younger audiences. To wit: 80% of fourth grade girls and 91% of college women in the US are dieting (Kurth et al., 1995).

Although reliable data are difficult to obtain, eating disorders appear to have risen steadily in the US during the past 40 years. This increase coincides with the changes in advertising detailed above. The etiology of eating disorders is obviously a complex bio-psycho-social-spiritual phenomenon (Cumella, 2002). But since the human genome has scarcely changed in the past 40 years, cultural changes are likely to be a driving force behind this increase in eating disorders. The sophisticated critiques of advertising's omnipresent impact on American's identities may indeed be correct. Recent controlled experimental studies support this conclusion. In one study (Hawkins et al., 2004), women exposed to magazine images of thin models evidenced increased body dissatisfaction, negative moods, and eating disorder symptoms, and decreased self-esteem, when compared with women exposed to neutral images. In another study (Tiggemann & Slater, 2003), women who viewed music videos featuring thin female bodies experienced increased body dissatisfaction and compared themselves more to others than those exposed to neutral music videos. Research is moving beyond qualitative anthropological surveys to quantitative experimental science and finding confirmatory results regarding the impact of culture on eating disorder symptoms.

The body hatred cultivated by advertising may also be intensified by other trends in our culture. Modern America appears to be obsessed with youth and thinness (Maine, 2000). Because maturing bodies naturally widen, Americans may feel compelled by our culture to fight the inevitabilities of biology—a fight that cannot be won. American culture also exhibits obvious weightism—a prejudice against those who are overweight. Large people are routinely subjected to ridicule, derision, and even violence (Koppleman, 2003). America's youth and weight obsessions coexist with supersized eating options—an abundance of rich desserts, large restaurant portions, and fast foods with enormous numbers of calories. Barraged by quantities of high calorie foods, yet obsessed with a youthfully thin body, Americans find themselves in an irresolvable contradiction. This contradiction can be circumvented primarily through disordered eating behaviors such as serial dieting, compulsive exercise, self-starvation, bingeing, purging, cosmetic surgery, and so on. Some analyses (Jhally, 2000) even suggest that advertising deliberately promulgates these eating disorder behaviors as a normal and desirable resolution to this contradiction.

Finally, it is important to recognize the role of sexism in advertising, and hence in our cultural milieu. Because these issues are explored elsewhere in depth (e.g., Buchwald, Fletcher, & Roth, 1993; Jhally, 2000; Maine, 2000), we will describe them only briefly here. Again and again, women are offered extreme thinness as the ideal of feminine beauty. Some authorities have suggested that by offering an impossibly thin ideal of feminine beauty, women are literally being cut down to size—made to believe that their mature bodies are unacceptable and relegated to a diminished, waif-like presence in the world. In addition, women's body parts—rather than images of complete female bodies—are routinely displayed in advertisements, promoting an objectification of the female body and, perhaps unconsciously, a disrespect for and normalization of violence toward women's bodies. Images of women in advertising are often nearly naked, essentially pornographic. Exposure to such images would appear to promote continued dehumanization and objectification of the female body. Collectively, these trends may intensify women's disconnection from their own bodies and experiences of body loathing. It is self-evident that sexism, violence, and dehumanization of women depart from the fundamental biblical imperative: "Show respect for everyone" (1 Peter 2:17 TLB).

Ethnicity, Subculture, and Assimilation

Inconsistent research results regarding the relationship between ethnicity and eating disorders have led most researchers to posit that there is no clear relationship between the two. One conclusion often repeated is that the more ethnic minorities assimilate into mainstream American culture, the more similar their risk of eating disorders to White Americans. This supports the notion that cultural influences indeed have a significant impact on eating disorder development.

Inconsistent research results have also occurred when examining eating disorders in relation to socioeconomic status and sexual orientation. Once again, the influences of the predominant US culture on eating disorder development may be stronger than many subcultural factors.

International studies also suggest that the more American culture influences a foreign culture, the greater the risk of eating disorders in the foreign population. Ann Becker's well-known Fiji studies are telling in this regard (Becker, et al., 2002). During the 1990s, American television was widely introduced into Fiji. Within a few short years, a 500% increase was observed in girls' vomiting to control weight, along with enormous increases in girls' dieting and feeling fat. Ancient Fijian culture, which had long valued robust women's body types, appears to have been overwhelmed by images portrayed in American television shows and advertising.

Forces for Cultural Change

Many organizations and individuals are working to offer Americans healthier and more realistic messages about body image. They include organizations that promote public awareness of eating disorders, offering such services as school-based prevention curricula and congressional lobbying. Organizations of this kind include the National Eating Disorders Association (NEDA) and the National Women's Health Information Center. Many organizations are devoted to media literacy education, such as the Center for Media Literacy, About-Face, Media Watch, and The Media Foundation. Some media have also accepted that the human images they display affect women's and girls' self-concepts, and now endeavor to portray "plus-sized" models. The popular magazine for teenage girls, YM, is an example of this phenomenon. New Moon is an advertising-free magazine edited by and for girls ages 8 to 14. Teen Voices is similar, but targets 13 to 20 year olds. YSB addresses African-American youth. Brio is a Christian magazine for teenage girls that encourages a healthy, biblically-based self-concept.

MODE is a magazine for adult women, emphasizing body esteem regardless of weight.

Some organizations are taking a more combative rather than purely educational approach, countering weightism directly with messages and social action intended to bring about greater weight acceptance. The Healthy at any Weight journal, the International Size Acceptance Association, the National Association to Advance Fat Acceptance, The Council on Size & Weight Discrimination, Body Peace, and Body Positive are examples of this latter trend.

Organizations listed here are by no means alone in their efforts to reshape US culture. Many others exist. As yet the impact of such organizations on American culture and advertising may be small because the rates of eating disorders are continuing to rise. Many experts believe that eating disorders are also becoming more common among preteen girls, middle-age women, elderly women and men, and young men. This increase in eating disorders throughout our society would suggest that greater and more visible efforts are needed to wrest our culture away from its obsession with thinness and to transform America into a society that promotes health, self-respect, and acceptance for all its citizens. As the Bible commands: "You shall love your neighbor as yourself. Love does no wrong to a neighbor; therefore love is the fulfillment of the law" (Romans 13:9-10 NASB). Or even more succinctly, "encourage one another and build each other up…" (1 Thessalonians 5:11).

References

Becker, A.E., Burwell, R.A., Gilman, S.E., Herzog, D.B., & Hamburg, P. (2002). Eating behaviors and attitudes following prolonged exposure to television among ethnic Fijian adolescent girls. *British Journal of Psychiatry, 180,* 509-14.

Buchwald, E., Fletcher, P., & Roth, M. (1993). *Transforming a rape culture.* Minneapolis: Milkwood Editions.

Burkett, L. (1996). *The complete guide to managing your money.* New York: Inspirational Press.

Cumella, E. (2002). Bio-psycho-social-spiritual: Completing the model. *The Remuda Review: The Christian Journal of Eating Disorders, 1,* 1-5.

Cumella, E. (2003). Examining eating disorders in males. *Behavioral Health Management, 23,* 38-41.

Ewen, S. (1988). *All consuming images.* New York: Basic Books.

Fuller, D. (1999). Figuratively speaking. In S. Torres (Ed.), *That body image thing: Young women speak out* (pp. 31-33). Ottawa, ON: Canadian Research Institute for the Advancement of Women.

Hawkins, N., Richards, P.S., Granley, H.M., & Stein, D.M. (2004). The impact of exposure to the thin-ideal media image on women. *Eating Disorders: The Journal of Treatment and Prevention, 12,* 35-50.

Jacobson, M.F. & Mazur, L.A. (1995). *Marketing madness: A survival guide for a consumer society.* Boulder, CO: Westview Press.

Jhally, S. (1991). *The codes of advertising: Fetishism and the political economy of meaning in the consumer society.* New York: Routledge.

Jhally, S. (Director/Producer). (2000). *Killing us softly 3: Advertising's image of women* [Motion picture]. United States: Media Education Foundation.

Kilbourne, J. (1999). *Can't buy my love.* New York: Touchstone.

Koppleman, S. (2003). *The strange history of Suzanne LaFleshe and other stories of women and fatness.* New York: Feminist Press.

Kurth, C.L., Krahn, D.D., Nairn, K., & Drewnowski, A. (1995). The severity of dieting and bingeing behaviors in college women: Interview validation of survey data. *Journal of Psychiatric Research, 29,* 211-25.

Lucado, M. (2001). *Traveling light.* Nashville: Thomas Nelson.

Maine, M. (2000). *Body wars: Making peace with women's bodies.* Carlsbad, CA: Gurze Books.

Pipher, M. (1994). *Reviving Ophelia: Saving the selves of adolescent girls.* New York: Ballantine Books.

Smolak L. (1996). *Next door neighbors: Eating disorders awareness and prevention puppet guide book.* Seattle: National Eating Disorders Association.

Swenson, R.A. (1992). *Margin: Restoring emotional, physical, financial, and time reserves to overloaded lives.* Colorado Springs: NavPress.

Tiggemann, M. & Slater, A. (2003). Thin ideals in music television: A source of social comparison and body dissatisfaction. *International Journal of Eating Disorders, 35,* 48-58.

Chapter 15

Body Image: Concepts and Treatment

Marian C. Eberly, RN, MSW, LCSW, DAPA and Eileen Adams, MS, LMSW

Don't be concerned about the outward beauty...Be beautiful inside, in your hearts... (1 Peter 3:3-4 TLB)

Body image is sometimes defined as "an inner view of one's outer self" (Freedman, 1989; Thompson, 1996). This definition indicates that body dissatisfaction lies primarily in how we think about ourselves. Some might say that the problem is "from the neck up."

Many researchers recognize three primary influences on body image disturbance:

- Developmental—effects of maturation and peer/family experiences
- Sociocultural—influence of Western cultural ideals, gender roles, and mass media
- Perceptual—cortical deficits, adaptive failure, and perceptual artifact theories

The last is typically an issue for chronically ill patients with anorexia. The first two—developmental and sociocultural factors—affect the entire population. Developmentally, puberty is a critical milestone in the shaping of body image. It is marked by numerous physical and psychological changes for both genders. Nevertheless, sociocultural factors account for the majority of body image disturbance in Western societies. In an important research investigation, Stormer and Thompson (1996) found that the majority of variance in body image is accounted for by the tendency to make social comparisons and to be aware of and internalize sociocultural norms regarding thinness and attractiveness.

Of course, there is not a one-to-one relationship between sociocultural influences and body image disturbance. Research has concluded that individuals exposed to the same ideals of thinness fall on a continuum of dissatisfaction, with some reporting very little disturbance and others developing eating disorder behavior (Waller, Hamilton, & Shaw, 1992). More study is needed to explore how some individuals manage to refute societal messages of thinness and escape body image disturbance (Heinburg, 1996). Perhaps some individuals challenge societal messages because their self-understanding is faith-based. Indeed, acquiring a biblically-based awareness of one's identity may enhance resilience against powerful societal messages (Newman, 2002).

Children have a great capacity to love, accept, socialize, and play well together. However, from early adolescence onward, they generally do not have a high tolerance for difference. Fear of rejection begins to dominate the psyche in a powerful way; the worst fear is being unacceptable to peers. Beginning in early adolescence, teens learn to conform to the socially approved images they see and to believe the messages they hear about what kind of appearance is valued and expected of them. Certain interests spend a great deal of money offering these "approved" images. For example, the 50 billion dollar a year diet industry profits from those who are afraid of being rejected because they appear different from the approved images. (For more details on economic interests and body image, see the chapter in this book, American Culture and the Production of Eating Disorders.)

A central message, continually reinforced in the media, is the need to obtain a beautiful outward appearance at any cost, with "beautiful" defined narrowly by a repetition of similar images. One of the symptoms of narcissistic personality disorder is "...being preoccupied with fantasies of unlimited success, power, brilliance, beauty, or ideal love" (American Psychiatric Association, 2000). Our culture appears to be suffering from narcissism, because we are preoccupied with these issues, perhaps beauty or physical attractiveness above all others.

The sociocultural standard of beauty, as we know it today, is confusing at best. Being beautiful is touted as the road to happiness. This is a lie we are encouraged to believe as propagated by all forms of media and crafty marketing (e.g., Kilbourne, 1999). If beauty equates to happiness, contentment, peace, and joy, then why are so many of the physically beautiful people we see on magazine covers suffering so much? We need only open the magazines to read that many are beset with the heartaches of broken relationships, addiction, spiraling depression, and thoughts of suicide. Lives are falling apart, and the beautiful outward appearances stand impotent to prevent the tragedy.

We have long known that humans have an innate tendency to derive information about themselves through social comparison (Festinger, 1954).

More recent research indicates that a tendency to compare one's physical appearance to others is strongly related to body dissatisfaction (Heinburg & Thompson, 1992; Striegel-Moore, McAvay, & Rodin, 1986; Thompson, Coovert, & Stormer, 1999). The media and culture as a whole foster this often envious and shame-producing social comparison. Computer enhanced supermodels are held up as the standard of comparison for women. This can create a profound narcissistic wound, i.e., a wound to the sense of self.

Self-demeaning social comparison has been an age-old problem. It was Gideon's problem thousands of years ago (Judges 6). His inferiority complex left him hiding in the bottom of a winepress, fearful and afraid. Gideon had to be small in stature to fit into the bottom of a winepress. His physical appearance evidently had a great influence on how he viewed himself. But the Bible tells us that God spoke to Gideon about God's plans for him, addressing him as a "mighty warrior." Gideon basically responded by saying, "You must be kidding! Don't you know that I'm the least of my clan?" Gideon had beliefs about himself that he had to overcome to accomplish God's plans for him. He began this process by placing his trust in God at a time when everything else seemed hopeless.

Discerning the truth about one's identity is a central theme in preventing and recovering from negative body image. Although the world's values include such characteristics as beauty and wealth, the Bible tells us that "what is highly valued among men is detestable in God's sight" (Luke 16:15). The things we treasure can block what God wants to accomplish in our lives. "...no longer tossed here and there by waves...by the trickery of men, by craftiness in deceitful scheming" (Ephesians 4:14 NASB). The bait of comparison to others is an enticing one; for those with a negative body image, this measuring rod continually leaves the person feeling exposed and inferior.

Seeing ourselves as God does is key in overcoming insecurities. The biblical standard of beauty does not generally focus on outward appearance (Elwell & Comfort, 2001). The Hebrew Scriptures speak of God's creation and nature as beautiful (Genesis 2:9; Job 26:13; Psalm 19:1-6; Jeremiah 3:19). But physical beauty was considered secondary to resourcefulness and traditional piety in women (Proverbs 31:30). The Hebrew concept of beauty had deeper meaning than simply physical attractiveness. It affirmed God's essential glory: the Lord's favor is called his "beauty" (Psalm 90:17). The Greek term for beauty, used in the New Testament, refers more to virtue and character—goodness, fairness, gladness, graciousness, and love—than to physical manifestations of beauty. There are many instances of this usage in the New Testament. Christ's followers are encouraged to "adorn" the teaching of the Savior, making it attractive to nonbelievers by their integrity and honest actions (Titus 2:10). Those who preach the gospel are referred to as "beautiful" (Romans 10:15). The apostles Peter and Paul warn women against being satisfied with outward beauty (1 Timothy 2:9-10). It is apparent then that the majority of women in the Bible are not specifically noted for physical beauty. The New Testament underscores this powerfully because it does not support physical beauty as the measure of a woman's worth. Scripture encourages us to focus instead on inner qualities, relationships, attitudes, and love for God. This provides a model and perspective from which a woman can build a healthy identity: refusing to measure her worth by the shape of her body.

God does not view us as we view ourselves and others: "God sees not as man sees, for man looks at the outward appearance, but the LORD looks at the heart" (1 Samuel 16:7 NASB). In contrast to the world, then, Christians must also view beauty from the inside out: a teachable spirit, open to constructive criticism, and capable of learning from mistakes; self-control; consideration and wisdom in the timing of speech; not insisting on "my way"; selflessness; willingness to listen to others' needs/perceptions; not insisting on putting one's needs first. These qualities are exemplified by at least two women of the Bible: Esther and Ruth. These qualities are necessary components of the portrait of a truly beautiful woman (Kole, 2001).

According to the Bible, our worth and value have nothing to do with being physically beautiful or fit. As Psalm 139:14 says: "I praise you because I am fearfully and wonderfully made: your works are wonderful..." God made us. We are of great value and worth to him. When we begin to realize that we are valued, cherished, and loved deeply by the Maker of the universe—that he created each person to be unique and different from every other living being on the planet—we may be moved to step back in awe, knowing that we are worthy even to be called his children.

To further drive the point, the Bible reveals that God has chosen to house his Holy Spirit in a place of great worth: within the believing Christian. "For we are the temple of the living God, just as God said: 'I will dwell in them and walk among them; I will be their God and they will be My people'" (2 Corinthians 6:16 NASB).

God has chosen to inhabit our hearts, to dwell among us and in us. It is an awesome and holy thing to consider this truth. And once we grasp it, we begin to realize that this life is not about the appearance of the temple called the body, but about the relationship we have to God and he to us. That he would find each of us of such great value and worth to him to cause his Holy Spirit to dwell in us puts many concerns into perspective. The God of the universe has chosen to live in us with all our issues, flaws, and shortcomings. There is no need for the temple to meet some idealized worldly notion of perfection before he will abide within it. He loves and values us as we are. For those who consider themselves to be "damaged goods," this truth can bring necessary perspective and healing. God considers us worthy—worthy to pour his life into. As this mystery unfolds in our lives, it brings deepening self-acceptance: "May the Lord bring you into an ever deeper understanding of the love of God…" (2 Thessalonians 3:5 TLB).

Treatment

Body image can be understood simply as one's relationship with one's body. In eating disorders, this relationship focuses primarily on appearance. As with any relationship, if one area is emphasized and others ignored, the relationship becomes unhealthy and unbalanced. When conceptualizing a patient's body image issues, it is helpful to think in terms of relationship. How does the patient need to improve her:

- physical relationship with her body—e.g., self care, clothes, distorted perceptions
- emotional relationship—e.g., alexithymia, feelings skills, self-talk
- cognitive relationship—e.g., ineffective beliefs, identity, comparisons with others
- spiritual relationship—e.g., gratitude, competition with others, priorities

The essence of body image treatment across these four domains is encapsulated in Psalm 139:14: "I will give thanks to You, for I am fearfully and wonderfully made; wonderful are Your works…" (Psalm 139:14 NASB). Does the patient:

- see her body as a good work? → physical relationship
- feel awe about the way God made her? → emotional relationship
- know about the beauty and love with which and for which she was made? → cognitive relationship
- experience gratitude that she was born and made as she is? → spiritual relationship

Answers to these questions give direction for continued body image work, helping the patient to build a biblical foundation for a healthy, right relationship with her body. For many with eating disorders, distorted body perception is the symbolic core of the eating disorder. It often manifests as follows:

- The patient literally sees herself as fat, even if her weight is within normal parameters. Because she hates fat, she hates her body and mistreats it. Her physical relationship with her body is damaged.
- The patient feels fat—a shorthand way of expressing a variety of complex and difficult emotions, including shame, depression, anxiety, and fear. Her emotional relationship with her body is confusing and troubling.
- The patient believes she is fat and that she is therefore unworthy, unlovable, and inferior to others. Her cognitive relationship with her body demeans her.
- The patient alienates herself from God and others, competing with others who appear thinner, longing to be someone else. Her spiritual relationship with her body has been pinched off and depleted of joy.

The books below describe specific step-by-step techniques that can be used to assist patients in body image recovery within this biblical framework.

Cash, T. (1997). *The Body Image Workbook.* Oakland, CA: New Harbinger.

Hornyak, L.M. & Baker, E.K. (Eds.). (1989). *Experiential therapies for eating disorders.* New York: Guilford Press.

Newman, D. (2002). *Loving your body: Embracing our true beauty in Christ.* Wheaton, IL: Tyndale.

References

American Psychiatric Association. (2000). *Diagnostic and Statistical Manual of Mental Disorders, Text Revision* (4th ed.) *(DSM-IV-TR).* Washington, DC: Author.

Elwell, W.A. & Comfort, P.W. (2001). *Tyndale Bible dictionary.* Carol Stream, IL: Tyndale House Publishers.

Festinger, L. (1954). A theory of social comparison processes. *Human Relations, 7,* 117-40.

Freedman, R. (1989). *Bodylove: Learning to like our looks and ourselves, a practical guide for women.* New York: Harper and Row Publishers.

Heinburg, L.J. (1996). Theories of body image: Perceptual, developmental and socio-cultural factors. In J.K. Thompson (Ed.), *Body image, eating disorders and obesity: An integrative guide to assessment and treatment* (pp. 27-48). Washington, DC: American Psychological Association.

Heinburg, L.J. & Thompson, J.K. (1992). Social comparison: Gender, target importance ratings, and relation to body image disturbance. *Journal of Social Behavior and Personality, 7*, 335-44.

Kilbourne, J. (1999). *Can't buy my love.* New York: Touchstone.

Kole, S. (2001). *Seeing yourself through God's eyes.* Artesia, CA: Shannon Publishers.

Newman, D. (2002). *Loving your body: Embracing our true beauty in Christ.* Wheaton, IL: Tyndale House Publishers.

Stormer, S. & Thompson, J.K. (1996). Explanations of body image disturbance: A test of maturational status, negative verbal commentary, social comparison, and sociocultural hypotheses. *International Journal of Eating Disorders, 26*, 43-51.

Streigel-Moore, R., McAvay, G., & Rodin, J. (1986). Psychological and behavioral correlates of feeling fat in women. *International Journal of Eating Disorders, 5*, 935-47.

Thompson, J.K. (1996). *Body image, eating disorders and obesity: An integrative guide to assessment and treatment.* Washington, DC: American Psychological Association.

Thompson, J.K., Coovert, M.D., & Stormer, S.M. (1999). Body image, social comparison, and eating disturbance: A covariance structure modeling investigation. *International Journal of Eating Disorders, 26*, 43-51.

Waller, G., Hamilton, K., & Shaw, J. (1992). Media influences on body size estimation in eating disordered and comparison subjects. *British Review of Bulimia and Anorexia Nervosa, 6*, 81-87.

Part V

Spiritual Dimensions of Eating Disorders

Chapter 16

Bringing the Spiritual into Treatment

Marian C. Eberly, RN, MSW, LCSW, DAPA

I am sometimes asked: "Why do you have to bring God in to everything? Can't you just counsel your patients without all that God stuff?" The answer at Remuda is simple: "No." Because some have difficulty accepting this answer, let me explain our understanding of why spirituality is indispensable in treatment.

Why Spirituality?

We practitioners want the same things for those entrusted to our care: to see our clients get well, to heal where they are broken, to learn to do things differently, to make better choices, for their suffering to be soothed, for wholeness mysteriously to happen.

In the Christian worldview, God permeates everything. "[I]n him all things hold together" (Colossians 1:17). He created the world, and its people were made in his image (Genesis 1:26) to fellowship with him (1 John 1:3). From this perspective, treatment without God would inevitably be incomplete, bordering on a crisis of meaning, with difficulty pointing clients toward wholeness.

The Bible is the Christian's handbook for living (2 Timothy 3:16). It tells us that we are spiritual beings—in other words, that we have a spirit, and that our spiritual nature needs to be cared for in specific ways (Wall & Eberly, 2002). If we ignore spiritual care, we are only treating part of the patient. How then can we guide a patient toward the desired outcome of wholeness? Without spiritual direction and relatedness, it is a basic Christian belief that human beings will continue to strive to fill a place within them that yearns to know God (e.g., Psalm 42:1; 69:32; John 10:10; 1 Corinthians 1:9). As Augustine wrote early in the Christian era, reflecting on Scripture: "Thou hast made us for thyself, O Lord, and our hearts are restless until they rest in thee" (1960).

Philosophers have debated human spirituality for centuries, as have psychologists and psychiatrists in more recent times. Some have simply given up on the notion of spirit, and dismiss it as ridiculous. Others believe that human beings possess a body, soul, and spirit, intricately entwined, symbiotically collaborating with each other, each part needing the other for optimal functioning. Often when one part fails to thrive, the whole system breaks down and needs to be healed. There may be exceptions, such as when a terminally ill patient matures and flourishes spiritually in response to their illness. But more often than not, problems in one area will impact the whole person. More and more, this perspective is on the ascendant in modern medicine (e.g., Benson & Stark, 1997; Koenig & McConnell, 2001). Luminaries in medicine and psychotherapy are embracing and promulgating the role of spirituality in healthcare. In its emphasis on spirituality in treatment, Remuda is therefore not outside the mainstream thinking of our day.

In keeping with the emerging recognition that spirituality has a significant place in healthcare, studies bridging the worlds of psychotherapy and faith have seen burgeoning growth during recent decades in the US. Textbooks, books, and peer-reviewed articles and journals by mental health professionals on the subject of faith and counseling reflect a heightened awareness of the need to understand and deal with the client's spiritual world (Scafranske, 1996). There is also an abundance of research on religion and coping (Koenig, George & Siegler, 1988; Mattlin, Wethington & Kessler, 1990; Wicks, 1990). Graduate programs in psychology have been formed that explicitly attempt to integrate spirituality with psychological theories and methods: e.g., Fuller Theological Seminary, Biola University, Azusa Pacific University, George Fox University, Wheaton College, John F. Kennedy University. Prestigious medical schools are offering courses on spiritual counseling (Gundersen, 2000). In this context, Remuda offers an opportunity whereby seasoned professionals schooled in spiritual counseling can utilize their knowledge and experience effectively to address the needs of the whole patient. In fact, healthcare professionals are in a strategic position to assist those searching and struggling with spiritual matters. In one study of terminally ill patients in a nonsectarian medical center, 76% indicated they would like to talk with their nurses about God, 55% wanted nurses to assist them with prayer, and 46% wanted nurses to acknowledge their religious beliefs (Soderstron & Martinson, 1987). Surveys by *USA Today* and *Time* magazine indicate that 2/3 of Americans would like their healthcare providers to address religion with them, and 1/2 want their doctors to pray with them (Gundersen, 2000).

For those struggling with an eating disorder, the relationship with God has often suffered greatly. Why is that? Because God sees all, is in all, and we are aware of his presence even when we are otherwise alone. Hence, the desperate desire to hide our self-destructive actions from him becomes a priority. This is not new regarding human behavior, but indeed a primeval response to shame. Even at humanity's beginning, Adam and Eve tried to hide their shame about their behavior from God: "They hid from the LORD God among the trees of the garden" (Genesis 3:8). We push God out of the picture because we want what we want through the methods we have chosen, and because we are not thinking about or focusing on whom we may hurt in the process, least of all ourselves. Slowly, God becomes silent to us, perhaps nonexistent. This is followed or accompanied by a moving away from others, or at least attempts at isolation. We become more and more evasive, less available, and more detached from a range of feelings and emotions. The numbing process is well underway.

Caring for the spirit is indeed essential in such circumstances, because there has been a tearing away of the relationship with God, a separation. Human beings can live like this for a long time, usually in misery. But ultimately, when people desire complete healing, they want their spirit healed too. They want to be in communion with God again and to know and experience him as they once did or never have before. In Psalm 40 through 45, King David expresses this well, crying out to God while buried in his sins.

> Do not withhold your mercy from me, O LORD; may your love and your truth always protect me. For troubles without number surround me; my sins have overtaken me, and I cannot see. They are more than the hairs of my head, and my heart fails within me. Be pleased, O LORD, to save me; O LORD, come quickly to help me.
>
> You are my help and my deliverer; O my God, do not delay.
>
> I waited patiently for the LORD; he turned to me and heard my cry. He lifted me out of the slimy pit, out of the mud and mire; he set my feet on a rock and gave me a firm place to stand. He put a new song in my mouth, a hymn of praise to our God. (Psalm 40:11-13,17,1-3)

Although there have been advancements recognizing the role of spirituality in healthcare and ample literature is accumulating on the prominent role of spirituality in eating disorders, some healthcare professionals still seem to tread very lightly regarding spiritual counseling with eating disorder clients. Occasionally there are explicit criticisms of nonclerical mental health professionals who have educated themselves to provide this service. Perhaps, then, some clinicians and researchers have yet to explore the evidence for the role and impact of spirituality in recovery and healthy living.

Why Christianity?

At Remuda, we address the needs of the body, soul, and spirit simultaneously for optimal healing, treating the whole person. Many practitioners, aware of the growing recognition of spirituality's legitimate role in healthcare, come with us this far. But then they may ask: "Why does Remuda choose to address spirituality from the perspective of biblical Christianity? Why not take a more generic approach to spirituality?" The answer is once again simple: "Christianity is our faith."

By faith I do not merely mean the system of beliefs to which we adhere, although this certainly pertains. But more than this, faith in Christ, for us, is a living experience, a gift from God that enables us to believe in and follow his Son (Romans 10:17). Our spirits are alive because of this faith. We cannot authentically live spiritual lives, or communicate about spiritual matters, apart from this faith. It is the cornerstone of our spirituality (Ephesians 2:20).

We are certainly not alone in the United States. Up to 88% of Americans report Christianity as their faith system (Kosmin & Lachman, 1993). Interventions that approach spiritual care from a Christ-centered perspective are therefore able, without modification, to reach the large majority of patients seeking treatment in this nation. This is an important point not often recognized among healthcare professionals or scholars.

Furthermore, of the many spiritual traditions, by far the greatest quantity of research and theory on the integration of spirituality into mental health has occurred in the Christian tradition. The field of integration studies endeavors to integrate counseling and Christianity into a unified conceptual and treatment model. Accredited universities and seminaries support this work, as do scientific journals dedicated exclusively or predominantly to this work, such as *The Journal of Psychology and Christianity* and *The Journal of Psychology and Theology*. Thousands of books have been written on recovery and healing from a Christian perspective. Thus, the mental health professional wishing to follow current standards of the field and incorporate spirituality into his or her research or clinical work can draw on an extensive literature and evidenced-based content regarding the integration of patient care and Christianity. For other spiritual traditions, the resources are less extensive. As such, Christian-based mental health programs are not only following the standards of current practice by integrating spirituality into treatment, but they are also doing so in perhaps the most scientifically-defensible manner possible given the present state of knowledge.

At Remuda, we see God acting daily in multiple ways, continually confirming our faith. We have the blessing of seeing him move among us: families coming together, remembering and talking about their deep and abiding love for one another, their suffering in the grip of such love, the effects of their secret behaviors, their hunger to find a way out and restore their relationships. We see families rejoined after years of separation. We see crushed and devastated marriages take the first steps toward reconciliation. We see children and adolescents literally regain the joy and enthusiasm of youth. We believe that spiritual renewal of this magnitude is ever more possible when Jesus Christ is brought openly and fully into the equation, for he is the source of all reconciliation and redemption. "All things are possible with God" (Mark 10:27).

What About Non-Christians?

What about those who have never had a relationship with God? Are their spirits in need of succor, if they truly *don't care*? Because of our biblical understanding of human nature (Cumella, 2002; Wall & Eberly, 2002), we believe that all human spirits need care when they are suffering. If we provide treatment for the body and mind, and leave out the spirit, the result will be less than optimal. There is also ample scientific evidence of the need to attend to spirituality during treatment (e.g., Benson & Stark, 1997; Koenig & McConnell, 2001). All patients who come to Remuda are informed before admission of our emphasis on spirituality throughout treatment and they assent to our holistic model. In fact, they are carefully informed that they will be exposed to expressions of biblical Christianity, and they explicitly consent to this prior to admission. If they strongly prefer another approach, they may not elect to seek treatment at Remuda.

At our facility, we ask many questions about clients' spiritual condition. This assessment process is as critical as any of the seven clinical evaluations performed during the admission process. We want to know how the patient perceives God. Is there spiritual distress, a broken and hurtful relationship with a church or faith community, disappointment with God, or a crisis of faith? The Remuda Spiritual Assessment Questionnaire (Wall, Cumella, &

Darden, 2003) was developed and validated psychometrically to assess objectively a broad range of spiritual issues with which patients may be dealing. We thus assess each client's individual and personal needs for spiritual care. These issues are addressed during treatment with patient consent.

The Remuda Program includes classes to explore spiritual issues in greater depth. Patients attend chapel daily, including a devotional message and songs of spiritual praise and worship. Support group models are taught and opportunities given to experience these groups. For example, Celebrate Recovery and 12 Steps for Christians are offered on campus and made available for patients to participate in at their choosing.

Remuda's patient care staff are compassionate people, highly skilled and fully credentialed in their professions, and also professing to know Christ. Through them, patients have the opportunity to be exposed to Christianity "with skin on," and hopefully more is "caught" than taught at Remuda. We have often said that Christianity is more about *relationship* than *religion*. Someone once said, "No one cares how much you know until they know how much you care." As Scripture says: "Your lives are echoing the Master's Word...The news of your faith in God is out. We don't even have to say anything anymore—*you're* the message!" (1 Thessalonians 1:8 MSG). We desire that those who come to Remuda have an opportunity to meet Jesus through the love we demonstrate in the way we perform our duties.

Once they surmount initial obstacles, the women and girls who come to Remuda for treatment are often not afraid: they are some of the most courageous people one will ever be blessed to meet. They inspire us with their courage and strength. They are not afraid to ask hard questions about God, the purpose of life, and the mystery of death, and they want answers that make sense and that they can count on. Throughout their lives they want to know. They have already been hearing answers to these questions through our culture, answers that have left them empty, confused, and ill. Someone, somewhere, is going to offer them spiritual answers, so why not us? They need not accept our answers to these potent questions, but often they do, because the answers ring true for them and derive from a book which they have either long revered or recently come to appreciate as sacred, the Bible.

It goes without saying that, in all cases, Remuda respects the spiritual and religious backgrounds and choices of our clients. This is a standard of ethics in all healthcare professions. If a patient elects not to be exposed to Christian messages and ideas while at Remuda, we respect that boundary. In fact, many patients from other faith backgrounds have renewed their particular faith and spiritual joy through their experiences at Remuda. Our internal research shows that patients from non-Christian backgrounds experience short- and long-term outcomes equivalent to our Christian patients. Thus, the vital spirituality experienced at Remuda can be accessible to, and healing for, clients from many faith backgrounds.

Forgiveness: From Anger to Peace

Mainstream psychotherapy researchers and practitioners and other helping professionals have begun to apply spiritual methods of coping and counseling quite broadly. These methods include discussion of and training in the use of forgiveness to help people release old patterns of resentment and move forward toward new goals and relationships (e.g., McCullough, Sandage, & Worthington, 1997). Even before the popularity of forgiveness counseling in mainstream mental health, forgiveness counseling was one of the hallmark spiritual issues that patients and families were addressing at Remuda. It continues to be so.

In *The Psychology of Religion and Coping*, Dr. Kenneth Pargament (1997) writes:

> There are many things forgiveness is, and many things it is not. Forgiveness is neither pardon, nor forgetting, nor denial, nor an act of moral superiority over a perpetrator. It is not a form of passive reconciliation, a way to quickly restore an unhealthy relationship, placing a person at continued risk. It is not simply a protective method of coping, one designed to limit the pain and hurt of injustice.

Instead, forgiveness is viewed by a growing body of healthcare professionals as an important and profound process. Giving up the right to bring retaliatory harm may seem counterintuitive to some who have witnessed the mistreatment of others or have been mistreated themselves. Yet those who practice forgiveness find themselves restored and radically changed.

David Augsburger, in his classic writing, *Caring Enough to Forgive, Caring Enough Not to Forgive* (1981), states that "forgiveness is one of the hardest things in the world to do, and one of the greatest of human achievements. It calls for change at many levels: relational, cognitive, behavioral, affective, volitional and spiritual." It is one of the essential recreating events that is performed every week by patients and families at Remuda, and it is the place where true healing begins on every level. Yet this transforming act arises from the human spirit. It is a spiritual decision that affects the rest of the person as well as those around them.

Unforgiveness reaps destruction. The powerlessness and anger one feels over injustice has the potential to leave one in the grips of paranoia, alienate one from sources of support, and intensify the physical signs of stress. The freedom gained by the act of forgiveness means that one is no longer held hostage by painful memories of mistreatment. Forgiveness offers one the possibility of emotional, mental, spiritual, and physical peace.

Forgiveness is rarely instantaneous. Although forgiveness involves a decision, that decision oftentimes must be made again and again—a process. Because forgiveness involves action, attempts are made to change one's thinking, feeling, and relating to others. With changes in behavior, changes in thinking and feeling deepen.

Forgiveness is but one aspect of recovery, but one of the most essential in healing a person's heart and spirit. It is for many the essence of spiritual care, whether from a Christian perspective or other faith. Christianity takes forgiveness to new heights by recognizing that it is the very source of spiritual salvation and central event in human history, epitomized in Christ's crucifixion. As Christ said the night before he was crucified: "This is my blood of the covenant, which is poured out for many for the forgiveness of sins" (Matthew 26:28). As Christians, we deeply recognize the value of forgiveness and we are awed to participate with our clients and their families in the unfolding of this mysterious spiritual process that renews lives and relationships.

References

Augsburger, D.W. (1981). *Caring enough to forgive, caring enough not to forgive.* Ventura, CA: Regal Books.

Augustine. (1960). *The confessions of Saint Augustine.* (Trans. John K. Ryan) New York: Doubleday.

Benson, H. & Stark, M. (1997). *Timeless healing: The power and biology of belief.* New York: Fireside.

Cumella, E.J. (2002). Bio-psycho-social-spiritual: Completing the model. *The Remuda Review: The Christian Journal of Eating Disorders, 1*, 1-5.

Gundersen, L. (2000). Faith and healing. *Annals of Internal Medicine, 132*, 169-72.

Koenig, H. & McConnell, M. (2001). *The healing power of faith: How belief and prayer can help you triumph over disease.* New York: Simon & Schuster.

Koenig, H.G., George, L.K., & Siegler, I.C. (1988). The use of religion and other emotion-regulating coping strategies among older adults. *Gerontologist, 28*, 303-10.

Kosmin, B.A. & Lachman, S.P. (1993). *One nation under God: Religion in contemporary American society.* New York: Harmony Books.

Mattlin, J.A., Wethington, E., & Kessler, R.C. (1990). Situational determinants of coping and coping effectiveness, *Journal of Health and Social Behavior, 31*,103-22.

McCullough, M.E., Sandage, S.J., & Worthington, E.L. (1997). *To forgive is human: How to put your past in the past.* Downers Grove, IL: InterVarsity Press.

Pargament, K.I. (1997). *The psychology of religion and coping: Theory, research, and practice.* New York: Guilford Publications.

Scafranske, E.P. (Ed.) (1996). *Religion and the clinical practice of psychology.* Washington, DC: APA Books.

Soderstron, K.E. & Martinson, I.M. (1987). Patients spiritual coping strategies: A study of nurse and patient perspectives. *Oncology Nursing Forum,14*, 41-46

Wall, A.D., Cumella, E.J., & Darden, R.A. (2003). *Remuda spiritual assessment questionnaire professional manual.* Wickenburg, AZ: Remuda Ranch Center for Anorexia and Bulimia, Inc.

Wall, A.D. & Eberly, M. (2002). Five biblical factors in eating disorder development. *The Remuda Review: The Christian Journal of Eating Disorders, 1*, 6-10.

Wicks, J.W. (1990). *Greater Toledo area survey.* Bowling Green, Ohio: Population and Society Research Center.

Chapter 17

Spiritual Development: Growing in God's Love

A. David Wall, PhD, Marian C. Eberly, RN, MSW, LCSW, DAPA, and Edward J. Cumella, PhD, CEDS

> *I am convinced that neither death nor life, neither angels nor demons, neither the present nor the future, nor any powers, neither height nor depth, nor anything else in all creation, will be able to separate us from the love of God.* (Romans 8:38-39)

Her name is Katie. For all the world, she looks like a healthy young American woman. Her sweet spirit is evident, especially when she smiles. Bright and personable, she should have the world by the tail. How did she end up needing intensive inpatient treatment for an eating disorder?

We discuss her family, school, friends, and her religious background.

"I'm a Christian," she replies.

"Tell me who God is—not necessarily what you've been taught, but who you experience him to be."

"He's awesome. He is someone I can turn to, someone who loves you. I know he died for me."

"If he were to suddenly stand before you right now, what do you think he would say?"

At first she stumbles for words. Then she hesitantly replies, "He would tell me he loves me."

"What do you think he would say about your eating disorder?"

"He wants me to stop. I'm destroying my body—that he gave me—and I'm wasting the gifts he gave me." Tears flow, just slightly.

As she continues, her shame emerges. She is ashamed not just about her eating disorder. A trusted Christian boyfriend, Michael, slowly wore her down and pushed her into having sex.

"I said 'no,' but he wouldn't stop. He knew where I stood. It's my fault. I never should have allowed that to happen."

So much of what she values—her plans and dreams—disappeared in one night. Shame replaced her dreams.

Although devastated, and in spite of her boyfriend's persistent physical advances, Katie continued her relationship with him. One day he didn't call when he was supposed to. Days went by. Then Katie learned from a friend that he was dating another girl. Something inside her began to die: not simply because of the rejection, but because of what this relationship had cost her. For what? She was so ashamed of herself.

Within a matter of weeks, Katie's preexisting focus on healthy foods erupted into an eating disorder. Her list of healthy foods shrank to precious few. Exercise became a compulsion. Her dietary rules and exercise regime demanded obedience. When she obeyed anything less than perfectly, she experienced unending waves of obsessive guilt. Her standards for herself were always just a bit higher than her achievements, so feelings of guilt became the norm.

Katie still garnered attention from young men, but pulled back in fear. She did not trust them, and more importantly, did not trust herself. She wanted to be physically attractive. Yet at the same time, she wanted men to see her as repulsive. This was just one of many areas in her life that seemed conflicted and confusing.

Katie gave of herself to everyone. She felt obligated to live out her faith by always being there for anyone who needed her and to "point them to the Lord."

After listening for some time, I interjected. "What is your vision for your life?"

"I just want to get better so I can help other people, to be an inspiration to them. This illness has me so focused on myself and so tired all the time, I can't be the kind of friend I should be to other people."

"Is God disappointed in you?"

"Yes. I know he is. I keep praying and praying for God to take my eating disorder away, but he doesn't. I want to stop, I should be able to overcome this, but I can't. I cry out to him; I beg him to help me. I would never kill myself, but I wish he would just take me home. Maybe he wants me to suffer to teach me and make me strong, so I can minister to others, but how can I, not like this? I say I love God, but I don't show it. I am so wrapped up in myself. I guess being thin is more important to me than obeying God."

"What do your parents say?"

"My mother is supportive, but Dad just doesn't get it. He tries, but he just thinks that all I need to do is start eating. But I can't. I just can't. Sometimes he gets so mad. He scared me with how angry he got a couple weeks ago. We used to be really close, but now…"

Soon our interview ended.

Works and Shame

A week later, Katie's treatment team reported that she was having a significant impact on other patients in the milieu, reminding them of God's love for them and helping them to trust in his grace for the difficult tasks of recovery. Yet she remained unable to apply this knowledge to herself.

Did Katie fail God? Is she simply reaping what she has sown? Did God fail Katie? She reads the Bible, attends fellowship, mourns the things she has done, pleads for God's help, and cries quietly in the night. But she is not recovering from her eating disorder.

There are moments after meeting with young women like Katie when we wonder: "God, she is such a sweet young lady. She honestly loves you. Why haven't you heard her cries?"

Katie appears to truly love and seek God. She has done the right things according to her faith system. So why haven't her efforts sent her flying into recovery?

Katie is filled with shame. Dictionaries define *shame* by reference to other words, particularly *disgrace* and *humiliation*. *Disgrace* means a loss of honor, respect, favor, and trust. *Humiliation* means degradation, loss of respect for oneself, complete defeat. Regarding relationship with God, disgrace indicates the feeling that one has lost God's favor and broken his trust. Humiliation indicates self-hatred and feeling powerless against a powerful, malignant force— complete defeat. Ultimately, the word *disgrace* seems to capture this human experience best: *disgrace*, or the state of being removed from God's grace, love, favor, and aid.

This is precisely the experience of many patients with eating disorders. They believe they have so disappointed God that he has withdrawn his grace, love, and help from them. Feeling as though one has been forsaken by one's Maker is a crushing, even terrifying, experience. Many patients with this belief are desperately trying to get God's love back; some, in anger and disappointment, have given up the quest. But all who struggle with this profound spiritual devastation ultimately believe that in order to receive God's love again, they must earn it back. They believe that until and unless they change their behavior, God will not show his love to them. Enter the focus on performance. So often women and girls with eating disorders have come to believe, through a series of life events, that their performance determines how much love they receive, if any at all. They must outperform everyone to feel lovable and receive love.

According to the Christian Scriptures, this approach cannot succeed. It is, in fact, completely antithetical to Christianity. If there is one thing that distinguishes Christianity from other religious perspectives—one thing that so many Christians stumble over and struggle with—it is the belief that God's love, forgiveness, and spiritual restoration come not by our own efforts but from God's free, unmerited grace. Much of the book of Romans is devoted to this topic. Here, describing the unmerited grace and forgiveness of God, the apostle Paul writes: "And if by grace, then it is no longer by works; if it were, grace would no longer be grace" (Romans 11:6). The Living Bible translates this same verse even more illustratively: "And if it is by God's kindness, then it is not by their being good enough. For in that case the free gift would no longer be free—it isn't free when it is earned."

The Truth About Love: The Christian View

How do we assist patients at Remuda to make this fundamental shift in thinking, to absorb this counter-intuitive understanding? We begin by sharing this most basic, yet essential truth: God is love (1 John 4:16). It is not necessary to do anything to earn his love, it is a free gift. There is nothing we can do to make God love us any more, or any less. He already loves us completely and this will not change based on our behavior. Hence, patients do not need to remain on the performance treadmill. It's time to turn off the machine.

Explaining this to patients, showing them scriptures that make this clear, and modeling this kind of love often have an impact. But it is not easy for the human mind to grasp the free nature of God's love. Jesus irritated his contemporaries mostly because he spoke about love: love for God, love for one another...and God's great love for us. How do you begin to tell someone of their incredible worth? Parents can tell their children that they love them, but that does not necessarily mean the children believe it. A therapist can tell a patient she is loved by God, but sometimes the words slide off like an egg on a Teflon pan. The knowledge doesn't stick; she doesn't believe she is loved by anyone.

One patient wrote the following poem, recording the struggle to understand the concept of grace.

Again I sinned, I turned away.
I broke your law, I defiled the Way.

Yet your response leaves me amazed—
Your love persists, you expand your grace.

You give me gifts when I least deserve.
You forgive me over and over.
You pick me up and clean me off
And clothe me again with your power.

You keep on giving—no matter what I do.
You boggle my tiny mind.
I haven't yet grasped that you are the Gift
Which has nothing to do with these deeds of mine.

Good or bad, you love me still,
For love is your unchanging will.

Can I ever take such grandeur in?
That you live your life inside my skin
Carrying my helplessness all the while
Like Mary with her newborn child.

Many Christians struggle to understand God's love and grace. In fact, even when we professionals think we "get it," we may find ourselves surprised all over again by the depth of his love. It is a lifelong journey to grow deeper in our understanding of and trust in God's love and forgiveness. As we do, we grow closer to God and become more like him.

God, in his wisdom, knew that we doubt our own value and worth, and that we would doubt his love for us. So he did the greatest thing imaginable: He became a human being like us, leaving behind his abode of holiness, dwelling among us in a frail human body, and experiencing the injustice and suffering common to us all. And then he died for us. He allowed himself to be put to death to show us something about his unconditional love for us and our great worth to him. He knew we might be able to understand the depth of a sacrifice of life. "Greater love has no one than this, that he lay down his life for his friends" (John 15:13).

It has been said that the point Jesus was trying to communicate with his arms outstretched on the cross was this: "I love you." For Christians, healing, growth, and wholeness begin with this realization: We are loved unconditionally and irrevocably by God. God loves us! This is the foundation of our self-worth. Not our actions, achievements, successes, appearance, talents, or intelligence—but the fact that the Creator of the universe made us in an act of love and loves us as we are. This is meant to be a eureka experience—"I am valuable because I am loved by God himself!" For someone like Katie, this realization is a dramatic and unexpected reversal. She no longer needs to strive and perform to earn God's love. Her self-worth and dignity arise from the fact that he loves her already.

Spiritual Development

It can be difficult and time consuming to encourage patients to grow in their understanding of and trust in God's love. We do so not by imparting to them from our great depth of wisdom, via lectures and sermons, but by asking them *questions,* and lots of them. It is not as though we are seeking information through these questions, but are instead encouraging patients to ask these questions of themselves. As they consider and reconsider these questions in light of what they know or are learning about God through Scripture and experience, they often begin to understand.

The kind of questions we encourage in our patients are:

- From where do I obtain my self-worth?
- Am I growing in love toward myself and others?
- How do I really view myself and those around me?
- How do I feel about the sins I commit?
- Is something wrong with me because I am afraid to die?
- Why do I find it so hard to forgive?
- What do I *really* believe about God?

From a spiritual perspective, these questions and others like them hang on one nail: God's love. God's love is the foundation of human self-worth, healthy relationships, intimacy, forgiveness, and peace about death and afterlife. As Christians, we also believe that the Christian life centers on the love that flows through us from Jesus to others. Therefore, if patients grasp nothing else at Remuda, the message of love is the one that we hope is caught as well as taught. Learning what love is and how to experience and practice it is a lifetime journey that becomes the engine of continual spiritual development, also known as sanctification.

Most people think of love as a feeling or an emotion. Love is more than a feeling. In fact, it may not involve feelings at all. Love is about relationship. C.S. Lewis (2001) wrote, "Love is...a steady wish for the loved person's ultimate good as far as it can be obtained." But love goes beyond merely wishing for the ultimate good; it is an active commitment to the well-being of the one who is loved, regardless of internal emotions. Emotions can be volatile and fragile. Real love is anything but volatile and fragile. Affectionate expressions of love—along with validating verbal and nonverbal messages—are usually essential in love relationships, but love is not limited by the current emotional state of the one who loves.

Love is neither abusive nor indulgent, because neither abuse nor indulgence manifests a commitment to someone's well-being. Love isn't guided by emotions such as guilt or anger. Guilty parents may be indulgent of a child. Their indulgence is not guided by a commitment to the child's well-being, but rather by their desire not to feel guilty. Angry parents may punish to express and release their anger, but are not disciplining out of a commitment to the child's well-being.

The focus on love as an emotion causes a plethora of problems: "I don't love you anymore." "I don't feel God's love for me." We often base our perceptions of reality on how we feel. If I feel stupid, I am stupid. If I feel that no one loves me, no one loves me. If I feel fat, I am fat.

As Christians, we are often reminded to show our love for God and others, to be committed to their well-being. The Bible instructs us how to love others: "Love your neighbor *as* yourself" (Matthew 22:39, emphasis added). *As* means "to the same degree or amount." So we are being told to love others to the same degree and amount that we love ourselves. Sometimes love for self is perceived as unchristian, hedonistic, or worldly. But Christ does not *ask* us to love ourselves, he *commands* us to do so.

And yet, we are also commanded by the Bible to be humble. Therefore, being humble is not mutually exclusive with loving oneself. "Perfect humility dispenses with modesty" (Lewis, 2001). Feeling worthless or superior are extreme conditions of self-concept that have nothing to do with humbleness. Jesus was humble, because humbleness indicates an absence of false pride—pride based on an unrealistic appraisal of oneself. Instead, humbleness indicates an honest and realistic appraisal of oneself—which includes an awareness of both one's strengths and weaknesses. Love for oneself therefore has much to do with humbleness, since we can only authentically love when we honestly know who we are.

Yet loving oneself can sound discordant to the Christian's ear—not because it isn't biblical, but because our culture links self-love to hedonistic egotism. When we love ourselves, we do not worship ourselves. Rather, we are committed to our well-being. We do not indulge ourselves. Rather, we follow God's plan for healthy living. We do not put our needs above others' and our comfort above all else. Rather, we are secure enough to be self-sacrificing for the sake of others. Our self-sacrifice is not generated by an inner sense of worthlessness or need to compensate for shame—both of which are compulsive and self-centered expressions. Rather, we *choose* to sacrifice because we are loved and have been granted infinite worth by God, as with Jesus: "This is my Son, ...with him I am well pleased" (Matthew 3:17). God has made us his children.

Once, the apostle Peter brashly declared that he would die for Jesus (Luke 22:33). But that statement arose from his egocentric need to be seen as great. Later Peter betrayed Jesus rather than dying for him. He failed in his own efforts at self-sacrifice. Then and only then, through Christ's forgiveness and tenderness, Peter learned how much he was loved, valued, and considered worthy by God. Then, not because of his performance, but in spite of it, out of his knowledge of how much he was loved, Peter did die for Christ. History tells us that he was martyred in Rome in 63 AD (or thereabout). From his intimate knowledge of how much he was loved by God, this same Peter sought to build up the individual Christian's sense of self-worth and value. He wrote: "...you are a chosen people, a royal priesthood, a holy nation..." (1 Peter 2:9).

Perhaps the number one problem for patients who come to Remuda is that they do not love themselves. Some pity themselves, some hate themselves, some indulge themselves, some promote themselves, and some hide themselves. But they seldom truly love themselves. Experiencing God's love is the pivotal first step in change. What does experiencing God's love do for us? Does it shame us or drive us to perform harder and harder? No. Christ said: "Come to me, all you who are weary and burdened, and I will give you rest...For my yoke is easy and my burden is light" (Matthew 11:28,30). Rather than demanding or depleting us with expectations, Jesus' love empowers us.

Katie has already experienced that love. Why then is she having many problems? Eating disorders are complex, but one of Katie's most enslaving issues is that, although she originally found freedom and love through Christ's grace, she now seeks it by performance. Although grace saves us, often we unconsciously believe something like this: "Now that I am a Christian I have to work to be good." With this mind-set, we can become painfully aware of our failings. Paradoxically, perhaps Katie's best chance for recovery is when she realizes that she doesn't *have* to recover in order to be loved. Rather, her recovery begins with the release from shame and guilt brought about by the experience of God's love and her consequent ability to love herself.

Katie doesn't know how to love herself. When she thinks about herself, she feels only shame and anger. When we tell Katie, "You need to love yourself in order to recover," her immediate response is hopelessness. This is because people like Katie often view love as an emotion. Because she has no sense of emotional love for herself, just feelings of worthlessness and shame, self-love seems alien and far away. If she has to stir up love for herself, she knows she cannot do it. Because feelings are reality for her, and because she feels worthless, she fully believes that she is worthless. "I can try to love myself, but it would be fake, it wouldn't be real."

"Why is it fake?"

"Because, I don't feel it."

"So if you don't feel something it cannot be real?"

"Well, no." She looks puzzled.

"If you had a daughter and she had done something very wrong, would you tell her she was worthless?"

"No, never. Of course not!"

"Why not?"

"Because it would hurt her and because it isn't true."

"You wouldn't call her worthless because you would love her. And in your love for her, you would be able to see beyond her mistakes. You would know who she really is, her value to you."

"Yes, I would. She's my daughter."

"Katie, you need to tell yourself what you would tell her. God loves you the same way—even more than—you would love your daughter, no matter what. Can you take that in, see yourself as loved, regardless of how you feel."

She tears up.

"Katie, I've seen how you act toward other people. You know how to love and you really desire to love others. You've made a real impact on people here. Doesn't the Bible say to love your neighbor *as yourself*?"

"Yes."

"What is love, Katie? Feeling mushy all the time? What does God say love is?"

At this point, 1 Corinthians 13 may become the focus. In 1 Corinthians, the apostle Paul offers a tutorial on love, telling us what love is and is not. The passage in 1 Corinthians 13 is among the Bible's most well-known. It is often read at weddings and quoted by Christians. But the most amazing thing about Paul's tutorial on love—something often missed—is that it is a tutorial about the nature of God himself. For God is love. And it is by experiencing the depth of his love for us that we learn to love *ourselves* and other people. "We love because he first loved us" (1 John 4:19). Our love for ourselves and others—our good works—are a fruit that develops from our experience of God's love for us.

Paul begins his tutorial on love by informing us, foremost, that "Love is patient" (1 Corinthians 13:4). *Patient* means long-tempered and long-suffering. Do we recognize that God is patient with us, loving us all along, accepting us as we are, not expecting perfection, liberally forgiving us, and rejoicing in our little steps? As we absorb this and live in the reality of God's unconditional love for us, we can begin to love ourselves and others as we are loved, unconditionally. Are we patient with ourselves, gently forgiving our errors, again and again, and allowing ourselves room to grow? Or do we expect perfection today? Patience does not retaliate when a wrong has been done—neither wrongs we do against ourselves or experience from others. Patience is truly love in action, and we learn it because of God's gentle patience with us.

The apostle Paul continues: "Love is kind..." (1 Corinthians 13:4). *Kindness* means proactively and enthusiastically doing good and showing compassion for the afflicted. This is how God treats us—with kindness, actively pursuing ways to bless us, showing compassion and mercy when we err, and joining us in our sufferings. As we believe in and receive this love from God, we can begin to love ourselves with the same kindness, and to offer it to others, allowing his love to flow through us toward the people around us.

The apostle proceeds on love: "It does not envy..." (1 Corinthians 13:4). *Envy* is a discontented feeling that arises in the human heart. It occurs when one person is confronted with another person who possesses something of value to the first person. This can be a physical possession, special knowledge or skill, talent one has not mastered, and so on. Envy can recede, however, when we know how deeply we are loved by God: that we are made unique creations, each a child whom he is shaping and guiding to become in time the full person he has designed us to be. *There is nothing more that we need to be or have today*. Through this experience, we can enjoy ourselves in our uniqueness and others in theirs. We can celebrate others' blessings and gently affirm them as they, too, grow toward wholeness. Remuda is often a classroom in which patients can learn these valuable lessons. Love, rather than envy, builds true Christian community. Knowing that we are all loved by God as his unique creations is a powerful unifying experience.

The apostle continues on love: "...it does not boast, it is not proud. It is not rude, it is not self-seeking, it is not easily angered..." (1 Corinthians 13:4-5). Outward actions demonstrate what is going on inside. How we treat ourselves and others reflects our inner attitude. Do we treat ourselves and others with respect and dignity, or with contempt and as objects intended only to meet needs and goals? The attitudes of love include humbleness, mutuality, and compassion rather than contempt, self-centeredness, and anger. By believing in and opening to God's gracious love for us, we learn more about who we are, we become honest about our strengths and weaknesses, and humble yet secure in our self-concept as unique beings created by God. When we discover that God loves us, seeks relationship with us, and above all wants to know us intimately, we recognize that we are not objects to him and we cease to objectify ourselves and other people.

Paul continues on love: "...it keeps no record of wrongs" (1 Corinthians 13:5). Keeping a ledger, noting the debits and credits we have earned by our good and bad behaviors and those of other people—this leads to a hard heart. It places us in the role of judge, and judgment limits mercy. Learning to let go, to step back and think before impulsively acting out of offense or woundedness, and to overlook minor offenses against us and errors we may make—this ultimately leaves a soft heart. A soft heart is capable of mercy, forgiveness, and gratitude for the forgiveness that God continually offers us. Such a heart is humble, because it recognizes its dependency on God's unending mercy and the extent to which he freely and continually offers mercy to us. Such a heart can receive forgiveness from God and from others, and can offer forgiveness to self and others. Such a heart is unburdened by the past and set free to live and love today.

Paul proceeds: "Love does not delight in evil but rejoices with the truth" (1 Corinthians 13:6). In Psalms 51 we read, "Surely you desire truth in the inner parts" (verse 6). God is less concerned with our outer appearance, actions, successes, and failures, and more concerned with honesty and integrity. He delights in honesty. Learning about the tenderness of his love and forgiving nature enables us to become honest with ourselves in his presence, to experience being loved for who we are, exactly as we are, without expectations. This is a radical, transforming truth. It empowers us to be authentic with others and to invite them into authenticity as well. People who can be honest with one another become great supports to each other, rejoicing together in God's love and acceptance for them. They can help each other with accountability regarding mistakes and sinful choices, and gently restore one another when problematic choices have been made.

Paul concludes his discourse on love: "It always protects, always trusts, always hopes, always perseveres. Love never fails" (1 Corinthians 13:7-8). These words are a description of God: God always protects us, trusts, hopes, and perseveres. God never fails us, and God never fails, period.

Protection means taking care of people, shielding from harm and loss, even absorbing harm and loss to guard others from it. It means holding up, supporting, and coming alongside another. These are the things that

God has done and does for us. There are clearly many times in believers' lives when they experience this protection. There are also times when difficult events may lead to questioning about God's protection. But we hold in faith to this belief: "...in all things God works for the good of those who love him" (Romans 8:28). We recognize that, because God has the whole picture—past, present, future, all interactions and consequences of every event—his thoughts and his choices are higher than ours (Isaiah 55:8-9) and perhaps inscrutable to us. Yet his choices can be counted on to protect and promote his goal for us: our continued spiritual growth. Because we experience and believe in God's protection for us no matter what, we can offer this same quality of love to others.

Trust means that, in his love, God believes the best of us. He lets go of our past mistakes and starts again with us every day on a clean slate. "The steadfast love of the LORD never ceases, his mercies never come to an end; they are new every morning" (Lamentations 3:22-23 RSV). He sees who we will ultimately become, not just who we are today. Thus, he trusts the process of our spiritual growth, even when something seems amiss. He can do so because the outcome of the process depends on him: "...he who began a good work in you will carry it on to completion" (Philippians 1:6). We, too, can learn to trust God with the proper unfolding of our lives, in spite of our mistakes. And we can learn to trust his work in the lives of others, in spite of theirs.

Hope means that God believes in the best for us, and is optimistic about the choices we will make. no matter how often we may have chosen poorly. He instills us with hope– the attitude of knowing that he is in control and has a future planned for each of us (Jeremiah 29:11). Scripture promises: "...in all things God works for the good of those who love him" (Romans 8:28). This becomes the source of our own optimism toward ourselves and other people. Because of God's steadfast hope for us, we can learn to expect the best of others even when they have disappointed us many times, giving space to the possibility that they may come through this time. Of course, in doing so, we would not open ourselves to harm from others, because in addition to hoping, "love always protects."

Perseverance means commitment and responsibility. God is committed, forever and unshakably, to our well-being. "For great is his love toward us, and the faithfulness of the LORD endures forever" (Psalm 117:2). God will never give up on us, never. "...no one can snatch them out of my Father's hand" (John 10:29). As we learn about God's persistent, unchanging love for us, we become more able to offer the same to ourselves and others.

Finally, love never fails. God never fails us and never falters. He is stable. We can count on his enduring love and power to bring about the things he has promised. God's love will always, eventually, patiently and persistently, triumph over evil. "The one who is in you is greater than the one who is in the world" (1 John 4:4).

As we experience God's immense love for us in these ways, we become able to treat ourselves with the same patience, kindness, mercy, and optimism with which our Maker treats us. We also strengthen our relationships and communities as we become able to offer this love to others. This, indeed, is the heart of the Christian life and the source of ongoing spiritual growth: The experience of God's love for us becomes contagious.

Learning to love God, ourselves, and others perfectly fulfills Christ's commandments to us: "Love...God with all your heart and with all your soul and with all your mind and with all your strength...Love your neighbor as yourself. There is no commandment greater than these" (Mark 12:30-31). We fulfill these commands not because we strive to, but because God's love is experienced within us and overflows into the world. "...but whoever drinks the water I give him will never thirst. Indeed, the water I give him will become in him a spring of water welling up to eternal life" (John 4:14).

This is the good news that Jesus Christ came to preach. Sharing the reality of God's love with eating disorder patients like Katie has the potential to help them break free from the performance trap that ensnares them. It takes a lifetime to absorb this message fully, but as we gradually do, we grow slowly, subtly, and continuously into wholeness and holiness as the children of God.

References

Lewis, C.S. (2001). *The weight of glory*. San Francisco: Harper San Francisco.

Chapter 18

Spiritual Assessment and Treatment Strategies

Edward J. Cumella, PhD, CEDS, Robert A. Darden, PhD, and Marian C. Eberly, RN, MSW, LCSW, DAPA

In recent years the healthcare community has come to recognize that spirituality plays a role in recovery from medical and mental illness and the promotion of physical and mental well-being (e.g., Gartner, Larson, & Allen, 1991; Gundersen, 2000; Larson, Swyers & McCullough, 1998; Levin, 1994; Worthington, Kurusu, McCullough, & Sandage, 1996). For example, Larson and colleagues reviewed 300 studies on the relationship between religious factors and psychopathology and found considerable evidence for a positive relationship between religious participation and mental well-being (Larson, Swyers, & McCullough, 1998). Equally important, healthcare recipients desire opportunities for their spiritual beliefs to be addressed by their providers. A 2000 Gallup poll found that 86% of Americans believe in God and an additional 8% believe in a higher power. Accordingly, surveys by *USA Today* and *Time* indicate that 2/3 of Americans would like their healthcare providers to address religion with them, and 1/2 even want their doctors to pray with them (Gundersen, 2000). In keeping with these data, treatment providers are becoming increasingly aware of the need to address patient spirituality (Hodge, 2001; Richards & Bergin, 1997).

Richards and Bergin (1997) suggest that a spiritual assessment should be part of a multi-model assessment with each patient. Consistent with its bio-psycho-social-spiritual model, Remuda has been incorporating careful spiritual assessment into its programs for many years. Richards and Bergin (1997) indicate that, in addition to traditional components of an assessment, healthcare providers do well to conduct a spiritual assessment through broad and ecumenical inquiries using language that is devoid of denominational terms and underpinnings. It is often useful to begin by obtaining information about patients' spiritual beliefs and practices, along with religious participation. Other areas of inquiry to consider include congruency of patients' lifestyles with their values, history of religious experiences and relationships, issues pertaining to shame, guilt, and performance, and the concept of forgiveness. Of course, information regarding patients' willingness to address spiritual and religious issues should also be included. Then, depending on the information obtained during the initial assessment process, clinicians can proceed with more in-depth assessment if significant spiritual issues appear to be present with particular patients.

A spiritual assessment can also include objective measures. In fact, numerous measures of spirituality have been developed and can be found in the literature. However, many have theoretical and/or psychometric weaknesses (Hall, Tisdale, & Brokaw, 1994; Hill & Hood, 1999). Others are limited by a narrow scope of questions (e.g., Standard, Sandu, & Painter, 2000). Consequently, Remuda Ranch developed the Remuda Spiritual Assessment Questionnaire (RSAQ; Wall, Cumella, & Darden, 2003). The RSAQ represents a broad spectrum of clinically meaningful spiritual beliefs and experiences, fully addresses psychometric considerations in design features and in the demonstration of instrument reliability and validity, and can be used to assess spiritual growth and change through repeated administrations during the course of treatment. It is also relatively short and easy to administer: 41 questions, taking 10 to 15 minutes for the average patient to complete, and not requiring clinician involvement to administer. Scoring and interpretation are automated.

There are several advantages to using an objective assessment of patient spirituality. First, a properly selected objective assessment is comprehensive and thorough, reflecting more questions and domains of spirituality than it is possible to review quickly through face-to-face clinical assessment. As such, an objective assessment may have a greater likelihood of discovering areas of spiritual concern. Research suggests that, especially early in treatment, patients may be more likely to reveal difficult experiences through paper-and-pencil tests than in face-to-face interactions with clinicians. Finally, objective assessments are just that—objective. They reveal the extent to which specific issues are causing distress to an individual when compared with the "average" person. Thus, they may make it easier to determine how much attention a spiritual concern merits during time-limited therapy.

Remuda Spiritual Assessment Questionnaire (RSAQ)

The lead developer of the RSAQ was a doctoral-level licensed psychologist with an additional master's degree in theology and extensive clinical experience with spiritual integration. Others experienced in mental healthcare, including two additional doctoral-level licensed psychologists, also contributed. Combining the knowledge of these experts, a 41-question version of the RSAQ was designed to reflect the broad, multidimensional construct of spirituality plus three important dimensions of spirituality (see below).

Because 86% of the US population self-identifies as Christian (Kosmin & Lachman, 1993), the authors wrote questions to be most meaningful and conceptually appropriate to this large majority of Americans. The authors also believed it important to develop a questionnaire that any English-speaking person could use. As such, two versions of the RSAQ were developed. The Christian version includes such words as "Bible," "Jesus Christ," and "church." A parallel, interfaith version uses words such as "spiritual texts," "higher power," and "religious service."

Between 6/1/1999 and 6/30/2002, RSAQ data were collected from 1905 mental health patients. A normative sample of 208 non-patient women and men also completed the RSAQ. A random sample of 50 individuals from the normative population was asked to complete a second RSAQ one week following their initial testing. Using these data, great attention was paid to item selection, reliability demonstrated through item stability and internal consistency, and validity demonstrated through criterion-related, construct, convergent, and discriminant methods. (For psychometric details, see Wall, Cumella, & Darden, 2003.)

The RSAQ reflects the broad, multidimensional construct of spirituality, and examines three specific domains which have been found by the authors and their colleagues to be particularly relevant when working with thousands of mental health patients. As such, the RSAQ produces the following scores:

Total Spirituality Index, indicating either: a) overall spiritual well-being, including positive spiritual attitudes, beliefs, and experiences, or b) overall spiritual distress, including negative spiritual attitudes, beliefs, and experiences.

Current Spiritual Wellness, indicating either: a) current spiritual well-being, typically including intimacy with God and supportive spiritual relationships, meaningful spiritual practices, faith as a source of strength, a clear spiritual identity, the experience of spiritual joy, and a desire to grow spiritually, or b) spiritual distress, typically including distance from and disappointment with God, unsupportive spiritual relationships, meaningless or absent spiritual practices, a lack of spiritual joy, and little interest in growing spiritually.

Experiences of Shame and Judgment, indicating either: a) the extent to which patients have beliefs and experiences of an accepting, forgiving, and unconditionally loving God, as well as accepting and supportive relationships with other people, or b) beliefs and experiences of a judgmental and condemning God who does not easily forgive human frailty or weakness but expects perfect works before offering love, as well as stringent expectations and judgments from other people.

Past Spiritual Experiences, indicating either: a) childhood experiences of spiritual warmth, love, and grace in one's family and place of worship, or b) childhood experiences of spiritual abuse and self-righteousness in one's family and place of worship.

For each of these scales, spiritual distress may be mild, moderate, severe, or extreme.

The RSAQ has been useful at Remuda, in other facilities, and among outpatient practitioners in conducting spiritual assessments with patients, clients, and church members. Both scale scores and individual questions from the RSAQ can be used as part of treatment planning. It is not uncommon, for example, for eating disorder patients to score high on Experiences of Shame and Judgment. With this information available, treatment teams are better equipped to address the cluster of related issues—shame, forgiveness, grace, and the patient's view of God as judgmental versus unconditionally loving and forgiving. Cognitive therapy may be combined with religious or spiritual interventions. For example, cognitive disputation of distressing beliefs, and the reframing of perceptual schemas, might be sought through reading and memorization of appropriately selected scriptures (e.g., 1 John 1:9, Jeremiah 29:11). (For more details on cognitive distortions common to patients with eating disorders, see the companion chapter in this book, Spiritual Development: Growing in God's Love.)

Treatment Strategies

Spiritual interventions are contraindicated when patients do not want them or are psychotic or delusional. If spiritual interventions are warranted, it is important to inform patients at the start of treatment that you may use spiritual interventions and to obtain their informed consent, in writing if possible. Spiritual interventions are most effective once time has allowed for the development of a trusting therapeutic relationship. It is always essential to work within a patient's value framework. However, as Christian counselors we have an obligation to express the commonly understood, interdenominational gospel truth, including Christ's atoning sacrifice, forgiveness rather than punishment, and God's unconditional, unmerited grace and love rather than legalism, performance, or the need for perfection.

Primary spiritual interventions for patients with eating disorders include:

- teaching spiritual concepts
- spiritual bibliotherapy
- prayer with patients
- spiritual imagery and meditation
- encouraging forgiveness
- referrals for spiritual counsel from pastors or spiritual directors
- encouraging involvement in a faith community
- cognitive restructuring focusing on:
    - — self hatred or perfectionism as obstacles to receiving God's love
    - — the nature of God
    - — a mature understanding of suffering
    - — application of patients' values to their own lives to reduce cognitive dissonance

Self-help groups, such as Christian Recovery International or Survivors of Spiritual Abuse, may also be recommended for patients emerging from backgrounds of religious abuse. Greater detail on treating religious abuse can be found in a separate chapter of this book. A detailed approach to spiritual development can also be found in a separate chapter of this book. As a part of treatment, it may be necessary to guide patients toward finding healthy faith communities. We explore this in more depth below.

Finding a Healthy Church Community

How do Christians find a healthy church to worship in? This is not a new question. It's age old. It is predicated on a basic assumption: Churches are intended to be healthy communities. In the course of spiritual assessment with patients, it is not unusual to encounter those who have struggled with this concern. They often request guidance on a basic issue: What does a healthy church look like?

Identifying a healthy church can be difficult, because churches are made up of hurting, broken people. In some ways, churches are magnets for those who have been hurt, are hurting, or will hurt in the future. And there are two sides to this coin: It has been said that "hurting people hurt people." It is important to emphasize, then, that a healthy church does not and cannot mean a church composed of only healthy people. Health in a church is something different altogether.

Consider the earliest church: In the second chapter of Acts, seven weeks after Jesus had risen from the dead, he gave the gift of the Holy Spirit to his church—to instruct, guide, equip, comfort, and empower them (Acts 1,1 Corinthians 12, Romans 12). And shortly thereafter we read of the earliest church:

> They joined with the other believers and devoted themselves to the apostles' teaching and fellowship, sharing in the Lord's Supper and in prayer...They worshiped together at the Temple each day, met in homes for the Lord's Supper, and shared their meals with great joy and generosity—all the while praising God and enjoying the goodwill of all the people. And each day the Lord added to their group those who were being saved. (Acts 2:42,46-47 NLT)

These scriptures describe critical aspects of the earliest church—the very elements to look for when choosing a church today. Although today's churches may have different callings and visions—e.g., some minister to the elderly or youth, others focus primarily on evangelism through specific forms of outreach—the scripture in Acts 2 evidences four aspects of health in the Christian church which remain a model for us.

Healthy Churches: The Four Fs

Food. "They...devoted themselves to the apostles' teaching..." (Acts 2:42 NLT). After reflecting on this scripture, when considering a particular faith community one must ask: Is the Bible—the apostles' teaching— treated with honor and respect? Is the Bible the centerpiece of what is taught? Are the Scriptures reverenced? Christ is the head of the church (Colossians 1:18). His Word—the Bible—is therefore key. "The words I have spoken to you are spirit and they are life" (John 6:63). We are told that "all Scripture is inspired by God and is useful to teach us what is true and to make us realize what is wrong in our lives" (2 Timothy 3:16 NLT). One must therefore ask of a particular church: Is the Bible accepted as the authoritative word of God? Is the Bible the instrument that the pastor uses to teach from? Are the church members being fed "real food" (John 6:55)?

One must also ask whether the *substance* of the apostles' teaching, the gospel, is practiced in a particular community, for this, too, is spiritual food. Christ reveals: " 'My food...is to do the will of him who sent me and to finish his work...And this is the will of him who sent me, that I shall lose none of all that he has given me, but raise them up at the last day. For my Father's will is that everyone who looks to the Son and believes in him shall have eternal life, and I will raise him up at the last day' " (John 4:34; 6:39-40). We should then ask of each church: In addition to honoring the Bible, is there a loving concern for those who do not know Christ, shown in ways that are not punitive or harsh, but gentle and caring, with opportunities for those who may not yet know Christ to learn about him in an accessible, non-judgmental way? Simply put—is the gospel preached, and its truth spoken in love (Ephesians 4:15)? For this is the substance of "devoting oneself to the apostles' teaching"—not just hearing the words, but being doers thereof (James 1:23). This is food for the soul, and promotes its growth.

Fellowship. "They...devoted themselves to...fellowship, sharing the Lord's Supper and...prayer" (Acts 2:42 NLT). The church is about a common love, a common life, a common longing—a *koinonia*, the New Testament Greek term for fellowship, which means *eating out of the same pot.* First John 3 (11,16-24) speaks of the love we have for one another in the body of Christ. First Corinthians 13 clarifies the expressions of that love. Fellowship is an essential part of Christian community. It implies relationships that encourage our walk with the Lord, and do not tempt us to sin or to be self-destructive. It includes the safety to share our heart and pain with trust, receiving forgiveness and comfort rather than shame or pity. It is having someone come alongside us not to fix us, but to pray with us. It is being around other believers who not only love and accept us, but also equip us to be the people God intended us to be. It implies accountability. "...where two or three come together in my name, there am I with them" (Matthew 18:20). In his power and grace, the church community becomes a place where burdens and gifts are shared, wise counsel is offered, and people grow into the character of Christ because they love one another with his love and sharpen one another with his truth.

Because the church is often called the "Body of Christ" then one can ask regarding it, *what is a healthy body?* The church is called the body many times throughout Scripture to help us understand the concept of purposeful, planned, harmonious, and integrated interaction with other Christians. "Love your neighbor as yourself" (Matthew 19:19).

There are many correlations between how we treat our own bodies, temples of the Holy Spirit (2 Corinthians 6:19), and how we treat others. When choosing a church, it is wise to reflect honestly on what we bring to it, and to evaluate what *we* contribute. How well do we care for the body, the church? Do we sustain it with our prayers and petitions, or criticize and tear it down? Do we have the pastor *for* lunch instead of *over to* lunch? Do we "make every effort to keep the unity of the Spirit through the bond of peace" (Ephesians 4:3)?

Fit. "They worshiped *together* at the Temple each day..." (Acts 2:46 NLT, emphasis added). Finding a good fit in a place of worship can be more challenging than one might think. Today, there is a wide variety of churches to choose from, and each has stylistic, structural, doctrinal, and historical differences. Stylistically, one might prefer hymns, contemporary music, or liturgical forms of worship. It may be better to find a church that is compatible with one's intuitive style, rather than trying to change a church's current style and stirring up unneeded conflict. It is important to learn about church structure: How are decisions made, collectively or by a leadership board? Where one disagrees with the leadership structure, it may be prudent to keep looking. Doctrinal issues have split many churches. All believers should learn what is essential for them in the Christian faith, and learn not to quibble over nonessentials. If everything is important, nothing is important. Pray for discernment in this regard so that you do not find yourself needlessly arguing over doctrine and thus compromising Christ's desire for churches to have unity (John 17:23). Finally, some may find that they are in a church for no other reason than history—this is where their family has been coming for generations. Yet, they may feel as if they are dying on the vine. Although family traditions and history matter, they must be weighed against the strong personal need to grow spiritually by finding a church in which one's style and beliefs fit well.

I liken "fit" to wearing an outfit that you just feel good in...it's comfortable. For some, it will be jeans and a sloppy shirt. For others, it's a suit and tie. Be comfortable in your own skin. There is a reason God designed you this way rather than some other way. If you are not comfortable where you are worshipping, the small things can become big things and create problems and conflict that only serve to distract from what God desires to do in that place and through those people.

It is sad, but true, that for some their experiences of church raise the question: Is the church a *life-giving* or a *life-taking* community? Some, whose church experiences may have been abusive, avoid reconnection with a church because of the pain they have suffered (see chapter in this book, Religious Abuse). However, even reasonably healthy churches have conflict. We must remember that churches consist of imperfect people, because the world consists of imperfect people. What matters is that the church ultimately deals with conflict in a healthy, thoughtful, biblical, and healing manner (e.g., Sande, 1997). The conflict in regard to the care of widows in Acts 7 demonstrates that even the early biblical church experienced conflict. It is noticeable that this conflict was not front and center in the life of the church. In short, when conflict occurs, it need not become the focal point of the church. A healthy church experiences conflict without losing its priorities or mission.

It is also important to recognize that the absence of conflict does not necessarily signal health in a church community. False unity, born of forced conformity, is often a feature of an abusive church rather than a healthy one.

Fruit. "They...devoted themselves to...prayer...shared their meals with great joy and generosity—all the while praising God and enjoying the goodwill of all the people. And each day the Lord added to their group those who were being saved" (Acts 2:42,46-47 NLT). A sign that you are in the right church is when your life evidences good fruit (John 15:1-8). This is less about *doing* and more about a state of the heart. The New Testament life cannot be lived in isolation, because it is completely relational to God and others. We find ourselves serving God in particular ways that are compatible with our unique gifts, talents, and personality. And it is in this giving that we receive. "It is more blessed to give than to receive" (Acts 20:35). Serving God and others for the sheer joy it brings may be a new concept to many, but this is the attitude described of the New Testament church. There is a new sense of connectedness and commitment that was not there before. A precursor to experiencing fruitfulness in the life of the believer is being committed to Jesus Christ and his teachings. There is new fruit in one's life: no longer a desire to sin but a desire to please God (1 John 3:21-24). This is evidence that the Holy Spirit lives in one's heart. In this, one grows spiritually, and the fruit of the Spirit—love, joy, peace, patience, kindness, goodness, faithfulness, gentleness, and self-control—becomes increasingly manifest in one's maturing Christian character (Galatians 5:22-23).

A healthy church also evidences good fruit in its corporate activity—prayer for and among the members, service for and together with other members, service to the community, spiritual growth and maturation of the members, and/or growth in the size of the church itself.

Conclusion

We often have expectations of our churches that are unrealistic. I once heard a pastor tell his congregation with tongue-in-cheek humor, "If you find the perfect church, don't join it, because you'll ruin it!" He made the point well: There are no perfect churches because there are no perfect people. Instead of perfection, we do well to seek a church where grace is not only taught, but lived, and to build up this church by offering God's grace liberally to the other members of this body to which we have been joined.

References

Gallup, G. (2000). *The Gallup Poll: Public Opinion 1999.* Wilmington, DE: Scholarly Resources.

Gartner, J., Larson, D. B., & Allen, G. D. (1991). Religious commitment and mental health: A review of the empirical literature. *Journal of Psychology and Theology, 19*, 6-25.

Gundersen, L. (2000). Faith and healing. *Annals of Internal Medicine, 132*, 169-72.

Hall, T.W., Tisdale, T.C., & Brokaw, B.F. (1994). Assessment of religious dimensions in Christian clients: A review of selected instruments for research and clinical use. *Journal of Psychology and Theology, 22*, 395-422.

Hill, P.C. & Hood, R.W. (Eds.). (1999). *Measures of religiosity.* Birmingham, AL: Religious Education Press.

Hodge, D.R. (2001). Spiritual assessment: A review of major qualitative methods and a new framework for assessing spirituality. *Social Work, 46*, 203-14.

Kosmin, B.A., & Lachman, S.P. (1993). *One nation under God: Religion in contemporary American society.* New York: Harmony Books.

Larson D.B., Swyers, J.P., & McCullough, M.E. (Eds). (1998). *Scientific research on spirituality and health: A consensus report.* Rockville, MD: National Institute for Healthcare Research.

Levin, J. S. (1994). Religion and health: Is there an association, is it valid, and is it causal? *Social Science and Medicine, 38*, 1475-82.

Richards, P.S., & Bergin, A.E. (1997). *A spiritual strategy for counseling and psychotherapy.* Washington, DC: American Psychological Association.

Sande, K. (1997). *The peacemaker.* Grand Rapids, MI: Baker Books.

Standard, R.P., Sandu, D.S., & Painter, L.C. (2000). Assessment of spirituality in counseling. *Journal of Counseling and Development, 78*, 204-10.

Wall, A.D., Cumella, E.J., & Darden, R.A. (2003). *Remuda Spiritual Assessment Questionnaire Version 1.0.* Wickenburg, AZ : Remuda Ranch Center for Anorexia and Bulimia, Inc.

Worthington, E. L., Kurusu, T. A., McCullough, M. E., & Sandage, S. J. (1996). Empirical research on religion and psychotherapeutic processes and outcomes: A 10-year review and research prospectus. *Psychological Bulletin, 119*, 448-87.

Note: We thank J. Mark Martin for the initial conceptualization of the 4 Fs.

Chapter 19

Religious Abuse

Edward J. Cumella, PhD, CEDS

> *Woe to the shepherds of Israel... You have not strengthened the weak or healed the sick or bound up the injured... You have ruled them harshly and brutally.* (Ezekiel 34:1-5)

Religious abuse is as old as humankind. It first appeared in the Garden of Eden when Satan twisted God's words and persuaded Adam and Eve to listen to him rather than God. This primeval event epitomizes all religious abuse.

Religious abuse occurs across denominations, in nondenominational churches, and across faiths—Christianity, Judaism, Islam, Buddhism, et al. It normally does not arise from the beliefs of any particular religion, but from the personality pathology of individual religious leaders. Those with certain Axis II features—particularly narcissistic, antisocial, obsessive-compulsive, borderline, paranoid, and histrionic—are at greatest risk of becoming religiously abusive toward those whom they lead. For more details on these personality disorders, see Millon et al. (2004). Leaders with these personality issues have serious emotional, relationship, and cognitive difficulties that engender a distorted understanding of the Bible, theology, and church relationships. The distortions can sometimes be so significant that church members are seriously harmed.

Christians believe that human beings literally have a *spirit*—an aspect of our being that connects us to God. Religious abuse interferes with this connection. Religious abuse includes a range of actions by pastors, counselors, and other people that harm our relationship with God and/or separate us from him. Because human identity arises from knowing who we are in relation to God, religious abuse also harms our self-concept and sense of personal value. In addition, religious abuse often includes both mental and emotional abuse. In the most severe instances, it involves physical and sexual abuse rationalized by the abuser as God's will through distorted interpretations of Scripture or sacred texts.

For those who may not believe in the existence of a literal human spirit, religious abuse can be readily conceptualized in terms of the clear emotional and mental abuse which it inevitably entails, as well as any physical or sexual abuse present in the most extreme instances.

Victims of religious abuse can suffer profound, negative consequences. As such, religious abuse can be a legitimate focus of care for counselors or pastors. It is important to note that religious abuse often includes acts—such as the mental, emotional, physical, and sexual abuse, or even neglect, of children—that professionals are legally bound to report to state child protection agencies. Where religious abusers are themselves licensed or certified counselors or pastors, professionals should also report the abuser's actions to licensing boards or church and denominational oversight authorities.

For various reasons, religious abuse is usually more serious in churches than counseling settings. Pastors, ministers, priests, and other church leaders are typically regarded with high degrees of respect, even reverence, and may wield substantial authority in believers' lives. Church leaders offer authoritative teachings covering issues critical to daily life—e.g., marriage, sexuality, relationships, finances, childrearing. Churches are also communities in which membership offers an experience of belonging, fellowship, and support. Along with these benefits comes social pressure. If abuse takes places in this context, many aspects of a person's life can be negatively impacted. As such, this chapter primarily considers religious abuse in a church context.

The Bible teaches us about religious abuse. Perhaps the most important passages appear in Matthew 23 and Luke 11, where Jesus issues a series of "woes" to the Pharisees—religious leaders of his time. In many ways, the Pharisees are paragons of the religiously abusive leader. Their behavior evidences Axis II features.

Religious abuse is best understood as a continuum. Some churches may be virtually free of religious abuse; others may be occasionally and mildly abusive; still others may abuse their members frequently and with great intensity. The subjective experience of religious abuse is also related to the mental and emotional functioning of each individual. Certain individuals—e.g., those with perfectionistic traits or prone to obsessions and compulsions, fear, and/or low self-esteem—are apt to interpret teachings legalistically or as condemnation. Others in the same church and hearing the same teachings might not experience trauma.

When we search the Bible, we find that religious abuse includes one or more of the following 13 features.

Authoritarianism

A subtle shift occurs in the messages of abusive leaders. Instead of urging believers to obey God, these leaders are so convinced that they are exercising God's authority that they expect believers to obey *them*. Likewise, abusive leaders also fully expect that church leadership bodies and other associate ministers/pastors/deacons will fully support the leaders' intentions instead of offering input and accountability. Accordingly, a Bible verse frequently repeated by religiously abusive leaders is Hebrews 13:17, "Obey your leaders and submit to their authority." Leaders with narcissistic, antisocial, obsessive-compulsive, and paranoid personality traits are most likely to engage in this form of religious abuse. Christ's words make plain that authoritarianism has little place in his church: "But you are not to be called 'Rabbi,' for you have only one Master and you are all brothers. And do not call anyone on earth 'father,' for you have one Father, and he is in heaven. Nor are you to be called 'teacher,' for you have one Teacher, the Christ. The greatest among you will be your servant. For whoever exalts himself will be humbled, and whoever humbles himself will be exalted" (Matthew 23:8-12).

Coercion

Instead of honoring the personal freedom and conscience of believers, as God does, with teachings that convince the mind because of their biblical accuracy and logic, abusive leaders will use any tactic at their disposal to coerce believers into disregarding their better judgment and meeting the leaders' demands. Leaders with antisocial, narcissistic, and obsessive-compulsive personality traits are most likely to engage in this form of religious abuse. God's Word makes plain that coercion has little place in the church: "But the goal of our instruction is love from a pure heart and a good conscience and a sincere faith. For some men, straying from these things, have turned aside to fruitless discussion, wanting to be teachers of the Law, even though they do not understand either what they are saying or the matters about which they make confident assertions" (1 Timothy 1:5-7 NASB).

Intimidation

Instead of offering Christ, whose yoke is easy and whose burden is light, and emphasizing the covenant of forgiveness, abusive leaders routinely threaten punishment, disfellowshipping, and excommunication, and raise the specter of eternal condemnation in an effort to force believers into submission and continued church membership. Leaders with narcissistic, antisocial, and paranoid personality traits are most likely to engage in this form of religious abuse. Christ's words make plain that intimidation has little place in his church: "Woe to the shepherds of Israel...You have ruled them harshly and brutally" (Ezekiel 34:1,5).

Terrorism

Instead of inviting people to follow Christ with the gospel of love, abusive leaders terrorize believers by manipulating their fears, shame, and guilt. They overemphasize that believers' problems have arisen because of believers' sins, without offering believers a corresponding message of redemption and deliverance through Christ. Leaders with narcissistic, antisocial, borderline, paranoid, histrionic, and obsessive-compulsive personality traits are most likely to engage in this form of religious abuse. Christ's words make plain that terrorism has little place in his church: "Woe to the shepherds of Israel...You have not strengthened the weak or healed the sick or bound up the injured. You have not brought back the strays or searched for the lost..." (Ezekiel 34:1,4).

Condemnation

Instead of heeding Christ's admonition, "judge not lest ye be judged," abusive leaders make a point of condemning those who leave their church, outsiders, and whomever else they define as sinners. Such leaders teach that believers will join the ranks of the condemned if they deviate from the leaders' teachings or leave the leaders' church or denomination. Individual church members are scapegoated when problems arise in the church. Leaders with narcissistic, antisocial, borderline, paranoid, histrionic, and obsessive-compulsive personality traits are most likely to engage in this form of religious abuse. Christ's words make plain that condemnation has little place in his church: "Do not judge, or you too will be judged. For in the same way you judge others, you will be judged, and with the measure you use, it will be measured to you. Why do you look at the speck of sawdust in your brother's eye and pay no attention to the plank in your own eye?" (Matthew 7:1-3).

Classism

Christ was no respecter of persons. Nevertheless, abusive leaders are preoccupied with power, promoting church hierarchy, referring to and treating people according to their titles and roles. Those lower on the hierarchy are taught that their needs are less important. Leaders with narcissistic, antisocial, and obsessive-compulsive personality traits are most likely to engage in this form of religious abuse. Christ's words make plain that classism has little place in his church: "Woe to you Pharisees, because you love the most important seats in the synagogues and greetings in the marketplaces" (Luke 11:43).

"Everything they do is done for men to see: They make their phylacteries wide and the tassels on their garments long; they love the place of honor at banquets and the most important seats in the synagogues; they love to be greeted in the marketplaces and to have men call them 'Rabbi' " (Matthew 23:5-7).

Conformity

Abusive leaders usually exert the greatest influence over inexperienced, naïve, and dependent individuals who are seeking a strong leader. These individuals suppress their objections to the leader's teachings for fear of being shamed or rejected by the leader or ostracized by the church community. Because of this self-censorship, abusive churches may appear unified. Yet there is often much discontent, anguish, whispering, and secrets hidden beneath the veneer of unity, with many members wanting to leave. Leaders with narcissistic, antisocial, paranoid, and obsessive-compulsive personality traits are most likely to engage in this form of religious abuse. Although true unity in the spirit is Christ's will for his church—"May they be brought to complete unity" (John 17:23)—disagreements do occur. Scripture indicates that pastors must be confronted when their teachings deviate from sound biblical doctrine: "When Peter came to Antioch, I [Paul] opposed him to his face, because he was clearly in the wrong" (Galatians 2:11-12).

Manipulation

Instead of interpreting the Bible with the Bible, according to long-held Christian beliefs, and in context, abusive leaders manipulate Scriptures so that they appear to endorse the leaders' personal opinions. Leaders with narcissistic, antisocial, borderline, and paranoid personality traits are most likely to engage in this form of religious abuse. God's word makes plain that manipulation of Scripture has little place in the church: "Woe to you experts in the law, because you have taken away the key to knowledge. You yourselves have not entered, and you have hindered those who were entering..." (Luke 11:52). "...ignorant and unstable people distort...Scriptures, to their own destruction" (2 Peter 3:16).

Irrationality

Because abusive leaders twist the Scriptures, their various interpretations of Scripture may contradict one another. Interpretations may even contradict reason and reality. To remain in such churches, members must suspend critical thinking. Some abusive leaders claim to receive messages directly from God about their church or individual members. These messages usually diverge from Scripture and reality. Some engage in a self-proclaimed "healing ministry," where church members are pressured into dramatic confessions of sin and professions of deliverance that are highly exaggerated and have little lasting effect in believers' lives. Leaders with narcissistic, antisocial, borderline, paranoid, and histrionic personality traits are most likely to engage in this form of religious abuse. God's word makes plain that irrationality has little place in the church: "For God is not the author of confusion, but of peace, as in all churches of the saints" (1 Corinthians 14:33 KJV).

Legalism

Abusive leaders do not extend much grace. Instead, they communicate that one's value and the amount of love one should receive depend on performance and position in the church. As such, abusive leaders expect church members to make extreme sacrifices of money, time, and energy for the church. Leaders with antisocial, borderline, paranoid, and obsessive-compulsive personality traits are most likely to engage in this form of religious abuse. Christ's words make plain that legalism has little place in his church: "Woe to you Pharisees, because you give God a tenth of your mint, rue and all other kinds of garden herbs, but you neglect justice and the love of God. You should have practiced the latter without leaving the former undone" (Luke 11:42).

Isolation

Instead of honoring family bonds, community obligations, and the importance of friendship, abusive leaders teach that these relationships will negatively influence the believer. Abusive leaders therefore encourage believers to minimize contact with family, friends, and the outside world. Such leaders also routinely excoriate the outside world as a place of egregious sin and temptation, lacking in anything positive and redeeming. Encouraging believers' isolation enables the abusive leader to consolidate his power over his flock, removing possible challenges to his authority. Leaders with narcissistic, antisocial, and paranoid personality traits are most likely to engage in this form of religious abuse. God's Word makes plain that, for most believers, isolation from family and the world is not part of God's plan: "If anyone does not provide for his relatives, and especially for his immediate family, he has denied the faith and is worse than an unbeliever" (1 Timothy 5:8). "Honor your father and mother…" (Ephesians 6:2).

Elitism

Instead of practicing and teaching humility, abusive leaders are filled with false pride and teach believers to feel the same emotion. In such churches, the following belief ensues: "We're the chosen ones! Everyone else is condemned!" This belief partially compensates for the shame and worthlessness that believers feel due to other experiences in the abusive church. In line with this elitism, abusive leaders insist that believers protect the church's image at all costs. Hence, an atmosphere arises of secrecy and denial of error and sin in the church. Leaders with narcissistic, antisocial, and obsessive-compulsive personality traits are most likely to engage in this form of religious abuse. Christ's words make plain that elitism has little place in his church: "Woe to you, teachers of the law and Pharisees, you hypocrites! You are like whitewashed tombs, which look beautiful on the outside but on the inside are full of dead men's bones and everything unclean. In the same way, on the outside you appear to people as righteous but on the inside you are full of hypocrisy and wickedness" (Matthew 23:27-28).

Ensnarement

Instead of guiding their flock to Christian maturity, the methods of abusive leaders promote self-doubt, guilt, and identity confusion. Members are confused by the contradictions between what their conscience and reason tell them and what the leader is teaching them. This ambivalence, joined with fear of condemnation and loss of direction and fellowship, make it difficult and painful for believers to leave abusive churches. Abusive leaders may work deliberately to create this interior conflict in church members, because the interior conflict weakens members' clarity and resolve and thereby strengthens the leaders' grip on them. Leaders with narcissistic, antisocial, borderline, paranoid, and obsessive-compulsive personality traits are most likely to engage in this form of religious abuse. God's Word makes plain that ensnarement and entrapment have little place in the church: "The wind blows wherever it pleases. You hear its sound, but you cannot tell where it comes from or where it is going. So it is with everyone born of the Spirit" (John 3:8). "It is for freedom that Christ has set us free" (Galatians 5:1).

It is easy to remember and conceptualize religious abuse if one considers that religious abuse, at its most extreme, resembles a cult. A religiously abusive church, like a cult, has departed substantially from accurate biblical teaching and become dependent on the authoritarian rule of a single leader. It has become a house of idolatry where God is no longer worshipped because he has been displaced by the leader and the leader's errant teachings. "Who cut in on you and kept you from obeying the truth? That kind of persuasion does not come from the one who calls you. A little yeast works through the whole batch of dough...Be on your guard against the yeast of the Pharisees..." (Galatians 5:7-10, Matthew 16:6).

Although the features of religious abuse may occur in a counseling setting, in such settings religious abuse is typically less severe when compared to church settings. There are several constraints on religious abuse in the counseling domain. First, because of their psychotherapeutic training, counselors tend to be client-centered, to prioritize listening over speaking, and take pains to respect clients' personal beliefs and choices. Counselors are therefore less apt to demand that clients accept only the counselors' perceptions and beliefs. Second, counselors do not generally command the same degree of authority as church leaders, because counseling is not usually seen as conveying the authority of God. Third, counseling relationships are short-term and readily terminated, while church membership may be seen as a lifetime or family-wide commitment. Finally, termination of counseling does not entail separation from family and friends, but leaving a church may indeed have this implication.

Assessing Religious Abuse

Religious abuse must be assessed carefully. When clients themselves define their religious experiences as abusive, counselor intervention can follow. However, when clients fail to recognize the potential religious abuse in their backgrounds, counselors must proceed with caution:

- Counselors are bound ethically to respect adult clients' religious preferences. Defining a client's religious background as abusive when the client does not agree risks undue interference with the client's rights to free religious choice. Because different people experience similar events differently, seemingly abusive religious experiences may not be traumatic for everyone who has lived through them. Nevertheless, counselor authenticity, integrity, and responsibility compel an exploration with clients of the possibility that they have been subject to religious abuse. It is useful to coach clients in identifying and describing their potentially abusive experiences so that they can draw their own informed conclusions.
- It is best to rely on an objective definition of religious abuse. Most healthcare professionals agree that religious abuse has definitively occurred when the experience has led to *serious* and *diagnosable* behavioral, cognitive, emotional, or mental disorders. Unless this criterion is met, it would be imprudent to use the word "abuse" to describe a client's religious background.
- When a reasonable suspicion exists that a minor has been or is currently subject to religious abuse according to the definition above, healthcare providers and pastors must report this abuse to the

appropriate state child protective agency as a form of emotional/mental abuse.

Because of the implications when religious abuse has been documented, it can be helpful to rely on objective assessment tools. Remuda has developed a psychometrically valid and reliable questionnaire that can be employed in this assessment: the Remuda Spiritual Assessment Questionnaire. This questionnaire includes a factor score that measures religiously abusive experiences. It is short, easy to use, with either paper-and-pencil or computerized administration. Remuda offers this instrument free of charge to healthcare professionals (www.remudaranch.com).

Common problems to assess for in individuals who have lived through religious abuse include:

- Feelings of worthlessness instead of a sense of personal dignity and self-respect
- Need for control instead of healthy surrender and trust in God
- Shame instead of self-acceptance
- Excessive and unremitting guilt instead of forgiveness
- Hopelessness instead of optimism
- Fear of punishment instead of assurance of God's love
- Rigid morality and legalism instead of grace and unconditional love
- Fear of intimacy instead of belonging and authenticity
- Addictions instead of adaptive coping
- Expectations of betrayal and mistrust instead of trusted relationships
- Poor boundaries instead of healthy boundaries
- Spiritual confusion instead of clarity about the gospel and God's love
- Possible distance or separation from family instead of family support
- Loss over wasted years instead of meaning and purpose

It is not possible in this short chapter to lay out detailed instructions for treating survivors of religious abuse. Useful information and resources regarding treatment can be found in a companion chapter in this book and in the materials listed under Resources below.

Resources

Churches that Abuse by Ronald M. Enroth

Damaged Disciples by Ron & Vicki Burks

Faith That Hurts/Faith That Heals by Stephen Arterburn & Jack Felton

Healing Spiritual Abuse by Ken Blue

Healing the Shame that Binds You by John Bradshaw

Recovering from Churches that Abuse by Ronald M. Enroth

Searching for a God to Love by Chris Blake

Stealing Jesus by Bruce Bawer

Subtle Power of Spiritual Abuse by David Johnson & Jeff VanVonderen

Tired of Trying to Measure Up by Jeff VanVonderen

Toxic Faith by Steve Arterburn

Twisted Scriptures by Mary A. Chrnalogar, Paul M. Howey, & Stephen D. Martin

Understanding Difficult Scriptures in a Healing Way by Dennis Linn, Sheila Fabricant Linn, & Matthew Linn

References

1996. *The Holy Bible (King James Version).* New York: Alfred A. Knopf.

1977. *The Holy Bible (New American Standard).* Anaheim, CA: Lockman Foundation.

Millon, T., Millon, C.M., Meagher, S., Grossman, S., & Ramnath, R. (2004). *Personality disorders in modern life* (2nd Ed.). Hoboken, NJ: John Wiley & Sons.

Part VI

Eating Disorders in Context: Frequent Co-Occuring Issues

Chapter 20

Athletes and Eating Disorders

Kenneth Littlefield, PsyD, Juliet Zuercher, RD, Rachel Daberkow, MS, RD, Jennifer Hazel, MA, LPC, and Brenda K. Woods, MD, FAAFP

Athletes constitute a significant subgroup of women with eating disorders (ED). Recent research with 1022 ED inpatients found 53% were athletes (Day, 2003). Yet educators, coaches, families, and treatment professionals sometimes overlook ED evidence in athletes. Due to a relative lack of available information, they may not fully grasp the unique challenges that ED athletes face.

Awareness of ED's signs and symptoms and the female or elite athlete triad is crucial for athletes, parents, and coaches to identify ED problems. As with all EDs, early identification predicts good outcome. The female athlete triad consists of disordered eating, amenorrhea, and osteopenia or osteoporosis. Depending on symptoms and severity, it is diagnosed as anorexia, bulimia, or eating disorder not otherwise specified. It especially affects those in sports where low body weight may be beneficial, such as long-distance running.

The Physiologic Screening Test, available online, is a brief screening tool that may be used by healthcare and athletic professionals as an early detection tool for disordered eating among female athletes (Black, Larkin, Coster, Leverenz, & Abood, 2003). Athletes in higher risk categories, such as White female athletes (Johnson et al., 2004) and those involved in certain judged sports, should be carefully monitored. Research suggests that initiatives such as ATHENA—Athletes Targeting Healthy Exercise and Nutrition Alternatives—may reduce athletes' use of diet pills and performance-enhancing substances and increase healthy exercise, proper eating, and self-efficacy (Elliot et al., 2004). It is therefore important to ask whether a particular athlete is participating in such initiatives, to promote their use, and to closely monitor athletes who are not participating.

Current treatment approaches do not automatically recommend abstinence from exercise and sport competition for ED athletes. Abstinence may be counterproductive *(Beals, 2004, p. 133)*. Hence, athletes' appropriate return to sport must be addressed. In addition, although there are some compulsive exercisers for whom physical activity quickly becomes exercise abuse, this is not the case for many ED patients. Making these distinctions, however, is often difficult for treatment providers. The problem is compounded for a patient whose identity, self-esteem, and motivation for recovery arise from her role as an athlete (Heyman & Andersen, 1998).

The large population of athletes in Remuda's inpatient milieu necessitated a systematic, objective method for making recommendations about: 1) the appropriateness of athletes' involvement in training/competition during ED recovery, and 2) their long-term athletic participation. To develop our methodology, we combined research, clinical experience, and common sense. We have thus established a process for determining the risk factors involved in athletics and individuals' readiness for return to sport and exercise.

Research on Eating Disorder Athletes

A review of the research regarding ED athletes reveals the need for a comprehensive, multidisciplinary assessment of many factors to predict the most likely effects of athletic involvement on each individual. Treatment professionals, athletic departments, and families do well to collaborate together and with the athlete to improve comprehensive evaluation and formulate congruent goals.

Influential in the decision to return to athletics is the kind of sport in which a patient is engaged. EDs are not equally distributed among sports. In some sports, ED behaviors are pervasive. Zucker, Womble, Williamson, and Perrin (1999) demonstrated that judged sports like gymnastics, figure skating, diving, and dance have an ED prevalence rate of 13%. In contrast, ED prevalence in refereed sports is only 3%, comparable to a nonathlete population. Furthermore, participants in judged sports score significantly higher on measures of overconcern with weight and size. Such overconcern is the most significant psychosocial characteristic associated with ED among female athletes (Williamson et al., 1995). Judged sports may produce ED risks because they allow physical appearance to influence performance evaluation, whereas refereed sports do not (Best, 1988).

Powers (1999) indicated that judged sports are not the only athletic endeavor to increase females' risk for ED. Endurance sports, sports with weight categories, individual sports, female sports with revealing clothing, and lean sports all are risky. Lean sports are described as those that prefer or give an advantage to participants who lack adequate body fat. Petrie (1996) defined lean sports as those "where appearance or weight are important for success, such as gymnastics," and non-lean sports as those "where weight is noncentral, such as basketball." Lean sport athletes may be more likely to engage in pathological weight control behavior, particularly excessive exercise and strict dieting, to achieve their desired weight or appearance (Petrie, 1996). Accordingly, men involved in sports that focus on weight and appearance, such as wrestling and body building, face ED risk (Choi, Pope, & Olivardia, 2002; Pope, Gruber, Choi, Olivardia, & Phillips, 1997; Williamson et al., 1995).

No discussion of athletics' influence on ED development would be complete without mention of perfectionism. Sport participation can engender an obligatory, perfectionistic attitude towards exercise and training. Perfectionism increases the likelihood of ED behaviors and attitudes, such as strict dieting and negative evaluation of one's weight and body (Seigel & Hetta, 2001). Female athletes who are more perfectionistic show significant increases in ED behaviors, especially in dietary restraint (Hopkinson & Lock, 2004).

It is critical to note that certain female sports may also be protective against ED. Although the research contains some contradictory results, non-lean sport athletes report higher self-esteem, greater perception of control over external events, and fewer feelings of worthlessness, insecurity, emptiness, and inadequacy (Petrie, 1996). Overall, female athletes have less body dissatisfaction than nonathlete counterparts (Davis & Cowles, 1989). Thus, women in certain sports evidence greater self-esteem and less body dissatisfaction—key factors that protect against ED development.

It is theorized that social influence, performance anxiety, and self-appraisal each contributes to body dissatisfaction (Williamson et al., 1995). If these factors can be influenced in a positive direction, then athletes may have further insulation against EDs. One of the best influences in all three areas is an athlete's coach or athletic department. Accordingly, Biesecker and Martz (1999) view coaching style as a significant factor in preventing athletes from developing EDs. They suggest a "person-oriented" coaching approach and discourage a "performance-oriented" approach. Their research indicates that coaching styles emphasizing the value of the individual over the outcome of their performance result in less body dissatisfaction and fear of fat.

The concept of person-oriented coaching can be extrapolated to parenting. Parents who are involved in their children's athletics often function as primary or secondary coaches. Parents may have a deeper influence on motivation for competition and desire to perform than coaches do. Athletes are constantly subject to parents' expectations and criticisms, and these influences may endure for a lifetime.

Treatment professionals should therefore consider the following questions to help determine a particular coach's or parent's style. Does the coach or parent focus more on the athlete's well-being or performance? The level of competition may dictate the extent of performance focus to some degree, but not completely. What costs to the athlete are communicated as acceptable sacrifices for the sake of athletic achievement?

Our personal experiences in both athletics and ED treatment reinforce our support of person-oriented coaching. We have seen the attitudes of wrestling, track, and cross-country coaches exert positive influences in the nutritional and training practices of athletes at risk for ED behavior. We have also seen the opposite and witnessed damaging effects. We thus believe that educating coaches and athletic departments and enlisting their participation in preventing and treating EDs are essential to the athletic community's long-term health and its influence on popular culture.

Several studies have shown that athletes are a distinct subgroup of ED sufferers. They have unique presentations, strengths, and challenges (Day, 2003; Johnson, Powers, & Dick, 1999; Petrie, 1996), with both advantages and disadvantages in treatment and prognosis (Sundgot-Borgen, Skarderud, & Rodgers, 2003). Athletes may expect more positive outcomes in treatment, possibly because they are used to conforming to the expectations of coaching and training programs. In general, athletes have less Axis II pathology than nonathletes. Disadvantages for some athletes may include limited psychological-mindedness, limited social experiences from spending much time within a narrow athlete subculture, and parents who focus primarily on their child's competitive success rather than balance or health.

Yet most of what we know about general ED etiology, personality, treatment, and prognosis is applicable to athletes. For females, the need to perfect their bodies to fit America's lean cultural ideal trumps all other factors, including the influence of sport participation (Hopkinson & Lock, 2004). Hence, we are best informed about ED athletes by utilizing available research on ED individuals in general. We may then refine our understanding of ED athletes by applying findings specific to this group.

Remuda's Sports Return Assessment

It is imperative to assess the appropriateness of athletic participation given mounting evidence that permanent physiological damage is possible if EDs go untreated among athletes (Devlin, Jahraus, & Dobrow, 2004). We therefore combined research results, clinical experience, and common sense to develop Remuda's Sports Return Assessment for Athletes with EDs. In a word, the most expedient path of return to competition is not the goal of intervention with the ED athlete. Instead, the guiding principles in making recommendations for athletes' sport participation are to: 1) minimize factors that increase risk of ED relapse or jeopardize current or future health, and 2) maximize the individual's opportunity for full recovery both physically and psychologically.

Remuda's Sports Return Assessment includes a hierarchical list of six factors to consider in triaging acuity and making determinations for athletic participation. Using Remuda's Sports Return Assessment, a multidisciplinary treatment team may determine under what circumstances or terms involvement in sport and training are permissible or even encouraged. Remuda's Sports Return Assessment includes:

1. medical status
2. nutritional status
3. eating disorder behaviors
4. prognosis
5. environment
6. internal milieu

The first three are objective factors, such that these criteria can be objectively measured or observed. They are non-negotiable and consistent for all athletes. If specific criteria in each of these three areas are not met, it is generally considered unsafe or inappropriate for the individual to participate in athletics.

The second three are subjective factors. Without psychological testing, these are more difficult to measure or observe. Thresholds may also vary from one individual to another, depending on unique needs and circumstances. None of these factors alone is generally enough to decide for or against continued sport participation. They may be viewed cumulatively as trends that tip the balance from total participation toward respite or even retirement, or vice versa.

Remuda uses its Sports Return Assessment to develop an individualized, written Terms of Participation Contract that serves as a forum for collaboration between athletes and their treatment team, coach, athletic department, and, when appropriate, family. It is a tool for communicating expectations for sport participation to the athlete. Specifics include medical, nutritional, therapeutic, and behavioral criteria necessary for continued competition or training. Listing specific logical consequences is encouraged. Athletes may view the Terms of Participation Contract as less punitive, more objective, cooperative, and binding because it is a collaborative process that is written and signed by all parties involved.

We detail below each element of the Sports Return Assessment and how it culminates in an individualized Terms of Participation Contract for a specific ED athlete.

Medical Status

Remuda's Sports Return Assessment begins with a fundamental question about the ED athlete patient: *Is the patient medically stable?*

Obviously, assessing current medical status is critical. This is best done by medical providers experienced with ED (Thompson & Sherman, 1993). Physical exertion may exacerbate ED's medical complications, including orthostatic pulse and blood pressure, dehydration, bradycardia, metabolic acidosis or alkalosis, electrolyte imbalance, and seizure. Chronic complications, such as cardiomyopathy, osteoporosis, and stress fractures may indicate that demanding athletic participation may need to be discontinued permanently (Devlin et al., 2004; Mehler & Andersen, 1999).

Depending on the individual athlete's situation, different indices measure medical stability. These include but are not limited to: lab values (e.g., liver enzymes, cardiac enzymes, electrolytes, bone morphogenetic protein), electrocardiogram, bone mass as evidenced by dual energy x-ray absorptiometry (DEXA), injury-free status, disease state (e.g., diabetes, in or out of control), and hydration status. A primary care provider should make the determination about which indices need to be within normal limits to support the athlete's participation in sport.

If "yes" is the answer to the fundamental question of medical stability when each of the necessary factors is considered for a particular athlete, then participation in sport can be cleared medically without Terms of Participation in the medical status domain. Providers would then proceed to assess the remaining five factors. If "no" is the answer, then the individual patient requires Terms of Participation in the medical status domain. Terms of Participation is a behavioral contract delineating medical issues that need to be measured and addressed. Terms of Participation specifies how they will be measured, how often, and what results are needed. It also points out what behaviors or medical treatments are necessary to correct any insufficiency.

For example, if lab results—such as high bicarbonate and highly elevated amylase—indicate suspicion of continued self-induced vomiting (SIV), the Terms of Participation might read as follows:

- I agree to have labs drawn 2 times/week for 2 months.
- I recognize that I will not be medically cleared for athletic participation or training until my labs are within normal limits for 2 consecutive weeks.
- If at any time my lab draw is abnormal I may be medically unable to train again until my labs are within normal limits for 2 consecutive weeks.

Nutritional Status

Remuda's Sports Return Assessment continues with a second fundamental question: *Is the patient nutritionally stable?*

Individuals who cannot comply with nutritional recommendations or are significantly underweight should not participate in training/competition until these issues resolve. Assessment parameters include but are not limited to:

- Maintenance of weight within Ideal Body Weight (IBW) range
- No physical evidence of malnutrition (e.g., no pattern of cracked lips, dry skin, hair loss, etc.)
- Adequate body composition (percent body fat and muscle mass)

If "yes" is the answer to the overarching question of nutritional stability when each necessary factor is considered, then participation in sport is cleared nutritionally without Terms of Participation in the nutritional status domain. Providers would then proceed to assess the remaining four factors. If "no" is the answer, then the individual patient requires Terms of Participation in the nutritional status domain. Examples of entries in the Terms of Participation read as follows:

- I will increase caloric intake by 300 kcals per day and reduce intensity of cardiovascular training by one hour per day until weight is restored to (specify weight).
- I will maintain my weight within my Ideal Body Weight (IBW) range consistently.
- I will not participate in athletic conditioning or competition until I have maintained my IBW for two consecutive weeks.
- I will meet with a Registered Dietitian two times per week for meal plan accountability until weight remains within my IBW range for three consecutive weeks during athletic participation.

Eating Disorder Behaviors

Remuda's Sports Return Assessment continues with a third fundamental question: *Is the patient abstaining from ED behaviors?*

Athletes currently engaging in significant ED behavior are rarely appropriate for full sport participation. Evidence of ED behaviors will be specific to the individual. It may include but is not limited to the following:

- Symptoms of self-induced vomiting (SIV):
  - Petechiae (burst capillaries in the facial region, especially the eyes)
  - Chelosis (corners of the mouth cracking)
  - Unusual callusing on the knuckles or fingers
- Rapid weight loss/gain (+/-10 lbs. in one month)
- Isolation (secretive binge eating)
- Bizarre food rituals or restricting food
- Physical exam revealing enlarged parotid or submandibular glands

If "yes" is the answer to the question of abstention from ED behaviors when all relevant factors for an individual patient have been considered, then the individual patient can be cleared for participation in sport without Terms of Participation in the ED behaviors domain. Providers would then proceed to assess the remaining three factors. If "no" is the answer, then the individual patient requires Terms of Participation in the ED behaviors domain. The Terms of Participation may read as such:

- I will eat with an accountability partner (teammate, therapist, coach/trainer, etc.) for every meal and snack and stay with this person one hour after each time I eat.
- I will surrender all laxative and diuretic products and commit in writing to abstain from use of these products for weight manipulation.
- My exercise will be restricted to workouts approved by coaches and medical staff.
- Any ED behaviors may be considered a breach of this contract, but not necessarily lead to limited participation. I understand that I need to demonstrate a trend of abstinence, but no one expects me to be perfect.

Prognosis

Remuda's Sports Return Assessment continues with a fourth fundamental question: *Is the patient's prognosis good?*

This question is answered by considering two sets of issues.

Research Indications. Research offers some guidance concerning prognosis and risk factors that need to be taken into consideration when making recommendations about athletic participation.

The American Psychiatric Association Practice Guideline for the Treatment of Patients with Eating Disorders (Yager et al., 2006) indicates that persons who develop symptoms at a younger age have a better prognosis for recovery. Patients with ED symptoms of longer duration have poorer prognosis. White female athletes are more likely to engage in ED behaviors than male or black female athletes (Johnson et al., 1999; Johnson et al., 2004). The type of sport and the level of competition can also have a significant positive or negative impact on risk factors for relapse (Best, 1988; Fulkerson, Keel, Leon, & Dorr, 1999; Williamson et al., 1995; Zucker, 1999); see above.

There are several risk factors for initial ED development that may predispose patients to ED relapse as well. These include but are not limited to childhood anxiety disorders (Bulik, Sullivan, Fear, & Joyce, 1997), childhood obsessive-compulsive personality traits, perfectionism (Anderluh, Tchanturia, Rabe-Hesketh, & Treasure, 2003), and a family history of ED (Agras, Hammer, & McNicholas, 1999; Russell, Treasure, & Eisler, 1998; Scourfield, 1995; Stein, Woolley, Cooper, & Fairburn, 1994; Ward et al., 2001). Low self-esteem, anxiety, social pressure, and poor body image appear to be the most prevalent risk factors in collegiate athletes (Berry & Howe, 2000).

These research indications can be considered in relation to an athlete's sport participation. We recommend an increasingly conservative approach to athletic participation as risk factors mount.

Testing. Several measures can be utilized in combination to provide prognostic data. It is important to emphasize that none of these measures should be used alone to make decisions about athletic participation. The same test results in two individuals may also be interpreted differently depending on other factors specific to the individual.

A comprehensive literature review suggests that the Minnesota Multiphasic Personality Inventory-2 (MMPI-2) predicts outcome for ED patients (Cumella, in press). Higher elevations on scales 1 and 2 at admission consistently predict poorer outcomes, while admission elevations on scales K and 9 predict better outcomes.

Day (2003) found two distinct EDI-2 clusters, one significantly more pathologic across EDI-2 subscales. For ED athletes whose EDI-2 scale scores place mostly above the top of the ED range using college female norms, sport recommendations should be more conservative. For those whose

EDI-2 scale scores place mostly at or below the bottom of the ED range using college female norms, return to sport would be more likely.

If "yes" is the answer to the overarching question about good prognosis, then the prospect of continued athletic involvement is more likely and no specific Terms of Participation are required in this domain. Providers would then proceed to assess the remaining two factors. If "no" is the answer based on any particular concern, then Terms of Participation can be developed to bring awareness of potential weaknesses, avoid pitfalls, and bolster other areas that may improve prognosis. Terms of Participation may read as such:

- Admission MMPI-2 elevated on scale 1: I will continue to work with my outpatient treatment team to accurately identify, label, and discuss emotions, learning to express myself assertively rather than through physical symptoms.
- History of perfectionism: I will continue to challenge my automatic, rigid, perfectionistic thoughts and replace them with healthier cognitions.

Environment

Remuda's Sports Return Assessment continues with a fifth question: *Does the athlete's environment support recovery?*

A range of environmental factors may support or hinder ED recovery. Examples follow:

- Athletic involvement
  - Support: A basketball team that offers positive support and provides a sense of belonging
  - Hindrance: A gymnastics team that is focused on body image and centers on competition between individual team members
- Living situation
  - Support: Living with teammates who have healthy attitudes toward food and exercise
  - Hindrance: Living in a dorm with ED roommates or hallmates
- Coaching/training staff
  - Support: Person-centered approach
  - Hindrance: Performance-centered approach
- School scholarship
  - Support: Provides the athlete with sense of relief from financial responsibilities
  - Hindrance: Pressures the athlete with difficult conditions

- Expectations from family/classmates
  - Support: Unconditional acceptance
  - Hindrance: Conditional acceptance, judgment, unyielding expectations, attention and validation based primarily on performance or star status

If there is an abundance of positive and protective environmental factors, then "yes" is the answer to the fundamental question about positive environmental influences. The prospect of continued athletic involvement would be more likely and no specific Terms of Participation would be required in this domain. Providers would then proceed to assess the remaining factor. If "no" is the answer, then develop Terms of Participation. Athletes should not train or compete if there is significant evidence that environmental factors will play a role in perpetuating their ED (Thompson & Sherman, 1993). Hence, a goal of treatment planning is to eliminate potential environmental stressors and cultivate protective factors. Terms of Participation may include items such as:

- I commit to living in an environment conducive to recovery:
  - Moving back home and commuting to school and practice (or, as appropriate)
  - Moving away from home and choosing a supportive environment
- I will transfer to a new athletic program with a coach who understands my situation and will support my recovery over my athletic performance.
- I commit to completing my educational goals by attaining my degree regardless of my ability to participate in athletics, the quality of my athletic performance, or the status of my scholarship.

Internal Milieu

Remuda's Sports Return Assessment culminates with a sixth question: *Does the patient want to recover from the ED?*

In assessing internal milieu, treatment teams should understand patients' motives for athletic participation and attitudes toward athletics. ED patients who engage in training/competition primarily to control weight or for other compulsory reasons are unlikely candidates for prompt sport return. A healthy attitude concerning exercise is that exercise occurs in the context of an athletic event or specific training for that event. Exercise is a means to an end, not an end in itself. It is therefore important to ask why the ED patient is interested in sport and exercise. Does she exercise only to lose weight and burn energy, or is she lifting weights so she can perform to her potential on game day? It is also useful to assess the patient's goals for school and adult life. If she reports, "I only went to this school to compete in my sport," such external motivation could be problematic. Internal, broader motivation would be preferred, such as "I am in school first to get an education."

Athletes' motivation for ED recovery may benefit from objective evaluation. Formal measures exist for assessing motivation for change in ED (e.g., Connors, Donovan, & DiClemente, 2001; Rieger, Touyz, & Beumont, 2002). The Anorexia Nervosa Stages of Change Questionnaire (ANSOCQ) is a strong predictor of weight gain for anorexics (Rieger et al., 2000). Athletes in pre-contemplation or contemplation stages are likely to be given more conservative recommendations for involvement in athletics and more behaviorally-oriented specifications in the Terms of Participation, such as increasing caloric intake by 300 kcals per day or meeting with a Registered Dietitian two times per week. It is important to carefully assess motivation even for athletes who state a desire to recover from their ED. They may, for example, be motivated to stop binge eating because it is associated with the fear of weight gain, but unwilling to reach their ideal body weight, stop purging, or curtail excessive exercise. Athletes in the latter stages of action or maintenance may need less behaviorally-oriented Terms of Participation contracts.

Individuals with strong internal motivation for change are better candidates for athletic participation than those who have entered treatment and gained weight due to external pressures. Some athletes with strong internal motivation for ED recovery may even choose not to return to their sport because of the risks that training and competition may pose for them. On the other hand, athletes have often been mandated to treatment by parents, schools, or employers. They may have learned to mask ED behaviors and gained only enough weight to pacify others. Especially at higher levels of competition, the highest priority for athletes, parents, and coaches alike may be the athletes' swift return to competition rather than long-term health. Athletes with such external motivation for change may be more likely to collaborate with those who prioritize performance and achievement over health and should be given more conservative recommendations for sport return.

Recreational athletes or compulsive exercisers are more difficult to hold accountable to a behavioral contract than professional or collegiate athletes. For those who are internally motivated for recovery, we suggest assembling an outpatient treatment team. But those who seem only externally motivated or clearly prefer to continue ED behaviors may require continual monitoring. In these cases, a residential or step-down program may be needed until internal motivation for recovery develops.

Spiritual assessment of ED athletes is also important (Darden, 2005). Societal pressures and standards often contradict God's purpose for our lives. We are inundated with images of what we are supposed to look like, value, and strive after. We have been conditioned to perform—to achieve and build our identity on how successful we are. We are taught that we are accepted and valued if we excel in school, athletics, business, and so on. Thus, our self-worth may be based on accomplishments and we may feel that our value derives from achieving more than, or out-competing, other people. Because of these cultural pressures, for any ED athlete with an active spirituality it can be useful to ask several questions. Does she believe that God loves her unconditionally, or does her spiritual thinking suggest a need to earn God's approval from athletic performance? Does she experience her identity and self-worth as lovingly given by God (Romans 8:14-17)? Is she able to compete in her sport while still remembering others' needs and making time to serve them (Mark 10:35-45)? Is there balance in her life—does her sport leave enough time for relationships, interests, work, and spiritual growth? In light of such questions, a thoughtful discussion of spiritual issues may be warranted to assess the risk of relapse.

In short, it is the responsibility of the treatment team to know and understand the ED athlete's internal world, discerning the difference between healthy motivation for athletic participation and a pathologic need to exercise or achieve. Using this information, treatment teams can evaluate the athlete's best interest in the context of a full and productive life and make recommendations that will be beneficial for the rest of the athlete's life. Above all, treatment teams should be careful not to sacrifice the athlete's future for better statistics in next year's athletic program or scholarship maintenance in the near term.

If "yes" is the answer to the question about the patient's desire to recover, and more than anything else the patient wants to be healthy again, continued athletic involvement is more likely without specific Terms of Participation in this domain. If "no" is the answer, then develop Terms of Participation as needed. Terms of Participation may include items such as:

- Work with outpatient treatment team to move through the Stages of Change
- Meet at least monthly with a spiritual director to explore the concepts of grace and unconditional love in your faith system

Conclusion

Making recommendations for athletes' return to sport is a multifaceted and individualized process that requires thorough assessment and knowledge of patients' unique needs, social context, and perceptions. We recommend a systematic approach to this process. We owe it to our athlete patients to offer recommendations that will promote their physical, psychological, interpersonal, and spiritual health for many years to come.

Case Study

Paige is a 20-year-old female, African American, college dancer, diagnosed with anorexia nervosa, binge-eating/purging type. At admission, she was 5' 7", weighed 90 lbs., and was eating only 800 calories a day. She was abusing laxatives and exercising up to five hours a day. She clearly exhibited the classic female athlete triad—disordered eating, amenorrhea, and osteopenia. In recent months, she had become depressed because stress fractures and chronic fatigue were preventing her from dancing competitively.

Psychological testing indicated low ego strength, feelings of worthlessness, perfectionism, shame, hatred of her body, spiritual distress, and trouble understanding and managing her emotions. As such, her chief coping mechanisms consisted of repressing emotions, denial, and minimization.

Paige often mentioned the high expectations she experienced within her family. Her parents were both collegiate athletes. Currently, her father coaches at the collegiate level and her mother manages her own business. Her older brother was an all-star basketball player during college and is now in medical school. She reflected that her family has always emphasized excelling in school and showered attention on her for her performance. She had a younger sister who died several years ago. She felt responsible for her sister's death and was trying to be the perfect daughter to make up for her parents' loss. She was slightly overweight when younger but had received praise for subsequent weight loss and the thin appearance that she attained. Because of her current appearance, she was frequently awarded leading dance roles and often asked on dates by popular men on campus. These experiences further reinforced the value that Paige placed on being thin.

Due to Paige's low body weight at admission, her treatment team recommended nocturnal nasogastric tube feeding. She accepted the recommendation. During the first weeks of treatment, she progressed to a weight gain meal plan. Her labs were stabilizing and her activity status was increased. She had gained five pounds in three weeks. Then a peer disclosed that Paige was secretly exercising in her room during the night. As such, therapeutic interventions were initiated to help Paige identify the pros and cons of her decision to exercise using a tool called Behavior Chain Analysis (BCA; Eberly, Wall, & Cabrera, 2003; Linehan, 1993). BCA assesses vulnerabilities and triggers to eating disorder (ED) behaviors and challenges patients to explore how they can use their newly learned cognitive-behavioral skills to reduce these vulnerabilities and make more effective choices.

The treatment team challenged Paige to be open and honest with peers and staff and established an accountability plan for Paige to follow. In group therapy and in the milieu, her peers helped her to confront her habitual defenses of denial, minimization, and repression. During group and individual therapy, Paige began to notice, identify, and talk about her difficult emotions, including guilt and shame, sadness and loss, and anger. These emotions and related themes such as control, performance, and perfectionism were explored in relation to her ED. On her diary cards, she began to connect these emotions and themes with her behavioral choices to restrict, exercise, and ruminate about her body.

Part of her treatment included body image sessions to explore body image distortion, body shame, and identity apart from her appearance and performance. During spiritual direction, Paige discussed the shame and judgment she felt from God and explored the concepts of grace and forgiveness. Experientials with equine and adventure programming also assisted with problem solving, risk taking, trust building, and assertion.

The week before Paige's family was to arrive for weeklong intensive family sessions, Paige was highly anxious about what her family would think about her eight-pound weight gain. During this stressful week, she restricted by refusing some tube feedings. Her treatment team therefore asked her to develop a plan for maintaining her nutritional intake. On her plan, she emphasized communication, emotion regulation skills, and confronting her obsessive and irrational thoughts.

Family Week provided deeper understanding of her ED. Her family acknowledged their emphasis on performance. They finally began to grieve the loss of the patient's sister. They explored how insufficient attention devoted to the grief process had left each of them less able to talk about feelings and more likely to deny and suppress emotional difficulties.

After Family Week, Paige worked with her treatment team to set goals for a return to dance. She developed the goals of: 1) challenging her fears, irrational thoughts, cognitive distortions, and comparisons, and 2) making the most of her remaining weeks in treatment. Although she had setbacks, including restricting caloric intake on three more occasions and another episode of exercising in her room, she gained an additional 12 pounds during treatment, for a total of 20 pounds. She was also accepting more food challenges. In accordance with her spiritual values, she worked on appreciating her body for what it does, rather than focusing only on what she would like to push it to do. She was learning to give herself permission to relax and to have times of struggle, as opposed to criticizing herself immediately for not being good enough. Her activity status continued to progress and many of her medical diagnoses were resolving. A final, significant piece of the puzzle was continued grief work regarding the loss of her sister.

Paige's discharge psychological testing indicated that her depression, perfectionism, body dissatisfaction, drive for thinness, alexithymia, and spiritual distress were improving. Paige was verbalizing hope and coming to build her identity on her character as opposed to her appearance and performance. She was also working towards other goals outside of dance, such as relationships and career planning. Her family was supportive of her recovery and was engaging in family therapy back home to consolidate gains made during Remuda's intensive Family Week, such as modulating their performance-based expectations. Fortunately, Paige's dance instructor verbalized clear support of her recovery goals and recommendations, and had long embraced the person-centered approach to dance instruction.

The treatment team assessed Paige's barriers to recovery to include the competitive atmosphere of dance, relationships with other dancers, peers who were struggling with EDs, and Paige's continued body focus. Due to her relatively short five-year history of ED, her commitment to follow recommendations, and identified support factors in her environment, her prognosis appeared to be fair to good. Paige also appeared to be internalizing more motivation, developing non-dance-related short- and long-term goals, discovering the joy of relationships outside the dance world, and growing spiritually by truly applying her spiritual values to her experiences. By her discharge date, she had progressed to the action stage in the Stages of Change.

The Remuda treatment team scheduled a teleconference with Paige's outpatient therapist, parents, and dance instructor, with Paige participating fully. Together, the inpatient and outpatient teams reviewed aftercare recommendations, explored ways to assist Paige with continued skill building, and addressed vulnerabilities and environmental barriers to recovery. The teams agreed on the need to assist Paige in de-emphasizing body weight, rejecting pathological weight techniques practiced by other dancers, choosing not to attend dance group weigh-ins, and recognizing and celebrating physical differences related to individual genetics. During the teleconference, Paige's family and outpatient team were struck by what her peers at Remuda had already begun to see: Paige's emerging personality with a gentle spirit and relaxed demeanor, coupled with spunkiness.

To structure preparation for discharge, her treatment teams used Remuda's Sports Return Assessment to develop a Terms of Participation Contract. This contract delineated when it would be appropriate for Paige to return to competitive dance. The six factors considered in this process are medical status, nutritional status, ED behaviors, prognosis, environment, and internal milieu.

Paige's Terms of Participation Contract is reproduced below as a detailed, case-specific example of using this technology effectively in planning sport return parameters for ED athletes. The Terms of Participation were written separately for each of the dance-related activities that Paige wanted to engage in following discharge, since the criteria for each varied somewhat.

1. Criteria to engage in stretching and leisure walking for a total of 2-3x/week, 20-30 minutes per episode:

Medical Status

- Agrees to weekly monitoring for stabilization of labs
- Cannot participate until malnutrition resolves
- Cannot participate until stress fractures are showing evidence of healing, by x-ray

Nutritional Status

- Weight restoration must continue at 1-2 lbs/week until weight range is reached
- No physical evidence/signs of malnutrition
- Agrees to meet with an RD 2x/week for meal plan accountability

Eating Disorder Behaviors

- Accountability plan for laxatives and exercise
- Must follow meal plan and experience weight restoration

Prognosis

- Positive Indicators:
    - Moderate duration of illness, 5 years
    - Relatively young age of illness onset
    - Admission EDI-2 scores resemble positive prognosis cluster
    - African American female athlete
    - Admission MMPI-2 elevated on scales K and 9
- Indicators of Concern:
    - Lean sport
    - Female sport with revealing clothing

  - Judged sport
  - Admission MMPI-2 elevated on scale 1: I will continue to work with my outpatient treatment team to accurately identify, label, and discuss emotions, learning to express myself assertively rather than through physical symptoms
  - History of perfectionism: I will continue to challenge my automatic, rigid, perfectionistic thoughts, replacing with healthier cognitions
- OVERALL PROGNOSIS: FAIR TO GOOD

Environment

- Positive Indicators:
  - Supportive family (following Family Week)
  - Person-oriented dance coach
  - Outpatient treatment team and coaches on board with recommendations
  - Accountability established for comparisons and triggers with competition
- Indicators of Concern:
  - Social milieu of dance and at-risk peers: Paige will make efforts to develop friendships with non-ED peers outside of the dance community
  - Challenging expectations of sport: Paige will continue to work with her outpatient therapist on developing balanced expectations in light of her long-term recovery and life goals
- OVERALL ENVIRONMENT: LARGELY SUPPORTIVE

Internal Milieu

- Positive Indicators:
  - Appears motivated for recovery
  - Testing suggests in Action Stage
  - Internal motivation
  - Goals to finish college whether or not she dances
  - Cultivating spiritual values of unconditional, instead of performance-based, self-acceptance
- Indicators of Concern: None
- OVERALL MOTIVATION: VERY POSITIVE

The Terms of Participation appears again below for three additional dance-related activities in which Paige wanted to engage. The last three factors remain the same as above, such that only the first three are detailed below.

2. Criteria to engage in strength training and dance 2-3x/week, 20-30 min per episode

Medical Status

- Cannot participate until stress fractures are healed, by x-ray
- Must have completed DEXA Scan within past calendar year
- Cannot participate until anemia resolves

Nutritional Status

- Must maintain low end of IBW range for 1 month
- Must follow meal plan without restricting or ED behaviors
- Must replace calories burned with snacks to maintain weight
- Must consume 2 challenge foods/week
- Must be working toward body composition of appropriate body fat and BMI

Eating Disorder Behaviors

- Must abstain from restricting, laxatives, and overexercise
- Must meet regularly with accountability partners
- Will replace ED urges with cognitive-behavioral skills
- Will cultivate identity outside of performance and appearance

3. Criteria to engage in dance practice with college 3-5x/week, 45-60 min per practice

Medical Status

- Cannot participate until stress fractures are healed, by x-ray
- Must obtain medical provider's clearance that bone density is sufficiently stable for this level of activity
- Cannot participate until anemia resolves
- Cannot participate until menses have resumed

Nutritional Status

- Must maintain IBW
- Must follow meal plan without restricting or ED behaviors
- Must replace calories burned with snacks to maintain weight
- Must consume 2 challenge foods/week
- Will continue weekly sessions with RD
- Must maintain appropriate body fat and BMI

Eating Disorder Behaviors

- Same as for strength training and dance 2x/week

4. Criteria to return to competitive dance

Medical Status

- Cannot participate until stress fractures are healed, by x-ray
- Must obtain medical provider's clearance that bone density is sufficiently stable for this level of activity
- Regular menstrual cycle, remaining consistent throughout training

Nutritional Status

- Weight maintenance @ IBW with body fat at least 18-19% for 6 months
- Must follow meal plan without restricting or ED behaviors
- Must replace calories burned with snacks to maintain weight
- Must consume 2 challenge foods/week
- Will continue weekly sessions with RD

Eating Disorder Behaviors

- Same as for strength training and dance 2x/week

Following discharge, Remuda's aftercare coordinator contacted Paige at predefined intervals. Paige appears to be doing well, and has met full criteria for resumption of participation in competitive dance.

References

Agras, W. S., Hammer, L. D., & McNicholas, F. (1999). A prospective study of the influence of 6 eating-disordered mothers on their children. *International Journal of Eating Disorders, 25,* 253-62.

Anderluh, M. B., Tchanturia, K., Rabe-Hesketh, S., & Treasure, J. (2003). Childhood obsessive-compulsive personality traits in adult women with eating disorders: Defining a broader eating disorder phenotype. *American Journal of Psychiatry, 160,* 242-47.

Beals, K. (2004). *Disordered eating among the athletes: A comprehensive guide for health professionals.* Champaign, IL: Human Kinetics.

Berry, T.R. & Howe, B.L. (2000). Risk factors for disordered eating in female university athletes. *Journal of Sport Behavior, 23*(3), 207.

Best, D. (1988). The aesthetic in sport. In W.J. Morgan & K. B. Meier (Eds.), *Philosophic inquiry in sport* (pp. 377-98). Champaign, IL: Human Kinetics.

Biesecker, A., & Martz, D. (1999). Impact of coaching style on vulnerability for eating disorders: An analog study. *Eating Disorders: The Journal of Treatment and Prevention, 7,* 235-44.

Black, D. R., Larkin, L. J., Coster, D. C., Leverenz, L. J., & Abood, D. A. (2003). Physiologic screening test for eating disorders/disordered eating among female collegiate athletes. *Journal of Athletic Training, 38,* 286-97.

Bulik, C. M., Sullivan, P. F., Fear, J. L., & Joyce, P. R. (1997). Eating disorders and antecedent 9 anxiety disorders: A controlled study. *ACTA Psychiatrica Scandinavica (Copenhagen), 96,* 101-07.

Choi, P. Y., Pope, H. G., Jr., & Olivardia, R. (2002). Muscle dysmorphia: A new syndrome in 20 weightlifters. *British Journal of Sports Medicine, 36,* 375-376.

Connors, J., Donovan, D., & DiClemente C. (2001). *Substance abuse treatment and the stages of change: Selecting and planning interventions.* New York: Guilford Press.

Cumella, E.J. (2006). MMPI and MMPI-2 in the assessment of patients with eating disorders: Comprehensive literature review and meta-analysis. Manuscript submitted for publication.

Darden, R. A. (2005). Spiritual assessment and treatment strategies. *The Remuda Review: The Christian Journal of Eating Disorders, 4,* 14-16.

Davis, C., & Cowles, M. (1989). A comparison of weight and diet concerns and personality factors among female athletes and nonathletes. *Journal of Psychosomatic Research, 33,* 527-36.

Day, K. (2003). A statistical investigation of the Eating Disorder Inventory (2nd ed.). Unpublished doctoral dissertation, Argosy University, Phoenix, AZ.

Devlin, M.J., Jahraus, J.P., & Dobrow, I.J. (2004). Eating disorders. In J. L. Levenson (Ed.), *Textbook of psychosomatic medicine.* Washington, DC: American Psychiatric Publishing, Inc.

Eberly, M., Wall, A.D., & Cabrera, D. (2003). Cognitive-behavioral therapy: Applications and skills. *The Remuda Review: The Christian Journal of Eating Disorders, 2,* 1-8.

Elliot, D., Goldberg, L., Moe, E., DeFrancesco, C., Durham, M., & Hix-Small, H. (2004). Preventing substance use and disordered eating: initial outcomes of the ATHENA (Athletes Targeting Healthy Exercise and Nutrition Alternatives) program. *Archives of Pediatric and Adolescent Medicine, 158,* 1043-49.

Fulkerson, J. A., Keel, P. K., Leon, G. R., & Dorr, T. (1999). Eating-disordered behaviors and 29 personality characteristics of high school athletes and nonathletes. *International Journal of Eating Disorders, 26,* 73-79.

Heyman, S. & Andersen, M. (1998). When to refer athletes for counseling and psychotherapy. In J. M. Williams (Ed.), *Applied sport psychology; Personal growth to peak performance,* (3rd ed., pp. 359-71). Mountain View, CA: Mayfield Publishing Co.

Hopkinson. R., & Lock. J. (2004). Athletics, perfectionism, and disordered eating. *Eating and Weight Disorders. 9,* 99-106.

Johnson, C., Crosby, R., Engel, S., Mitchell, J., Powers, P., Wittrock, D., & Wonderlich, S. (2004). Gender, ethnicity, self-esteem and disordered eating among college athletes. [Electronic version]. *Eating Behaviors, 5,* 147-56.

Johnson, C., Powers, P. S., & Dick, R. (1999). Athletes and eating disorders: the National Collegiate Athletic Association study. *International Journal of Eating Disorders, 26,* 179-88.

Linehan, M. (1993). *Skills training manual for treating borderline personality disorder.* New York: Guilford Press.

Mehler, P. & Andersen, A. (1999). *Eating disorders, A guide to medical care and complications.* Baltimore, MD: The Johns Hopkins University Press.

Petrie, T. (1996). Differences between male and female college lean sport athletes, non-lean sport athletes, and nonathletes on behavioral and psychological indices of eating disorders. *Journal of Applied Sport Psychology, 8,* 218-30.

Pope, H. G., Jr., Gruber, A. J., Choi, P., Olivardia, R., & Phillips, K. A. (1997). Muscle 32 dysmorphia. An underrecognized form of body dysmorphic disorder. *Psychosomatics, 38,* 548-57.

Powers, P. (1999). The last word, *Eating Disorders, 7,* 249-55.

Rieger, E., Touyz, S.W. & Beumont, P. J. V. (2002) The anorexia nervosa stages and change questionnaire (ANSOCQ): Information regarding its psychometric properties. *International Journal of Eating Disorders, 32,* 24-38.

Rieger, E., Touyz, S.W., Schotte, D., Beumont, P. J. V, Russell, J., Clark, S., et al. (2000). Development of an instrument to assess readiness to recover in anorexia nervosa. *International Journal of Eating Disorders, 28,* 387-96.

Russell, G. F., Treasure, J., & Eisler, I. (1998). Mothers with anorexia nervosa who under-feed their children: their recognition and management. *Psychological Medicine, 28,* 93-108.

Scourfield, J. (1995). Anorexia by proxy: are the children of anorexic mothers an at-risk group? *International Journal of Eating Disorders, 18,* 371-74.

Seigel, K. & Hetta, J. (2001). Exercise and eating disorder symptoms among young females. *Eating and Weight Disorders, 6,* 32-39.

Stein, A., Woolley, H., Cooper, S. D., & Fairburn, C. G. (1994). An observational study of mothers with eating disorders and their infants. *Journal of Child Psychology and Psychiatry, 35,* 733-48.

Sundgot-Borgen, J., Skarderud, F., Rodgers, S. (2003). Athletes and dancers. In J. Treasure, U. Schmidt, & E. van Furth (Eds), *Handbook of eating disorders (2nd ed.).* West Sussex, England: John Wiley & Sons.

Thompson, R. A. & Sherman, R. T. (1993). *Helping athletes with eating disorders.* Champaign, IL: Human Kinetics.

Ward, A., Ramsay, R., Turnbull, S., Steele, M., Steele, H., & Treasure, J. (2001). Attachment in anorexia nervosa: a transgenerational perspective. *The British Journal of Medical Psychology, 74,* 497-505.

Willamson, D. A., Netemeyer, R. G., Jackman, L. P., Anderson, D. A., Funsch, C.L., & Rabalais, J.Y. (1995). Structural equation modeling for risk factors for the development of eating disorder symptoms in female athletes. *International Journal of Eating Disorders, 17,* 387-93.

Yager, J., Devlin, M.J., Halmi, K.A., Herzog, D.B., Mitchell, J.E., Powers, P., et al. (2006). Practice guideline for the treatment of patients with eating disorders (3rd ed.). *American Journal of Psychiatry*. Retrieved November 10, 2006, from http://www.psych.org/psych_pract /treatg/pg/prac_guide.cfm

Zucker, N., Womble, L., Williamson, D., & Perrin, L. (1999). Protective factors for eating disorders in female college athletes. *Eating Disorders. 7,* 207-18.

Chapter 21

Self-Injurious Behavior in Eating Disorders

Marian C. Eberly, RN, MSW, LCSW, DAPA and
Kari B. Anderson, MS, LPC

Although the psychiatric community first recognized self-injurious behavior (SIB) in the nineteenth century, SIB has warranted treatment professionals' attention most significantly in the last decade. In recent years, eating disorder professionals are talking about SIB as a common co-occurring condition with both anorexia and bulimia. We do not see this phenomenon mitigating in the near future. Thus, there is a need to increase awareness of SIB's many functions and effective treatment strategies for eating disorder patients who engage in SIB.

To respond to the growing incidence of SIB among eating disorder patients, in fall 2003 Remuda established a multidisciplinary task force to explore SIB in depth. Our objectives were:

1) To come to a greater understanding of the conceptual framework of SIB and the functions it serves, i.e., "what is the meaning behind the behavior?"
2) To evaluate areas of risk in our patient care practices.
3) To evaluate current treatments of SIB.
4) To develop a comprehensive bio-psycho-social-spiritual treatment approach for use with Remuda's SIB patients.

The current chapter describes the work Remuda has completed in recent years to better understand SIB in eating disorders and the comprehensive treatment program we have developed for eating disorder patients with SIB.

Defining SIB

SIB has been analyzed in many publications. It is evident that diversity exists in the terminology used, including *self-harm, self-injurious behavior,* and *self-mutilation*, as well as in how these terms are defined. We prefer the term SIB, but will use these several terms interchangeably to reflect authors' preferred usage when citing their works.

Within this chapter, SIB—and the related terms—are defined as: Any socially unacceptable behavior, involving immediate, deliberate, direct, and usually repetitive physical injury to one's own body, resulting in mild to moderate harm, usually without suicidal intent, and not due to psychiatric organicity.

As such, SIB describes individuals' mild to moderate wound infliction on their body surface, encompassing the range of parasuicidal gestures that are generally not truly suicidal in nature but which may mimic suicide attempts. SIB typically includes behaviors such as scratching, cutting, carving, burning, rubbing, abrading, punching, pinching, biting, head banging, and hair pulling. In cutting, the tool most often used is a razor blade and the most common body parts cut are the wrists and forearms, followed by the legs.

A case is made by some (Claes, Vandereycken, & Vertommen, 2004; Favaro & Santanastaso, 1996; Favaro & Santanastaso, 2000) to define SIB to include a broader spectrum of self-defeating and damaging behaviors, such as binging and purging, drinking and smoking, substance misuse, and laxative, diuretic, and diet pill abuse. The use of medications to self-injure would also be placed in this category, including diabetics' inappropriate use of insulin to maintain or prolong an eating disorder. For the purposes of this chapter, we do not endorse this broader definition. In addition, we do not include piercing and tattooing in our definition, since most persons in the US who engage in these behaviors do so for cultural and aesthetic reasons, not as a form of SIB.

Favazza (1996) believes there is enough research and knowledge about SIB to argue for the diagnosis of a new disorder, "deliberate self-harm disorder." Favazza's (1996) argument is particularly compelling in that self-injury is not always associated with personality disorders. Those who self-injure simply do not always meet the strict criteria for a personality disorder, and thus, their SIB may not be captured in a diagnosis in spite of its clinical significance. In particular, Favazza (1996) argues that self-mutilation is an impulse disorder, occurring frequently with other impulse disorders such as kleptomania and, in his opinion, eating disorders. In support of this perspective, research suggests that among patients who self-injure, those without personality disorders often have more extensive treatment histories than those with personality disorders or even those who commit suicide (Suyemoto, 1998).

Favazza (1996) divides superficial, moderate self-harm into two categories: compulsive and impulsive. Impulsive SIB includes both episodic and repetitive forms.

Compulsive SIB

Compulsive self-harm differs in character from the impulsive forms and is more closely associated with obsessive-compulsive disorder (OCD). It is a pattern of skin-picking and excoriation that is prompted by anxiety. As such, Favazza (1996) suggests that compulsive self-harm has a different intention and root than do the impulsive forms.

Impulsive/Episodic SIB

Both episodic and repetitive self-harm are impulsive acts. The difference between them may be only a matter of degree. Episodic self-injury is defined as SIB that is not premeditated and occurs in response to an emotional trigger event. Individuals who engage in episodic self-harm do not typically see themselves as "self-injurers." However, what begins in this manner can escalate under certain stressors into a pattern of repetitive or habitual self-injury.

Impulsive/Repetitive SIB

Distinguishing features of repetitive self-injury are rumination about the self-injury, even when not actually carrying out the behavior, and the self-identification as a self-injurer. Repetitive self-harm becomes an impulsive, reactive response to positive and negative stressors. In a manner similar to how some use tobacco in response to stress, the repetitive self-harmer reaches for a sharp instrument. Several researchers have suggested that repetitive self-harm should be characterized as a separate diagnosis in an upcoming edition of the Diagnostic and Statistical Manual of Mental Disorders (American Psychiatric Association, 2000). Short of having its own diagnosis, Favazza (1996) suggests that practitioners diagnose repetitive self-injury as impulse control disorder not otherwise specified.

Functions of SIB

It is incredibly important to understand the functions of SIB—to view the behavior as a message. The practitioner has the opportunity to receive the message and help the patient decode it. The patient may or may not have full insight into why s/he self-injures.

The literature describes various functions at work in SIB (Osuch, Noll, & Putnam, 1999; Suyemoto, 1998). The most common functions have been well explained by authors Vanderlinden and Vandereycken (1997) as follows:

Stimulation. Escaping dissociative experiences through an intentional gesture to feel one's body, thereby utilizing SIB as a self-grounding technique.

Punishment. Imposed when feeling guilt, intense shame, weakness, and anger at oneself for demonstrating behaviorally a lack of discipline.

Relaxation. A pleasure response to the warmth of the blood and the physical sensation of pain, a form of tension reduction through direct abreaction and endorphin release.

Diversion. Inducing dissociation or a trance-like state to avoid attending to an emotional trigger, issue, subject, or suicidal thoughts.

Social motives/attention. Obtaining self-affirmation by showing oneself and others one's strength, and achieving nurturance and protection through others' responses.

Alteration. To become unattractive to self and others through scarring.

An interesting feature of SIB is that it is often performed with a sense of deliberate control, even when impulsive. In those who repeat the action, there seems to be a sense of empowerment and craft—a definite ownership of the behavior.

There is a great deal of agreement among patient self-reports about SIB. The events that often precipitate SIB are: 1) the perception of loss and abandonment—e.g., canceling an appointment, breaking a date; and 2) the experience of shame—e.g., failure on the job, feedback perceived as judgment or criticism. Isolation almost always occurs before an act of self-injury (Suyemoto, 1998). In one study of 101 eating disorder patients (Claes, Vandereycken, & Vertommen, 2004), the most frequently mentioned motive for SIB was to diminish negative feelings, followed by self-punishment and, to somewhat lesser degrees, to avoid painful memories and place oneself in a trancelike state. For all types of SIB, anger at oneself and sadness were most often mentioned as feelings both preceding and consequent to SIB. Seventy percent of SIB patients report a release of tension and anxiety and a sense of satisfaction following SIB, since they experience the behavior as ending their anger, dissociation, or painful memory intrusion. The vast majority of patients speak of this emotional release as a key reinforcing factor for the behavior (Brown, Comtois, & Linehan, 2002).

One researcher's definition gives a glimpse into the world of those suffering with self-injury, viewing it not as a self-destructive act but one of self-preservation. This applies particularly to those who have trauma history. Favazza (1996) describes habitual self-mutilation as "a purposeful act of self-help which enables the subject to re-establish contact with the world." Self-medication or self-soothing and protection are often evident in the transcendent and sometimes dissociative experience of self-injury. Though the pain of SIB may be horrifically unbearable physically, it is preferred over the mental and emotional anguish and is believed by the injurer to effectively assuage their anguish and deep inner suffering. Imperative to theories surrounding SIB behavior is the understanding that many authorities have today: SIB sometimes, if not most of the time, has the ring of self-saving, not self-rejection and self-annihilation, and should be distinguished from pathologies with clear suicidal and self-destructive intent.

SIB and Eating Disorders

Estimates of SIB in the general US population range from 14 to 600 per 100,000 annually, or less than 1% (.014 % to 0.6%). Given the current US population of approximately 280 million, this indicates that between 39,200 and 1,680,000 people engage in SIB each year. Rates seem higher in adolescents and young adults: 1.8% in those aged 15 to 35, and 12% in college populations (Suyemoto & Kountz, 2000). Research suggests that most persons who self-injure are unmarried and female.

Western culture has long been known for its influence on the rest of the world, and this influence has continued with eating disorders. Recent cross-cultural research has found that eating disorders are emerging in societies, cultures, and ethnic groups that had earlier been presumed immune to these disorders (Becker et al, 2002; Nasser, 1997). Likewise with SIB. When rates of SIB were compared among indigenous populations in Australia, New Zealand, Canada, and the United States, researchers concluded that youth were quite vulnerable to breakdowns in traditional culture and roles spawned by Western influences, and attributed SIB predominantly to this factor (Hunter & Harvey, 2002).

Among patients with mental health disorders, the prevalence of SIB ranges from 4.3% to 13%, higher than in the general population but low in comparison to that found in eating disorders. In eating disorders, prevalence ranges from 25% to 45% (Claes, Vandereycken, & Vertommen, 2003; Herpertz, 1995; Paul et al, 2002). Correspondingly, Walsh and Rosen (1988) found that self-mutilating teens were significantly more likely to have an eating disorder, and Favazza (1996) concluded that as many as 50% of those who self-injure have a documented history of an eating disorder. Evidently, then, there is a high rate of co-occurrence between eating disorders and SIB. Quite interestingly, in one study with 35 patients (Solano et al, 2005), SIB had simultaneous onset with the eating disorder in 48.5% of patients, later onset in 40%, and previous onset in only 11.5%. The authors suggest that perhaps SIB serves differential functions in the three groups.

Differences in SIB rates between patients with anorexia and bulimia have not reached statistical significance (Favaro & Santonastaso, 1998; Fichter, Quadflieg, & Reif, 1994; Matsunaga et al, 2000). Furthermore, although patients with purging symptoms showed a higher frequency of SIB than non-purgers, the difference again did not reach statistical significance (Solano et al, 2005). This suggests that all eating disorder patients, regardless of diagnosis or subtype, have an equal risk of engaging in SIB. What differentiates one eating disorder patient from another in terms of SIB appears to lie beyond the diagnostic categories.

Overall, SIB research leaves us with some lack of clarity. Despite many studies on impulsivity and its relationship to eating disorders, few studies address self-harm specifically, and those that do have unclear clinical implications. Some of the contradictory results in the literature are due to imprecise and divergent definitions of SIB—heterogeneous criteria. Some definitions are very broad. Others include suicidal attempts and other forms of self-harm such as poisoning, which leads to overestimates of SIB. Still others choose to deal with only very mild forms of self-harm, leading to underestimates. Additional problems include limited sample sizes and mixing levels of care such as inpatients and outpatients. Future studies must explore the prevalence of SIB in greater depth and detail. There remains the unanswered question of the role that culture plays in the dynamic of self-injury. What roles do one's geographic, ethnic, socioeconomic, religious, and/or racial backgrounds play in the development of SIB? This requires further study and may affect the prevalence estimates of SIB.

Trauma

A relationship between childhood sexual abuse and SIB has often been raised. The assumption is often made by practitioners that patients who self-injure are likely to have a history of childhood sexual abuse. Among Remuda's eating disorder patients (*N*=6033), 49% report a sexual abuse history prior to age 18. Of those with sexual abuse histories, 37% report engaging in SIB, while only 21% of those without a sexual abuse history report SIB. Sexual abuse thus appears to increase the likelihood of SIB in eating disorder patients. Consistent with Remuda's data, Paul and colleagues (2002) reported a significantly higher rate of trauma in eating disorder patients who engage in self-harm versus those who do not. Researchers and practitioners agree that trauma does appear to play a significant role in the propensity to self-harm.

There is also a substantial body of empirical work demonstrating an association between sexual abuse and eating disorders themselves (e.g., Palmer et al, 1990; Schmidt, Humphries, & Treasure, 1997). In the context of the eating disorder, self-harm has been said to represent a language of its own that crosses cultural, racial, and ethnic barriers. Even as the eating disorder has been called the patient's "voice," SIB is said to express past trauma experiences, repeatedly. In the words of one patient who engaged in self-harm: "When I could not find the words, cutting had become the language to describe the pain, communicating everything I felt" (Pembroke's study, as cited in Takemoto, 2001).

To summarize, findings in the literature suggest that childhood sexual abuse appears to be a nonspecific risk factor for a range of psychiatric issues, including both eating disorders and SIB (Anderson & Bulik 2002). Among eating disorders, childhood sexual abuse has been found to be most closely correlated with bulimia nervosa (Kendler et al, 2000; Wonderlich et al, 1997), although there are no demonstrated differences in rates of SIB between anorexia and bulimia.

Other Psychopathology

In the general population, SIB is positively correlated with impulsiveness and antisocial behaviors (Simeon et al, 1992; Stephens, 2003), sexual promiscuity and high risk for HIV (DiClemente, Ponton, & Hartley, 1991), and suicide attempts (Dulit et al, 1994). Among psychiatric patients, those with SIB demonstrate significantly more anxiety, depression, hostility, feelings of anger, traumatic experiences, dissociation, and cluster B personality disorders than those without SIB (Claes, Vandereycken, & Vertommen, 2003; Newton, Freeman, & Munro, 1993).

The prevalence of personality disorder is one of several contributory factors to SIB in eating disorder patients. The inability to self-regulate emotions and tolerate distress have been identified as key underlying problems in many Axis II disorders as well as in SIB (Linehan, 1993). Other common features in the backgrounds of those with personality disorders—early abuse histories, high levels of dissociative defenses, highly chaotic family environments, lack of sufficient parental support, extensive psychosocial stressors, and severe mood disorders—are also risk factors for SIB (Levitt, Sansone, & Cohn, 2004).

In the eating disorder population specifically, SIB has been positively linked to neuroticism and conscientiousness, and negatively with extraversion and openness (Claes, Vandereycken, & Vertommen, 2004). There is a very high correlation between substance/alcohol abuse and SIB in all types of eating disorders (Claes, Vandereycken, & Vertommen, 2004). SIB in eating disorders is further associated with purging behaviors, generalized impulsiveness, suicide attempts, mood disorder, sexual abuse history, dissociation, co-morbidity, severity of illness, higher treatment dropout rates, and poor treatment outcome (Favaro & Santonastaso, 2000; Pierloot, Wellens, & Houben, 1975; Solano et al, 2005).

It has also been noted that eating disorder SIB patients are considerably body-focused, demonstrating a love/hate relationship with their bodies. As such, they demonstrate greater body dissatisfaction than those who do not self-injure (Claes, Vandereycken, & Vertommen, 2003). Remuda's data accord with this perspective, in that Remuda's patients who self-harm evidence higher scores on measures of somatization (Minnesota Multiphasic Personality Inventory-2; Butcher, Dahlstrom, Graham, Tellegen, & Kaemmer, 1989) and body dissatisfaction (Eating Disorder Inventory-2; Garner, 1991), with both differences being highly statistically significant using analysis of variance. The notion of using one's body as an expressive outlet for emotional tension would seem worthy of continued reflection among eating disorder professionals (Claes, Vandereycken, & Vertommen, 2004).

The Spiritual and Sacred in SIB

The suffering we speak of in SIB is of a profound, almost sacred, type. Most practitioners are no longer shocked or dumbfounded by the behavior itself. That is not to say that one ever becomes immune to hearing about or seeing SIB, but it has indeed become an epidemic among young people across the world (Nasser, 1997; Nasser, Katzman, & Gordon, 2001). SIB tests the limits of normality and rationality from a psychological perspective. And from a spiritual perspective it still causes us to pause, in a quiet, sorrowful grief when we hear the stories told. The notion that one would need to go to the depths of physically carving, cutting, or burning one's own body to be released from the burden of interior anguish, even for a single moment, is deeply troubling. And so it should be.

In the Hebrew Scriptures, we read of the prophets of Baal who felt the need to mutilate their bodies through acts of carving and cutting their skin. They became agitated and "shouted louder and, as was their custom, cut themselves with knives and swords until the blood gushed out. They raved all afternoon until the time of the evening sacrifice, but there was no reply, no voice, no answer" (1 Kings 18:28-29 TLB).

These men did many of the things we hear about self-injurers doing today. But one thing was quite different: Their motivation was not to avoid a painful memory or to reject themselves in some way. Their self-injurious acts were done as a ritual sacrifice to a god named Baal. They believed that if they could show this god devotion by imposing severe physical suffering upon themselves they would be seen as worthy. They believed their actions would render a response from Baal, a figure of power in their lives. In return they believed they had the power to convince this god to be moved by their actions: He would respond to their cries and show himself to be real and true, validating their identity as belonging to him, and delivering them from their difficulties. But he did not validate their beliefs or reinforce the identity they had in relation to him. As the story goes, Baal did not show up for dinner. They had a whole bull ready to be barbecued in his honor, but he never came. He abandoned them in their hour of need. But Jehovah did show up that day. "Then, suddenly, fire flashed down from heaven and burned up the young bull, the wood, the stones, the dust, and even evaporated all the water in the ditch! And when the people saw it, they fell to their faces upon the ground shouting, 'Jehovah is God! Jehovah is God!'" (1 Kings 18:38-39 TLB).

It is imperative to know to whom one belongs and in whom one can trust. Adolescents and young adults often experience a loss of trust in significant others. There is a constant theme of being left, abandoned, and betrayed that pours forth from those who self-injure. It is a repetitive theme, and their response to this repetitive injury is to repeat the injury on themselves. They are searching for meaning and identity. When their world is shaken and they are left or abandoned in one form or another by those they trust, they punish themselves, then search for something or someone else to believe in, someone to believe in them, and someone or something to help them control their inner chaos. As Suyemoto and Kountz (2000) reflect:

> Youth who self-mutilate may choose this behavior because it meets a multitude of needs at one time. The most common functions of self-mutilation reported by clients and practitioners are *expressing and controlling overwhelming emotions*, and maintaining a coherent sense of self when threatened with *the loss of identity* (emphasis added).

From a biblical viewpoint, we can teach patients that God already believes in them and that they belong to him. He sent his son, Jesus Christ, to die for them. Jesus gave his life for theirs, sacrificing all he was and all he had. "Once for all time he took blood into that Most Holy Place, but not the blood of sacrificial goats and calves. He took his own blood, and with it he secured our salvation forever" (Hebrews 9:12 NLT). He did this so that we might have peace, identity, and a secure future through eternal life. This is a powerful relationship based on unconditional love, not simply a metaphor of exchange.

There is much to explore in the spiritual life, but chasing after false gods, whatever they may be, is not going to bring the acceptance, identity, and inner security one desires. Many who self-injure are searching not only for a cure from the pain inflicted upon them, but also for meaning and purpose in their lives. What they find in Jesus Christ is one who loves them unconditionally, has a purpose for their lives, and delivers on his promises. They are searching for God, an authentic relationship of love, and when they find it, we see lives restored.

Those who are suffering with self-injury need to have a new tool put in their hands to replace the razor blades and matches. The word of God is meant to be that tool which renews our minds, restores our emotions, establishes our identity, and guides our decisions for life. The author of Hebrews uses this telling analogy: "For the word of God is full of living power. It is sharper than the sharpest knife, cutting deep into our innermost thoughts and desires. It exposes us for what we really are. Nothing in all creation can hide from him. Everything is naked and exposed before his eyes" (Hebrews 4:12-13 NLT).

God knows our thoughts before we think them, and understands our suffering to the deepest extent possible. He is the source of healing. As patients expose their deepest sorrow to him, God restores them, bringing comfort and true healing (e.g., Psalm 71).

The research reviewed in the earlier part of this chapter is helpful in aiding us to come to greater awareness of what to call it? *More than a malady, more than a disorder, from the depths of hell pain?* Clearly, by additionally reflecting on the spiritual dimension of self-injury, we recognize that comprehensive understanding and treatment must be derived from a holistic perspective. If we fail to do that, we have failed the patient because there is an undeniable aspect of her person that is spiritual (Wall & Eberly, 2002). As such, in addition to a careful scientific understanding of SIB drawn from the latest research and theoretical endeavors, the spiritual dimension must be recognized. Within the comprehensive bio-psycho-social-spiritual model of treatment, we can best offer patients tools and understanding that can guide them into healthier lives free of self-mutilating behavior.

Treating Self-Injurious Behavior in Eating Disorders

Remuda's program to treat self-injurious behavior (SIB) is extensive and broad. Treatment teams utilize an extensive battery of multidisciplinary assessments to understand patients' needs and history of self-harm. Using these assessments, a plan is designed to prevent patients from self-harming. If SIB occurs, it is addressed immediately. Psychotherapeutic interventions are premised on cognitive behavioral therapy, emphasizing assisting patients to make connections between their thoughts, feelings, and behaviors. Patients are actively engaged in the process from beginning to end, with self-assessments and participation in Remuda's Skills Program (Eberly, Wall, & Cabrera, 2003).

Remuda's self-harm task force began in fall 2003 and completed its first phase in fall 2004. The program has progressed further in 2005. It was determined early on that Remuda's adult and adolescent programs would each develop their own self-harm committees, with the committee chairs remaining part of the central self-harm task force. Using structured performance improvement methodologies, each program developed a plan to address its patients' specific needs with an awareness of their unique developmental issues. The central self-harm task force continues to meet regularly to evaluate processes and communicate change throughout the Remuda system.

Staff are trained throughout the year in the SIB protocols used at Remuda. All disciplines work conjointly to establish a safe environment for the patient. It is important that interdisciplinary treatment teams work closely to achieve cohesion and consistency in practice as they carry out these protocols. Milieu-wide behavioral programs of this kind cannot succeed without shared vision and training among patient contact staff (Linehan, 1993).

Assessment and Treatment Protocols

Assessment is the key to preventing and teaching patients to live successfully without SIB. Safety is the guiding principle behind thorough assessment. All gears turn toward safety when a patient is struggling with SIB. We start the assessment process prior to admission with a comprehensive prescreen. When self-harm is acknowledged on this prescreen, patients are asked to sign a Safety Commitment upon admission and are placed on a proactive high risk precaution status, which alerts the treatment team of their SIB history and the need to continue evaluating for self-harm and suicidal risk. This precautionary status is slowly reduced to lesser precautions as patients adjust to treatment.

A thorough psychosocial self-assessment tool is utilized following admission to gain information about self-injury from the patients' perspective. The self-assessment tool asks patients about their history, frequency, urges, methods, severity, subjective experiences, triggers, and consequences of self-harm, as well as their motivation to change the behavior and perceived level of control over the behavior. The results are evaluated by a licensed psychologist and the patients' primary therapist. A self-harm reassessment is performed halfway through treatment and again at discharge.

Patients also complete an objective spiritual assessment at admission and discharge, and spiritual issues related to self-harm are integrated into treatment planning. Comprehensive, holistic assessment is critical to healing. Someone once said: "If we fail to plan, we plan to fail." At Remuda, we hear this mantra over and over again because we know from research and experience that assessment is critical to good outcomes. Spiritual assessment is thus as important a part of the assessment process as clinical information gleaned from patients, their families, and other treating professionals. Spiritual assessment allows us to identify what matters to each patient spiritually at this point in her life. Has she been wounded spiritually? Does she perceive God to be a part of her healing and recovery? What does she think and feel about spiritual matters in general? What is her experience of God in the midst of her pain and suffering? Another chapter in this book details the content of a spiritual assessment.

Patients are also seen by a psychiatric provider on admission and repeatedly thereafter to evaluate the need for medications to proactively manage psychiatric conditions that predispose to impulsive and destructive behaviors such as SIB. Body checks to assess for self-harm may be initiated by doctor's orders as needed. These are carried out by nursing staff and documented on a self-harm flow sheet.

In keeping with the proactive approach upon admission, nursing staff explains the Safety Commitment and the patient signs this. The patient then reviews the Safety Commitment again with her primary therapist during their first meeting. The message given to the patient is deliberately repetitive. We want her to understand early on that she will be taking an active, participatory role in her treatment, working together with staff to remain safe as she processes through difficult issues.

Nurses practice *neutral nursing*, a nonemotionally charged response to patient self-harm episodes. Neutral responses assist patients with the immediate medical care they need without offering unneeded nurturance that could inadvertently reinforce the self-harm behavior.

Primary therapists have the range of assessment information available as they begin counseling sessions early in the course of treatment. In light of the assessments, sessions with patients who have a history of SIB are planned to accomplish several objectives:

- Building initial trust and rapport
- Reviewing opportunities to assist patients in recovery from self-harm
- Interventions and supports, as follows:

Basic skills group. Patients attend a basic skills group weekly, where they are introduced to the pragmatics of skills. The skills are taught comprehensively in a six-week curriculum. They are reinforced in application-based process groups throughout treatment, as well as in all aspects of program and activities. Upon admission, those with an active self-injury history receive one-to-one coaching in skills to help understand and use the skills effectively, which they then apply to a personalized safety plan.

One-to-one sessions. Attending one-to-one appointments with the primary therapist, since some patients may require additional support and encouragement as they continue to practice their new behavioral skills.

Safety plan. Collaboration between patient and primary therapist to develop a personalized safety plan based on discussions about what has and has not been helpful in self-harm reduction. The safety plan is used to support patients with resources to prevent them from engaging in self-harm. The therapist explains how self-harm is handled behaviorally at Remuda. Patients are coached on preventive skills, identification of triggers, and healthier responses to them. These plans are placed on a card and given to patients to keep with them as a reference. A copy is placed in the front of patients' medical records to educate members of the treatment team about how best to identify signs of distress and the skills each patient has chosen to use when needing support.

As needed supportive tools. Patients with impulsive self-harm are given multiple supports throughout their stay to help them remain focused on what is helpful. For example, diary cards are a tool used by patients to individually track which skills they use for which triggers. This helps patients to identify what is most useful in preventing impulsive acts against themselves, and in gaining strength to combat the obsessive thoughts which often accompany self-injury. Other tools used as needed with patients are beyond the scope of this chapter.

Behavior chain analysis. A behavior chain analysis (BCA) is another supportive tool that is used to gain insight regarding an undesirable behavioral event or maladaptive behavior, such as self-injury. The patient works collaboratively with the treatment team to carefully identify what thoughts and feelings were triggered precipitously and to link the thoughts, feelings, and behaviors to the resulting event. As each small link in the chain is identified and discussed, the therapist questions the patient about the details of her responses: "what the patient was doing, feeling (emotions and sensations), thinking (both implicitly and explicitly, as in expectations and assumptions), including imagining" (Linehan, 1993, p. 259). Insight gleaned from the BCA aids in identifying risk factors for future self-harm and establishes or modifies the patient's preventive Safety Plan. After processing her BCA and safety plan fully with her primary therapist and psychiatrist, the patient resumes full participation in her normal treatment program. Patients use this tool as often as necessary, and may at times become weary of it, but simultaneously they see how they are gaining insight into their thoughts and feelings and become better able to manage their subsequent behavior.

Precautions protocol. It is critical that treatment teams respond in a consistent manner to patient self-injury. Therefore, Remuda has developed a Precautions Protocol which provides our treatment teams a standardized set of responses to patient self-injury, consistent across all disciplines. This protocol identifies specific supports that are put in place depending on the level of ideation or injury experienced. For example, if a patient self-harms but does not require medical attention for the injury, she must remain within nursing eyesight for 24 hours and complete and process a BCA with her primary therapist, including one-to-one coaching. For adolescents and children who self-injure, Remuda uses a modified version of this protocol, adjusted for developmental needs. For those in lower levels of care, such as the Remuda Extended Care, Day Treatment, or Outpatient Programs, staff also utilizes the same protocol, modified to suit each care level.

Aftercare planning. Aftercare planning includes the development of a harm prevention plan executed by the patient with support from her treatment team. This information is shared with her outpatient treatment team for accountability and support. Should the patient remain in our care and transfer to the Remuda Life Extended Care Program, the treatment team there will consistently carry out the same philosophy of treatment utilized in the intensive setting, with skills classes continuing and BCAs available to the patient as needed.

Spiritual Care

As appropriate, patients are also helped to understand self-harm from a spiritual perspective. Appropriately selected scriptures can be used as part of cognitive-behavioral interventions to assist Christian patients in developing an accurate understanding of their faith, and can be used as meditations, prayers, and affirmations during times of distress. The following scriptures have proved helpful in working therapeutically with patients to overcome SIB. These scriptures minister to the person's spirit, helping them to understand—and hopefully to experience—that they belong to a loving God who intends to comfort them during times of suffering and bring meaning to their lives.

> Do not be afraid, for I have ransomed you. I have called you by name; you are mine. When you go through deep waters, I will be with you, when you go through rivers of difficulty, you will not drown. When you walk through the fire of oppression, you will not be burned up; the flames will not consume you. For I am the…Holy One of Israel, your Savior…and I love you. (Isaiah 43:1-4 NLT)

> That is why we have a great High Priest who has gone to heaven, Jesus the Son of God. Let us cling to him and never stop trusting him. This High Priest of ours understands our weaknesses, for he faces all the same temptations we do, yet he did not sin. So let us come boldly to the throne of our gracious God. There we will receive his mercy and we will find grace to help us when we need it. (Hebrews 4:14-16 NLT)

> God can be trusted to keep his promise. (Hebrews 10:23 NLT)

> Your words are what sustain me; they are food to my hungry soul. They bring joy to my sorrowing heart and delight me. (Jeremiah 15:16 TLB)

> By his mighty power at work within us, he is able to accomplish infinitely more than we would ever dare to ask or hope. (Ephesians 3:20 NLT)

> Yet now God in his gracious kindness declares us not guilty. (Romans 3:24-25 NLT)

> …nothing in all creation will ever be able to separate us from the love of God that is revealed in Christ Jesus our Lord. (Romans 8:39 NLT)

> "For I know the plans I have for you," declares the LORD, "plans to prosper you and not to harm you, plans to give you hope and a future...you will call upon me and come and pray to me, and I will listen to you. You will seek me and find me..." (Jeremiah 29:11-13)

Outcomes

Remuda's self-harm intervention plan has been evaluated each quarter to determine its effectiveness. Prior to implementation, we had an average of 29 self-harm incidents per quarter across our treatment centers. After implementation of the plan, this decreased to 10 incidents per quarter. Overall, then, we observed a 66% decrease in self-harm at the inpatient treatment level since our comprehensive approach was instituted. Approximately 50% of Remuda's adult inpatients admit with a self-harm history. Likely due to our comprehensive self-harm reduction program, only 5% of our patients actually self-harm while at Remuda. Therefore, our program appears to be effective in preventing self-harm in 9 out of 10 patients with self-harm in their histories. Of those who do ultimately self-harm at Remuda, approximately 75% attempt SIB one to three times early in treatment, but the vast majority do not continue to self-harm as treatment progresses. With our interventions, their SIB falls off dramatically as they learn to cope with emotional distress using newly learned skills.

We believe our program for treating self-harm has been successful for several reasons. Patient care leadership had a solid commitment to the establishment of a comprehensive bio-psycho-social-spiritual approach to the treatment of SIB and led the way in developing the program. Staff have been unified in carrying out the protocols in a consistent manner across all disciplines. This was challenging at the beginning, but with continued training and coaching milieu-wide consistency has become a reality. The multidisciplinary team has been trained and is continually retrained to develop a clear understanding of motivational and cognitive behavioral theories. A spiritual assessment and ongoing counseling for these concerns is thoroughly integrated into the treatment process. Patients are not viewed as manipulative or victims, but as agents of change—people capable of change. Patients have benefited from the evidence-based tools we have incorporated and the structured intervention plans we have developed. They are helped not only to understand what is driving their self-harm behavior, but to acquire healthy skills that effectively replace self-harm by accomplishing the same goals without the compromises SIB entails. They are thus empowered to live without self-harm as they discharge from Remuda's structured environment and return to everyday life.

Case Study

A preliminary assessment prior to admission identified this college-age adult as having anorexia, binge-eating/purging type. The patient weighed 90 pounds, which was 80% of her ideal body weight. The patient had a history of depressive symptoms and reported suicidal thoughts and fantasies within the past six months. The patient denied self-injurious behaviors (SIB). Given the history provided for the treatment team, the patient was admitted to Remuda on proactive high risk precaution status, which alerted the team to maintain the patient within eyesight of staff for 72 hours and to further assess her suicide risk. After initial psychiatric assessment at admission and 72 hours of close observation, precautions were reduced and the patient was required to check in every nursing shift, reporting her suicidal thoughts on a 1-10 scale. This continued for one week until the staff deemed the patient safe to discontinue this final precaution.

Although preliminary assessments did not disclose a history of SIB, Remuda's online screening procedure performed soon after admission, called the Self-Harm Assessment, identified a pattern that the patient had been too ashamed to reveal during her initial interviews. The patient indicated that within the last three months she had engaged in SIB that had caused mild tissue damage. Hitting herself on her upper legs, buttocks, and upper arms helped her inner pain to be externalized. The primary function of her SIB was self-punishment. When her eating disorder behaviors did not suffice in this regard, she progressed to SIB to punish herself. Triggers to this punitive form of SIB were feelings of guilt or hatred toward her body. Self-harm in this situation is not an act of attention seeking. In fact, it was very important to the patient that others not find out about her SIB.

Upon learning of this SIB from the Self-Harm Assessment, the patient's psychologist immediately notified her primary therapist to meet with the patient regarding the results and to formulate an individualized safety plan as part of a Safety Commitment signed by the patient. The safety plan included events that led the patient to engage in SIB and other ineffective behaviors, followed by skills that she could use to replace these behaviors.

Further assessment interviews revealed a long history of depressive symptoms dating to the same year of eating disorder onset. The prompting event was the death of the patient's sister in a car accident. The patient wished it were she herself who had died instead of her sister. Her survivor guilt was reinforced when she overheard her father, in a time of grief, stating the same wish.

Following the accident, the patient's mother overly attached to the patient in an effort to compensate for the loss of her other child. Meanwhile, her father, who had been very close to the deceased sister, withdrew from the family and devoted himself to work. The patient admitted that from a family systems perspective her eating disorder communicated anger as a way to "get back at Dad" and also, somewhat paradoxically, to seek his approval. Family dynamics were significant, as the family had never completely grieved the sister's loss, creating a conflict between mother and father. This marital conflict further reinforced the enmeshed attachment of mother and daughter and the distancing of the father, resulting in a dysfunctional pattern of triangulation where the mother and daughter bonded against the father and pushed him out of the picture.

Psychological testing revealed that this patient tended to feel sad and unhappy, pessimistic about her future, and self-critical, with low self-esteem. Disabling feelings of guilt and shame were present along with self-punishing thoughts. She had difficulty expressing her anger directly and was often unaware of her angry feelings. Consequently, her anger manifested itself in indirect and passive-aggressive ways. Defenses included repression, denial, and somatization. The patient's Eating Disorder Inventory-2 (EDI-2; Garner, 1991) underscored these results, indicating feelings of worthlessness, emptiness, inadequacy, and low self-esteem. The Remuda Spiritual Assessment Questionnaire (RSAQ; Wall, Cumella, & Darden, 2003) reflected significant spiritual distress. In spite of her Christian beliefs, the patient's responses indicated that she likely viewed God as judgmental and condemning, seeing God as having difficulty forgiving human frailty and weakness.

The patient's purging behaviors by self-induced vomiting were usually precipitated by feelings of regret, shame, and guilt. Typically, she restricted during times of loneliness and when feeling insignificant. She described this aspect of her eating disorder as a "slow kind of suicide." Later in treatment she also elaborated on her suicidal ideation and fantasies of killing herself. She had imagined killing herself by driving into oncoming traffic, smothering herself, and hanging herself. She stated that she had never acted on her thoughts and that she did not have plans to carry them out. Upon learning of the extent of her suicidal ideation, the patient was again placed on a preventive precautions program requiring her to check in with nurses every hour, rating her suicidal thoughts on a 1-10 scale, and meet daily with her psychiatrist. Precautions were eventually discontinued when the patient's skills were demonstrated to be securely in place.

In addition to a nutritional protocol that restored 22 pounds during her 9 week stay, the patient's treatment plan focused on transforming her shame-based beliefs and equipping her with more effective tools to manage her life. Her depression was treated with Paxil® and followed by her psychiatrist. Therapeutic interventions focused on emotional identification and expression, recognizing ineffective patterns and creating new responses, exploring family relationships, and promoting healthier communication skills. Individual therapy with her primary therapist concentrated on the underlying issues, mainly shame, which prompted her eating disorder and self-harm behaviors. The therapist facilitated personal and spiritual growth emphasizing grace and forgiveness. The body image specialist addressed the patient's shame in relation to body dissatisfaction.

Each week in the patient's weekly self-assessment and diary cards she rated her SIB urges and reinforced her commitment to safety. As a result of these interventions, the patient did not self-harm throughout the first 7 weeks of treatment. Her safety plan seemed quite effective. But urges to self-harm became increasingly pronounced as her intensive Family Week approached. Also, as the patient's weight restored, her body image distress increased. The patient did not verbalize the extent of her growing anxiety, yet revealed later in treatment that the days approaching Family Week were the most difficult of her treatment.

On the weekend prior to Family Week, the patient was struggling with a desire to purge. With the intention of finding a time of peaceful reflection and meditative prayer, the patient asked to visit the Remuda chapel during her free time. Since she was not on precautions at this juncture, she was allowed to leave the community for a short time. As she began to pray in the chapel, an intense sense of shame, unworthiness, and personal disgust began to overwhelm her. She was having a difficult time understanding how God could accept her and believed that the concept of grace was impossible to comprehend. She reflected on her past behaviors and felt that she had brought disgrace to her family. She thought, "Why in the world would God want me to be his daughter?" She did not understand the gospel message that Christ had already forgiven her when he chose to die on the cross for her sins. Instead, she felt that she could not accept forgiveness and entry into God's family without punishing herself.

Historically, this patient would turn first to purging when she felt the urge to punish herself. But she had committed to Remuda staff that this would no longer be an option for her. In a state of despair, the patient picked up a tambourine in the chapel room and began beating her arm with its sharp side. Within minutes, the patient realized that God would not want this and stopped the behavior. She returned to the community with plans to hide the incident. Upon discovery of the bruising on the upper portion of her arm by nursing staff, the patient stated that she had fallen while going downstairs. After receiving comfort and medical attention from the staff, she felt guilty and disclosed the incident. Staff learned that she had indeed tried to utilize cognitive-behavioral skills taught in Remuda's Skills Program and that they had worked to a certain point prior to the SIB.

Following Remuda's Self-Harm Protocol, the patient was immediately assigned a support staff person to keep her within eyesight at all times. She was also taken out of regular program so that she could focus on and grow from the SIB incident through a Behavior Chain Analysis (BCA).

The patient's BCA showed that the events leading to the SIB began the day before. The patient found herself vulnerable from anxiety as Family Week approached. She found herself thinking that she was unworthy of her family's care and guilty that her father would have to miss work to spend a week with her. She felt shameful. In the past, she had used purging behaviors to temporarily resolve these feelings. Using her skills of radically accepting the reality that purging was no longer an option, she had resolved not to purge. She tried several additional distress tolerance skills, including distracting with activities, pushing away thoughts, self-soothing through self-care activities, and plans to find meaning through time with God and prayer. As such, her plan to visit the chapel was well-intentioned. Yet it ended up being the prompting event or trigger for her self-harm.

In reviewing her BCA, she listed skills that could have prevented her SIB. The patient realized that all of her interventions were isolative and that the key factor necessary was to reach out to others. The patient also understood that the skills of keeping her self-respect and acting opposite to emotion could have been useful. The patient was able to see that the self-harm actually created more guilt and shame, and that the behavior had not been effective in giving her relief. In exploring the spiritual struggle that had occurred in the chapel, she further found that sharing her difficulty through prayer and listening to God's will through meditation on the Scriptures might have given her the answers she needed during the difficult time. She was encouraged to ask for guidance from staff when spiritual dilemmas would occur. The patient was able to formulate a safety plan to prevent further self-harm incidents. The patient's support precautions were slowly diminished as she earned the trust of staff that she would indeed be able to keep herself from SIB. She did, in fact, remain free of self-harm for the remainder of treatment.

Family Week was effective in that the patient verbalized her current eating disorder patterns and how the events in her life had shaped her ineffective beliefs. Although the family had an understanding of her problem and learned new communication tools, unresolved grief and marital discord diminished the family's ability to reach full resolution of certain issues. The family was encouraged to seek ongoing individual and family counseling in their home state.

The patient's discharge planning involved a detailed self-harm prevention plan. Contracting to stay safe, the patient was admitted to a lower level of care to provide a transition prior to outpatient treatment. The patient was vulnerable to purging as she reached her ideal body weight. Continued skill building and practice to reinforce her confidence were necessary for her to continue in recovery. The patient also needed continued support in her spiritual growth to fully accept the grace and forgiveness inherent in her Christian beliefs. Staff communicated verbally and through medical records to the team who would be taking over her care and the patient discharged with optimism about her future.

References

American Psychiatric Association. (2000). *Diagnostic and Statistical Manual of Mental Disorders, Text Revision* (4th ed.) *(DSM-IV-TR)*. Washington, DC: Author.

Anderson, C.B., & Bulik, C.M. (2002). Self-harm and suicide attempts in bulimia nervosa. *Eating Disorders: The Journal of Treatment and Prevention, 10*, 227-43.

Becker, A.E., Burwell, R.A., Gilman, S.E., Herzog, D.B., & Hamburg, P. (2002). Eating behaviours and attitudes following prolonged exposure to television among ethnic Fijian adolescent girls. *British Journal of Psychiatry, 180*, 509-14.

Brown, M.Z., Comtois, K.A., & Linehan, M.M. (2002). Reasons for suicide attempts and nonsuicidal self-injury in women with borderline personality disorder. *Journal of Abnormal Psychology, 111*, 198-202.

Butcher, J.N., Dahlstrom, W.G., Graham, J.R., Tellegen, A., & Kaemmer, B. (1989). *Minnesota Multiphasic Personality Inventory-2: Manual for administration and scoring.* Minneapolis: University of Minnesota Press.

Claes, L., Vandereycken, W., & Vertommen, H. (2003). Eating disordered patients with and without self-injurious behaviours: A comparison of psychopathological features. *European Eating Disorders Review, 11,* 379-96.

Claes, L., Vandereycken, W., & Vertommen, H. (2004). Personality traits in eating disordered patients with and without self-injurious behaviours. *Journal of Personality Disorders, 18,* 398-403.

Darden, R. (2005). Spiritual assessment and treatment strategies. *The Remuda Review: The Christian Journal of Eating Disorders, 4,* 14-16.

DiClemente, R.J., Ponton, L.E., & Hartley, D. (1991). Prevalence and correlates of cutting behavior: Risk for HIV transmission. *Journal of the American Academy of Child and Adolescent Psychiatry, 30,* 735-39.

Dulit, R.A., Fyer, M.R., Leon, A.C., Brodsky, B.S., & Frances, A.J. (1994). Clinical correlates of self-mutilation in borderline personality disorder. *American Journal of Psychiatry, 151*, 1305-11.

Eberly, M., Wall, A.D., & Cabrera, D. (2003). Cognitive-behavioral therapy: Applications and skills. *The Remuda Review: The Christian Journal of Eating Disorders, 2*, 1-8.

Favaro, A., & Santonastaso, P. (1996). Purging behaviors, suicide attempts, and psychiatric symptoms in 398 eating disordered subjects. *International Journal of Eating Disorders, 20*, 99-103.

Favaro, A., & Santonastaso, P. (1998). Impulsive and compulsive self-injurious behavior in bulimia nervosa: Prevalence and psychological correlates. *Journal of Nervous and Mental Disease, 186*, 157-65.

Favaro, A., & Santonastaso, P. (2000). Self-injurious behavior in anorexia nervosa. *Journal of Nervous & Mental Disease, 188*, 537-42.

Favazza, A.R. (1996). *Bodies under siege: Self-mutilation and body modification in culture and psychiatry* (2nd ed.). Baltimore: Johns Hopkins University Press.

Fichter, M.M., Quadflieg, N. & Reif, W. (1994). Course of multi-impulsive bulimia. *Psychological Medicine, 24*, 591-604.

Garner, D.M. (1991). *Eating Disorder Inventory-2: Professional manual.* Odessa, FL: Psychological Assessment Resources, Inc.

Herpertz, S. (1995). Self-injurious behavior: Psychopathological and nosological characteristics in subtypes of self-injurers. *Acta Psychiatrica Scandanavica, 91*, 57-68.

Hunter, E., & Harvey, D. (2002). Indigenous suicide in Australia, New Zealand, Canada, and the United States. *Emergency Medicine, 14*, 14-23.

Kendler, K.S., Bulik, C.M., Silberg, J., Hettema, J.M., Myers, J., & Prescott, C.A. (2000). Childhood sexual abuse and adult psychiatric and substance use disorders in women: Epidemiological and co-twin control analysis. *Archives of General Psychiatry, 57*, 953-59.

Levitt, J.L., Sansone, R.A., & Cohn, L. (2004). *Self-harm behavior and eating disorders.* New York: Brunner-Routledge.

Linehan, M. (1993). *Cognitive behavioral treatment of borderline personality disorder.* New York: Guilford Press.

Linehan, M. (1993). *Skills training manual for treating borderline personality disorder.* New York: Guilford Press.

Matsunaga, H., Kiriike, N., Iwasaki, Y., Miyata, A., Matsui, T., Hagata, T., Yamagami, S., & Kaye, W.H. (2000). Multi-impulsivity among bulimic patients in Japan. *International Journal of Eating Disorders, 27*, 348-52.

Nasser, M. (1997). *Culture and weight consciousness.* London: Brunner-Routledge.

Nasser, M., & Katzman, M. (1999). Eating disorders: Transcultural perspectives inform prevention. In N. Piran, M. Levine, & C. Steiner-Adair (Eds.), *Preventing eating disorders: A handbook of interventions and special challenges* (pp. 26-43). Philadelphia: Brunner-Routledge.

Newton, J.R., Freeman, C.P., & Munro, J. (1993). Impulsivity and dyscontrol in bulimia nervosa: Is impulsivity an independent phenomenon or a marker of severity? *Acta Psychiatrica Scandinavica, 87*, 389-94.

Osuch, E.A., Noll, J.G., & Putnam, F.W. (1999). The motivations for self-injury in psychiatric inpatients. *Psychiatry, 62*, 334-46.

Palmer, R.L., Oppenheimer, R., Dignon, A., Chaloner, D.A., & Howells, K. (1990). Childhood sexual experiences with adults reported by women with eating disorders: An extended series. *British Journal of Psychiatry, 156*, 699-703.

Paul, T., Schroeter, K., Dahme, B., & Nutzinger, D. (2002). Self-injurious behavior in women with eating disorders. *American Journal of Psychiatry, 159*, 408-11.

Pierloot, R.A., Wellens, W., & Houben, M.E. (1975). Elements of resistance to a comorbid medical and psychotherapeutic program in anorexia nervosa. *Psychotherapy and Psychosomatics, 26*, 101-17.

Schmidt, U.H., Humphries, H., & Treasure, J.L. (1997). The role of general family environment and sexual and physical abuse in the origins of eating disorders. *European Eating Disorders Review, 5*, 184-207.

Simeon, D., Stanley, B., Frances, A., Mann, J.J., Winchel, R., & Stanley, M. (1992). Self-mutilation in personality disorders: Psychological and biological correlates. *American Journal of Psychiatry, 149*, 221-26.

Solano, R., Fernandez-Aranda, F., Aitken, A., Lopez, C., & Vallejo, J. (2005). Self-injurious behaviour in people with eating disorders. *European Eating Disorders Review, 13*, 3-10.

Stephens, M.B. (2003). Behavioral risks associated with tattooing. *Clinical Research and Methods, 35*, 52-53.

Suyemoto, K.L. (1998). The functions of self-mutilation. *Clinical Psychological Review, 18*, 531-54.

Suyemoto, K.L. & Kountz , X. (2000). Self-mutilation. *The Prevention Researcher*, 7, 1-4.

Takemoto, T. (2001). Open wounds. In S. Ahmed & J. Stacey (Eds.), *Thinking through the skin. Transformation: Thinking through feminism* (pp. 104-23). New York: Brunner-Routledge.

Vanderlinden, J., & Vandereycken, W. (1997). *Trauma, dissociation, and impulse dyscontrol in eating disorders.* New York: Brunner/Mazel.

Wall, A.D., Cumella, E.J., & Darden, R.A. (2003). *Remuda Spiritual Assessment Questionnaire Version 1.0.* Wickenburg, AZ : Remuda Ranch Center for Anorexia and Bulimia, Inc.

Wall, A.D. & Eberly, M. (2002). Five biblical factors in eating disorder development. *The Remuda Review: The Christian Journal of Eating Disorders, 1*, 6-10.

Walsh, B.W. & Rosen, P.M. (1988). *Self-mutilation: Theory, research and treatment.* New York: Guilford Press.

Wonderlich, S.A., Brewerton, T.D., Jocic, Z., Dansky, B.S., & Abbott, D.W. (1997). Relationship of childhood sexual abuse and eating disorders. *Journal of the American Academy of Child and Adolescent Psychiatry, 36*, 1107-15.

Chapter 22

Anxiety and Eating Disorders

A. David Wall, PhD, Edward J. Cumella, PhD, CEDS, and Kenneth W. Littlefield, PsyD

> *An anxious heart weighs a man down...Do not be anxious about anything.* (Proverbs 12:25; Philippians 4:6)

I boarded my airplane. We taxied from the terminal to the runway and were cleared for takeoff. But the pilot suddenly steered the plane to the side of the runway and stopped. Before long, we taxied back to the terminal. The pilot informed the passengers that a warning light had come on in the cockpit, indicating a serious mechanical problem.

Mechanics poured over the plane. An hour later the problem was located. The problem was not the mechanical feature that the warning light was intended to monitor, but the warning light itself. The warning light had an electrical short causing it to illuminate even though the mechanical apparatus it was monitoring was functioning normally. With this reassurance, we were cleared again for takeoff.

This story illustrates the anxiety process. Anxiety is the warning light within us that triggers us to search for danger. Sometimes, we feel anxiety, check out our concerns, and find nothing of consequence. Our anxiety signal turns off. For example, we hear a noise in the night and become anxious. We get up and find that the cat has knocked over a bowl. We realize there is no danger; our anxiety subsides and we go back to sleep. Sometimes there is real danger. While driving, we hear a loud popping sound and experience a rush of anxiety. We scan our surroundings and notice rubber shards flying out behind our vehicle. We slowly decelerate and stop on the roadside. Our anxiety subsides—we are safe. We then call our emergency road service and have the blown-out tire replaced by a spare. Danger averted.

But some individuals—through a combination of genetic and biochemical proneness and learning—have anxiety "warning lights" that come on very quickly and/or unnecessarily. Such persons may take unneeded evasive actions that harm their quality of life. When this happens frequently, an anxiety disorder arises. In my airplane experience, the warning light came on while the plane was safely on the ground. But what if that light had suddenly illuminated as we were actually lifting off? The pilot might have become quite concerned and taken serious evasive actions. If there had been real danger, these actions would have reduced it. But the evasive actions may have also had some element of risk in them. Because they would have been triggered by a faulty warning light, the evasive actions might have put the plane in more danger than it was truly in.

Anatomy of Anxiety

Each human being is wired with a life-saving, genetically-derived, biological system called *anxiety* that resembles the airplane warning light. Anxiety is a *feeling*—a specific physiological arousal involving shakiness, perspiration, racing heart, rapid and shallow breathing. Individuals differ in their ability to tolerate anxiety. Sometimes small amounts of anxiety are experienced as stimulating and positive; e.g., some people pay good money to ride on roller coasters. But as anxiety intensifies, it is ultimately experienced as aversive.

The aversive nature of anxiety motivates us to eliminate or reduce it. Anxiety reduction involves two processes: 1) an instinctive response of retreat or escape—"let me out of here"; and 2) a drive to determine the source of the anxiety and danger level. If immediate escape is unsuccessful in reducing anxiety or not possible, motivation to find the source intensifies.

Let's use an analogy. Imagine you feel pain in the center of your chest. If the pain is barely perceptible, you may ignore it. If more intense, you are likely to ask, "What is that?" If it soon goes away, you may give up searching for its cause and move on. If it remains, you will likely continue focusing on it, seeking its meaning. Similarly, the noxious experience of anxiety causes us to become hypervigilant when it intensifies and/or persists.

Trying to find the source of anxiety is a cognitive or thinking process. Our search for the cause of anxiety is not random, but directed by clues from our current environment and learning history, such as what we have come to believe is dangerous. Sometimes the source of our anxiety is immediately apparent—e.g., being robbed. At other times, we are unsure and the process prolongs.

When we begin to focus on a specific source of our anxiety, we are using a mental process called *attribution*. We see a snake; we *attribute* danger to the snake's presence and take action based on this attribution. This example makes common sense, because our anxiety correctly led us to assess the environment for danger, the danger was real, and our fleeing response reduced the danger.

Fear is the emotion that results when we causally attribute the noxious feeling of anxiety to a particular situation. We begin to fear that situation. Our fear level is directly correlated with the perceived danger of the situation. A situation's dangerousness is always related to our belief in its power to take away something we value. Fear level increases proportionate to how much we value what we may lose.

Always is a strong word, but applies in this case. If I fear physical attack by an animal, the fear is based on my belief that the animal has the power to take away something I value—my physical well-being. So I avoid that animal. If, on the other hand, that animal is a threat to my daughter, I may approach and neutralize the animal because I value my daughter's welfare more than I value my own. Hence, the fear of one event can override the fear of another. With one question, it becomes clear that fear level is always directly correlated with the value we place on what we might lose. Which creates more fear for a parent: a stolen car or a kidnapped child? The difference derives from the value we place on the child versus the car.

From Functional Process to Disorder

Problems can arise with the genetic/biological basis of anxiety and the cognitive attribution process by which we determine what in the environment is causing our anxiety. Both classical and operant conditioning also play a role in the development of anxiety disorders.

First, genetics renders individuals more or less vulnerable to anxiety problems. Some people are born high-strung and have anxiety warning lights that turn on with less or little provocation. Anxiety proneness is not dichotomous, but falls on a continuum. In addition to psychotherapeutic interventions, individuals who are genetically prone to anxiety may benefit from nonaddictive medications that partially correct this biochemical proneness, such as selective serotonin reuptake inhibitors; or, for short-term relief during acute anxiety states, from anxiolytic medications such as benzodiazepines.

Second, growing up in dangerous situations renders certain people more prone to anxiety problems. When children grow up in stressful environments that are physically and/or emotionally dangerous, their brains' anxiety warning lights come on frequently and accurately. Over time, constant arousal and need for vigilance creates an anxiety response with a hair trigger. When such persons are adults and move into safe and stable environments, the sensitivity to danger that they needed to develop during childhood leaves them with near-constant anxiety. Much like individuals with genetically-based anxiety proneness, these individuals likely have a neurochemical tendency to experience anxiety, and may benefit from pharmacological interventions in addition to psychotherapy.

Third, anxiety problems can arise based on modeling. Even children who grow up in stable environments learn to define danger by watching how their parents react to various situations. If parents react with great fear to relatively benign situations, children also learn to attribute danger to, and thus to fear, those situations.

Fourth, classical conditioning can create anxiety problems. Our brains not only look for dangerous situations, but also for cues suggesting that danger is present or imminent. When we encounter danger, our brains remember the situation as well as the events leading up to it, even if we cannot consciously recall these events. Reacting to the lead-up events or *cues* is a basic survival issue. It increases the speed with which we can detect danger, making it more likely that we will escape unharmed. This process is largely the result of classical conditioning. Classical conditioning occurs when a cue that is not normally capable of triggering a specific response develops the capacity to trigger that response. This happens when a neutral cue is paired in time with a cue that is capable of triggering the specific response. For example, if a young child lives in a family where the mother and father fight every night at dinner, food—which normally does not trigger anxiety—can become a cue that triggers anxiety in the child, because it is paired in time with the parents' arguments—something that naturally triggers the child's anxiety.

Fifth, operant conditioning can reinforce anxiety problems. When we repeatedly avoid situations that we believe to be dangerous, the avoidance behavior reduces our anxiety about those situations. Our actions of avoiding are reinforced and strengthened because they reduce our anxiety. The process by which a behavior is strengthened because it reduces anxiety is called *negative reinforcement*. Situations that we repeatedly avoid will continuously be perceived by us as dangerous, because we will not have an opportunity to challenge that perception by entering into the situation and experiencing it differently.

For a more detailed cognitive-behavioral understanding of anxiety, anxiety disorders, and the treatment thereof, see Barlow (2004) or Beck, Emery, & Greenberg (1990).

Developing a Specific Anxiety Disorder

One patient with obsessive-compulsive disorder used the word "spinning" to describe her horribly distressing mental condition. One imagines a front-loading clothes dryer spinning endlessly around and around. This spinning process is largely inherited—a genetic and neurobiological proneness to anxiety—although environment may play a role. The spinning is the alarm going off—constant anxiety about something, leading to worry and rumination in an effort to understand the source of the anxiety.

Clothes dryers usually have something in them as they spin around and around. Contents may differ from dryer to dryer and over time. Dryers may be filled with socks, shirts, pants, or combinations of clothes. The contents of the "spinning" anxiety process can change from one person to another, and may also change for one individual over time. In short, the anxiety is a constant; the object of the anxiety may shift.

Let us look at this developmentally. A young child is genetically anxiety-prone. She experiences the noxious feeling of anxiety. Anxiety pushes individuals to seek a causal object. The attribution the child ultimately makes about the content or target of her anxiety will be developmentally appropriate. A child at an early age is not likely to be overly concerned about peers, finances, or grades, but may be concerned about the developmentally appropriate fear of losing a parent. Her anxiety may therefore manifest as separation anxiety disorder. Later, as the child grows and begins to understand death, she may fear illness and develop a related germ phobia. Later still, in adolescence, peer acceptance becomes extremely important, so now she worries about whether she is overweight.

Research suggests that anxiety disorders often precede eating disorders (Bulik, Sullivan, Fear, & Joyce, 1997; Godart, Flament, Lecrubier, & Jeammet, 2000; Yaryura-Tobias et al., 2000). In many ways, eating disorders can be understood as anxiety disorders with specific food and weight-related content. In fact, at Remuda we often see patients who had obsessive-compulsive disorder prior to their eating disorder. Their earlier obsession with germs was replaced by an obsession with calories. Their earlier compulsion to wash was replaced by a compulsion to purge. Is this a normal developmental route for a single anxiety process? Is there really only one disorder present with different contents? For some patients, this is a possibility.

Some Remuda patients were once obese which can be socially dangerous in our society, especially for children. Some patients have been actively teased to the point of being emotionally tortured; some have been rejected and ignored. Either way, obesity created trauma—a hypervigilant, ever-present anxiety. Anxiety pushes for escape behaviors. An obsess girl may have tried many things, but nothing worked until she developed an eating disorder. She lost much weight and the teasing and rejection have ended. Patients with post-traumatic anxiety experience fear in response to any cue that reminds them of their trauma. They go to extremes to avoid these cues. For someone who has experienced emotional trauma due to obesity, the cues are food and weight gain. Fear always involves losing something of value. Such patients value not being emotionally tortured and socially rejected. They attribute their pain to obesity. Asking such patients to give up an eating disorder is asking them to risk a return to the past when life was filled with emotional pain.

Family and cultural differences also influence the attribution/content selected by each individual. In the US, women are more vulnerable to eating disorders, in part because they model their concerns and behaviors after mothers and female friends who are weight-obsessed and they are told "you can never be thin enough." Seldom will you hear that phrase spoken to a man. Men and women may both have spinning dryers—anxiety-prone brains—but the content may be very different because of cultural influences.

Although people sometimes perceive body image issues in eating disorder patients as indicating a desire to look like a supermodel, this is often not the case. Some patients do not want to be sexually attractive; they may, in fact, want just the opposite. We often see adolescents from Christian families that have heard about other girls having sex and are very aware of girls who flaunt their sexuality. They are taught that this is wrong and they may have learned from their parents to fear sexuality as dangerous. As they begin to mature physically, peers may tease and boys may make sexually charged comments. Although parents may attempt to be supportive and inform adolescents that their development is normal, it is difficult for them to understand how something can be good and bad at the same time. Such adolescents may attribute their anxiety to their sexual development. Their natural instinct is to avoid the source of their anxiety. How do you avoid physical development? Anorexia nervosa stops—and may even reverse—physical development in teens. It offers an escape that removes individuals from peer pressures and from their own guilt about sexual development, which they may view as bad or dirty.

Over the years we have also observed many patients who can be described as having "impulse phobia." These individuals have developed intense fear of their own impulses. If they date, they fear losing control and engaging in unwanted sexual activities. If they get angry, they fear losing control and hurting someone emotionally. If they eat, they fear they will not stop and will become obese. If they express feelings directly, they fear being unable to contain themselves. Fear always involves losing something of value. These individuals value what they define as "being good" and "feeling in control," as well as family approval for these attributes. There are particular psychological, familial, and cultural reasons why they have come to value these attributes. They know that emotions and impulses, if given enough rein, can overwhelm and rob them of what they value.

Co-Occurrence of Anxiety and Eating Disorders

There is evident overlap between anxiety and eating disorders. A recent study found 64% of eating disorder patients having one or more co-occurring lifetime anxiety disorders (Kaye, Bulik, Thornton, Barbarich, & Masters, 2004). Among Remuda's 6753 inpatients, point-prevalent percentages with an anxiety-related disorder are nearly identical—64%. Furthermore, 61% of Remuda's inpatients evidence significant anxiety on the MMPI-2 or MMPI-A (Butcher, Dahlstrom, Graham, Tellegen, & Kaemmer, 1989; Butcher et al, 1992), and 85% evidence significant anxiety on the Beck Anxiety Inventory (Beck & Steer, 1993). (See Table 1.)

Table 1. Co-Occurring Anxiety-Related Disorders and Measures for Remuda's Patients

	Children (Ages 9-12)	Adolescents (Ages 13-17)	Adults (Ages 18-69)	All Patients
N	100	1841	4812	6753
Diagnosis:				
Post-Traumatic Stress Disorder	2%	12%	23%	20%
Obsessive-Compulsive Disorder	25%	19%	18%	18%
Generalized Anxiety Disorder	11%	16%	18%	17%
Social Anxiety Disorder (Social Phobia)	6%	6%	5%	5%
Anxiety Disorder Not Otherwise Specified	42%	31%	25%	27%
Avoidant Personality Disorder	2%	6%	11%	10%
At Least One Anxiety Disorder	68%	62%	64%	64%
Measure:				
MMPI Pt Scale indicates anxiety	N/A	26%	75%	61%
Beck Anxiety Scale indicates anxiety	N/A	78%	88%	85%

Anxiety issues are clearly far more prevalent among eating disorder patients than non-patients. Research also suggests that at least certain anxiety disorders are also significantly more common among eating disorder patients compared to other psychiatric patients (Grilo, Levy, Becker, Edell, & McGlashan, 1996; Kaye, Bulik, Thornton, Barbarich, & Masters, 2004). The relationship between anxiety and eating disorders may indeed be more than mere co-occurrence, implying common underlying etiological mechanisms—genetic (Silberg & Bulik, in press), neurobiological, and psychosocial. It is not surprising that the range of treatments with evidence-based efficacy for anxiety—primarily cognitive-behavioral interventions such as cognitive restructuring, systematic desensitization, and exposure with response prevention—have been found effective in treating certain eating disorder symptoms as well (Yager et al., 2006).

Anxiety's Spiritual Dimension

Remuda uses a bio-psycho-social-spiritual model to understand and treat eating disorders and other illnesses. We have already reviewed the biological bases of anxiety disorders as a malfunction in the natural warning system that protects against danger; the psychological bases in learning theory; and the social bases in family, relationship, and cultural influences. Anxiety disorders also have a spiritual dimension.

The most common commandment in the Bible, appearing 365 times, is "fear not," or some variant thereof. This is likely so common in Scripture, because God understands our propensity towards fear and wants to emphasize its danger and ultimate emptiness.

Fear can have great control over us. At Remuda, we see women who would literally starve to death due to fear of weight gain. People panicking in a fire may trample each other to death. Fear arises from the potential of losing something we value. When we fear loss of money, possessions, status, or power, our values and priorities are not in harmony with God's. When we cease to value those things, we have no fear of losing them.

We are told in Scripture to fear one thing only—God himself. "The fear of the LORD is the beginning of wisdom" (Proverbs 9:10). To those of us who recognize God as the source of all love, this call to fear God can be hard to comprehend. Why would we fear an all-loving and grace-giving God? Because fear is directly related to the potential of losing something we value–the greater the value, the greater the fear. Fear of God is therefore recognition of his value. This is a protective fear. Without God, we have lost everything. As Christ so aptly puts it: "What good is it for a man to gain the whole world, yet forfeit his soul?" (Mark 8:36-37). Fear of God places everything into perspective. Nothing that we physically possess or that happens to us in this world is of any lasting consequence, so it is not spiritually healthy to fear the loss of such things. Ultimately, we will lose them all anyway at the time of physical death. "Do not store up for yourselves treasures on earth, where moth and rust destroy, and where thieves break in and steal. But store up for yourselves treasures in heaven, where moth and rust do not destroy, and where thieves do not break in and steal" (Matthew 6:19-20).

Given fear's ability to control our lives, it is better to fear God than anything in this world. But the Bible does not stop with the idea of fearing God. As we spiritually mature, there is another step. We are told that "perfect love drives out fear" (1 John 4:18). No one will ever explain the seemingly paradoxical concept of fearing God *and* having love cast out fear more eloquently than John Newton in his hymn, Amazing Grace: "'Twas grace that taught my heart to fear and grace my fears relieved."

Thus, the command "fear not!" is not issued as a harsh rule where failure is met with rebuke, but rather a message of hope. "The fear of the LORD is the *beginning* of wisdom" (Proverbs 9:10, emphasis added), for it leads us to value God above all else and to grow to the point where the world and its passing attractions cease to have unneeded value and sway in our lives. We may enjoy the world's offerings, but learn not to attach too deeply to what is inherently transient. Simultaneously, in our relationship with God we can grow to the point where we understand God's love for us so deeply that we are fully attached to him—valuing him above all else—because we adore him more than anything; and, where we so trust God and his plans, that our fear of life's vicissitudes has been slowly replaced with peace. Such "perfect love drives out fear" (1 John 4:18).

For those with anxiety disorders and anxiety-related eating disorders, the process of spiritual renewal starts slowly. Distorted attributions about feared objects are challenged; the fear itself is extinguished by preventing avoidance and its negative reinforcement through a process called *exposure with response prevention.* Eventually, deeper spiritual truths are grasped through an ongoing relationship with God, replacing belief systems that lead to unneeded anxieties about worldly losses. An example of this multimodal approach can be found in the case study at the end of this chapter.

Case Study

There is a strong relationship between anxiety and eating disorders (ED) and their treatments have similarities. We examine the overlap specifically between anorexia nervosa and obsessive-compulsive disorder by considering Lara, a 15-year-old girl with a history of treatment failures.

Lara admitted to Remuda at 74% of her medically expected weight. Like most adolescents entering treatment she was functionally a mandated patient, since her parents sent her to treatment against her will.

Sitting sideways in a chair and hugging her knees, she hung her hair in front of her face and avoided all eye contact. She was severely depressed. Conversations between us consisted of my talking, and her shrugging her shoulders in response. Lara refused all group and individual therapy. She refused meals and supplemental feedings. She even refused to look at food and pushed away water.

Lara also announced her atheism when she arrived for treatment. She did not want to hear about God or spirituality. She believed that life was meaningless, expressed no hope for her future, and saw no reason to try recovery. She wanted to die. Her perfectionism and consequent sense of worthlessness seemed to penetrate to her bones. She indicated that she was not worth the labor to produce food that would be better utilized by someone else. Lara believed that there was nothing good about her and she was worthy only of punishment.

Not surprisingly, Lara soon needed regular trips to the hospital to be rehydrated. Her treatment team began asking if she needed a higher level of care where compulsory feedings could be administered.

Needing to help this patient progress, I employed the "door in the face" technique (Tusing & Dillard, 2000). In this technique, the therapist makes a large and unreasonable request of the patient, knowing it will probably be refused. The objective is to get the patient to agree to a smaller request that follows, because by comparison it will seem reasonable. The large request gets you the "door in the face" when you ask it, but the smaller request gets an "OK."

So I offered Lara a minimal reward if she ate an entire meal—a large request with little incentive. Of course, she immediately refused this unreasonable recommendation. I then continued by offering increasingly larger rewards for decreasingly less consumption, until we reached a balance that she believed to be reasonable and agreed to do. Because Lara loved to play cards, we ended our first negotiation with Lara eating two baby carrots and my teaching her a new card game that she wanted to learn.

For dinner we settled on her drinking an eight-ounce glass of water and my taking her out to the horse corral. She fed a snack to a horse that would be assigned to her when she started eating what was recommended by her dietician. Lara loved horses, and this motivated her. Interestingly, as much as she loved the experience she washed herself thoroughly immediately after petting the horse. I soon learned the extent of Lara's obsessions and compulsions.

Table 2. Comparison of Obsessive-Compulsive Disorder and Eating Disorder Behaviors

Experience	**OCD**	**Eating Disorder**
Feared Stimulus	Doorknob	Food
Specific Fear	Germs	Calories/Fat Grams
Fear Category	Contamination	Contamination
Body Location	Hands	Stomach/thighs/etc.
Means of Avoidance	Sterile Environment	Restricting
Eliminating Consequences of Contact	Washing	Purging/Exercise
Feared Outcome	Sickness	Weight Gain/Fat
Ultimate Feared Outcome	**Dying**	**Rejection by Others**

After weeks of this approach, Lara still talked minimally, but she was allowing nasogastric tube feedings which supplied full nutrition, drinking the minimum required water, and eating selected fruits and vegetables. We were moving along.

I then introduced a variable reinforcement schedule rewarding Lara when she ate solid foods. Finding rewards she wanted and foods she believed she could at least try eating was the hardest part. I added the expectation that she talk during individual therapy.

For certain patients, EDs, particularly anorexia, can be effectively viewed as a hybrid or subset of OCD. EDs and OCD have high comorbidity rates. Many more ED patients have histories of obsessions and compulsions. Others have no obsessions or compulsions except those related to their ED, but they usually identify with OCD through general knowledge or popular figures such as Jack Nicholson in the movie *As Good As It Gets* (Brooks & Andrus, 1997). For some patients, previously existing OCD concerns have become redirected to food and weight concerns. Patients with OCD histories notice a clear decline in their previous obsessions and compulsions when ED-related obsessions and compulsions begin.

By definition, OCD is an anxiety disorder. Generally, obsessions result in anxiety and compulsions relieve the anxiety. Like Lara, patients with EDs often find that no matter what they are anxious about, their ED relieves their anxiety. In the long run the ED increases their anxiety, but the fact that it provides immediate relief reinforces ED behavior and increases the likelihood that the person will repeat the behavior. In essence, the ED behaviors may serve the same function of managing anxiety and are analogous to their stereotypic OCD counterparts. (See Table 2.)

Patients with OCD and ED are conditioned over time to react to the feared stimulus as though it were the ultimate feared outcome. Over time they may lose sight of the relationship of the fear to the feared outcome or ultimate outcome, if they were ever consciously aware of it. Consequently, becoming aware of the fact that their obsessions are based on a greater fear often helps patients tolerate the obsessions.

More detailed information about the diagnosis and treatment of OCD is available on the internet at www.ocfoundation.org or in the following references: Kozak & Foa, 1997; March & Mulle, 1998; Steketee & White, 1990.

Lara was anxious. She likely exhibited a genetically/biologically-based proneness to anxiety. Superadded to her preexisting anxiety about germs was anxiety about weight gain, a developmentally-appropriate fear for a 15-year-old girl in our culture. For both fears, she had a solution in her OCD and ED symptoms. Lara had already become familiar with her OCD at Remuda, speaking about her "OCDs" and recognizing that she was a captive of her anxiety. So I showed her the table above. Quickly she saw similarities between her OCD and ED that she had previously missed. She saw that the ED had a concrete function in her life—to reduce anxiety.

Treatment for OCD includes exposure therapy with response prevention (ERP). Similarly, treatment for certain EDs that resemble OCD can benefit by incorporating ERP. ERP involves exposure to the fear without giving in to it or engaging in compulsive behavior. Over time the fear subsides when the feared outcome is not realized. ERP is thus based on an extinction of behaviors by breaking the bonds formed by previous conditioning processes.

Lara was able to understand this, but she did not like it. I needed to enlist her cooperation. There are many resources available for information on how to educate and enlist children's cooperation with ERP (e.g., Jablonsky, Moritz, & Geary, 2001; Niner & Swearingen, 2004). Cultivating hope had also been a goal written into Lara's treatment plan. By watching and listening to others in Remuda's Christian atmosphere, she was beginning to understand the fundamental Judeo-Christian principles of grace, forgiveness, and intrinsic worth. She was experiencing a restoration of hope and self-esteem and an incipient belief in a higher power offering assistance for her recovery. With her newfound hope, she cooperated and agreed to try ERP. She wanted to get well.

Once she agreed to ERP, we created a hierarchy of fears that paralleled each other—one for the OCD and one for the ED. I repeated that we would challenge only fears she believed she could resist. Giving in to fears and engaging in the compulsion or avoiding the stimulus reinforce the behavior and increase the conditioned fear. We would not challenge any fear that she knew she would end up giving into. Note that we look for the "sweet spot"—between the fears that are too powerful to resist and those that can be easily resisted and concentrate our efforts on that area.

We never challenge fears of things that are actually perilous. ERP only addresses exaggerated fears of objects or situations. The exposure task places patients in such situations to raise their level of anxiety. Patients endure the anxiety, and the conditioned responses are extinguished over time when the fears are not realized.

Lara had an exaggerated fear of weight gain from a variety of foods. Eventually she disclosed that she had an irrational fear that she would gain weight from the smell of food. She also believed that she could absorb calories through her skin by touching food.

We created a hierarchy list of fears. Lara first listed examples of foods that caused various degrees of anxiety. Then we ranked what sensations were most aversive for the foods. For example, tasting them was the scariest, followed by smell, then touch and sight. Hearing the foods, such as bacon frying, or simply hearing about food in conversation raised no anxiety by Lara's report.

Lara suffered from several other OCD fears, involving counting, numbers, perfectionism, and superstitions. This complicated the application of ERP. Normally patients are asked to rate their subjective anxiety throughout the exposure task on a traditional 1 to 10 scale. This helps the therapist judge when to change the task by adjusting the intensity or bringing the session to an end. This was not possible with Lara: she would always rate her anxiety as a "6" because of her preoccupation with this number. Even if she could overcome the obsession with the number 6, she would avoid assigning another number because she feared that doing so would permanently lock her anxiety at that level.

My eventual solution was to draw a picture of a cylinder on a white sheet of paper. The cylinder was exactly 10 centimeters tall. I asked Lara to choose a colored marker and fill the cylinder with ink to represent her rising anxiety. She was able to manage this style of rating without interference from her obsessions and compulsions about numbers. Following our sessions, I would take a ruler and measure the height of her markings to document objectively her anxiety on the traditional 1 to 10 scale. This allowed me to track Lara's anxiety and progress.

The task we agreed to begin working on with Lara was exposure to a food relatively low on her fear hierarchy. We wanted a food that would raise her anxiety based on smell and touch first, since eating it would be too anxiety provoking. It was unnecessary to have her eat it because she was already receiving sufficient caloric intake through Remuda's nutrition schedule and because contact with the food through the smell and touch would effectively raise her anxiety to the target range.

Finally, after much educating, negotiating, and contemplating, we began what Lara eventually dubbed "Banana Therapy." Two or three times each week we blocked two to three hours in our day to engage in ERP. The times were open-ended because the task needs to continue until there is a significant reduction in anxiety. ERP should not be ended prior to the reduction of anxiety.

Lara was initially petrified that she was gaining weight from the smell of the bananas. Later in the course of therapy she no longer worried about the olfactory transmission of calories, but she still feared weight gain by touching the bananas. This too waned by the end of treatment, such that one day she actually ate the bananas in session in lieu of her normally prescribed snack. We thus progressed from seeing to smelling to touching to eating the bananas. We used ERP with increasingly anxiety-provoking sensations instead of the traditional method of progressing to increasingly anxiety-provoking foods. To work on Lara's smell and touch fears, we engaged in activities such as smashing bananas into paste and having Lara smear the paste onto her hands. Activities included much food play.

"Banana Therapy" lasted for two months. Meanwhile, the normal modalities of therapy at Remuda continued.

Lara learned many of the principles of ERP through our sessions. She was able to generalize those skills to other obsessions and compulsions that were not related to specific food fears. For instance, her concerns about germs diminished and her focus on numbers no longer impaired her functioning. She left treatment after reaching a reasonable weight through a combination of normal eating for maintenance calories and nocturnal tube feedings for weight gain calories.

Lara also developed a good sense of humor about ERP as her anxiety decreased and she began to feel powerful over her OCD and ED. Her developing sense of humor prompted me to arrive for our final session wearing a cowboy hat, boots, and "six-shooter" holsters slung across my hips, each holster armed with a banana. Drawing the bananas gunslinger-style, I evoked uproarious laughter from Lara. This was quite a change for a girl who made no eye contact and spoke no words during the first week of treatment.

References

Barlow, D.H. (2004). *Anxiety and its disorders: The nature and treatment of anxiety and panic (2nd Ed.)*. New York: Guilford Press Press.

Beck, A.T., Emery, G., Greenberg, R.L. (1990). *Anxiety disorders and phobias: A cognitive perspective*. New York: Basic Books.

Beck A.T. & Steer, R.A. (1993). *Beck Anxiety Inventory Manual*. San Antonio: The Psychological Corporation.

Brooks, J.L. (Producer/Writer/Director) & Andrus, M. (Writer). (1997). *As good as it gets*. [Motion picture].

Bulik, C.M., Sullivan, P.F., Fear, J.L., & Joyce, P.R. (1997). Eating disorders and antecedent anxiety disorders: A controlled study. *Acta Psychiatrica Scandinavica, 96*, 101-07.

Butcher, J.N., Dahlstrom, W.G., Graham, J.R., Tellegen, A., & Kaemmer, B. (1989). *Minnesota Multiphasic Personality Inventory-2: Manual for Administration and Scoring*. Minneapolis: University of Minnesota Press.

Butcher, J.N., Williams, C.L., Graham, J.R., Archer, R.P., Tellegen, A., Ben-Porath, Y.S., & Kaemmer, B. (1992). *Minnesota Multiphasic Personality Inventory-Adolescent: Manual for Administration, Scoring, and Interpretation*. Minneapolis: University of Minnesota Press.

Godart, N.T., Flament, M.F., Lecrubier, Y., & Jeammet, P. (2000). Anxiety disorders in anorexia and bulimia: Comorbidity and chronology of appearance. *European Psychiatry, 15*, 38-45.

Grilo, C.M., Levy, K.N., Becker, D.F., Edell, W.S., & McGlashan, TH. (1996). Comorbidity of DSM-III-R Axis I and II disorders among female inpatients with eating disorders. *Psychiatric Services, 47*, 426-29.

Jablonsky, J., Moritz, E.K., & Geary, R. (2001). *Blink, blink, clop, clop*. Plainview, NY: Childswork/Childsplay.

Kay, W.H., Bulik, C.M., Thornton, L., Barbarich, N., & Masters, K. (2004). Comorbidity of anxiety disorders with anorexia and bulimia nervosa. *American Journal of Psychiatry, 161*, 2215-21.

Kozak, M.J. & Foa, E.B. (1997). *Mastery of obsessive-compulsive disorder: A cognitive-behavioral approach*. Oxford, England: Oxford University Press.

March, J.S. & Mulle, K. (1998). *OCD in children and adolescents: A cognitive-behavioral treatment manual*. New York, NY: Guilford Press.

Niner, H.L. & Swearingen, G. (2004). *Mr. Worry: A story about OCD*. Morton Grove, IL: Albert Whitman & Company.

Silberg, J. & Bulik, C. (in press). Developmental association between eating disorders and symptoms of depression and anxiety in juvenile twin girls. *Journal of Child Psychology and Psychiatry*.

Steketee, G. & White, K. (1990). *When once is not enough: Help for obsessive compulsives*. Oakland, CA: New Harbinger Publications.

Tusing, K.J. & Dillard, J.P. (2000). The psychological reality of the door-in-the-face: It's helping, not bargaining. *Journal of Language and Social Psychology, 19*, 5-25.

Yager, J., Devlin, M.J., Halmi, K.A., Herzog, D.B., Mitchell, J.E., Powers, P., et al. (2006). Practice guideline for the treatment of patients with eating disorders (3rd ed.). *American Journal of Psychiatry*. Retrieved November 10, 2006, from http://www.psych.org/psych_pract/ treatg/pg/prac_guide.cfm

Yaryura-Tobias, J.A., Grunes, M.S., Todaro, J., McKay, D., Neziroglu, F.A., & Stockman, R. (2000). *Nosological insertion of axis I disorders in the etiology of obsessive-compulsive disorder.* Great Neck, NY: Institute for Biobehavioral Therapy and Research.

Chapter 23

Depression and Eating Disorders

A. David Wall, PhD, Edward J. Cumella, PhD, CEDS, and Jennifer Lafferty O'Connor, PhD

> *How long must I wrestle with my thoughts and every day have sorrow in my heart?* (Psalm 13:2)

Depression is eating disorders' (EDs) most common co-occurring psychiatric problem (Bulik, 2002). Across studies, between 20 and 98% of ED patients have been diagnosed with some form of depression (Blinder, Cumella, & Sanathara, 2006). At Remuda, 90% of adults and adolescents, and 81% of children, have a depression diagnosis at admission. Because depression is so common with ED patients, ED practitioners need to understand the relationship between depression and ED and how to treat co-occurring depressive symptoms.

Many see depression primarily as sad or blue feelings. Although sadness is often at depression's core, it does not in and of itself define depression. In depressed adolescents, irritability rather than sadness is often the primary mood. On the widely-used Beck Depression Inventory-II (Beck, Steer, & Brown, 1996), people can indicate that they do not feel sad and still achieve scores indicative of depression, even extreme depression. Hence, depression manifests in a range of symptoms in addition to or even in lieu of sadness. These symptoms include anhedonia, weight fluctuations, fatigue, guilt, concentration and sleep problems, indecision, and others.

Depression can be primary or secondary. Both primary and secondary depression are typically diagnosed in *DSM-IV-TR* (American Psychiatric Association [APA], 2000) as major depression, dysthymia, or depression not otherwise specified. In primary depression, no other mental or physical disorder plays a significant etiological and/or maintaining role in the depression. The depression stands alone, or without significant relation beside another condition. However, in secondary depression, persons become depressed because of their emotional and mental reaction to another physical or mental condition. For example, someone just diagnosed with progressive vision loss may sink into deep depression due to impending blindness. People with obsessive-compulsive disorder often experience extreme depression because they are overwhelmed by the pervasive anxiety of their obsessions and the tyranny of having to engage in compulsive behaviors. Even when depression is secondary, it still requires treatment, because the triggering condition may not be fully treatable or, even if it is, the depression may not resolve when the triggering condition resolves.

Two additional *DSM-IV-TR* (APA, 2000) variants of secondary depression include depression due to the direct physiological effects of a medical condition and substance-induced mood disorder. In these situations, the individual manifests symptoms of depression, but the symptoms are definitively explainable by physiological mechanisms associated with the underlying medical condition. Common medical conditions that lead to such secondary depression are malnutrition, degenerative neurological illnesses, strokes, endocrine and autoimmune disorders, certain cancers and viral infections, and the use of a range of prescription and illegal substances. It is important to understand these forms of secondary depression when working with EDs because ED patients often abuse substances and may be chronically malnourished—both of which can produce secondary depressive symptoms. Screening for these conditions, especially for substance abuse, is therefore essential with ED patients.

One preliminary study suggested that many ED patients develop depression at some time *after* they have first developed their ED (e.g., Yaryura-Tobias et al., 2000). Thus, depression may often be a secondary condition caused by EDs or associated malnutrition. In other ED cases depression may come first and be primary.

A Synergy of Problems

In addition to high co-occurrence, there is also symptomatic overlap between depression and EDs. For comparison, Table 1 lists the *DSM-IV-TR* (APA, 2000) features of major depression and dysthymia juxtaposed with the primary features of EDs.

Depressed mood is not, in and of itself, a feature of EDs. Thus, when present, it indicates possible co-occurring depression. To help differentiate primary from secondary depression, it is useful to determine whether ED patients' depressed mood is chiefly in response to their being prevented from practicing their ED or is a more general experience that occurs even when they are able to engage in ED behavior.

Table 1. Features of Major Depression and Dysthymia Compared with Eating Disorders

Major Depression	Dysthymia	Eating Disorders
Depressed Mood	Depressed Mood	
Anhedonia/Loss of Interest or Pleasure in Most Activities		ED absorbs time, leading to removal from other activities
Weight Loss/Gain		Weight Loss/Gain
Decreased or Increased Appetite	Decreased or Increased Appetite	Eating Less or More
Insomnia or Hypersomnia	Insomnia or Hypersomnia	
Psychomotor Agitation or Retardation		Psychomotor Agitation or Retardation
Fatigue/Loss of Energy	Fatigue/Loss of Energy	Fatigue/Loss of Energy (when severe malnutrition is present)
Concentration Problems	Concentration Problems	Concentration Problems (related to malnutrition)
Feelings of Worthlessness	Low Self-Esteem	Body Hatred/Negative Body Image
Excessive Guilt		
Indecisiveness	Indecisiveness	
Recurrent Thoughts of Death		
Suicidal Ideation/Plan/ Attempt	Hopelessness	Hopelessness as ED gets out of control

Anhedonia, like depressed mood, is not in and of itself a feature of EDs. Thus, when present, it indicates possible co-occurring depression. It is important and often difficult, however, to differentiate whether the anhedonia is merely apparent or real. Apparent anhedonia can occur because the ED has so absorbed patients' time and mental energy that they have let go of other interests they once had. Upon probing, individuals with merely apparent anhedonia often state that they would still like to engage in various activities and express hope that these activities will one day be part of their lives again. In true anhedonia, patients more clearly indicate that they have lost interest in, or express a blasé attitude about, activities from which they once gained satisfaction.

Weight loss/gain as well as changes in appetite and eating are part of both depression and EDs. In both disorders weight loss or gain can be excessive. However, since weight loss/gain and appetite changes are the core symptoms of EDs, in practice it is difficult to use these symptoms to make a depression diagnosis in ED individuals. It may be useful to note that when appetite and weight changes are present in depressed individuals who do not have EDs, these patients are not obsessed with weight, calories, and food; they do not fear food; they do not have a desire for excessive weight loss or extreme fear of gaining weight; and they do not use compensatory behaviors to eliminate calories consumed.

Insomnia and hypersomnia are primarily features of depression and not EDs. Thus, when present, they often indicate co-occurring depression.

It is often difficult to differentiate whether psychomotor agitation/retardation, fatigue/loss of energy, and concentration problems are the result of depression or of the anxiety and/or metabolic changes secondary to an ED. As such, in practice it may be difficult to base a depression diagnosis on these symptoms. A careful, longitudinal history can sometimes assist with this differential.

Indecisiveness is not ordinarily a feature of EDs. Therefore, when present, it is a good indicator of co-occurring depression. Differential diagnosis can be complicated, however, when dealing with patients who are ambivalent about ED recovery. Their ambivalence may manifest as indecisiveness, but usually in these cases the indecisiveness pertains mainly to the issue of whether to engage in the recovery process. More generalized indecision likely suggests depression.

Recurrent thoughts of death also do not typically characterize EDs. Therefore, when present, they are good indicators of co-occurring depression. Differentiating primary from secondary depression can be difficult, however, for ED patients with severe medical complications or protracted EDs, especially those who have had multiple medical hospitalizations and/or treatment failures for their ED. These individuals may no longer deny that they may die from their ED. As such, they may be thinking regularly about death.

Excessive guilt about past actions or inaction is a *DSM-IV-TR* (APA, 2000) feature of depression. When such guilt predated the ED, or covers a range of past behaviors, it suggests co-occurring depression. But even when patients feel guilty chiefly about their ED behaviors, excessive guilt is, in and of itself, suggestive of depression. Likewise, hopelessness and suicidality are not ordinary aspects of EDs and are inherently suggestive of co-occurring depression. Even when patients are mostly hopeless about ever recovering from their ED, hopelessness, in and of itself, suggests depression secondary to the ED.

Finally, there are the issues of low self-esteem and feelings of worthlessness. When negative feelings about oneself are long-standing, predate the ED, and generalize to contexts beyond eating and body image, we are more likely looking at symptoms of depression. When negative feelings about oneself are confined to body image and failure to adhere to strict, self-imposed dietary or exercise rules, we are more likely dealing primarily with an ED. Sometimes, however, perceived failure to achieve one's ED goals, other losses related to the ED's absorption of personal time, and negative experiences with other people who are judgmental or distraught about the patient's ED, collectively diminish the patient's self-esteem across multiple domains. In such cases, the ED has contributed to a genuine depressive symptom.

Clearly, depression and ED symptoms have a complex and even confusing relationship. One disorder feeds the other. For example, individuals with a history of low self-esteem are vulnerable to develop EDs, in part because their generalized self-esteem deficits lead them to negative views of their bodies. The malnutrition associated with EDs can exacerbate depressive symptoms such as poor concentration and anergia. The loss of dreams and narrowed focus associated with severe EDs often lead to hopelessness and despair. There is evidence of a common biological vulnerability that predisposes some people to both depression and ED (Mangweth et al., 2003; Silberg & Bulik, 2005). We also outline below a prominent approach to depression called *learned helplessness* that further underscores its interweaving with EDs.

In addition, recent studies (Cooper, 2005; Cooper & Hunt, 1998; Waller et al., 2001; Waller, Kennerley, & Ohanian, 2005) suggest that the core cognitions of patients with both depression and ED overlap substantially, such that there is a common set of distorted attitudes, beliefs, and perceptions that predispose individuals to both depression and EDs. These include self-perceptions of personal defectiveness, shame, vulnerability to harm, abandonment, failure to achieve, and social isolation. It is important to note, however, that one study (Cooper, Rose, & Turner, 2006) found a relatively small subset of cognitions that may distinguish ED patients from depressed patients. Self-perceptions that may be relatively unique to ED patients include expectations of betrayal, feeling unintelligent, dependent, and as though no one has ever cared deeply for them, and a perceived need to caretake others.

There is also the psychoanalytic concept of *anaclitic depression*. This term describes depression beginning early in childhood, related to separation or neglect from primary caregivers. It indicates a deep, forlorn experience of being alone in the world with no one to meet one's needs. In recent days, aspects of anaclitic depression are addressed at least partially in the literature on attachment disorders. We have seen ED patients with severe attachment issues and concomitant (anaclitic) depression that appear to be etiologic of the ED. In such cases, the ED offers a sense of control to replace unstable and unpredictable relationships; it garners attention; it provides options for emotion regulation through the numbing and euphorogenic effects of starvation, bingeing, purging, and exercise; it fills the void of loneliness by occupying the person's time and attention; and it prescribes rewards and punishments based on clear, concrete behaviors in the absence of external feedback. A deeper exploration of attachment issues, anaclitic depression, and EDs is not possible in this chapter. Those with greater interest in this topic can consult attachment resources, such as Cassidy and Shaver (2002).

In sum, depression and EDs intensify one another, have overlapping symptoms and cognitions, and at some points their features blend and can no longer be differentiated with confidence. In a practical sense, then, it is often prudent to treat ED patients' depressive symptoms rather than assume that they are secondary to the ED and would spontaneously resolve when the ED or its physiological components resolve. Antidepressant medication in combination with cognitive behavioral interventions for depression may at a minimum assist patients to develop more rational and positive thinking, self-esteem, and coping skills. At a maximum, they will address a true depressive disorder in need of appropriate treatment.

Learned Helplessness and Depression

Depression is frequently conceptualized within the *learned helplessness* model derived from the work of psychologist Martin Seligman (Seligman, 1975). In Seligman's experiments, dogs received electric shocks while restrained. Later, even though no longer restrained and able to run away, the dogs stayed put and accepted the shocks. The principle was clear: Repeatedly experiencing an unavoidable aversive situation caused dogs to passively accept it, even when it could be easily escaped. The dogs had "learned helplessness."

This principle explains the helplessness that often accompanies depression in human beings. Those with histories of painful experiences over which they have had little or no control develop a pervasive sense of hopelessness and helplessness, manifested in the symptoms of clinical depression.

Seligman elucidated learned helplessness further by exploring the attributions of depressed persons (Alloy et al., 1988). When something painful happens individuals seek to determine why it happened; i.e., they seek to *attribute* a cause to the event. For example, people who have been abused often wonder, "Why me?" Attributional answers to the "why" question can be:

- Internal: Something in me is the cause OR
- External: Something in the environment is the cause

- Specific: The cause is limited to this situation OR
- Global: The cause will manifest in many situations

- Temporary: The cause won't continue OR
- Permanent: The cause will always exist

Let us consider an example. If I receive an "F" in a class, I may conclude:

- I failed because I am not good at math (internal)
- I am not good at math because I am stupid (global)
- I will always be stupid (permanent)

I may alternately conclude:

- I failed because I did not study enough (internal)
- I am fairly good at math (specific)
- I won't fail next time because I will study harder (temporary)

Or I may conclude:

- I failed because the teacher was unfair (external)
- Most teachers are fair (specific)
- I won't have this problem once I get rid of this unfair math teacher (temporary)

There are other combinations. Each possible set of attributions may be healthy or unhealthy, depending on its correspondence to reality.

Research demonstrates that when depressed people explain aversive experiences, they tend to make internal, global, and permanent attributions. The learned helplessness model purports that this is due to a history of painful events over which depressed individuals have had little or no control. Depressed persons' attributions may run thus:

- I am helpless (internal)
- In all situations (global)
- There is nothing I can do to change this (permanent)

Attribution research also considers how people explain positive experiences, such as good grades in school or a work promotion. When something positive occurs in the lives of depressed individuals, they make the opposite kinds of attributions—external, specific, and temporary—the least optimistic attributions possible. To wit:

- I got an "A" because it was an easy class (external)
- It was just one class; most classes are hard (specific)
- I received an "A" this time, but won't in the future (temporary)

Finally, depressed individuals also perceive their environment as negative in a global and permanent way. For example:

- People are mean (external)
- Nobody accepts me (global)
- No one will ever accept me (permanent)

Depressed persons' negative attributional styles reinforce a bleak view of their lives. They have determined that they have no control over negative or positive events—leading to an experience of helplessness. Negative events are likely to occur across life situations, while positive events are limited in scope; negative events recur, while positive events are occasional at best—leading to an experience of hopelessness. The primary cause of these problems is internal to the person him or herself—leading to an experience of worthlessness. Depression is built on this punishing triad of perceived helplessness, hopelessness, and worthlessness.

Aaron Beck, another renowned authority on depression, has a similar conceptualization involving self, world, and future (Clark, Beck, & Alford, 1999). In his view, individuals with a negative view of themselves (internal), the world at large (global), and the future (permanent) are prone to depression. Because Beck's perspective can be seen to correspond closely to Seligman's, it will not be addressed further in this overview chapter.

Learned Helplessness and Eating Disorders

In ED patients, a multifaceted relationship exists between depression and the ED. For many ED patients, secondary depression arises after the ED (Godart et al., 2000; Yaryura-Tobias et al., 2000). In these cases, negative attributions about the ED are often the source of the depression. These negative attributions manifest chiefly in two ways, with some variant of the following cognitions:

- Factors outside of myself (e.g., my parents) caused me to have an ED (external)
- I cannot escape these factors (global)
- I am helpless to change because these factors won't go away (permanent)

- I am a horrible person because I have this ED that is hurting my body and my family (internal)
- I cannot do anything right (global)
- I am so messed up that I am beyond hope and can never change (permanent)

In these cases, because individuals attribute their ED to global and permanent factors, they feel helpless and hopeless to change their lives and they become clinically depressed.

In some ED cases depression arises before the ED (Godart et al., 2000; Yaryura-Tobias et al., 2000). These patients may actually experience the ED as an escape from their learned helplessness/depression. Instead of "I am helpless (internal), in all situations (global), and there isn't anything I can do to change this (permanent)," ED patients may conclude: "I am helpless, except over what I eat; although I cannot control the world around me, I can control what I eat; controlling what I eat is the only thing I can do to change my experience of helplessness." Through these ED attributions, the ED modifies the crushing experience of helplessness and hopelessness by opening a door through which the individual can make an impact on the world. For those who live in controlling families or have experienced years of peer rejection and ridicule, the ED may therefore paradoxically express an impulse toward health and freedom inherent in the human spirit—an effort to preserve and express the spirit in very limiting circumstances.

Whether depression precedes or follows ED, treatment is similar. The best treatment for depression in ED usually involves cognitive behavioral therapy combined with antidepressant medication. The cognitive behavioral approach begins by helping people recognize their thinking style. It can be useful to validate individuals' histories of uncontrollable situations to help them understand how their thinking patterns developed. Validation is not a syrupy "you are a wonderful person!" approach. Although positive regard, genuine concern, and acceptance are critical, true validation comes when we listen to patients' stories and develop an understanding of how they became negative and helpless. We enable patients to see how their unhealthy patterns developed by pointing out significant themes from their lives and demonstrating how these experiences understandably led to their current ways of thinking and behaving.

Validation helps patients to feel better, but does not change their thinking patterns. Thus, we must next confront individuals with their ability to make new choices. They need to make conscious attempts to move beyond the past and elect new ways of thinking and behaving. Counselors help patients to see that, "Although you adapted the best you could back then, now you can make changes": or, "You may have been helpless then, but you are not helpless now." Counselors then assist patients to frame more accurate and positive cognitive interpretations of their life circumstances and events.

As patients begin to change their perceptions, they are held to increasing responsibility for more changes. Of course, responsibility must be distinguished from blame. Helpless patients were often subject to constant berating and abuse in the name of making them more responsible. This history would cause most anyone to become responsibility-avoidant and perceive calls for responsibility as an attack. This issue must be raised and clearly addressed. Responsibility is a call to take control; blame is a call for punishment. The patient can be helped to see the difference. At this juncture, therapy for depressed ED patients will often need to include skill building to help individuals make continuing positive changes.

With validation and confrontation combined, patients recover. But therapists must work to balance validation and confrontation in the proper amounts for each patient; significant clinical error lurks at the extremes. One error is to constantly validate: "Of course you react negatively, who wouldn't given what you've been through." If therapy stays here, patients do not improve and will likely become dependent on therapy. In addition, continual empathic responses to negative thinking reinforce such thinking. When patients say, "I am the worst person in the world," therapists may naturally respond, "No, you are wonderful, look at all of your wonderful qualities in spite of how mean people have been to you." If therapists do little more than respond in this manner, patients will remain stuck, repeating the refrain, "I am the worst person in the world," to receive more validation. Therefore, therapists cannot allow patients to constantly pull out the "horrible past" card, even when the past was truly horrible. If this continues, patients remain helpless.

The other extreme ignores the difficult real-life forces that have shaped individuals' current presentation. If therapists say: "You are engaged in negative thinking. All we need to do is change that and you'll be fine," such confrontation without validation will be experienced by patients as an attack and will demoralize them. They are unlikely to continue in treatment.

Many resources (e.g., Clark, Beck, & Alford, 1999) present greater detail on the cognitive-behavioral approaches described herein.

Biblical Understanding

At cursory reading, the Bible actually appears to endorse a posture of learned helplessness.

> For we know that the law is spiritual; but I am made out of flesh, sold into sin's power. For I do not understand what I am doing, because I do not practice what I want to do, but I do what I hate. And if I do what I do not want to do…I am no longer the one doing it, but it is sin living in me. For I know that nothing good lives in me, that is, in my flesh. For the desire to do what is good is with me, but there is no ability to do it. (Romans 7:14-18; Holman Christian Standard Bible)

"There is no ability to do it!" That is indeed a statement of helplessness. Fortunately, Scripture doesn't leave us there. It continues: "…in all these things we overwhelmingly conquer through Him who loved us" (Romans 8:37 NAS). We also read:

> But he said to me, "My grace is sufficient for you, for my power is made perfect in weakness." Therefore I will boast all the more gladly about my weaknesses, so that Christ's power may rest on me. That is why, for Christ's sake, I delight in weaknesses, in insults, in hardships, in persecutions, in difficulties. For when I am weak, then I am strong. (2 Corinthians 12:9-10)

And finally we read, "In this world you will have trouble. But take heart! I have overcome the world" (John 16:33). These scriptures validate our human struggles and feelings of helplessness—"there is no ability to do it!", but also confront us with the possibility for change through a relationship with God—"we overwhelmingly conquer through him who loved us" and "when I am weak, then I am strong." Scripture does not suggest that we simply tell depressed Christians to have greater faith and snap out of it, but rather that their feelings of hopelessness can be overcome with God's help. Scripture also explains *how* God helps us to overcome the experiences of hopelessness and helplessness.

Because human beings interpret past events, we can learn to perceive past events in new ways and cope using new behaviors. God created us with the capacity to overcome painful histories and gain understanding within a much larger moral, existential, and spiritual framework. For example, the apostle Paul states: "I consider that our present sufferings are not worth comparing with the glory that will be revealed in us" (Romans 8:18). He later indicates: "I have learned the secret of being content in any and every situation, whether well fed or hungry, whether living in plenty or in want. I can do everything through him who gives me strength" (Philippians 4:21-13). The apostle James likewise instructs: "Consider it pure joy, my brothers, whenever you face trials of many kinds, because you know that the testing of your faith develops perseverance. Perseverance must finish its work so that you may be mature and complete, not lacking anything" (James 1:2-4).

These almost paradoxical spiritual exhortations underscore the human capacity for subtle understandings that allow us to transcend difficult experiences and benefit from them in ways that animals cannot. We as helping professionals can rely on this capacity to assist our patients to transform their depressive attributions into more accurate, positive, and freeing attributions by incorporating biblical wisdom. This will assist them in developing a worldview that may help inoculate them against future depression by recognizing that their current pain is temporary and will produce something of lasting value in their lives. Scripture suggests a range of valuable gains that may come from suffering, including a deepened relationship with and reliance on God, greater compassion for others who are suffering, the ability to persevere and achieve long-term goals in spite of obstacles, stronger faith, and a heightened awareness of God's ability to work good in the world even through difficult events and experiences. Books such as Willcox's *Feelings: Converting Negatives to Positives* (2001), Yancey's *Where is God When it Hurts?* (1990), or Jantz's *Becoming Strong Again* (1998) can help patients to mine their troubling experiences for spiritual gold and overcome depressive cognitions.

Personality Disorders, Eating Disorders, and Depression

Inasmuch as the human capacity for complex understanding and interpretation allows us to overcome problems in creative ways, it also opens the door to maladaptive coping that goes beyond simply giving up. In short, the human ability to contemplate and plan allows us to develop strategies for temporary relief that result in long-term problems. EDs are one such example. For instance, EDs may afford individuals escape from oppressively controlling environments, but they bring new dilemmas and threats to personal safety. In some cases, maladaptive coping strategies become so pervasive that they fully color an individual's personality. Along with biological predispositions to certain maladaptive behaviors, the fact that these behaviors yield short-term gains reinforces these behaviors again and again to become the core of personality disorders. As such, we often see a triune diagnosis of personality disorder, depression, and ED.

Particularly in aversive and toxic environments, children develop maladaptive coping methods. These coping methods can be broadly categorized as *flight*, *fight*, or *submit* responses. Fighting involves the increasing development of defiant and rebellious behaviors. Flight or fleeing involves spending as much time out of the home as possible, isolation in the safest possible location, or mental escape through reading, music, the internet, or anything that decreases the frequency of aversive interactions. Submission is the strategy of the perfectionistic child who tries to avoid aversive situations by doing everything well and through submissive and placating behaviors designed to prevent hostility.

A fascinating aspect of EDs is that they are often a combination of all three coping methods—fight, flight, and submission. Many ED patients choose submit responses: They are perfectionistic and high achieving, meeting their parents' and teachers' expectations in every area except one, their ED. Through their ED, they fight against control by defying parental wishes and demands to eat or to stop bingeing and purging. This opposition often generalizes to healthcare providers. Finally, ED patients flee this irresolvable conflict between submission and rebellion by escaping into their ED world, where they are preoccupied with weighing and counting calories, fat grams, carbohydrates, and amounts of exercise; devising schemes to eat less or more, to hide food, and to increase their physical activity, each without being caught; reading, writing, and ruminating about ED behaviors; and so on. EDs are thus a paradox, a testimony to the complexity of the human mind and the spirit's reach for mastery against difficult odds.

The more aversive a child's environment, the more likely the range of maladaptive behaviors will expand. When these maladaptive coping behaviors are the only ones the person has found that work, they become deeply ingrained. Such pervasive, ineffective behaviors characterize the personality disorders. Repeated emotional pain from past abuse/neglect plus self-defeating behavioral patterns often comprise the core of a depressive disorder as well.

DSM-IV-TR (APA, 2000) Cluster C personality disorders, the anxious-fearful type, may be the most common in ED patients (Westen, Thompson-Brenner, & Peart, 2006). But the single most common personality disorder associated with EDs, especially in patients with anorexia and bulimia who binge and purge, is in Cluster B, the dramatic-erratic type; it is borderline personality disorder (BPD). Perhaps as much as 25 to 50% of ED patients may have co-occurring BPD (e.g., Wonderlich, 1995). Depression is quite common in those with BPD. Therefore, ED practitioners are likely to see patients with all three diagnoses: co-occurring ED, depression, and BPD. Depression related to BPD has similarities to and differences from depression not associated with BPD. Depression related to BPD can be more complex to understand and treat.

First, depressive symptoms in BPD likely have secondary gain: They help the person obtain what they want and avoid what they do not want. For example, those with BPD may be self-deprecating, manifest helplessness and hopelessness, and mention suicide—all depressive symptoms—as a way of obtaining needed attention from other people. People see the depression and spend a lot of time cheering and building the person up. Those with BPD may also manifest social withdrawal, anhedonia, and anergia—additional depressive symptoms—in an effort to repel those at whom they are angry or of whom they are afraid. Depression symptoms without BPD rarely entail this degree of secondary gain.

Second, for many observers the depressive behaviors of those with BPD are often so irritating that judgmental and angry responses to these behaviors are, sadly, normal and understandable. These angry responses reinforce BPD patients' perceptions that the world is threatening and unlikely to meet their needs, intensifying their depression and leading to more self-defeating, maladaptive behaviors aimed at garnering succor. Hence, in BPD, depression is likely to become a chronic condition characterized by chaotic interactions with others to meet needs in ways that are ultimately self-defeating. Here is an example. Josh has a strong need for approval coming from a childhood of parental neglect. He meets this need by people-pleasing. However, his need is so great that he requires constant affirmation. So Josh becomes ingratiating. This eventually wears on those around him. They pull back, reducing social affirmation. The decreased social affirmation causes Josh to use his maladaptive strategy even more to obtain approval—his people-pleasing intensifies. But this increase in ingratiating behaviors causes others to pull away even further. Josh becomes more depressed because his needs remain unfilled and because other people are now ignoring and ostracizing him. He re-experiences abandonment and neglect, changes his once positive perception of his friends, and now sees them as mean and awful people. So he moves onto new "friends." But with them he repeats the same self-defeating pattern, with the same eventual consequence of abandonment.

Third, depression with BPD can be more profound than depression without BPD. Patients with BPD typically have early childhood histories of abuse and neglect, so they carry longtime wounds and profound unmet needs for love and affirmation. Their depression has also been intensified by other people's negative reactions to the frustrating behaviors they have used to meet their needs. Because of these continuing experiences of emotional deprivation, the wounding in persons with BPD is often lifelong. When such persons have an ED, they may cling to it tenaciously, because it may be the only reliable method they have found to meet their profound needs. EDs do significant harm to people, but they also soothe emotions, give purpose to life, and structure one's time. EDs are there on demand, whereas other people may be unavailable.

Fourth, the attributions made by depressed persons with and without BPD also differ. Those with BPD may initially sound like those with pure depression:

- I'm the problem in this relationship (internal)
- I have so many things wrong with me (global)
- I have always been this way, have failed at attempts to change, so I have no hope that I will ever be different (permanent)

But because their sense of reality and attributions are black-and-white and shift suddenly, they may also have the following set of near-contradictory attributions:

- People are rejecting (external)
- No one cares about me (global)
- I will never be able to count on anyone (permanent)

Let's illuminate both sets of attributions. Such persons may say: "I am the worst person in the world. I hate myself." Then, 60 seconds later, they may cry out: "How can my boyfriend leave me?" These individuals do not see the logical inconsistency. If someone is the worst person in the world, why wouldn't her boyfriend leave her? Of course he would. People who completely hate themselves do not become demanding or feel they are being treated unfairly. Instead, they believe they deserve maltreatment. But inconsistent and oscillating attributions characterize depression with BPD and can be confusing for clinicians to deal with.

Finally, in depressed patients with BPD, there is a higher likelihood of self-injurious behavior. Such behavior can be life threatening and often derails therapeutic progress in other key areas because it rightly becomes the most pressing issue to treat.

When treating ED patients with depression and BPD, it is useful to rely on evidence-based methods established by Linehan (1993a, 1993b). Providers begin by collaborating with a psychiatrist to choose an appropriate antidepressant medication and dosage for the patient. Then, there is a hierarchy of interventions. First, providers focus on decreasing life threatening behaviors, such as severe self-mutilation with true suicidal intent. Second, providers focus on decreasing therapy-interfering behaviors, such as superficial self-injury or failure to complete therapy homework assignments. Finally, providers focus on quality-of-life interfering behaviors, such as lack of organization skills or anxiety. While pursuing these goals, therapists simultaneously teach patients new cognitive-behavioral skills, such as interpersonal effectiveness, emotion regulation, and distress tolerance. These skills supplant the older, maladaptive behaviors on which patients have been relying.

The diagnosis of BPD can also be openly discussed with patients in helpful and nonjudgmental ways. Focusing on the wounds that patients almost certainly experienced earlier in life, validating their experiences, and presenting their symptoms as a valiant effort to survive in a painful environment is a key initial step. Both depression and ED can be framed in this context. Then, as described earlier, patients must be challenged to take responsibility for their current behaviors and develop new skills to cope more effectively. Treatment of both the depression and ED focus on patients' choices, and not on the behaviors of other people, either past or present.

In summation, the relationship between depression and EDs can be complex and synergistic. When a personality disorder is present, such as BPD, the synergy grows in complexity. Co-occurring depression and EDs therefore require thoughtful assessment and sophisticated evidence-based tools to secure the best outcomes for patients with these co-occurring disorders.

Case Study

Lisa is a 16-year-old girl with a longstanding history of depressive symptoms and severe bulimia nervosa. She presented as a sad, withdrawn, and utterly ashamed young woman who could not even maintain eye contact during her intake interview. When asked to describe herself, Lisa used adjectives such as "disgusting, gross, pathetic, and messed-up." When asked about her family, Lisa explained that her father frequently drinks alcohol, and is unavailable and distant most of the time. When he does interact with Lisa, he tends to be angry and critical of her. Lisa's 10-year-old brother has attention-deficit/hyperactivity disorder, evidencing behavioral problems at home and school. Lisa's mother appears stressed, anxious, and overwhelmed with her family's problems.

As a child, Lisa responded to her stressful and unpredictable family environment by withdrawing and escaping through TV, internet, books, and comfort foods. These outlets were reliable and consistently provided temporary relief from depression, hurt feelings, fear, anger, and loneliness. Through these mechanisms, Lisa avoided many aversive interactions with her family.

At school, Lisa had been shy, insecure, slightly overweight, and remained on the outskirts of social circles. In middle school, her female peers were receiving increased attention from boys, but Lisa was ignored and occasionally became the brunt of "fat jokes" perpetrated by "queen bee" girls in her class.

Both at home and school, Lisa felt ignored, unimportant, unloved, and unlovable. She was deeply depressed.

When Lisa entered high school, she determined to avoid rejection. She began dieting in the hope that losing weight would protect her from further rejection. At first, Lisa was very successful in dieting. She restricted herself to 700 calories per day and used diet pills to suppress her appetite. After losing 20 pounds, a boy in her class showed interest in her and they began to spend time together after school. Soon he began pressuring her to become sexually involved with him. Lisa did not feel comfortable with this, but she was terrified of losing the attention and affection that she had long desired and was finally receiving. So she gave in to the pressure and had sexual intercourse. A week later, her boyfriend dumped her and began hanging out with a much thinner girl.

Lisa was devastated by this rejection. She immediately turned to her old coping mechanism of eating for comfort. Because she had been depriving herself of food for so long through strict dieting, she had overwhelming urges to binge on all the foods that had been off-limits during her diet. After satisfying these urges and attempting to fill up the aching hole in her heart with high fat and calorie dense foods, she immediately began to panic about gaining weight again. So she quickly forced herself to throw up and popped five more diet pills. Then she punished herself with 24 hours of fasting.

Bulimia's vicious cycle had begun. For the next two years, Lisa continued to restrict, binge, purge, and abuse diet pills and laxatives until she was risking cardiac arrest from severe electrolyte imbalance. When Lisa arrived at Remuda, she was filled with self-hatred and hopelessness.

To develop a deeper understanding of Lisa's worldview, I assisted her in creating a life story timeline in which she identified significant memories and events from her life. For each memory/event, I asked Lisa to identify the thoughts, feelings, and behaviors that accompanied it. As this project progressed, she began to see significant patterns in her thinking. Whether the past events involved peer rejection or criticism from family members, the thoughts she had in response to the events were, "There's something wrong with me. No one loves me. No one ever will." Lisa had internal, global, and permanent attributions about her life that were contributing to pervasive feelings of helplessness and hopelessness.

After Lisa completed her life story timeline, I pointed out that she had endured many painful situations over which she had little or no control. When these situations were occurring, she was coping in the best ways she knew—through escape strategies that provided immediate relief from the feelings of pain. I normalized her reliance on comfort foods and the lure of acceptance through weight loss as reasonable responses to an unstable and emotionally unsatisfying environment. I could almost see her shame lifting as I empathized with her past wounds and validated her efforts to cope. Lisa was able to see that her coping mechanisms made sense at the time.

Bingeing and purging had provided her with a sense of emotional numbness, offering escape from intense depression, feelings of shame, guilt, and loneliness. "I could just flush it all down the toilet. It was like I was getting rid of all the bad stuff inside me, and then I was clean and calm again." Bulimia was her antidepressant. In addition, restricting had allowed her to punish and alter her "disgusting" body which she viewed as one of the main causes of her social rejection and exclusion.

While normalizing her reliance on these maladaptive coping strategies, I also pointed out to Lisa that these unhealthy escape mechanisms had led to long-term problems. Her behaviors were not meeting her needs in an effective manner. I explained that although we could not erase the painful events of her past, we could change how she views them and how she chooses to respond to them. I began by challenging Lisa's internal, global, and permanent attributions. Together, we created new attributions for each event on her timeline, often relying on biblical truths to help Lisa develop cognitions consistent with her faith. These new attributions were external, specific, and temporary—the very opposite of her original pessimistic attributions. For example, we created the following attribution regarding her boyfriend:

- He was being a jerk, not acting as God would want. It's not my fault that he acted that way (external)
- Not all guys are like this. Many are trying to live according to biblical or moral principles (specific)
- Just because I was rejected this time doesn't mean I always will be, because God has a plan for my life that includes healthy relationships (temporary)

After challenging Lisa's distorted cognitions in this way, we began to work on new behavioral strategies to meet her emotional and interpersonal needs. Lisa attended skills groups utilizing a Christian version of Dialectical Behavior Therapy (Eberly, Wall, & Cabrera, 2003; Linehan, 1993a, 1993b). Here she learned new behavioral strategies for emotion regulation, distress tolerance, and interpersonal effectiveness. She was then provided with opportunities to practice these skills during weekly individual and family therapy sessions and process groups with peers. With prompting and support, Lisa was able to express past wounds to her family members and assertively state her needs for respect and support from her family. Lisa also learned how to initiate boundaries with peers when they failed to respect her feelings or needs. Lisa was no longer relying on escape mechanisms to cope with life situations or emotions.

Slowly Lisa developed confidence in her ability to use new behavioral strategies to manage her emotions and relationships. She also began to see that others responded in positive ways when she used these strategies. She no longer felt invisible and worthless, but began to feel understood and valued in both the therapeutic relationship and relationships with peers and family. The self-hatred and deep shame were abating. She was learning to accept herself as a valued child of God and no longer felt intense urges to escape from herself and her life through bingeing, purging, and withdrawal. While she did feel tempted to do so at times, she knew to remind herself that yielding to such temptations would only provide temporary relief and result in bigger long-term problems.

When new stressors occurred, Lisa often needed to turn to her therapist for support in challenging her habitual tendencies towards self-blame and hopelessness. Lisa was learning to recognize when old ways of thinking resurfaced, and often used her favorite skill—*catch it, challenge it, change it*—to put herself back on track. Lisa was warned that old behavior patterns such as comfort eating, isolating, or restricting might reemerge during stressful times as well. She learned that if this occurred, she could immediately ask her therapist for additional support. She learned that secrets breed shame, and she was beginning to enjoy living without a heavy cloud of shame and guilt overhead. She was truly accepting God's forgiveness and unconditional love for her.

When Lisa discharged from Remuda, her Beck Depression Inventory-II (Beck, Steer, & Brown, 1996) score had moved from the severe to the mild range. Her Eating Disorder Inventory-2 (Garner, 1991) scores also showed significant reductions in her eating disorder symptoms. Lisa chose and planned to work with an outpatient team to continue with cognitive-behavioral therapy, family therapy, and antidepressant medications.

Before leaving Remuda, Lisa selected and began carrying a Bible verse on an index card in her pocket: "Everyone who drinks of this water will be thirsty again, but whoever drinks the water I give him will never thirst. Indeed, the water I give him will become in him a well of water springing up to eternal life" (John 4:13-14). This verse so clearly illuminated her journey: Her old coping methods provided temporary relief from her emotional thirst, but kept her trapped in an unending cycle, like an addiction; her new coping skills and reliance on God offered her hope and a new way of life.

References

Alloy, L.B., Abramson, L.Y., Metalsky, G.I., & Hartlage, S. (1988). The hopelessness theory of depression: Attributional aspects. *British Journal of Clinical Psychology, 27*, 5-21.

American Psychiatric Association. (2000). *Diagnostic and Statistical Manual of Mental Disorders, Text Revision* (4th ed.) *(DSM-IV-TR)*. Washington, DC: Author.

Beck, A.T., Steer, R.A., & Brown, G.K. (1996). *Beck depression inventory-second edition manual.* San Antonio: Psychological Corp.

Blinder, B. J., Cumella, E. J., & Sanathara, V. (2006). Psychiatric comorbidities of female inpatients with eating disorders. *Psychosomatic Medicine*, 68, 454-62.

Bulik, C.M. (2002). Anxiety, depression, and eating disorders. In C.G. Fairburn and K.D. Brownell (Eds.), *Eating disorders and obesity: A comprehensive handbook*. New York: Guilford Press.

Cassidy, J. & Shaver, P.R. (Eds). (2002). *Handbook of attachment: Theory, research, and clinical applications.* New York: Guilford Press.

Clark, D.A., Beck, A.T., & Alford, B.A. (1999). *Scientific foundations of cognitive theory and therapy of depression.* Hoboken, NJ: Wiley.

Cooper, M.J. (2005). Cognitive theory of anorexia nervosa and bulimia nervosa: Progress, development, and future directions. *Clinical Psychology Review, 25*, 511-31.

Cooper, M.J. & Hunt, J. (1998). Core beliefs and underlying assumptions in bulimia nervosa and depression. *Behaviour Research and Therapy, 36*, 895-8.

Cooper, M.J., Rose, K.S., & Turner, H. (2006). The specific content of core beliefs and schema in adolescent girls high and low in eating disorder symptoms. *Eating Behaviors, 7*, 27-35.

Eberly, M.E., Wall, A.D., & Cabrera, D. (2003). Cognitive-behavioral therapy: Applications and skills. *The Remuda Review: The Christian Journal of Eating Disorders, 2*, 1-8.

Garner, D.M. (1991). *Eating Disorder Inventory-2: Professional Manual.* Odessa, FL: Psychological Assessment Resources.

Godart, N.T., Flament, M.F., Lecrubier, Y., & Jeammet, P. (2000). Anxiety disorders in anorexia and bulimia nervosa: Co-morbidity and chronology of appearance. *European Psychiatry, 15*, 38-45.

Jantz, G.L. (1998). *Becoming strong again: How to regain emotional health.* Grand Rapids, MI: Baker.

Linehan, M. (1993a). *Cognitive behavioral treatment of borderline personality disorder.* New York: Guilford Press.

Linehan, M. (1993b). *Skills training manual for treating borderline personality disorder.* New York: Guilford Press.

Mangweth, B., Hudson, J.I., Pope, H.G., Hausmann, A., De Col, C., Laird, N.M., Beibl, W., & Tsuang, M.T. (2003). Family study of the aggregation of eating disorders and mood disorders. *Psychology and Medicine, 33*, 1319-23.

Seligman, M.E.P. (1975). *Helplessness: On depression development and death.* San Francisco: Freeman.

Silberg, J.L. & Bulik, C.M. (2005). The developmental association between eating disorders symptoms and symptoms of depression and anxiety in juvenile twin girls. *Journal of Child Psychology and Psychiatry, 46*, 1317-26.

Waller, G., Kennerley, H., & Ohanian, V. (2005). Schema-focused cognitive behavior therapy with the eating disorders. In L.P. Riso, P.T. du Toit, & J.E. Young (Eds.), *Cognitive schemas and core beliefs in psychiatric disorders: A scientist practitioner guide.* New York: American Psychiatric Association.

Waller, G., Shah, R., Ohanian, V., & Elliott, P. (2001). Core beliefs in bulimia nervosa and depression: The discriminant validity of Young's Schema Questionnaire. *Behaviour Therapy, 32*, 139-53.

Westen, D., Thompson-Brenner, H., & Peart, J. (2006). Personality and eating disorders. In S. Wonderlich, J.E. Mitchell, M. de Zwaan, & H. Steiger (Eds.), *Annual Review of Eating Disorders, Part 2.* Oxon, England: Radcliffe.

Willcox, G. & Young, O. (2001). *Feelings: Converting negatives to positives.* Kearney, NE: Morris.

Wonderlich, S.A. (1995). Personality and eating disorders. In K.D. Brownell and C.G. Fairburn (Eds.), *Eating disorders and obesity: A comprehensive handbook.* New York: Guilford Press. (pp. 171–6).

Yancey, P. (1990). *Where is God when it hurts?* Grand Rapids, MI: Zondervan.

Yaryura-Tobias, J.A., Grunes, M.S., Todaro, J., McKay, D., Neziroglu, F.A., & Stockman, R. (2000). *Nosological insertion of axis I disorders in the etiology of obsessive-compulsive disorder.* Great Neck, NY: Institute for Biobehavioral Therapy and Research.

Chapter 24

Trauma and Eating Disorders

Marian C. Eberly, RN, MSW, LCSW, DAPA and
Kerry Heath, MS, LPC

> *In this world you will have trouble, but take heart! I have overcome the world.* (John 16:33)

Eating disorder (ED) professionals have long recognized a relationship between EDs and childhood sexual abuse (CSA). Therapists often find themselves working with ED and CSA simultaneously. We therefore explore the most current research and an established, scientific-ally-valid, biblically-based treatment model that addresses this complicated dual diagnosis.

ED professionals agree that CSA occurs at significant rates among ED patients. With quite possibly the largest cohort of ED patients ever evaluated for CSA (*N*=6033), Remuda has found that 49% of its ED patients report CSA. This is approximately 20% higher than in the general population (Connors & Morse, 1993). Clearly, CSA history should always be assessed when working with ED patients. Conversely, when counseling for CSA, providers should also consider the strong potential for EDs.

Initial research failed to find a clear etiological relationship between CSA and ED (Garner & Garfinkel, 1985; Pope & Hudson, 1992; Vize & Cooper, 1995). But more recent studies have challenged these initial findings. Researchers now agree that a history of CSA does play an important role as a nonspecific ED risk factor.

Everill and Waller (1995) found a link between CSA and bulimia nervosa. Wonderlich and colleagues (1997) found that CSA is a risk factor for bulimia more than restricting anorexia nervosa, particularly when psychiatric comorbidity is present. Others (Lating, O'Reilly, & Anderson, 2002) reported that CSA is a nonspecific risk factor not only for EDs but for a range of psychiatric disorders. Wonderlich's groundbreaking research has clarified that CSA increases binge-eating, purging, restricting, and body dissatisfaction, but that sexual trauma occurring in adulthood in the absence of CSA appears unrelated to ED behaviors (Wonderlich et al., 2000; Wonderlich et al., 2001a; Wonderlich et al., 2001b). However, CSA plus adult sexual trauma appears to lead to the greatest ED pathology.

The mechanisms by which CSA promotes ED behavior are not entirely clear. Researchers have offered three main explanations. First, CSA increases body shame. EDs may help victims cope with this shame and may modify the body in ways that reduce shame or distress, e.g., reducing breast size. Second, CSA results in a range of psychopathology, increasing the risk of ED. Third, CSA may lead to an impairment in self-regulation, producing pervasive psychobiological dysregulation and a spate of impulsive behaviors, including EDs. Each of these causal pathways may work synergistically as well.

Regardless of the exact causal pathways, research strongly suggests that those who have experienced CSA have difficulties regulating their intense negative emotions (Linehan, 1993). The cardinal symptoms of EDs—restricting, bingeing, purging, and excessive exercise—all numb emotions and/or create euphoria to displace negative emotions. In short, EDs are, especially for those with intense pain related to CSA, an emotion regulation method.

Treating co-occurring trauma and ED is complicated because, when we treat the trauma, we intensify the negative emotions that lead to ED behaviors; when we treat the ED and encourage patients to stop their ED behaviors, we are asking them to give up a powerful method of emotion regulation on which they have relied, and hence we intensify the trauma experience. Remuda's Trauma Treatment Model is designed to break through this conundrum.

The Experience of Trauma

In her groundbreaking work, *Trauma and Recovery* (1992), Judith Herman defined the traumatic experience: "It is an affliction of the powerless; a victim is rendered powerless by force, meaning and connection are destroyed, it is a threat to life or bodily integrity, differentiated from ordinary suffering."

Herman is attempting to describe the indescribable. Traumatic experiences take people to a place of intense fear, affecting a part of the mind that is only accessed in extreme situations. Bessel van der Kolk and colleagues (1996) further describe trauma:

> Despite the human capacity to survive and adapt, traumatic experiences can alter people's psychological, biological, and social

> equilibrium to such a degree that the memory of one particular event comes to taint all other experiences, spoiling appreciation of the present. This tyranny of the past interferes with the ability to pay attention to both new and familiar situations. When people come to concentrate selectively on reminders of their past, life tends to become colorless, and contemporary experience ceases to be a teacher.

In short, the traumatic experience can become the lens through which all other life experiences are filtered.

Yet trauma survivors who have expressed their suffering in art or literature have also demonstrated the healing power of telling their story. Their testimonies yield evidence of the mind's ability to adapt with strength and creativity to horrific life events. Our role as counselors is to help CSA survivors to do just that, without ED behaviors.

The Therapist's New Role

Diane Langberg, in *Counseling Survivors of Sexual Abuse* (1997), discusses counseling with CSA survivors who find it difficult to talk about their trauma:

> The paradox, of course, is that in order to heal at all, from such violence, one must learn to speak the unspeakable...What is too terrifying to hold for long moments, in the mind must be remembered and reflected upon. That which is utterly impossible to put into words, must finally be spoken about again and again. Not only must the indescribable be described, but that which so powerfully isolates one human being from others must be uttered within the context of relationship if healing is ever to occur.

The therapist needs to embrace a holy regard for the intolerable suffering of the afflicted and realize that it is a high calling to enter into a healing relationship with those who have the courage to reach out beyond this pain. Langberg reminds us of the words of Elie Wiesel, a Holocaust survivor who was able to articulate in writing his encounter with trauma. He says that one who was not there can never begin to understand it, and one who was there can never communicate it. Wiesel tells us that we cannot speak for, or instead of, the survivor. We are encouraged then to take the role of witness. "To be a witness is to know by personal presence and perception what has occurred" (Langberg, 1997). In treating CSA, the therapist has a new role, then—witness to the redeeming work of God in the lives of those who ask for his healing and our help.

Remuda's Trauma Treatment Model

So what does CSA treatment look like when blended with a complicated ED diagnosis? In June 2003, I facilitated a task force to develop a treatment model for the dual diagnosis of trauma and EDs. Although trauma recovery is God's redemptive work and there is no exact formula to follow, there is a need for practical guidance and the simultaneous use of sound biblical principles to ensure safe and effective clinical practice.

The treatment model is predicated on a commitment to the safety of patients, safe practice by clinicians, the highest ethical codes of conduct, scientifically-valid research, and the truth of God's Word. The goals in developing the model were multifactorial: to synthesize the plethora of research on trauma, to apply a biblically-based and cognitive-behavioral theoretical approach to the treatment of trauma with co-occurring EDs, and finally to determine how best to equip patients to cope more effectively by imparting new skills.

Remuda's Trauma Treatment Model is not intended to completely resolve all effects of trauma, since this is often an extended process; but rather to teach patients skills that assist them, at a minimum, in preventing further exacerbation of their ED and, optimally, in achieving recovery from their ED while they take significant steps to work through trauma issues. So often, ED patients use trauma as an explanation for their continued need to rely on ED behaviors. Remuda's Trauma Treatment Model aims to rapidly impart sufficient skills so that patient trauma issues are no longer so intense that ED recovery work is repeatedly frustrated and derailed. The model allows patients to manage their trauma issues satisfactorily so that they can make substantive progress on their ED. Once in recovery from their ED, they can return as needed to more in-depth trauma work without significant risk of ED relapse.

Remuda's Trauma Treatment Model has three phases.

Phase I: Preparation

> You also, like living stones, re being built into a spiritual house. (1 Peter 2:5)

Phase I involves three building blocks that lay the foundation for a stable recovery process: safety, education, and an awareness of living in God's truth.

Patients must be able to keep themselves consistently safe through changing moods and their emotional reactions to the memories they would rather forget. Among ED women, 50% self-injure in some way (Eberly, 2006). Most utilize their ED behaviors to self-soothe or regulate difficult emotions. This underscores the need for safety plans before therapy begins.

Safety starts with building a therapeutic relationship and establishing trust and positive rapport between patient and therapist. Safety also requires education and practice that enable patients to acquire adaptive coping skills. Patients learn to tolerate distress by attaining skills such as distraction, self-soothing, deep breathing, and relaxation. These replacement skills are best taught and *practiced* in Phase I while there are no crises or perceived dangers and prior to challenging discussions about patients' CSA. It is helpful to utilize a skills card listing the various skills. Patients can reference this card when feelings of fear, agitation, or distress occur, reminding themselves of the tools they can use to maintain their safety and prevent reliance on ED behaviors.

In this preparation stage, patients also consider their choices as adults. Educational discussions about responsible living and choice-making are significant at this juncture. People can make irrational behavioral choices based on emotions. Defining what it means to live responsibly throughout treatment can be helpful. Patients may or may not be aware of their own personal slippery slope and how they are most likely to act out when stressed. Discussing these issues honestly and early provides a safety net for patients: they have an explicit plan to use the skills they are learning when the time comes to use them.

Nurturing hope in someone experiencing hopelessness is the work of the Holy Spirit, but often the Spirit's conduit is an earthly servant. Exploring together the loving nature of God, the patient's identity in Christ, and the provision of his grace is necessary education to help rebuild crushed spirits. It is difficult to work with the hopeless, because there must simultaneously be respect for the loss and suffering and a tenacious desire not to leave anyone in that barren, lonely, desolate place. Walking out of the grave with someone is not easy. It requires great patience and trust in the Lord, who is, after all, the redeemer of the days the locust has eaten (Joel 2:25).

These spiritual explorations open the door for patients to learn how to live in God's truth. Adversity and suffering can lead to a place of spiritual healing and hope, and into the safe arms of a loving God. But we obviously cannot assume that CSA survivors feel God's presence or have an understanding of his love. Trauma "has the potential to draw one to God or away from God...but often to confuse one about God" (Langberg, 1997). A common question worthy of exploration is, "Where was God?" This familiar refrain is one of the most important questions that trauma survivors ask and is intensely important to explore with them. CSA survivors may have lost hope and trust in God, because they had believed that God would never allow them to suffer in this horrific way. For many survivors, this damage produces powerful despair: People can feel desperate because they experience their faith as shattered. Reestablishing hope is the key ingredient to begin resolving this grief and loss in a personally meaningful way.

Phase II: Transformation

You can be transformed by the renewing of your mind. (Romans 12:2)

Within the context established in Phase I, the process of transformation can begin, since patients now have the tools to speak about their trauma without relying on ED behaviors to cope with the emotions that arise.

Bessel van der Kolk and colleagues (1996) described trauma as coloring all present situations, infectiously invading one's worldview, such that "contemporary experience ceases to be a teacher." The constructivist narrative approach challenges this dimension of trauma and successfully battles it to the ground (Meichenbaum & Fitzpatrick, 1993). This cognitive therapy approach works for patients who can address trauma issues without severe emotional decompensation.

Narrative psychology studies the stories we tell and the meaning we assign to them: how we as a result construct our worldview. People construct narratives that tell others about them. Threatening and traumatic experiences can invalidate the most fundamental beliefs one holds. Narratives once held no longer make sense in light of the trauma, the new reality. Typically, new narratives are therefore created, often negative and false, to help make sense of the trauma.

Here's a basic example. A woman is raped by a man. As a result, she determines that all men are to be feared, untrustworthy, hostile, and dangerous. Because God did not protect her, she concludes that he does not exist. The woman is not merely overgeneralizing to the entire male population; the traumatic act has shattered her worldview and fundamental belief in God. "The basic tacit rules or implicit beliefs that guide a person's life can be challenged or nullified by stressful events" (Meichenbaum, 1995).

Recovery from such trauma is contingent upon rebuilding the victim's world. The constructivist narrative would support rebuilding by assimilating the victimization experience in an adaptive manner (Meichenbaum, 1995). The goal is to help patients tell their story and in the process reconstruct it. Patients are helped to find new meaning, salvaging something redemptive from the trauma. This enables patients to have a new sense of mastery, control, competence, and self-acceptance. It allows them to question and pry open the door of faith once again, and even to trust God.

Patients reconsider the trauma-influenced implications and conclusions they have drawn about themselves and the world. They can learn to cope more effectively as they explore these issues, developing meaningful and acceptable interpretations of stressful life events, such as "my family drew closer to each other than ever before, and certainly closer to God." Tim Hansel (1985), mountaineer turned author, constructed this narrative after a fall from a mountain which shattered his body:

> But one of the ways that our faith expresses itself is by our ability to be still, to be present and not to panic or lose perspective. God still does his greatest work in the most difficult of circumstances. The spirit is more powerful than the will, more powerful than pain, more powerful than our weakness and our doubt. We can experience the living God here and now, and our most difficult circumstances will be the very opportunity for our faith to grow.

This is also a time for patients to resolve losses and learn to grieve. This may entail naming losses, perpetrators, identifying negligence for what it was, and accepting what is in the present tense. Grief and loss work is an in-depth, individualized process. Patients may become impatient because it can take a long time and is frankly excruciatingly painful for them. Grief is dreaded by many, leading some to minimize and short-circuit it. Therapists must be vigilant about this potential minimization.

Other issues addressed in this phase are voice, relationships, and power (Langberg, 1997). Each must be explored one layer at a time in response to trauma. Finally, it is pivotal to move toward forgiveness in altering the narratives one has constructed about oneself, the world, and God. Patients are helped to understand the price paid for holding onto resentment. Many good resources exist for assisting patients with forgiveness, such as John Ensor's *Experiencing God's Forgiveness: The Journey from Guilt to Gladness* or John MacArthur's *Forgiveness: The Art of Giving and Receiving.* Ultimately, this phase of treatment allows persons to walk through the sorrow and suffering to the other side, finding peace.

Phase III: Integration

> Being confident of this, that he who began a good work in you will carry it on into completion. (Philippians 1:6)

The final phase is called *integration* because it provides opportunities to integrate the skills and truths one has discovered in the previous phases of trauma recovery and apply these to the everyday challenges of ED recovery. When tensions and fears escalate, the skills of the earlier phases are brought to bear on the situation. Patients can now focus squarely on ED recovery, including such areas such as body image and establishing a continuing care plan.

Patients often continue to grapple in Phase III with questions of personal safety, such as learning not to take out their frustrations and anger on themselves physically or emotionally through the ED. Choosing to trust in themselves and others in decision making on such issues as nutrition, medication, medical concerns, and aftercare plans can continue to be a challenge, but is an ongoing part of learning to make responsible life choices while recovering from an ED.

Many patients find group work to be beneficial at this point. Various groups provide opportunities for exploration and expression in ways that individual therapy cannot. Art therapy is one such modality which can foster new insights. Trauma recovery groups provide support, build community, reinforce skills, and prepare patients for life's daily challenges by offering a safe place to practice the skills learned in Phase I and reinforce the voice, relationship skills, and personal power explored with the therapist in Phase II.

Ultimately the goal of Phase III is simple: for patients to use the skills they mastered in the earlier phases to manage their trauma issues, so that trauma no longer derails or impedes ED treatment. Patients can now engage in full-scale ED treatment and achieve substantial ED recovery. Since EDs can be life threatening and are always medically compromising, it is essential to treat the ED right away. Once the ED is stabilized during Phase III, patients can later resume trauma work as needed without significant risk of ED relapse.

Summary

Trauma recovery work, combined with ED recovery, can be challenging and complicated. We harness the knowledge available to us and ask the Lord for his blessing as we go about this restorative work. And most of all, we harness our faith. As Langberg (1997) reminds us so frankly, "recovery from trauma never happens in a straight line."

Case Study

Trauma and eating disorders are often treated simultaneously, as with Jennifer. Jennifer was a college student, admitted to Remuda Ranch with a history of bulimia nervosa and major depression. She admitted at 134 lbs.,

96% of her ideal body weight. Jennifer also exhibited self-injurious behavior (SIB). SIB began only weeks prior to admission and typically involved scratching her arms with her fingernails when intrusive thoughts about her past came to mind.

Given her recent SIB, Jennifer was proactively placed on high-risk precaution status at admission. This alerted her treatment team to keep her within their eyesight for 72 hours following admission. Jennifer's therapist met with her during this time to teach her basic grounding skills and help her develop a safety plan that she could rely on should she experience urges toward SIB.

Jennifer's psychosocial assessment revealed an extensive childhood history of sexual abuse. Jennifer had been repeatedly molested by an older cousin from early childhood into her teenage years. She was also date-raped at a party just prior to treatment. She was open with her therapist about these experiences, but did not want to discuss them with her family. She was quite obviously ashamed and embarrassed about her sexual abuse history.

As Jennifer entered Phase I of Remuda's Trauma Treatment Model, she struggled. She was increasingly uncomfortable addressing her feelings of shame, grief, and loss, and experienced heightened anxiety from discontinuing her binge/purge cycle. She therefore required multiple one-to-one coaching sessions to help her learn the cognitive-behavioral skills needed to cope safely with her difficult emotions. Once she had practiced these skills sufficiently, she began using them daily. They replaced the eating disorder behaviors and SIB that she had previously believed were the only ways to alleviate the anxiety caused by her traumatic memories. This was a turning point. She was no longer resorting to bulimia and SIB to manage her moods.

Jennifer was now able to begin Phase II work. During Phase II, she routinely relied on distress tolerance skills to deal with difficult feelings. It was common to see her journaling or drawing after a distressing therapy session: She was using appropriate forms of distraction. She also frequently applied a favorite hand lotion during free time as a form of self-soothing. She had previously felt that she did not deserve to use this nice lotion.

During Phase II, if appropriate, patients are encouraged to salvage something redemptive from their trauma experiences. As Jennifer's scheduled week of intensive family therapy approached, she asked for assistance planning how to discuss her sexual abuse with her baby sister. She decided to do so at the beginning of Family Week. The carefully planned discussion with her sister went well. Jennifer was shocked to learn that her sister had also been molested by the same cousin. This revelation gave Jennifer a deepened feeling that she wasn't alone in her pain, that her experiences and struggles were truly not her fault but were normal and valid reactions to what she had endured. Jennifer also learned that using her voice to speak the truth could bring validation and healing rather than shame and pain.

The sisters' mutual validation and newfound alliance gave them both the courage to tell their parents about the abuse. During Family Week, Jennifer unveiled the secret that she and her family had been avoiding nearly her entire life. She spoke the truth in love, and in response her family embraced an emotional openness and vulnerability with one another that Jennifer had longed for but never imagined possible. In particular, Jennifer was able to talk to her father for the first time about their father-daughter relationship.

As Family Week ended, the family members continued to voice that a profound healing had begun to take root. Of her own accord, Jennifer realized that something redemptive had been drawn from her abuse. Her conviction in this deepened in subsequent weeks. She believed that without the need to talk openly about the horrible experiences she had endured, her family would never have learned to communicate soul to soul.

Following her intensive Family Week, Jennifer continued to work on grieving a childhood lost to sexual abuse and its aftermath. Through trauma recovery group she recognized that years of molestation had left her vulnerable to the date-rape that occurred in her freshman year of college. As a result, she no longer blamed herself or God for her perpetrator's willful actions. Anger at God receded and her relationship with God began to thaw.

Jennifer had now accomplished some preliminary, but powerful, reconstruction of her trauma story, finding new meaning and peace about the experience. She was ready for Phase III of her trauma work, shifting focus to deal primarily with the aspects of her eating disorder that had not yet been addressed. During Phase III, Jennifer successfully remained at her target weight and free of eating disorder behaviors and SIB. Although she began Phase III work at Remuda, she needed to continue it following discharge.

In her discharge plan, she arranged to continue addressing her abuse history and related issues with an outpatient treatment team with whom she made initial outpatient appointments even before leaving Remuda. She also found an outpatient trauma recovery and eating disorder support group. Jennifer expressed a desire to receive ongoing support in her efforts to fully embrace the concepts of grace and forgiveness that had helped in her trauma recovery. She began the process of locating a church that could promote this spiritual growth.

At discharge, she recommitted to remain free of self-harm and developed an updated safety plan with her treatment team to rely on during the transitional days ahead. She had significant body image work remaining, but life-threatening ED behaviors were in remission. She had successfully completed Remuda's Trauma Treatment Model and had built a foundation for continued recovery in the months ahead from both her trauma and her eating disorder. She left Remuda with much hope for her future, believing that she had crossed a threshold toward healthy living and would continue journeying in that direction for many years to come.

References

Connors, M.E. & Morse, W. (1993). Sexual abuse and eating disorders: A review. *International Journal of Eating Disorders, 13,*1-11.

Eberly, M.C. (2006). Understanding self-injurious behavior in eating disorders. *The Remuda Review: The Christian Journal of Eating Disorders, 4,* 26-30.

Ensor, J. (1997). *Experiencing God's Forgiveness: The Journey from Guilt to Gladness.* Colorado Springs: Navpress.

Everill, J.T. & Waller, G. (1995). Reported sexual abuse and eating psychopathology: A review of the evidence for a causal link. *International Journal of Eating Disorders, 18,* 1-11.

Garner, D.M. & Garfinkel, P.E. (1985). *Handbook of psychotherapy for anorexia nervosa and bulimia.* New York: Guilford Press.

Hansel, T. (1985). *Ya gotta keep dancing: In the midst of life's hurts you can find joy.* Colorado Springs: Victor Publishers.

Herman, J.L. (1992). *Trauma and recovery.* New York: Basic Books.

Langberg, D.L. (1997). *Counseling survivors of sexual abuse.* Wheaton, IL: Tyndale.

Lating, J.M., O'Reilly, M.A., & Anderson, K.P. (2002). Eating disorders and post-traumatic stress: Phenomenological and treatment considerations using the two-factor model. *International Journal of Emergency Mental Health, 4,* 113-8.

Linehan, M.M. (1993) *Cognitive behavioral treatment of borderline personality disorder.* New York: Guilford Press.

MacArthur, J. (2000). *Forgiveness: The art of giving and receiving.* Nashville: W Publishing.

Meichenbaum, D. & Fitzpatrick, D. (1993). Narrative constructivist perspective of stress and coping: Stress inoculation applications. In L. Goldberger & S. Brenitz (Eds.), *Handbook of stress (2nd ed.).* New York: Free Press.

Meichenbaum, D. (1995). *A clinical handbook/practical therapist manual for assessing and treating adults with post-traumatic stress disorder (PTSD).* New York: Institute Press.

Pope, H.G. & Hudson, J.I. (1992). Is childhood sexual abuse a risk factor for bulimia nervosa? *American Journal of Psychiatry, 149,* 455-63.

Van der Kolk, B.A., McFarlane, A.C., & Weisaeth, L. (Eds.). (1996). *Traumatic stress: The effects of overwhelming experience on the mind, body and society.* New York: Guilford Press.

Vize, C.M. & Cooper, P.J. (1995). Sexual abuse in patients with eating disorders, patients with depression and normal controls: A comparative study. *The British Journal of Psychiatry, 167*, 80-85.

Wonderlich, S.A., Brewerton, T.D., Jocic, Z., Dansky, B.S., & Abbott, D.W. (1997). Relationship of childhood sexual abuse and eating disorders. *Journal of the American Academy of Child and Adolescent Psychiatry, 36*, 1107-15.

Wonderlich, S.A., Crosby, R.D., Mitchell, J.E., Roberts, J.A., Haseltine, B., Demuth, G., & Thompson, K. (2000). Relationship of childhood sexual abuse and eating disturbance in children. *Journal of the American Academy of Child and Adolescent Psychiatry, 39,* 1277-83.

Wonderlich, S., Crosby, R., Mitchell, J., Thompson, K., Redlin, J. Demuth, G., & Smyth, J. (2000). Pathways mediating sexual abuse and eating disturbance in children. *International Journal of Eating Disorders, 29,* 270-9.

Wonderlich, S., Crosby, R., Mitchell, J., Thompson, K., Redlin, J. Demuth, G., Smyth, J., & Haseltine, B. (2001b). Eating disturbance and sexual trauma in childhood and adulthood. *International Journal of Eating Disorders, 30,* 401-12.

Chapter 25

Substance Use and Eating Disorders

A. David Wall, PhD, Marian C. Eberly, RN, MSW, LCSW, DAPA, and Kevin R. Wandler, MD

In Romans 7, the apostle Paul said: "I have the desire to do what is good, but I cannot carry it out. For what I do is not the good I want to do; no, the evil I do not want to do—this I keep on doing." This summarizes the experience of many who fight addictions. Indeed, addiction is a common human experience.

Twenty years ago, *addiction* meant alcohol or drugs. Now the literature describes addictions to sex, gambling, shopping, food, exercise, the internet, anger, and work. Ten years ago, *dual diagnosis* usually referred to someone with alcohol or substance use who also had depression or anxiety. Today we talk about *co-occurring diagnoses*, where many psychiatric disorders occur simultaneously.

Blinder et al. (1998) reported that 26% of eating disorder (ED) patients have co-occurring substance use disorders (SUDs). At Remuda, where acuity is high, 40% of ED inpatients have SUD. Nearly 90% of Remuda's ED patients also have co-occurring depressive and 50% anxiety disorders. One might think that patients with anorexia would more likely use stimulants to reduce appetite, while those with bulimia would more likely use alcohol and marijuana to deal with emotional chaos. But data show almost equivalent drug choices among patients with anorexia, bulimia, and ED not otherwise specified (EDNOS). This suggests that ED patients are choosing drugs for reasons beyond the ED itself—likely the same range of reasons that drive most people to addictions.

Substance abuse and dependence diagnoses differ. *DSM-IV-TR* (American Psychiatric Association [APA], 2000) defines *substance abuse* as a maladaptive pattern of substance use within a 12-month period that leads to clinically significant impairment or distress. The criteria include: any failure to fulfill major role obligations, such as work; use of the substance in ways that are physically hazardous, such as driving under the influence; legal problems; and/or continued substance use despite persistent and recurring problems, such as family conflict surrounding the use of substances.

According to *DSM-IV-TR* (APA, 2000), *substance dependence* involves the same 12-month time frame as *substance abuse*, but more extreme impairment. For example, important activities are given up or reduced, and/or significant time is spent obtaining the substance or recovering from its use. With *dependence* there are also criteria reflecting loss of control: e.g., larger amounts used over a longer period than intended, persistent desire or unsuccessful efforts to reduce or control use. When tolerance or withdrawal symptoms occur, the diagnostic specifier, *with physiological dependence*, is added. Tolerance means needing a significant increase in consumption to achieve intoxication or desired effects. Withdrawal involves a syndrome of physical and psychological symptoms following abrupt discontinuation or rapid decrease in substance intake.

The American Society of Addiction Medicine and American Psychiatric Association agree that therapies need to be individualized to specific patient needs and adjusted based on patients' responses to treatment. Detoxification is not a substitute for treatment, but is one component of a comprehensive treatment strategy. According to the American Psychiatric Association's Practice Guideline for the Treatment of Patients with Substance Use Disorders (American Psychiatric Association, 2006), SUD treatment programs should diagnose and treat associated psychiatric disorders. As such, many SUD programs are prepared to treat co-occurring depression, anxiety, trauma, Axis II, and certain other issues that frequently occur in SUD populations. However, many SUD programs are not equipped to offer the intensive monitoring needed by patients with anorexia and bulimia. Often, when patients with co-occurring SUD and ED begin SUD treatment and stop using substances, their ED intensifies. Most SUD programs are not set up to manage these patients, who begin bingeing, purging, and restricting food. Similarly, when patients with SUD and ED enter ED programs and reduce their ED behaviors, their cravings for substances intensify. Yet according to the American Psychiatric Association's Practice Guideline for the Treatment of Patients with Eating Disorders (Yager et al., 2006), concurrent treatment for ED and SUD should be attempted, since these patients have a range of medical complications, require longer inpatient stays, and are less compliant with treatment.

Because of ED's complexities and significant medical sequelae, we believe that most patients with co-occurring ED and SUD are best managed in inpatient ED treatment facilities that offer detoxification services. At Remuda, we treat ED and SUD together in safe, intensive programs. Because of their interaction, the detoxification and ED issues need to be addressed simultaneously. Treatment teams at such facilities should include at minimum a psychiatrist, primary care provider, dietician, family therapist, 24-hour nursing, and a therapist skilled in cognitive-behavioral therapy (CBT).

Remuda's post-discharge outcomes suggest that among patients we treat with co-occurring ED and SUD, 95% are in good ED recovery and 67% report complete abstinence from substance use at one-year post-discharge. This 95% ED recovery rate is substantially higher than the 50 to 75% one-year recovery expectation in the field (Richards et al., 2000). Likewise, the 67% substance use abstinence rate appears higher than the 25 to 50% one-year abstinence expectation for those who have completed a residential chemical dependency treatment program (Substance Abuse and Mental Health Services Administration, 2005).

Biological Considerations

Most people exposed to addictive drugs do not become addicted or dependent on them. Evidence suggests that the likelihood of addiction, especially to alcohol and nicotine, is strongly affected by heredity. Greater vulnerability to alcohol abuse, for example, has been identified on the A1 allele of the D2 dopamine receptor gene. An additional 20+ receptors are being studied to understand the genetics and possible treatment options for those with SUD. Clearly, the physiological effects of addictive drugs on the human body and brain are partially engineered by each person's genetic code. How a person responds physically to a drug also involves setting, mood, previous use experiences, and social/peer influences. We discuss these factors later.

Most drugs of abuse release dopamine and other chemicals that produce pleasure. As tolerance builds, drug dependence is further reinforced, because more of the drug is needed to obtain the same effect. Neurons in the brain change—possibly permanently. Cocaine, nicotine, alcohol, amphetamine, and cannabis all release dopamine in the nucleus accumbens, a brain site producing neuronal reinforcing effects. After detoxification, addicts' brains may be permanently altered, sensitizing them to relapse.

Our brains seek balance or homeostasis where we feel good. When our bodies need something to maintain homeostasis, we experience unpleasant feelings. Dopamine is a neurotransmitter associated with pleasure. Studies suggest that individuals with substance abuse problems have fewer dopamine sites and, thus, possibly need more dopamine. Many street drugs increase dopamine levels. It is believed that this abnormal need for dopamine makes individuals more prone to SUD. There is also some evidence that repeated drug use may decrease brain dopamine sites, exacerbating the need for dopamine.

Individuals with attention deficit/hyperactivity disorder (ADHD) are prone to SUD. Those with ADHD have brains that are congenitally under-stimulated. Thus, they seek stimulation to bring about balance. It is likely that individuals with ADHD self-medicate through SUD. Appropriately, medical treatment of ADHD involves stimulant medications. Individuals with anxiety disorders also have an elevated SUD risk. In this case, substances are used to reduce anxiety. Because substances can do this quickly with little effort, SUDs are readily reinforced.

The drugs we primarily see at Remuda include nicotine, alcohol, marijuana, cocaine, and amphetamines. Opiates, hallucinogens, solvents, and designer drugs like ecstasy are not common in our treatment setting and will not be discussed in this chapter, though many of the treatment principles are the same.

Whether legal or not, prescribed or not, all addictive substances must be carefully reviewed by a physician to obtain the information needed to treat the individual properly. At Remuda, a psychiatric provider includes lab results to determine whether to begin detoxification according to evidence-based protocols.

Nicotine

When offered a chance to quit smoking, most of our ED inpatients refuse because they believe they can only deal with one addiction at a time. In their perception, smoking helps with their anxiety. Many also fear weight gain following smoking cessation. There appears to be convincing evidence for the association between smoking cessation and weight gain, but the actual mechanisms are not well understood. We do know that weight gain is related to a decreased resting metabolic rate following nicotine cessation. Nicotine Replacement Therapy (NRT) appears to be effective in delaying post-cessation weight gain with nicotine gum being particularly effective. The post-cessation weight gain for women is generally 10 pounds in the first year, even if they do not eat more.

With nicotine withdrawal, initial symptoms include anxiety, increased appetite, nicotine cravings, irritability, frustration, anger, decreased heart rate, restlessness, and concentration difficulties. These symptoms begin within 4 to 24 hours. When patients choose to stop smoking, an individualized program may include NRT, such as nicotine patches and gum, plus cognitive-behavioral therapy and clinical support. With ED patients, it is important to directly address weight gain fears as part of smoking cessation interventions.

Alcohol

Alcohol is generally avoided by those with restricting anorexia because it contains calories. However, in individuals with anorexia nervosa, binge-eating/purging type, and in those with bulimia, alcohol is frequently used and then purged.

Alcohol is a sedative. Many ED patients start using alcohol to self-medicate anxiety. In low amounts, alcohol calms the nerves and creates disinhibition. Over time, it takes more alcohol to potentiate the anxiolytic effect, such that self-medication can become alcohol dependence.

All patients admitted to Remuda with alcohol dependence and some with alcohol abuse are placed on an evidence-based detoxification protocol. Detoxification is not a substitute for treatment, but is one component of a comprehensive treatment strategy. The long-term consequences of alcohol abuse/dependence may not be known for months. Mild mental confusion, common in the first weeks of detoxification, may be prolonged in severely malnourished ED patients.

Cannabis

Cannabis, commonly known as marijuana or pot, is the most commonly used illegal drug in the United States. It is likewise the most commonly used illegal drug among Remuda's ED patients. Nevertheless, cannabis is seldom used by our patients with anorexia because of its known appetite-stimulating properties.

Cannabis can cause undesirable side effects, increasing with high doses. Side effects may include dry mouth, red eyes, increased appetite, impaired perception and motor skills, decreased short-term memory, paranoia, mood swings, and hallucinations. The degree of and reaction to these side effects varies across individuals.

Fortunately, medical detoxification is not needed for cannabis cessation. Supportive interventions for headache, malaise, and sleep disturbance are indicated. If cannabis users also smoke cigarettes, cannabis relapse rates are higher. Therefore, such patients should be strongly urged to give up all smoking or they are apt to impair their recovery from cannabis abuse.

Stimulants

Stimulants are often used by ED patients for weight control. Stimulants described here include illegal amphetamines such as methamphetamine ("crystal meth") and prescriptive amphetamines such as Dexedrine®, Adderall®, and Phentermine (the *phen* in fen-phen). Cocaine and crack cocaine also fall into this general class. Nicotine and caffeine both have stimulant properties, but not to the same extent.

Amphetamines and cocaine are appetite-suppressing drugs. Although those with restricting anorexia generally do not use them because they are able to manage their appetite without drugs, these substances of abuse/dependence are used frequently by patients with bulimia. A patient with bulimia will often use them following a several day binge, to curb appetite and to resume restrictive ED behaviors.

Stimulant withdrawal signs and symptoms include aches, pains, anergia, increased appetite, drug craving, anhedonia, depression, chills, tremors, and hypersomnolence. No medications have demonstrated efficacy for detoxification from stimulants, but fortunately there are rarely life threatening symptoms. Medications that have been used to treat symptoms of stimulant withdrawal include tricyclic antidepressants and short-acting benzodiazepines such as lorazepam.

When someone uses stimulants, massive amounts of dopamine are released. Stimulants are very addicting, because dopamine creates pleasure. The consequence of chronic stimulant use is decreased dopamine activity. Ultimately, it may take months for recovering stimulant addicts to achieve stable dopamine levels so they are able to feel normal without using drugs.

A significant challenge exists for psychiatric providers treating patients with severe attention deficit/hyperactivity disorder (ADHD) and co-occurring anorexia. Medications for ADHD include stimulants such as Adderall® or Concerta®. These medications decrease appetite, further promoting weight loss and intensifying anorexic symptoms. Individuals with anorexia who need stimulants for ADHD should thus be treated in an inpatient setting or intensive lower level to monitor their ability to focus, concentrate, and gain weight.

Psychosocial Considerations

A carefully designed study found that non drug-using individuals with lower dopaminergic activity experienced an injection of a stimulant as pleasant; non drug-using individuals with normal or high levels of dopaminergic activity found the stimulant to be unpleasant. This suggests that fewer dopamine receptors may be a cause of stimulant abuse, whereas normal or high levels of dopamine receptors may reduce the likelihood of stimulant abuse.

Those who abuse cocaine and those with obsessive-compulsive disorder both have less dopaminergic activity in areas of the frontal lobe. Nora Volkow, Director of the National Institute on Drug Abuse, believes that this abnormal dopaminergic frontal lobe activity is "...likely involved in the obsessiveness of drug addiction...." (Macmillan, 2003). Here we have a biological condition—lower dopaminergic activity—apparently intensifying a psychological experience—obsessionality. Not surprisingly, those with SUD often have intrusive and obsessional drug-related thoughts resisting their control.

Just when we think it is safe to make a direct connection between biology and substance abuse, further research complicates the issue. In one study, primates were divided into two groups. One group was isolated by being housed individually; the other group was housed socially. Across the group of primates housed individually, no differences occurred in the numbers of dopamine receptors. However, in the socially housed primates, the dominant members of the social group had higher numbers of dopamine receptors than nondominant members. The dominant primates with greater numbers of dopamine receptors were less likely to self-administer cocaine than the members of the social group with fewer dopamine receptors. This research suggests that interpersonal and social factors may influence brain structure, particularly the numbers of dopamine receptors.

These several studies combined demonstrate the complex and synergistic interactions between genetics/biology, environment, and behavior in the development of substance abuse. The biological clearly interfaces with the psychosocial. We cannot neatly compartmentalize the biological and psychosocial dimensions in terms of their impact on substance abuse, because our biology/brain influences our behavior and our behavior influences our biology/brain. In short, it is true that biologically some people are more prone to abusing substances. At the same time, individuals are not simply helpless victims of their genes who have no choice or responsibility, nor do they exist in a vacuum apart from the influence of other people. As such, authorities recognize that psychosocial factors, such as peers and individual choice, play a role in the development of substance abuse and must be addressed in SUD treatment.

Psychological Dimension: A Functional Perspective

All human behaviors, including SUDs, have a purpose or *function*. The function of most behaviors is to reduce physical and/or emotional pain or obtain physical and/or emotional pleasure. It is critical to understand SUD's function(s) for each individual to help the person recover.

Behaviors are motivated by each person's perception of needs. We may or may not be able to accurately verbalize a specific need, but at some point we become aware of it because it creates an unpleasant feeling for us—uneasiness, discomfort, or pain. At some point, for example, we become aware of thirst and are motivated to drink. Our thirst isn't the actual need; fluid intake for bodily function is the true need. Thirst represents our awareness or perception of the body's need.

Needs can be subtle and hard to pinpoint or they can be intense and specific. As a need grows, the unpleasant sensation usually increases. Two or more needs can occur simultaneously and may compete for attention. There are many types of human needs, including physiological, emotional, security, relational, and spiritual needs. One of the developmental challenges all individuals face is learning behavioral strategies to meet their needs and gain control over when, how, and where to fulfill them.

Based on experiences, our brains learn which methods do and do not meet our needs. Behaviors that remove the aversive feelings of unmet needs are reinforced—more likely to be repeated in the future when we experience symptoms of the same need again. Behaviors that result in a sense pleasure are also reinforced—more likely to be repeated in the future. Some behaviors both remove aversive feelings and add pleasure; e.g., narcotics relieve pain and add a sense of euphoria. Most substances of abuse are of this type—they provide pleasure and also relieve aversive states.

As with any behavior, substance use will be more intensely reinforced when there is a short time interval between use of the substance and pain reduction or pleasure onset; i.e., when there is *instant gratification.* Most substances of abuse offer instant gratification, whereas many alternative ways of gaining pleasure or reducing aversive states take longer.

Punishment is the opposite of reinforcement: It suppresses behaviors, making them less likely to be repeated. Substance abuse almost always results in aversive consequences—punishment. However, the punishing consequences are often delayed by hours, days, months, or years—e.g., hangover the next day, liver disease years down the line. As such, the immediate gratification of substance abuse often outweighs the delayed punishment.

In short, substance use is reinforced because it takes away aversive and/or adds desirable experiences, usually does so quickly and without immediate punishing consequences. Substances therefore appear to meet our needs. As such, SUD assessment is not limited to diagnosis, but involves attempts to understand the function of the substance use in the individual's internal and external world, i.e., what needs does the substance meet? The reasons are seldom limited to a few needs, though some needs may predominate.

A behavior that is meeting needs cannot simply be terminated. It must be replaced by another behavior capable of meeting the same needs, or the needs will remain unmet and unpleasant feelings will mount. The individual must also believe that alternative behaviors can meet their needs, or they will be unwilling to try replacement behaviors.

Needs can be biological, psychological, social, and/or spiritual. Our biological needs are obvious—food, air, water, sleep, and so on. We all experience psychosocial needs, but they are not as easy to describe. Though not an exhaustive list, the following includes some of the most important psychosocial needs: the need to love, be loved, belong to a group, be autonomous, be creative, be secure, be special, contribute, and feel good about who we are. Psychosocial needs can be expressed in positive terms, such as the need for love, or in the negative terms, such as the need to avoid rejection. Negative needs are often more powerful. For example, the need to avoid rejection may overpower the need to belong, resulting in avoidance of others. Psychosocial needs are often more powerful than biological needs. Drug use for social acceptance may thus be a more powerful reinforcer than drug use to increase dopaminergic activity in the brain.

Need states change over time. We have all felt extreme thirst, but once we drink water, the need dissipates, losing its power to control our behavior. The need states underlying SUDs also come and go. When a need typically met by substance abuse goes away for awhile, those with SUD may truly believe, "I will never drink again," because they are unaware that the need driving their SUD may reappear later.

When a need is temporarily satisfied, other needs become more salient and powerful in influencing behavior. A woman who drinks to cover the pain of romantic rejection may cut back on alcohol when she meets a new boyfriend. However, if he breaks up with her, the drinking will likely increase again. Our sense of reality and predictions about our behavior, e.g., "I will never drink again," typically reflect whatever need(s) are strongest at any given time.

Social/Cultural Factors

A range of social and cultural factors are also associated with SUD, including poverty, access to drugs, perception that drug use is a low risk activity, perceived parental apathy, parental substance abuse, and perceived peer approval for drug use. There are also social and cultural factors that protect against SUD, including religious faith, goals that would be impeded by substance abuse such as academic or athletic success, perception of strong parental reaction against drugs, strong parent-child bonds, clear limits set by parents, consistent discipline, and perceived peer rejection of drug abuse. Among these social and cultural factors, the two primary groups of influence are family and peers. We explore these below.

People associate with groups by which they are accepted and receive affirmation. Peer groups have been referred to by several names, including social reference groups and social comparison groups. We have a sense of belonging and security in these groups and take from them our cues about how we should behave, what we should believe, how we should dress, and so on.

Developmentally, our first social comparison group is our family of origin. The family reinforces how we behave and what we value. Reaching school age usually means that exposure to groups outside the family increases significantly. The need for social acceptance by peers increases as children age. This need can have a dominant influence on the choice to use substances.

Young adolescents sometimes try to maintain inclusion in the family and peer group by living double lives, with one set of behaviors and values at home and another at school. This double life can include the use of substances. If parents do not have strong standards against substance use, the peer group often wins out.

Adolescents with extreme needs for social approval and popularity, and/or with tenuous social relations, are more vulnerable to peer influences. For these adolescents, peer acceptance may overpower needs for family acceptance, athletic and academic success, health, and spiritual values. Although needs may shift over time, by then, persons may have become psychologically and/or physically addicted to a substance such that, even when the need for social acceptance wanes, substance use continues.

As such, when patients have an ED with a co-occurring SUD, dealing with the issue of return to a substance-using peer group becomes imperative in treatment, family sessions, and aftercare planning. The chances of recovery from either the SUD or ED decrease if patients maintain a substance-using social reference group. Although the group may tolerate patients who don't use substances, it is often nearly impossible for patients to refrain at parties and gatherings where alcohol/drugs are used.

Psychosocial Assessment and Treatment

Twelve Step programs have been instrumental in leading millions with substance use problems into a lifetime of recovery. In this section, however, we will not discuss the 12 Steps, because a large body of literature already exists dealing with the 12 Steps from both secular and Christian standpoints. Instead, we discuss assessment and treatment issues that must be addressed in the complex, dynamically interacting, co-occurring world of ED and SUD, where research indicates that 12 Steps alone would be insufficient for recovery (Yager et al., 2006).

In treating SUD, it is important to assess whether the substance use is ego-syntonic or dystonic. *Ego-syntonic* refers to behaviors consistent with

Table 1. Substance Use Disorder Assessment Strategy

Assessment Area	**Sample Content of Assessment**
Need	Acceptance, belonging, respect, autonomy, etc.
Symptom	Loneliness, insecure feelings, anxiety.
Target	"I'm not attractive." "I need peer approval, guys paying attention to me!"
Behavioral Strategy	Lose weight, get toned. Do whatever it takes to fit in, including substance use.
Outcome: Did it work?	Reinforcement: Decreased anxiety, increased security, increased pleasure.

individuals' self-perception and values. *Ego-dystonic* refers to behaviors incongruent with individuals' self-perception and values. This assessment guides treatment. Table 1 outlines a SUD assessment strategy used at Remuda.

The treatment team pays particular attention to understanding patients' needs. Psychological needs are "felt" in the form of symptoms, such as sadness, anger, loneliness, and shame. Individuals attribute their symptoms to particular causes. For example, a patient may believe that she feels lonely because she is fat. These attributed causes are known as the target(s). The target then leads to a behavioral strategy. For example, if an ED patient believes she is lonely because she is fat, she may use ED behaviors to fix the targeted cause of her loneliness—weight. However, because the attributed target differs from the true need, the behavioral strategy will not meet the need and the negative feelings associated with the need will remain.

In the case of EDs, the true need is normally psychosocial or spiritual, and rarely physical. Therefore, even if the ED behaviors are reinforced, the unpleasant symptoms of the need soon return. For instance, if a patient loses weight and receives attention from guys, this attention will reinforce her ED behaviors. However, her true need was not attention from guys based on her appearance, but acceptance as a person. Hence, lonely feelings will return. ED patients erroneously conclude they must still be too fat and thus intensify their ED behaviors. This vicious cycle is hard to break unless the true need is identified.

The same logic applies to substance abuse. Fundamentally, almost all behaviors are motivated by needs. Hence, substance use is a behavioral strategy designed to meet needs by changing the felt or experienced symptoms of these needs.

Treatment, at least in part, involves helping patients to see the connection between the underlying need(s) and their SUD/ED behaviors. Then, treatment offers alternative ways for patients to meet their needs to prevent ED and SUD relapse. Often, SUD and ED are used by patients to meet the same underlying needs and must thus be treated simultaneously. If not, patients will lean more on the one when the other is removed. For more details on alternative methods that patients may use to meet their needs, see Eberly, Wall, & Cabrera, 2003 or Linehan, 1993.

Clearly, part of treatment is untangling the legitimate need from the behavioral strategy. We may say, "You need to stop drinking," but patients may hear, "You have to go back to extreme social anxiety and not have friends." It is easy for people to confuse a need with the method they have used to meet that need. For instance, people spend their whole lives pursuing money—and in so doing, sacrificing time with family and friends, recreation, and spiritual development—when the underlying need may be self-esteem or respect. The selected method or behavioral strategy for fulfilling the need can quickly become someone's focal point, such that people lose sight of the true underlying need. We see this often with ED patients, where thinness becomes the only obsession; whatever need they had hoped to achieve by being thin blurs and is lost in the past. The Bible eloquently describes this situation: "Why spend money on what is not bread, and your labor on what does not satisfy? Listen, listen to me, and eat what is good and your soul will delight in the richest of fare" (Isaiah 55:2).

As with any therapy, a critical component is the establishment of rapport. Most of us feel good when we talk with someone who listens and demonstrates that he or she truly understands our feelings. Helping professionals need to be able to see the world through their patients' eyes, to the point that they can understand the patients' logic, even when that logic is faulty and causing severe problems. Understanding and validation must precede confrontation. Confrontation without validation will simply be perceived as an attack. We earn the right to confront patients by careful listening, understanding their wounds, and demonstrating our understanding, combined with concern and empathy.

Of further use in treating patients with co-occurring SUD and ED is a stages of change model developed by Prochaska et al. (1995). The stages are not linear, progressive steps, but involve movement backward and forward. Remuda has adapted this approach in our assessments and interventions.

In Remuda's adaptation, there are four stages: Pre-Contemplation, Contemplation, Preparation/Action, and Maintenance. In Pre-Contemplation, patients are not even thinking about recovery. In Contemplation, patients have some ambivalence about their SUD and/or ED and are considering recovery. Preparation includes the decision that change is needed, which typically leads to Action—taking behavioral steps to achieve the change. Finally, maintenance involves relapse prevention.

Individualized interventions are based upon patients' stage of change. It would not make any sense to help a person who is not even contemplating recovery to develop a plan to avoid relapse. Without understanding stages of change, the timing and efficacy of even good interventions is compromised.

Interventions for Pre-Contemplation can involve increasing patients' awareness of the negative consequences of SUD and ED, creating cognitive dissonance. At this stage, power-struggles between provider and patient may occur. Motivational interviewing is a therapeutic technique that helps patients to navigate the Pre-Contemplation stage. "Motivational interviewing is a directive, client-centered counseling style for eliciting behavior change by helping clients to explore and resolve ambivalence…Motivation to change is elicited from the client, and not imposed from without" (Rollnick & Miller, 1995).

"Where there is no vision, the people perish" (Proverbs 29:18 KJV). Using this principle, one question I ask substance abusing patients in Pre-Contemplation is, "What is your vision for your life? What do you want?" This is important because it establishes that we are talking about the patients' goals and objectives, not the therapists', parents', or partners' goals. Once this is established, patients' substance use can be viewed in the context of their personal goals, which decreases time-consuming power struggles.

At Remuda, younger patients often state that they want to have a good career, to be married, and to have children. Having elicited their vision, we simply ask questions such as: "You said that you want to get married and have children. Do you want your husband to go out drinking on the weekends after you have children?" Almost always they reply, "No." "If you keep dating guys who get drunk with you, who love to party and get drunk with their buddies or use drugs, what makes you think they will stop when you get married or have children?" If nothing else, this creates an internal conflict between patients' drinking behavior and their own goals, as opposed to externally imposed value judgments. The ultimate question becomes, "Is your current substance use behavior moving you towards your goals or away from them?" The intention is to get them to contemplate change because change will help them achieve their own goals.

Patients in Pre-Contemplation and Contemplation can be derailed by words like "addict" or "alcoholic." Reviewing patients' behaviors with them and then discussing *DSM-IV-TR* (APA, 2000) criteria for substance abuse or dependence is a more productive approach. With this approach, we have had many patients who do not yet see themselves as "addicts" or "alcoholics" say, "Yeah, I do that stuff."

Other interventions are designed according to the remaining stages of change. The goal in the Contemplation stage is to have patients make a decision for recovery. The goal of Preparation and Action is for patients to take steps needed to move into recovery, such as pulling away from peers who abuse substances or have eating disorders, joining a 12 Step group, and so on. More detail about using stages of change with patients who have both ED and SUD can be found in Eberly, Cabrera, Wall, and Wolfe (2004).

Regardless of interventions used, a key challenge to recovery is that SUD and to some extent ED offer instant gratification, whereas healthier alternatives take longer, require more effort, and may not be as powerful. Here, support groups are vital, especially while new skills are being developed to meet underlying needs. In addition, finding ways to decrease stress, and learning to identify and avoid triggers are critical. The Maintenance stage deals with these issues of relapse prevention. Identification of high risk situations and development of specific plans to deal with these to avoid substance use and ED behaviors are foundational. A range of relapse prevention resources exist for those with SUD and ED.

In sum, behaviors become addictive when: 1) they fill a need; 2) they lead to desired outcomes quickly; 3) negative consequences are delayed; 4) they work consistently; 5) alternatives for meeting the need are unknown or not believed in; and 6) the behavior does not violate one's values and/or can be rationalized. Comprehensive treatment deals with each of these variables. The true need is understood and validated, and the long-term consequences are made more salient. Viable alternatives are developed and values examined. Ongoing support guides patients through the early days of skill acquisition so they are less likely to return to the instant gratification of their disordered ED and SUD behaviors.

Spiritual Considerations

Because most Christians affirm the doctrine of freewill, we believe there is a critical role in human life for individual choice. Freewill moves us beyond deterministic influences of our biology and the stimulus-response environment in which we live. Individual choice creates another dimension that must be considered when contemplating the assessment and treatment of SUD.

Freewill is an aspect of the human spirit. The spiritual component does not make us impervious to the extremely powerful forces of biology and environment, but it enables us to make choices that are not completely controlled by them.

It is helpful to know that the apostle Paul completely identified with those who are caught in the mire of addictions, destructive compulsive behaviors, and obsessive thoughts. Paul, like all human beings, struggled with his human nature. He poignantly wrote: "No matter which way I turn, I cannot make myself do right. I want to, but I can't. When I want to do good, I don't, and when I try not to do wrong, I do it anyway" (Romans 7:18-19 NLT). Paul described these behaviors as "foolishness" because they result in painful exploitation of self and others. In stern words, he wrote: "At one time we too were foolish, disobedient, deceived and enslaved by all kinds of passions and pleasures. We lived in malice and envy, being hated and hating one another" (Titus 3:3-4). Elsewhere, the Bible reminds us of humanity's fallen nature and its potential to nearly trounce freewill: "For a man is a slave to whatever has mastered him…" (2 Peter 2:19). Biblically, then, we hear about enslavement, a logical sequence of events where addictive behaviors run amok and lead to an out of control life. The 12 Step model echoes this perspective in Step 1: "We admitted we were powerless over our addiction, that our lives had become unmanageable."

In light of this strong biblical language, it is essential to recognize that the apostle Paul also preached the amazing news that "there is no condemnation…" for these behaviors (Romans 8:1). He was not interested in placing blame on those who are struggling, but in compassionately reaching out to them and introducing them to healing through Jesus Christ. We are not only flesh and bone. We have a spirit within us that responds to the encouragement and direction of the Scriptures and the still small voice of God speaking within us. We are loved by a God who offers us redemption. With these sources of strength, we can choose freedom. The 12 Step model echoes this perspective, particularly in Steps 2 and 3: "We came to believe that a power greater than ourselves could restore us to sanity," and "We made a decision to turn our will and our lives over to the care of God…" In these steps, a *decision* is made—an act of free will, assisted by a "power greater than ourselves…"

Yes, addictions are potent. Picture this. A man is walking in the woods and steps in a trap, getting caught up in it, snared to the point of frustration and confusion. While he is struggling to get out, the trap seems to grip tighter and tighter until he is desperate. There seems to be no relief, no release, and no escape from the situation. So the man sits down, exhausted, stops fighting, gives in, and stops trying. So many find themselves here at this hopeless place, where the addiction—a snare that has exhausted their efforts of escape—is now all they know.

God offers a special promise for those in this place of hardship and suffering, who have come to believe there is no escape. "But remember that the temptations that come into your life are no different from what others experience. And God is faithful. He will keep the temptation from becoming so strong that you can't stand up against it. When you are tempted, he will show you a way out, so that you will not give in to it" (1 Corinthians 10:13 NLT). Sometimes the "way out" is admitting that the problem has overwhelmed us and deciding to get help from a professional. Often the "way out" arrives when another human being comes alongside and becomes the hands and feet of Jesus for the one who is suffering. In order to escape the gravitational pull of both biology and environment, those who abuse substances typically need help from others—loved ones, professionals, support groups, and the church community. "A way out" or a "way of escape" often refers to a narrow mountain pass through which a trapped army can escape from an enemy seeking their destruction. One must decide to take the escape. The Bible assures us that it will be provided.

In the Hebrew Scriptures, there is the story of Benaiah (2 Samuel 23:20-21). Today we would call him, "Benny." Benny took on a battle with an armed and very strong man in a pit, "plucked the spear out of his hand and slew him with his own spear." Apart from the violent nature of this act, the premise here is that Benny faced his enemy squarely and fearlessly. This is the choice that one must make in recovery, to drive it out with deliberation fueled by a life or death, it's you or me, mentality. For Benny, there was a victory in the pit. Finding oneself doing battle with the lion-like men of Moab in the bottom of a pit is not unlike facing another drug deal, another gambling opportunity, or another night at the bar. In these battles, God is faithful to offer us strength.

The hopefulness we suggest may not come to the hurting easily. Emotions can be so numbed by drug use and a history of pain that hopelessness and despair seem to be the addict's closest friends. Christian health professionals have the opportunity to remind those with SUD of the hope of the resurrection and God's promises of deliverance. Life arises from the ashes.

At Remuda, we seek to provide exceptional clinical treatment combined with hope that life can and will be different without addictions and ED. It is not hard to be convincing, since thousands of patients have come through our doors and found peace, sometimes for the first time in their lives.

The book of Isaiah beautifully discusses community support and God's direct assistance in overcoming addictive and compulsive behaviors: "... strengthen those who have tired hands, and encourage those who have weak knees, say to those who are afraid, 'be strong and do not fear, for your God is coming to destroy your enemies. He is coming to save you' " (Isaiah 35:3 NLT).

Case Analysis

Background

Nursing staff brings Tiffany to my office wrapped in a blanket. She has unkempt hair and a tired face. Tiffany is a 19-year-old college student. She was sent to treatment by her parents, who threatened to pull her out of college if she doesn't change. Tiffany is not happy about being an inpatient, but is surprisingly pleasant given the circumstances. In spite of her tired appearance and messy hair, it is easy to see that she is an attractive young lady who typically pays attention to her appearance.

She comes from a successful family of high academic achievement and socio-economic status. Dad is a former college athlete, who owns a medium sized company. Mom has a college degree and taught grade school before Tiffany's older brother was born. Since then, she has stayed at home to care for the children.

As Tiffany continues to discuss her background it becomes clear that she has strong social skills and a likeable personality. While she presents as very nice, appearing open and motivated during the interview, she subtly suggests that she does not believe she needs treatment. She discusses her high school history in a non-boastful manner, but reveals that she was extremely popular and well-liked by most everyone in school regardless of their particular clique.

She appears open and honest about her family, mentioning serious problems and discussing positive points as well. Her father is heavily involved in his business. He is also an avid fitness buff who spends a lot of time exercising. He is very involved in her brother's sports. He himself was a three-sport all-star in high school. Her mother is extremely involved in social activities. Much like Tiffany, Mom had been homecoming queen and a cheerleader in high school and college. Tiffany belongs to the same sorority as her mother. It becomes clear that her family is focused on success and achievement. Neither parent had ever said anything openly, but A's on report cards are an unspoken expectation as is social and athletic leadership in school. Tiffany's parents are Christians and involved in a church. Tiffany had been involved as well, but school activities and a demanding social life had pulled her away by her sophomore year in high school.

Tiffany's paternal grandfather and grandmother had severe alcohol problems. Her father had a period of time in college and a short time before her brother was born when he used alcohol excessively. In college he had used alcohol for social reasons, and as an adult to handle the stress of a new business. Her mother drinks occasionally but has never abused alcohol.

Tiffany's openness during the interview suddenly shifts when we begin to talk about her alcohol use. She states that she is "not an alcoholic" and does "not have any problems with alcohol." Her alcohol use is "no different than any other college student."

I ask Tiffany when she first began to use alcohol, and she indicates that she began "drinking socially" with her ex-boyfriend, Sean, and their group of friends during her sophomore year of high school. Sean was one class ahead of her and every bit as popular and accomplished in academics and sports. Sean and his friends often went out after games and on the weekend to "party"; alcohol was part of those events. She admits that she "got buzzed and had a couple of blackouts," but believes that she never had any problems because of her drinking.

Sean broke off their relationship after his senior year as he thought it best if both of them were free to date in college. Tiffany was devastated. She continued drinking during her senior year and dated several guys. Until that time, she had only been sexually active with Sean, but during her senior year she had sex with four different guys. She also began to purge sporadically through self-induced vomiting early in her senior year, but this had become a weekly occurrence by the end of the year.

She joined a prestigious sorority at a large southern college. Alcohol was a central component of her social world. Her alcohol use increased, but she states that she does not drink any more than her friends and that "this is just the way it is in college; it's part of being a college student." She did well academically her first quarter, but then her grades began to slide. She denies that alcohol and her social life have had anything to do with this. She has a new boyfriend who, like Sean, is very popular and older than she. He drinks regularly and occasionally uses marijuana. Although she had purged in high school, she began to binge in college. Now she is extremely fearful of "getting fat" due to her binges. She still becomes intoxicated at least once a week, usually on Friday and/or Saturday nights. She normalizes this because, in her perception, just about all of her friends from the sorority and the fraternity guys do exactly the same. Her father also drank too much in college and "he's fine now."

Assessment and Treatment

Tiffany may have a genetic predisposition to substance abuse from her father. She recognizes some genetic risk, but also minimizes this since she has not experienced substance abuse firsthand in her family of origin. Her father's misuse of alcohol occurred before she was born.

Although Tiffany is popular, she is likely insecure. Her connections with her parents are not as strong as they might appear. Her father is gone much of the time and, on weekends, is busy with his own activities and her brother's sports. Time to deepen connection with her father is lacking, and he may be more interested in her brother than in her. Tiffany's bonding and intimacy with her mother may not be very strong because Tiffany has received praise from her mother conditional on appearance and accomplishments. Tiffany's family has therefore taught her that she needs achievement, physical attractiveness, and social status as evidence of self-worth. This leaves her vulnerable and insecure, because such a scenario bases her self-worth on external events that are difficult to control. Tiffany cannot allow herself or others to see her vulnerability and insecurity, because such inner experiences are not consistent with the persona she is expected to portray.

Tiffany's social group is high achieving and popular in spite of its alcohol use. Alcohol use has become ego-syntonic largely because it has been an accepted and even expected behavior in her social reference group. Neither do her parents have strong objections to alcohol use, so conflicts with family or peer group values would be minimal. Drinking has increased her status in her social reference group and has not, in her view, cost her status in terms of academic achievement or school activities such as cheerleading. Her eating disorder behaviors are also accepted within her sorority peer group.

Tiffany grew up with the influence of a church community and values. Although she has distanced herself from both at present, she continues to identify herself as a Christian. There may be a latent conflict between this identity and her current alcohol use and eating disorder behavior. Tiffany may be minimizing the extent and significance of these behaviors in an effort to harmonize her behavior with early internalized values.

I conceptualize eating disorders and substance use according to the model presented earlier in this chapter:

Need ➾ Symptom ➾ Target ➾ Behavioral Strategy ➾ Outcome

Tiffany's *needs* are to feel special, loved, and accepted unconditionally. The *symptoms* of her needs are painful feelings surfacing when she is alone, such as when her boyfriend abandoned her. Life has taught Tiffany that the fulfillment of her needs comes from external attributes that are superficial and difficult to control, such as appearance and achievement. To fulfill her needs, she therefore *targets* achievement, physical attractiveness, and social acceptance. Her chosen *behavioral strategy* is to fit in with the popular group by doing whatever that group requires for acceptance and approval. A major criterion for acceptance by her peer group is physical attractiveness. Alcohol use is central to this peer group's social gatherings and is expected of group members. The *outcome* of Tiffany's behavioral strategy is a high status boyfriend and external affirmation by the high status peer group that resembles her high status family.

Tiffany is in the Contemplation stage regarding her eating disorder, since it has become a burden leading to extreme fears of weight gain; hence, she is considering changing this behavior but has not yet committed to do so. Tiffany is in the Pre-Contemplation stage regarding her alcohol use: she does not see a need to change and is not interested in doing so. Pre-Contemplation is ripe for power struggles. The more one directly attacks the alcohol issue, the more resistant Tiffany is likely to become. Although Tiffany is in the Contemplation stage regarding her eating disorder, this resistance will likely generalize to eating disorder treatment as well.

Therefore, interventions need to be directed at moving Tiffany from Pre-Contemplation to Contemplation, where she is considering changing her alcohol use but has not yet committed to do so. Specific strategies to accomplish this movement from Pre-Contemplation to Contemplation are readily available and should be utilized. Tiffany may experience cognitive dissonance if she is helped to explore her substance use behavior in light of her Christian identity. This may open the door for her to consider the possibility of changing her behavior. As Tiffany progresses through the stages, interventions should shift to reflect her progressive level of motivation to change. As she enters the Preparation/Action stage, for example, more traditional treatment strategies can assist Tiffany with insight into her true needs and acquisition of the skills required to actually change her eating disorder and substance use behaviors and rely instead on healthier behaviors to meet her needs. Ultimately, relapse prevention strategies will assist her to maintain recovery.

Likely obstacles include her awareness that sobriety may result in social rejection or may require her to separate from her social reference group. Changing her substance use behavior will likely end her relationship with her boyfriend. If these possible losses are not dealt with openly and directly, and viable alternatives developed to meet her needs, she will be vulnerable to relapse.

Because Tiffany has a history of faith, this strength may offer a new social reference group and enable her to explore more internal views of personal value and worth.

References

American Psychiatric Association. (2000). *Diagnostic and Statistical Manual of Mental Disorders, Text Revision* (4th ed.) *(DSM-IV-TR)*. Washington, DC: Author.

American Psychiatric Association. (2006). *Practice Guideline for the Treatment of Patients with Substance Use Disorders*. Retrieved November 10, 2006, from http://www.psych.org/psych_pract/treatg/quick_ref_guide/SUD_QRG.pdf.

Blinder, B. J., Blinder, M. C., & Sanathara, V. A. (1998). Eating disorders and addiction. *Psychiatric Times, 15*, 30-33.

Eberly, M., Cabrera, D., Wall, A.D., & Wolfe, K. (2004). Resistance, motivation, and change in eating disorders. *Remuda Review: The Christian Journal of Eating Disorders, 3*, 1-8.

Eberly, M., Wall, A. D., & Cabrera, D. (2003). Cognitive-behavioral therapy: Applications and skills. *The Remuda Review: The Christian Journal of Eating Disorders, 2*, 1-8.

Linehan, M. M. (1993). *Cognitive-behavioral treatment of borderline personality disorder*. New York: Guilford Press.

Macmillan, L. (2003). *Imaging reveals secrets of addiction: Brain awareness keynote lecture*. http://www.mc.vanderbilt.edu/reporter/index.html?ID=2583 March 21, 2003 Dr. Nora Volkow delivered the 2003 Brain awareness keynote address.

Marlatt, G. & Gordon, J. (1985). *Relapse prevention: Maintenance strategies in the treatment of addictivebehaviors*. New York: Guilford Press.

Prochaska, J. O., Norcross, J., & DiClemente, C. (1995). *Changing for good*. New York: Harper Collins.

Richards, P. S., Baldwin, B. M., Frost, H. A., Clark-Sly, J. B., Berrett, M.E., & Hardman, R.K. (2000). What works for treating eating disorders? Conclusions from 28 studies. *Eating Disorders: Journal of Treatment and Prevention, 8*, 189-206.

Rollnick, S. & Miller, W. R. (1995). What is motivational interviewing? *Behavioural and Cognitive Psychotherapy, 23*, 325-334. Retrieved November 10, 2006, from http://motivationalinterview.org/clinical /whatismi.html

Substance Abuse and Mental Health Services Administration. Office of Applied Studies. (2005). *Services Research Outcome Study, 1995-1996: [United States]*. (SROS. #2691) http://oas.samhsa.gov/SROS/sros8020.htm#E14E10. Washington, DC: U.S. Department of Health and Human Services.

Yager, J., Devlin, M. J., Halmi, K. A., Herzog, D. B., Mitchell, J. E., Powers, P., et al. (2006). Practice guideline for the treatment of patients with eating disorders (3rd ed.). *American Journal of Psychiatry*. Retrieved November 10, 2006, from http://www.psych.org/psych-pract/treatg/pg /prac_guide.cfm

Author Index

G

H-I

J

K

T

V-W

Y-Z

Subject Index

A

B

C

D

E

L

M

N

O

P-Q

R

S